ATLAS OF FORENSIC PATHOLOGY

ATLAS OF FORENSIC PATHOLOGY

Nancy L. Jones, M.D.
Assistant Medical Examiner
Cook County Medical Examiner's Office
Chicago, Illinois
and
Clinical Associate Professor of Pathology
The Chicago Medical School
North Chicago, Illinois

IGAKU-SHOIN New York • Tokyo

Published and distributed by

IGAKU-SHOIN Medical Publishers, Inc.
One Madison Avenue, New York, New York 10010

IGAKU-SHOIN Ltd.,
5-24-3 Hongo, Bunkyo-ku, Tokyo 113-91

Library of Congress Cataloging-in-Publication Data

Jones, Nancy L. (Nancy Lynne), 1952–
Atlas of forensic pathology / Nancy L. Jones.
p. cm.
Includes bibliographical references and index.
1. Forensic pathology—Atlases. I. Title.
[DNLM: 1. Forensic Medicine—atlases. 2. Pathology—atlases. W 617 J78a 1996]
RA1063.4.J66 1996
614′.1—dc20
DNLM/DLC 96-1929
for Library of Congress CIP

ISBN: 0-89640-315-7 (New York)
ISBN: 4-260-14315-8 (Tokyo)

Printed and bound in the U.S.A.
10 9 8 7 6 5 4 3 2 1

Preface

This atlas has been designed to serve as an aid to nonforensic trained pathologists who find themselves performing forensic autopsies for the local county or state coroner when a trained forensic pathologist is not available. The American Board of Pathology requires that all candidates for Board certification in anatomic pathology have a minimum exposure, usually a one-month period, to forensic pathology in order to be eligible for the certification examination. This brief period of training, even if done at a busy facility, does not allow enough exposure to the wide variety of traumatic and nontraumatic deaths that an experienced forensic pathologist deals with on a regular basis. The ability to recognize and accurately interpret injuries and artifacts is as necessary to the forensic pathologist as the ability to recognize and accurately interpret the different types of malignant and nonmalignant changes is to the hospital-based anatomic pathologist.

This atlas is not meant as a reference text for practicing forensic pathologists. It is designed as a basic text to assist the inexperienced pathologist to recognize, accurately describe and to determine the causal mechanism of common injuries. It also describes many of the common postmortem artifacts which can be misinterpreted as evidence of injury by the untrained and inexperienced examiner. The information found within this atlas will allow the nonforensic pathologist to perform forensic autopsies with the same confidence and skill utilized when performing an autopsy on an individual who died from a natural disease process in a hospital setting.

Police officers, emergency medical personnel, and attorneys may also benefit from the information and examples contained in this atlas. It can assist police officers and detectives in evaluating scenes and apparent injuries on the body enabling them to differentiate wounds due to intentional violence from accidental injury which results from falls or a collapse. Familiarity with mongolian spot birth marks, senile purpura and the common skin changes which occur after death can save time and effort from being lost on the investigation of a nonexistent crime. Recognizing the characteristics of contact range, close range and distant range gunshot wounds of entrance can be useful in cases where a victim is found dead in the presence of others who say that the victim shot himself. If the wound shows none of the characteristics of contact or very close range fire, than it is very unlikely that the story given is true and the witnesses can be questioned accordingly.

Emergency medical personnel may find this information useful when treating patients, both those who survive and those who do not survive. Recognition of injuries, a knowledge of injury causation, and familiarity with the internal injuries associated with the various types of trauma can allow the clinician to more effectively treat victims of motorvehicle accidents, falls, and assaults with guns, knives and other weapons. Accurate description of injuries and care in preserving evidence and maintaining chain of custody can save a busy physician, nurse, paramedic, or laboratory worker a time-consuming trip to a courtroom at some later date to testify in a criminal or civil proceeding.

Prosecution and defense attorneys must read and interpret autopsy reports on a regular basis. The examples of various injuries and wounds found in this text will allow the attorney to better understand the autopsy findings. The information found herein may answer questions or provide insight into the issues of a given case, thus allowing the attorney to better judge the veracity or accuracy of testimony given by witnesses and/or the defendants. Direct and cross examination of witnesses, especially expert witnesses, is a skill which develops with experience and with familiarity with the language used by witnesses. This text provides a glossary of terms which can make learning the language of forensic pathology easier, thus improving the attorney's examination technique.

Nancy L. Jones, M.D.

Contents

1

Introduction

The field of forensic pathology deals with violence, trauma, unnatural events and the effects they have on the human body. Forensic pathologists routinely examine victims of homicides, accidents, suicides and natural disease. Injuries examined range from simple bruises on the skin to complete dismemberment of the body. The ability to recognize the type, the significance, and the cause of injury is one of the skills that the forensic pathologist develops during training and practice. The chapters in this atlas present the injuries commonly seen, the circumstances in which they occur, a discussion of the mechanism of injury, and a description of the characteristics which identify the injury. The knowledge and skills that the pathologist develops are important in the day-to-day performance of autopsy examinations, as well as during testimony in criminal and civil trials. With the introduction of cameras into American court rooms, the abilities of the forensic pathologist have become more public.

The autopsy examination in forensic cases does not end with the finalization and signing of the autopsy protocol as usually happens in hospital autopsies. The pathologist performing the examination becomes a witness at later trial proceedings. A subpoena duces tecum will often be the first document to arrive. This is a court document signed by the clerk of the local circuit court commanding that copies of the autopsy protocol, radiographs, photographs, and any other documents pertaining to a given death investigation be provided to the state's attorney or district attorney or to the defense attorney in criminal cases, or to the defense or plaintiff's attorney in civil cases. All information concerning the date and the place to send these documents will be on the subpoena. The next document to arrive, the subpoena, commands the examining pathologist to appear at the criminal or civil trial. The subpoena will have the name of the presiding judge, the courtroom, and the date the trial begins. The exact date and time that the pathologist must appear is usually not the date that the jury is chosen, which is the date that generally appears on the subpoena. The attorney sending the subpoena should contact the pathologist to set up a pretrial meeting to discuss the case and to set the date and time of the actual court appearance.

The pathologist will usually testify as an "expert witness". This requires that the educational background and experience of the pathologist be recited into the court record and that he or she be tendered to the court and accepted by the judge and the attorneys for both sides as an expert. Once accepted, the pathologist may testify to opinion and not just fact, and, in effect, act as a teacher to the court.

Even though the pathologist is most commonly subpoenaed by the prosecution in criminal cases, he or she should not consider himself or herself as a witness against the defendant. The pathologist is there as a witness for the victim, to relay to the court the autopsy findings and his or her opinion as to the cause of death based on those findings and the pathologist's own experience and expertise. It is not uncommon for the autopsy findings to support the case against the defendant. Occasionally the findings do support the statements and position of the defense.

While on the witness stand, the pathologist should address the jury, or the judge if the proceedings are a bench trial. It is important that answers be clear and in a language that the jury understands. The use of medical terms, which is second nature to physicians, may be confusing to the lay jury. If medical terms are used, it is helpful to immediately follow them with the colloquial or lay terms. Examples would be to follow the term *hemorrhage* with *bleeding,* or *clavicle* with *collarbone.* By testifying in a language the jury understands, the pathologist is allowing the members of that jury to clearly understand what happened to the victim. It is important for the pathologist to listen carefully to all of the questions that are asked by both sides. A brief moment of hesitation before answering a question will allow time for the attorneys to object to a question and allow the judge to sustain (accept) or to over rule (reject) that objection. It also allows the pathologist time to think before answering a question. If a question is not understood, the pathologist should say so. The attorney can then rephrase or repeat the question so that the meaning is clear. Answers should never be given to any question that is obscure.

During the court appearance, the pathologist will be shown, and asked to identify, photographs and evidence collected during the autopsy. It is helpful if an identifier, such as a case number or name and date, be present in each photograph to allow the pathologist to recognize the case. Any evidence removed during the examination, having been placed in clearly labeled envelopes or containers which the pathologist has initialed and sealed, is easily identified, allowing the pathologist to testify that the materials presented are truly those recovered from the victim during the autopsy. Reviewing the photographs and the autopsy protocol prior to the court appearance is vital.

In civil cases, and on occasion in criminal cases when the pathologist may not be available at the time of trial, instead of an appearance in a courtroom, the pathologist may be subpoenaed to appear at a deposition. This is a proceding attended by the pathologist, the attorneys for both sides and a court reporter who will take down the sworn testimony of the witness. In depositions, all questions must be answered, even if there is an objection. The deposition may be a discovery deposition, that is, taken so that the attorneys involved in a given case may find out what the witness has to say, or it may be an evidence deposition, which will be read into the court record at the trial.

2

The Forensic Autopsy

GENERAL PRINCIPLES

The primary purpose of the forensic autopsy is to determine the cause and manner of death (Tables 2.1, 2.2). The examination must be performed in a manner that will allow the pathologist to answer the questions raised by the sudden, unexpected, unexplained, or mysterious death of an individual. The first question, who is the deceased, is followed by when, where, and how did death occur, and sometimes by a final question, who caused the death. Identification of the deceased can be the easiest, or the most difficult portion of the examination. If a body is viewable, and family members are available to visually identify the body, or if photographic identification is found on the body, identification is easily accomplished. Fingerprint identification works well, if the deceased has fingerprints on file, either with the local authorities, or with the Federal Bureau of Investigation. Bodies that are severely decomposed, injured, or skeletalized are far more difficult to identify. In such instances, antemortem dental records or antemortem skeletal radiographs can be used for comparison with the postmortem dentition or postmortem radiographs. These comparison studies hinge on having at least a tentative identification of the remains so that the appropriate dental and medical records can be obtained. Advances in DNA fingerprinting have made the identification of partial remains possible (Table 2.3).

The answer to when an individual dies is easy if the death occurred in an emergency room or in the presence of others. It is more difficult to answer whenever bodies are found in various stages of decomposition.

It must be remembered that environmental conditions play an important role in the progression of rigor mortis, livor mortis, and decomposition. Cool environments will slow the progression of decomposition while warm or hot environments will accelerate the rate of change. The type and amount of clothing that the victim is wearing will also affect the rate of decomposition. Bodies found in water tend to decompose at a slower rate than bodies out in the open air, and bodies that have been buried decompose at a slower rate than those in water (Table 2.4).

The activities and physical condition of an individual prior to death also have an effect on these changes. Infants and elderly individuals with small muscle mass can go into and out of full rigor in a shorter time frame than more muscular adults. Physical exertion prior to death will also accelerate the progression of rigor. Rapid onset of decomposition is frequently found in individuals who are febrile prior to death and is also seen in some drug-related deaths and in the obese. Rapid decomposition is frequently found in victims of penetrating injuries to the gastrointestinal tract, as the microorganisms normally found in the large bowel are released into the peritoneal cavity.

If where the death occurred and the location where the body is found are one and the same, the "where" question is easy to answer. Unfortunately, this is not always the case. It is helpful for the forensic pathologist to visit the scene where a body is found, preferably while the body is still in situ. But scene investigations can still provide a great deal of information even when conducted after the body is removed or the autopsy is completed. In infant deaths, a scene investigation is mandatory.

Identifying the actual cause and manner of death can be the greatest challenge and the most rewarding accomplishment for the pathologist performing the examination. It is sometimes as easy as finding a single gunshot wound and recovering the spent bullet. At other times, the answer may never be found even after a complete autopsy, toxicologic workup, and thorough investigation have been done. Saying "I don't know" is difficult and sometimes necessary.

COLLECTION AND PRESERVATION OF EVIDENCE

Forensic autopsies are frequently done to assist law enforcement agencies in the identification, apprehension, and prosecution of the guilty. Careful examination of the victims of violent crime is vital, and must be done not only to determine the cause of death, but to search for clues as to the identity of the individual or individuals responsible for the crime. Careful examination can also turn up evidence on the deceased which may exonerate an individual who has been accused of a crime he or she didn't commit, or may prove that no crime has even occurred. A detailed examination of the clothing and the personal effects is done for clues to the identity of the deceased, but also for the location, identification, and collection of trace evidence such as fibers, hairs, metal or glass fragments, tissue, or blood. In cases where sexual assault is suspected, it is important to collect swabs and/or washings from the mouth, anus, and vagina. The swabs should be placed in clean cardboard boxes with air holes, or allowed to air dry before placing them in plastic containers. The head hair and pubic hair should be combed and the hair collected in clean evidence bags. Pulled samples of head hair and pubic hair should also be collected. It is important to pull samples from several different areas, that the hairs collected have follicles, and that a sufficient number, about 30 or so, be obtained.

Fingernail scrapings, using a clean blade can be done, or the entire nail tip can be carefully cut away and placed in evidence bags. All of the evidence collected should be carefully labeled with the date, victim's name, source of the evidence, and initials of the pathologist collecting the evidence. A receipt should always be obtained from the individual accepting the evidence collected so that the chain of custody is maintained.

PHOTOGRAPHY

During the examination, the pathologist, pathologist's assistant, or investigating police agency should take photographs. In noncriminal cases, an identification photograph should be taken. In trauma cases, an identification photograph and photographs of the injuries found on the body are needed. It is helpful to first take a photograph some distance from the body for location purposes, and then to take a close-up of the injury to document its appearance. In criminal cases, these photographs become part of the physical evidence presented to the jury at the time of trial. Clear, well-focused, color or black-and-white photographs of the injuries on the body allow the jury to better understand the nature of the events that lead to the death. It is important that the field of view is not blood-splattered and that the object to be photographed is dry, to prevent glare. The small amount of time that it takes to set up a good photograph is worth the effort. Not all photographs entered into evidence or presented during criminal or civil proceedings will make their way back to the jury room during deliberations. Some police agencies like to videotape the entire autopsy examination as well as their investigation of the scene. It is important to find out at the beginning of the examination if the video camera has audio capabilities and if the audio will be operating during the autopsy.

RADIOGRAPHY

Radiographs should be taken in all cases of firearm injury to assist in the location and recovery of the expended bullets. Anteroposterior (A-P) and lateral radiographs are desirable, but single view films can be adequate. Total body fluoroscopy is desirable in all deaths due to firearms, decomposed bodies, bodies with thermal burns, and motor vehicle accidents and pedestrian injuries. This is to assist in ruling out the possibility that the victim may have been shot or otherwise injured prior to the fire or thrown into the path of oncoming traffic. Total body radiographs are very useful in deaths in custody to answer any questions about fractures or other injuries. Radiographs should also be used to document skeletal injuries in all blunt trauma cases. For identification purposes in bodies that are not viewable, A-P and lateral head and chest films should be taken before performing the autopsy. This is done before the examination because the anatomy of the chest and the skull is distorted by the use of the autopsy saw.

HISTOLOGY

Histologic examination is not always necessary in forensic autopsies, especially in traumatic death. A histologic examination of bullet wounds of entry may be done to look for evidence of gunpowder within the wound that wasn't visible during the gross examination. All cases of fatal child abuse, and all natural deaths of children require that histologic examination be performed to rule out any natural disease process, and to clearly and unequivocally document the type and nature of any injuries found during the gross examination. It is helpful to take stock tissue in any type of examination and to preserve those samples so that they are available if any questions arise at a later date, as it is the common practice for forensic pathologists to return all of the organs to the body and to not retain them as is done in most hospital autopsies. Deaths due to natural disease can be documented with histologic examination of all organ systems, or the histologic examination may be confined to the organ system or systems affected and stock preserved from the other organ systems.

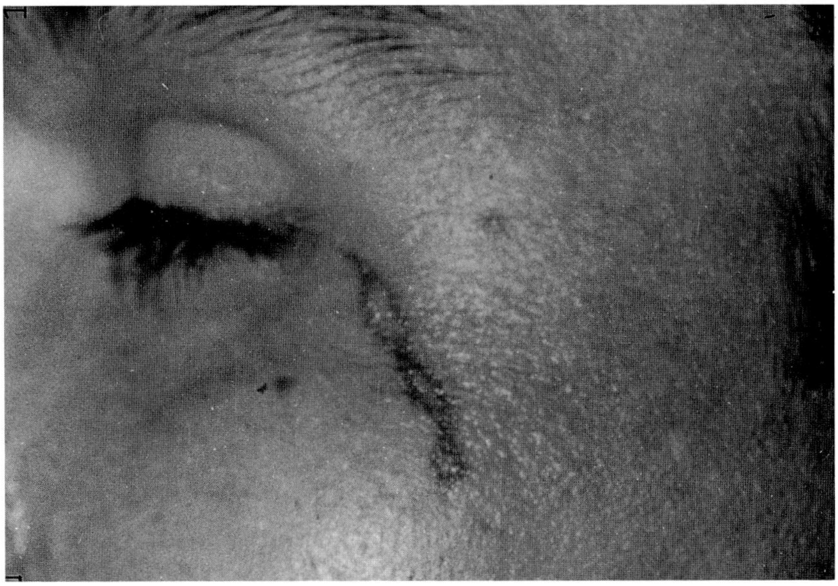

FIGURE 2.1 Tattoo of teardrops at the corner of the eye found on an unidentified Hispanic male victim of multiple stab wounds. This type of tattoo is commonly found on former prison inmates and identification was easily made through use of fingerprints. Tattoos can be used to confirm suspected identities in bodies that are decomposed or not viewable for other reasons. The dermal pigment of tattoos is visible even after the epidermis has sloughed.

FIGURE 2.2 Sweatshirt worn by drowning victim with logo of a local hot dog restaurant chain provided police with identification within hours of autopsy examination. Workers at the restaurant location nearest the recovery site of the body were able to provide information about a former employee who had not been seen for over a week. Clothing should always be checked for names or laundry marks. Sizes, colors, and manufacturers' names should be recorded. It is difficult to obtain fingerprints from drowning victims or decomposed bodies as the skin of the hands and feet sloughs, or degloves, and may not be recovered with the rest of the body.

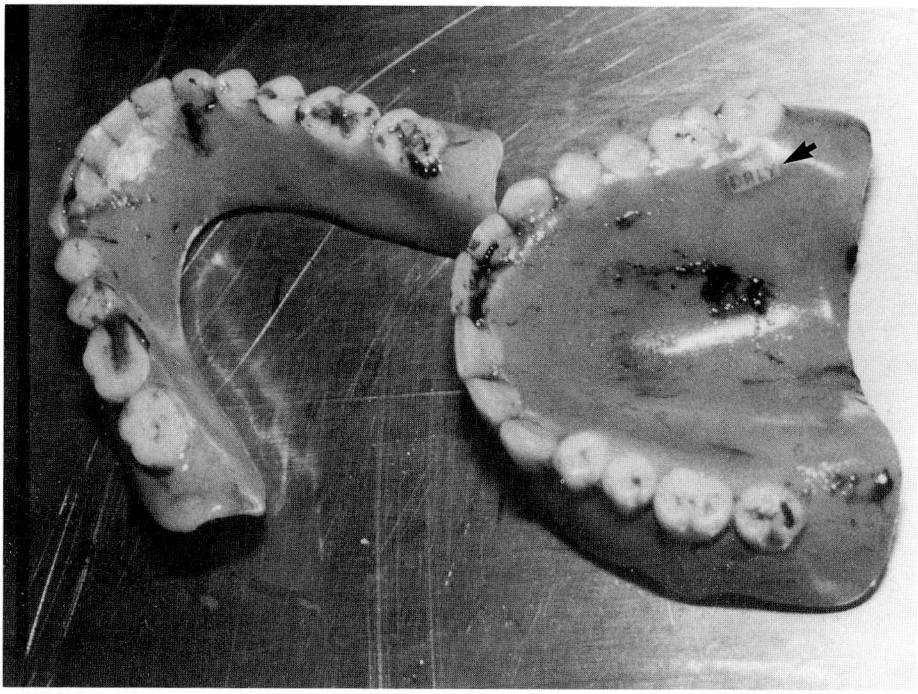

FIGURE 2.3 Denture plates frequently have the name of the owner etched on the palatal surface. These belonged to an elderly victim of a hit-and-run automobile pedestrian incident. The name was found on the left side of the upper plate (*arrow*). Dentures are durable and can be recovered intact from badly burned bodies, allowing for identification.

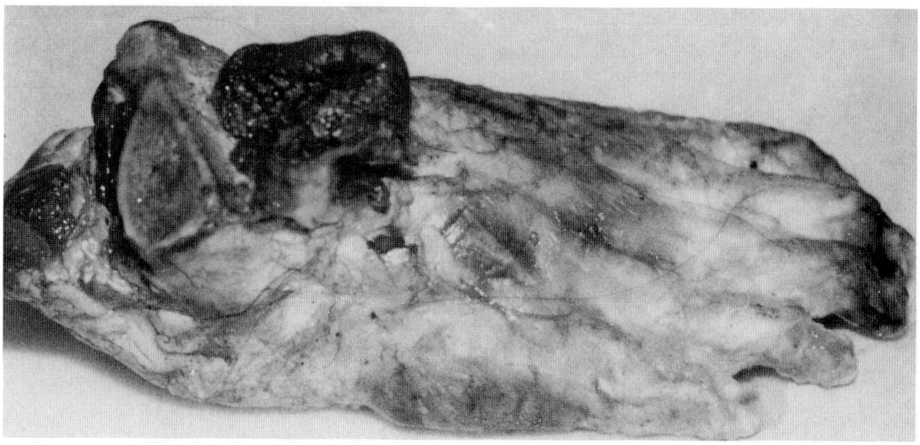

a

FIGURE 2.4a This rear bear paw was placed in a mailbox on Halloween. The local police and an emergency room physician were concerned that the specimen was human and were eager to begin searching for the rest of the body. The specimen does show striking similarities to a human foot. (The forepaws of bears look like the human hand.) When skinning bears, the distal phalanxes will be removed along with the claws to keep the foot pelt intact. Note that the distal phalanxes are absent in this specimen. Note the clean saw mark on the tibia and fibula.

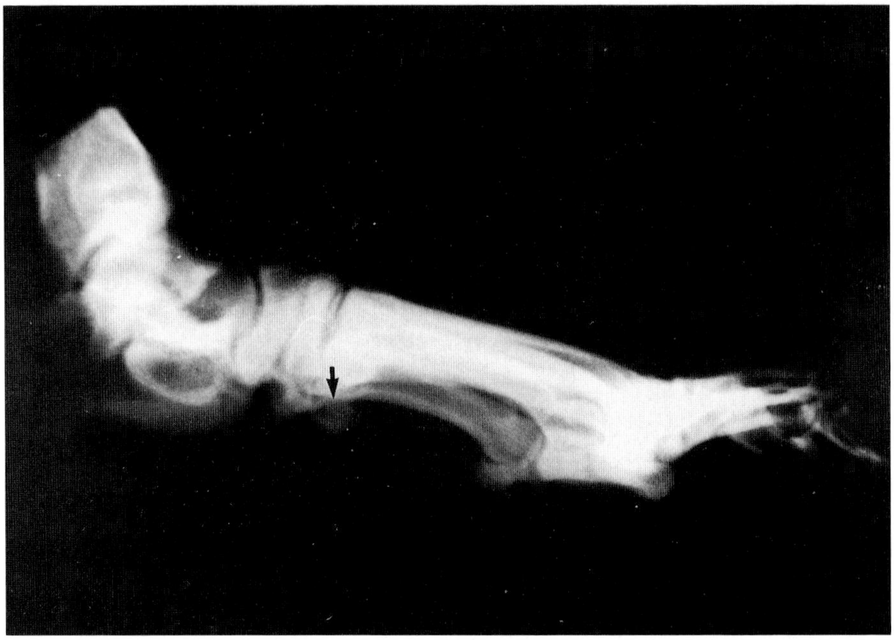

b

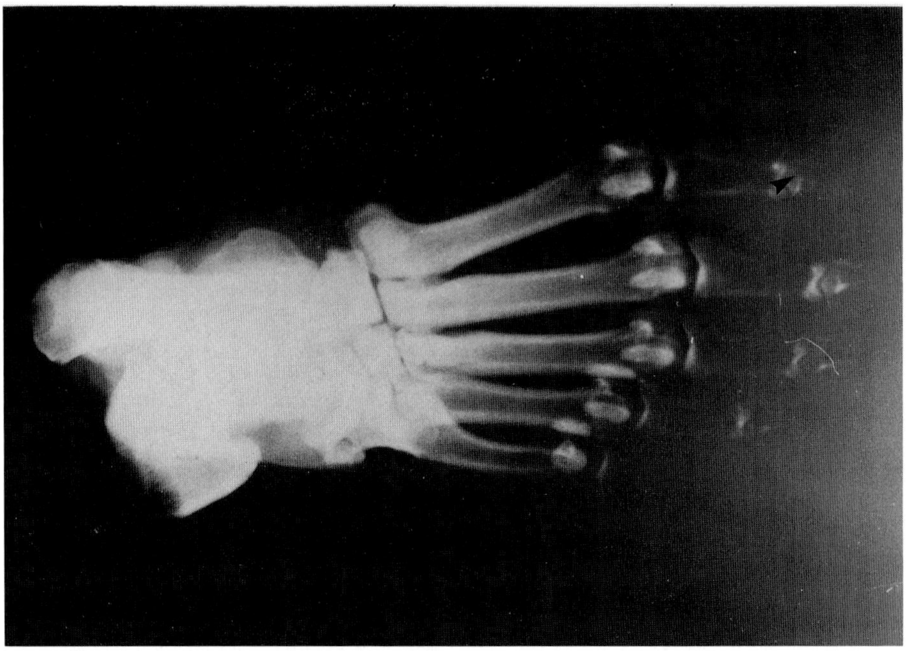

c

FIGURE 2.4b, c Radiographs of the bear paw show numerous sesamoid bones (*arrow*) in the joints and confirm the absence of the distal phalanxes (*arrow head*).

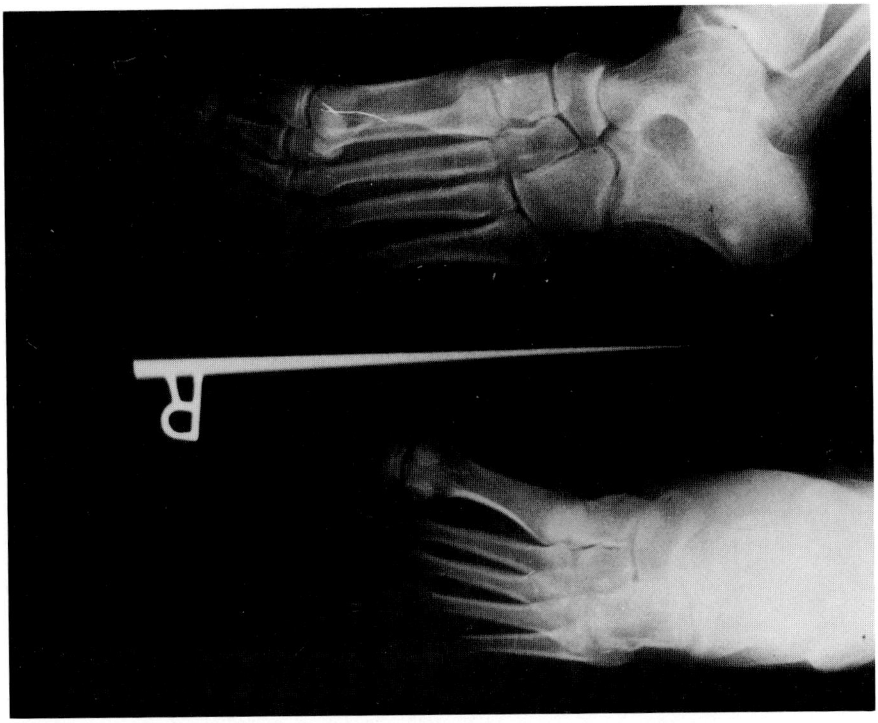

d

FIGURE 2.4d Radiographs of a normal adult human foot for comparison with those of the bear paw. No sesamoid bones are present.

FIGURE 2.5 Photograph of a scene where a body was found in an alley. Only one shoe is noted near the body, and there is significant head trauma. The victim may have been struck by a hit-and-run motor vehicle, dumped at the site or fallen from a height.

FIGURE 2.6 A canvas of the adjacent building provided the identity of the victim, who lived in the building. An open window with displaced screen through which the subject had jumped to his death, was found in the hallway on the floor where the victim lived.

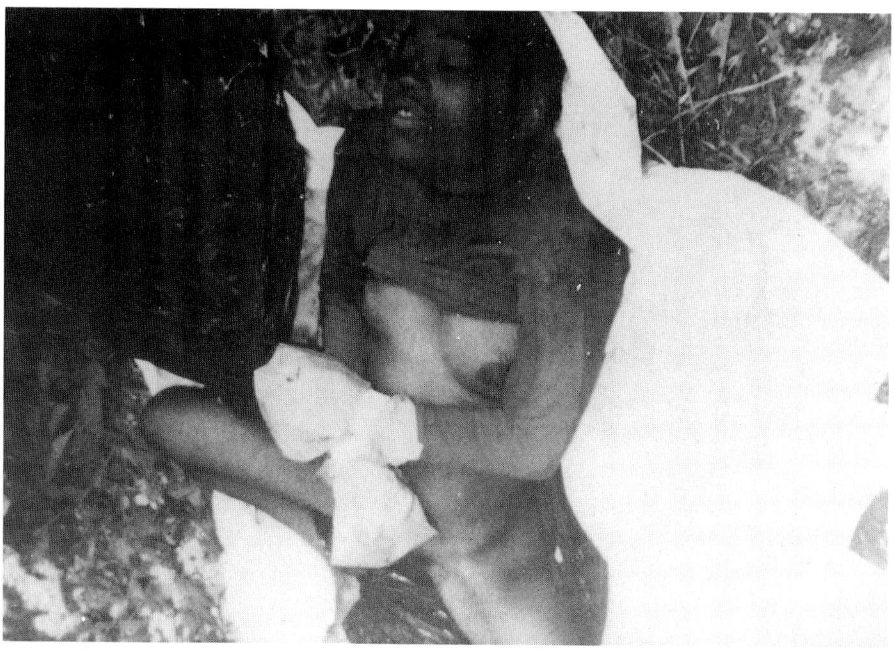

a

FIGURE 2.7a Scene investigation where a young African-American female was found wrapped in plastic bags and a blanket, partially clothed. The hands have been bagged by police officers at the scene to protect any evidence which may be present on the hands or under the fingernails. Note that the victim's top has been pushed up and away from the breasts and the genitalia are exposed.

b

FIGURE 2.7b Note that the jeans and underwear have been pulled off one leg and are around the thigh of the other leg. Cases of sexual assault require special care in collecting swabs and other evidence from the body prior to disrobing or washing the body. Loose fibers or hairs noted at the scene can be bagged and preserved before moving the body to ensure that they not be lost during transit (Table 2.5).

FIGURE 2.8 Weapons, especially knives, are sometimes found with the body or still within wounds on the body. They should be handled as little as possible with gloved hands, photographed, measured and then submitted to the investigating police agency.

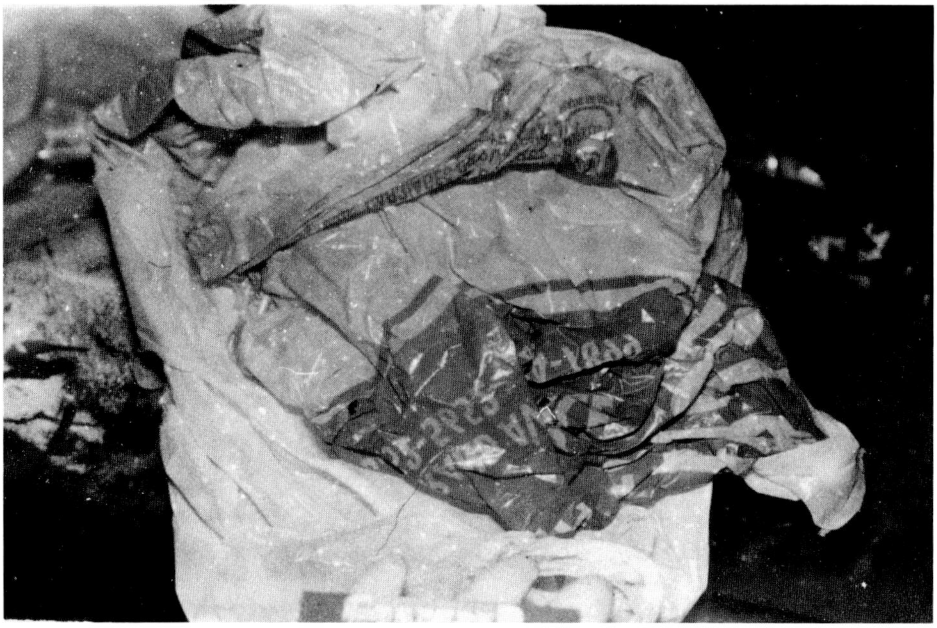

FIGURE 2.9 Plastic bag recovered from an asphyxia victim is photographed and then submitted for examination for fingerprints.

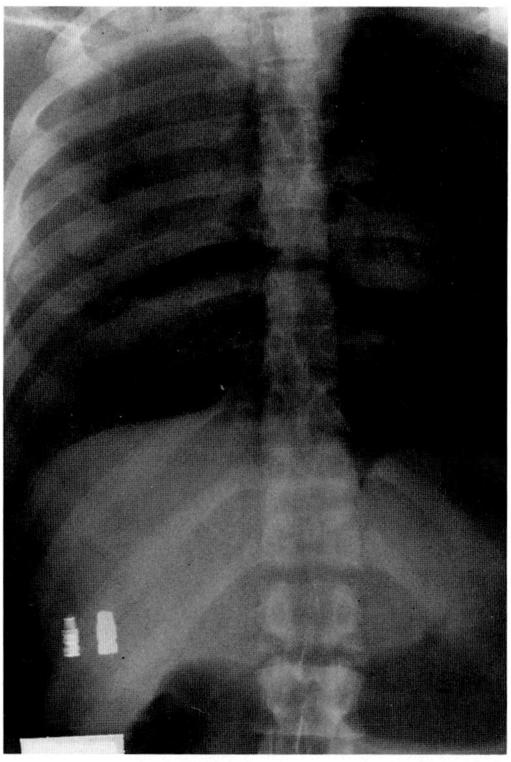

FIGURE 2.10 Radiograph taken of a gunshot victim with the recovered bullet placed next to the shadow of the bullet on the radiograph to demonstrate the magnification of the bullet in the film. This is a medium-caliber semiwadcutter bullet.

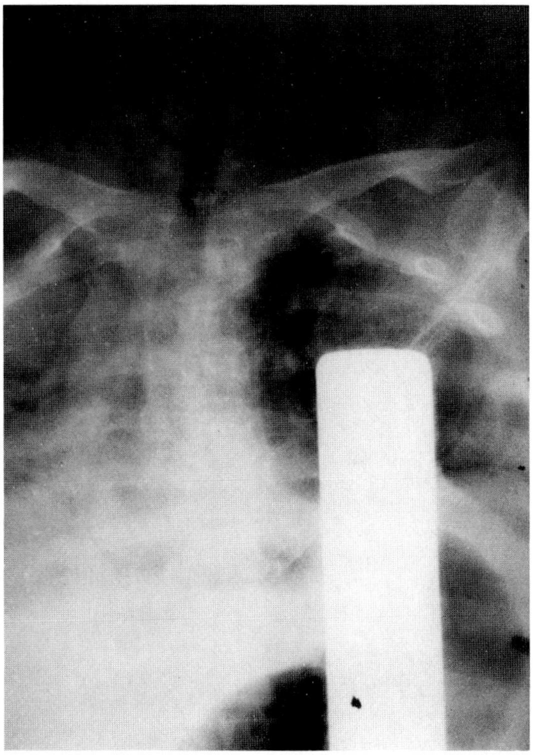

FIGURE 2.11 Chest radiograph taken of a construction worker who fell from a ladder and was impaled on a pipe. The displacement of the chest and abdominal organs by the pipe can be seen. There are several acute rib fractures on the left.

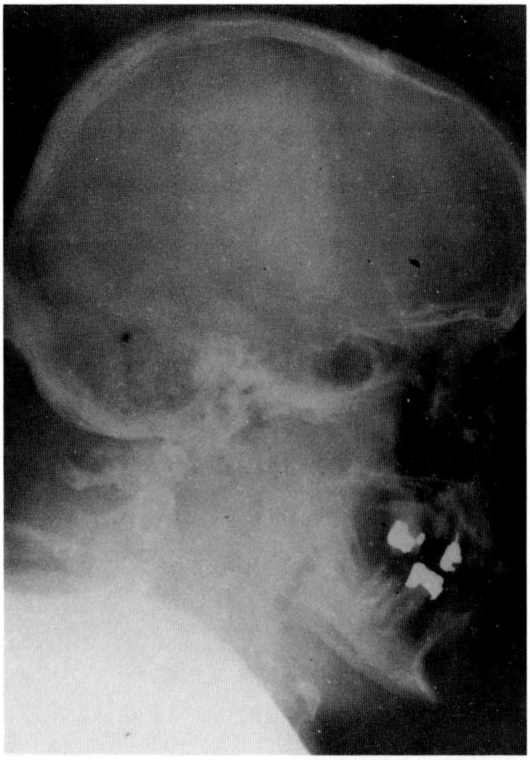

FIGURE 2.12 Lateral head and neck radiograph of a victim of a rear end motor vehicle collision. The victim was stopped at a red traffic signal and was struck from the rear by a car traveling at a high speed. The radiograph clearly demonstrates the posterior dislocation of the cervical spine.

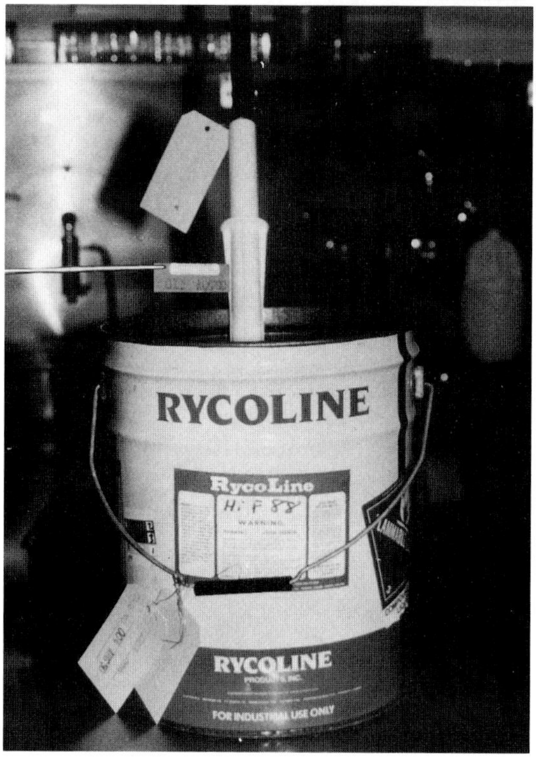

FIGURE 2.13 Industrial buckets, such as this, are used in the home as scrub buckets. The design makes them extremely stable and resistant to overturning. It is not uncommon for infants who can crawl and stand to drown in such containers if they are left out. This is not the white plastic bucket usually encountered in such tragedies. The bucket was removed from the home following the death so that studies to determine stability could be done, and also to prevent any further loss of life. These deaths are reported to the National Consumer Product Safety Commission.

3

Blunt Trauma Injuries

The most frequently encountered injuries in forensic medicine are those which are the result of blunt trauma. Blunt trauma injuries occur when the body impacts against something or something impacts against the body.

There are two major divisions of blunt injury, those where the skin is left intact and those where the skin is torn. The former includes abrasions and contusions, the latter, lacerations. Abrasions are friction type injuries where the surface epithelium is scraped away by the forces applied to the body. The abraded tissue piles up on the terminal margin corresponding to the direction of force. The appearance of the wound can give clues to the mechanism of injury. For example, brush burn abrasions are frequently encountered in pedestrian injuries, or in motor vehicle accidents where the passenger is ejected from the vehicle and scrapes along the pavement. Linear abrasions can also be seen if a victim is dragged from one location to another. Crushed abrasions, where the area of abrasion is depressed in relation to surrounding skin, can be seen when there is a direct perpendicular impact, sustained in a fall or from a blow. Bleeding may not occur if the wound is superficial and does not involve the blood vessels found within the dermal papillae. Abrasions are moist when they first occur due to the release of tissue fluids. In the dead, abrasions appear dry, leathery, and brown. Abrasions can occur during the postmortem period, and can be distinguished from antemortem or perimortem injuries by their translucent appearance and yellow color.

Contusions (bruises) occur when blunt force is applied to an area of skin, crushing blood vessels and releasing red blood cells into the surrounding tissue. Superficial bruises can appear immediately following trauma. Deeper bruises may not be visible immediately or may not appear for several hours, or never be visible at all. In large deep bruises, the hemorrhage may dissect along fascial planes causing the bruise to appear at an area distant from the actual point of impact. During a forensic autopsy, it is often necessary to dissect the deep soft tissues of the back, buttocks, and extremities in order to document injury not visible on the surface of the body. This posterior dissection is particularly helpful in cases of child abuse, pedestrian injury or deaths in custody (Tables 3.1, 3.2).

Bruises may be patterned and allow the examiner to identify the object that caused the injury. The color of bruises can be used to estimate the age of the injury, but it must be remembered that color is a factor not only of the age of a bruise, but the depth of the hemorrhage within the tissues, the natural skin tones of the individual, and the intactness of the red blood cells. Acute bruises tend to have a blue, red, or a purple coloration. There may also be swelling of the area if the victim survived for a time after the injury allowing the inflammatory process to begin. As the hemoglobin begins to break down, there will be a corresponding color change from red, blue, or purple to green, then to yellow and finally brown. This reflects the chemical changes of hemoglobin as it is converted to the storage form of iron, hemosiderin, which is a brown pigment. The time frame for bruises to heal and disappear is about 2 weeks to a month depending on the size and location of the bruise and the local circulation. Bruises in the red, blue, and purple range are thought to be about 1 to 5 days of age, green indicates an age of approximately 5 to 7 days, yellow indicates an age of approximately 7 to 10 days, and brown indicates an approximate age of greater than 10 days. These time frames are for reference, and will vary from individual to individual.

Microscopic examination is thought to be more reliable for aging bruises, and should be employed when possible. But even microscopic changes vary from individual to individual and must be interpreted cautiously. The presence of numerous bruises of varying color in a case of child abuse can mean that there have been multiple episodes of abuse over a period of time. It is not uncommon to find numerous bruises of different ages over the bony prominences on the body of chronic alcoholics. The size of a bruise may be a reflection of the amount of force applied to the area, but the size also depends on the vascular fragility and the clotting abilities of the individual and the looseness of the tissues surrounding the damaged vessels.

Lacerations are blunt trauma injuries where the epidermis is no longer intact. Lacerations are tears of the skin that occur when the tissue is stretched beyond the normal elastic limits. The margins of lacerations are usually irregular, and may show abrasions and bruises, or tissue bridges which are thin strands of intact elastic fibers, blood vessels, or nerve fibers that have a greater elasticity and that remain intact, stretching from one margin to the other. In lacerations caused by tangential forces, there may be undermining of one margin of the wound, on the side of the injury that corresponds to the direction of the force applied. Lacerations are more commonly encountered in skin that is over bone, such as the scalp, or over the long bones of the lower extremities. Some scalp lacerations may have very sharply defined margins similar to those of incised wounds. Examination of the hair over the injury can be useful. If the hairs are intact, and not cut, the injury is likely a laceration and due to blunt force. The presence of foreign material within the wound can also help identify the injury as a laceration and not an incision.

Abrasions are blunt trauma injuries unique to the skin. Contusions and lacerations are found within the body as well as on the surface of the body. Examination of victims of assaults, motor vehicle accidents, abuse, and falls will reveal lacerations and contusions of the internal organs. Subgaleal hemorrhages are found on the undersurface of the scalp in blunt head trauma. It is not unusual to find subgaleal hemorrhage where no obvious injuries are found on the scalp. This is due in part to the protection provided by the hair. Massive internal injuries to the abdominal organs may be found without obvious injury to the skin of the abdomen. This is particularly common in victims of child abuse, where lacerations of the liver, pancreas, and mesentery and rupture of the bowel may be found with little or no bruising noted on the body surface.

Bone fractures occur in blunt trauma as well as in penetrating trauma such as gunshot wounds. Long bone fractures of the legs are common in pedestrian and motor vehicle accidents. The presence of leg fractures in a pedestrian may be an important clue to the circumstances of the accident. Fractures of the feet and ankles in motor vehicle accidents help differentiate driver from passengers if all occupants of a vehicle are ejected. Location and type of skull fracture identified at autopsy can provide information as to the order in which injury occurred, or the mechanism of injury (Table 3.3). Fat or bone marrow emboli can result from bone fractures leading to pulmonary or systemic symptoms. Fat emboli can occur when fatty tissue alone is subject to trauma. Fat or bone marrow emboli may be identified on histologic examination or may be seen grossly as the presence of multiple petechial hemorrhages within the cerebral and cerebellar white matter.

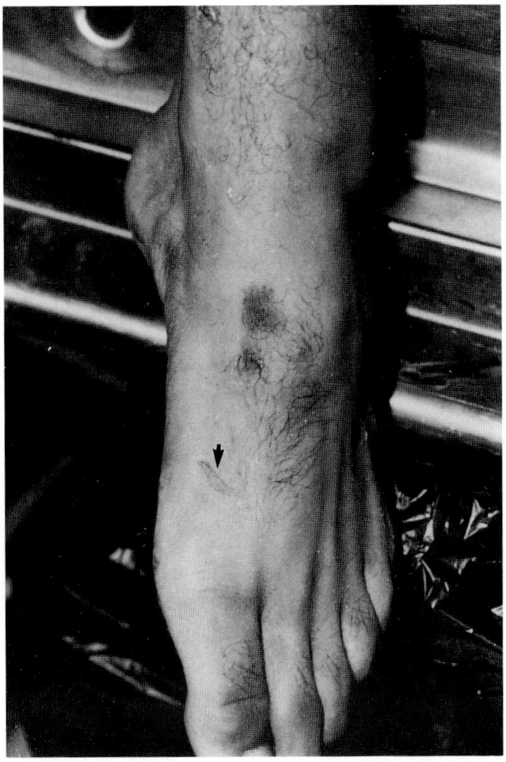

FIGURE 3.1 Superficial abrasion on the dorsum of the foot. Note the tissue piled on the terminal end of the wound (*arrow*), indicating the direction of force to be from ankle toward the toes. Fine striations are noted in the deeper portions of the injury near the ankle from the material of the sock the victim was wearing at the time the injury occurred.

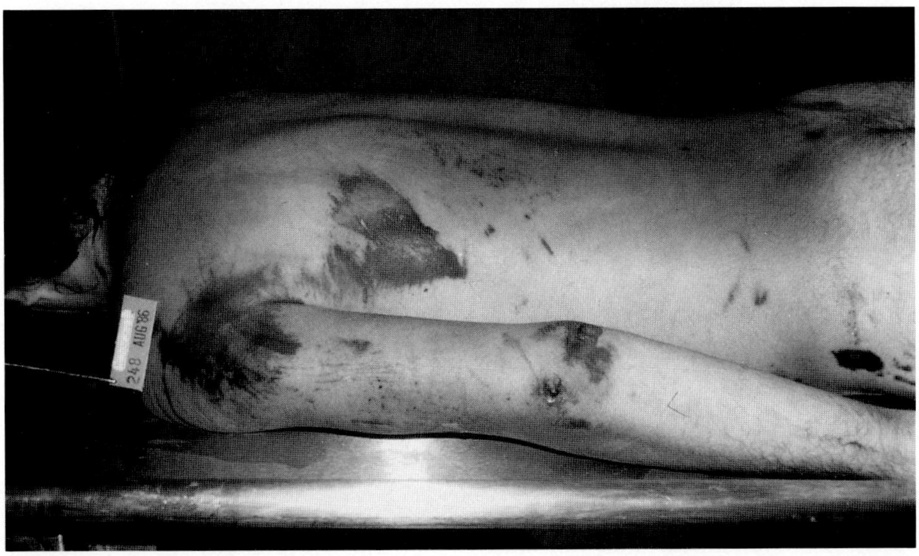

FIGURE 3.2 Brush burn or road burn abrasions on the back and shoulder of a pedestrian which were sustained from friction forces between the body and the road as the body slid along the road after being struck. The injuries have a dry brown appearance.

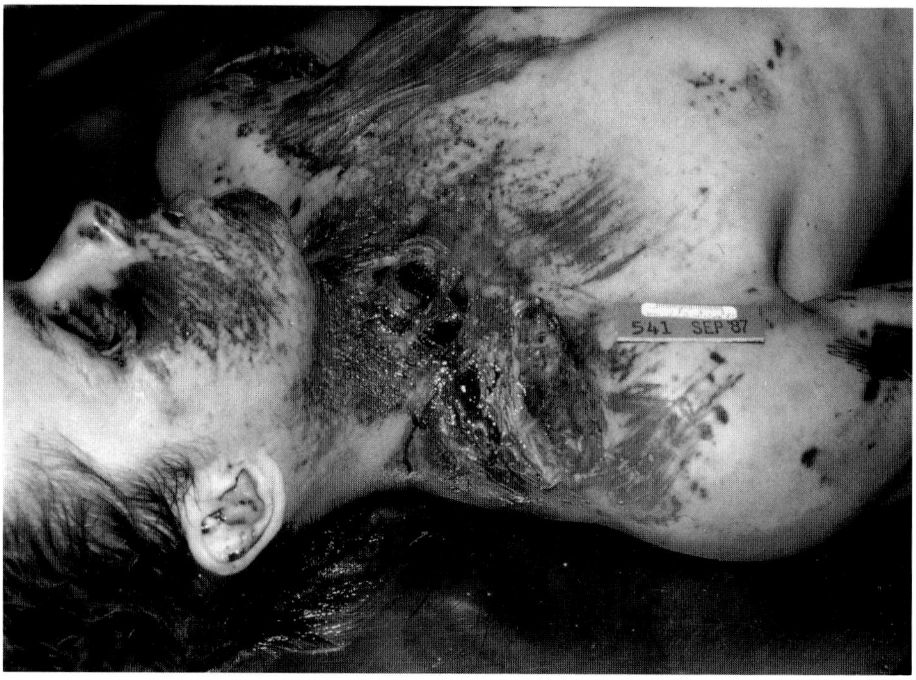

FIGURE 3.3 Abrasions on the chest and shoulders showing a linear pattern on a young motorcycle rider who was involved in a high-speed accident and was dragged along the ground by the motorcycle. Note that there are no injuries to the head above the level of the ears as he was wearing a helmet.

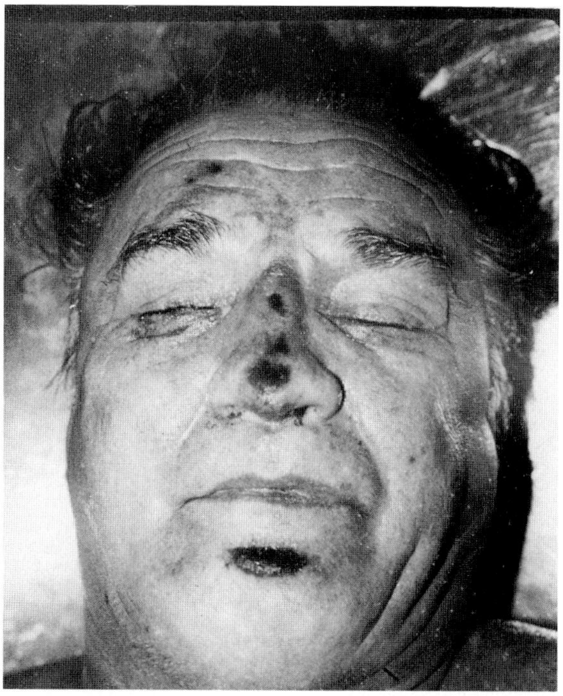

FIGURE 3.4 Crush abrasions on the forehead, nose, and chin of a middle-aged man who collapsed face down following a massive myocardial infarction. The abrasions are depressed in relationship to the surrounding skin and are found over the prominent portions of the face. Some bruising of the nose is also present. By the location and appearance of the injuries, it can be determined that they all occurred at the same time from a single impact, such as sustained in a fall, and that the victim died around the time the injuries were sustained.

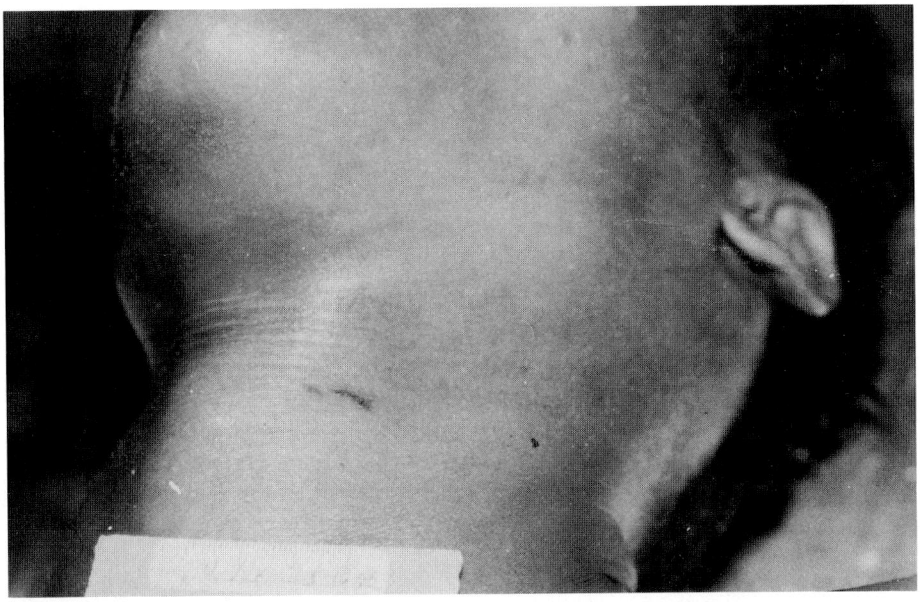

FIGURE 3.5 Fingernail abrasions on the neck of the victim of a strangulation. The curve of the nail is convex upward. These marks were made by the victim as she tried to pull the offender's hands from her neck. There are bruises on the skin above and to the right of the abrasions which were made by the offender.

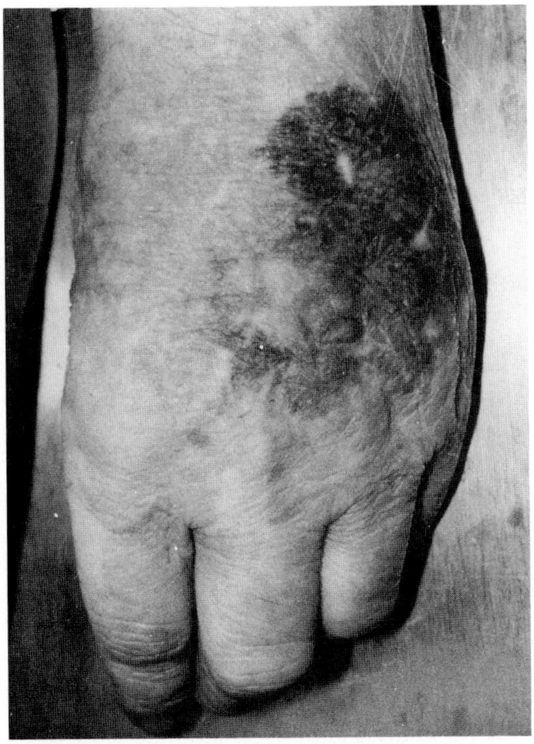

FIGURE 3.6 Senile purpura on the dorsal surface of the hand of an elderly man. The elderly have increased vascular fragility and loose soft tissues which leads to the development of bruises from minor day-to-day trauma. These areas of purple or purple-red discoloration can become permanent. They are common on the backs of the hands, the elbows, and the forearms. They are sites of trauma, but are not evidence of abuse or assault.

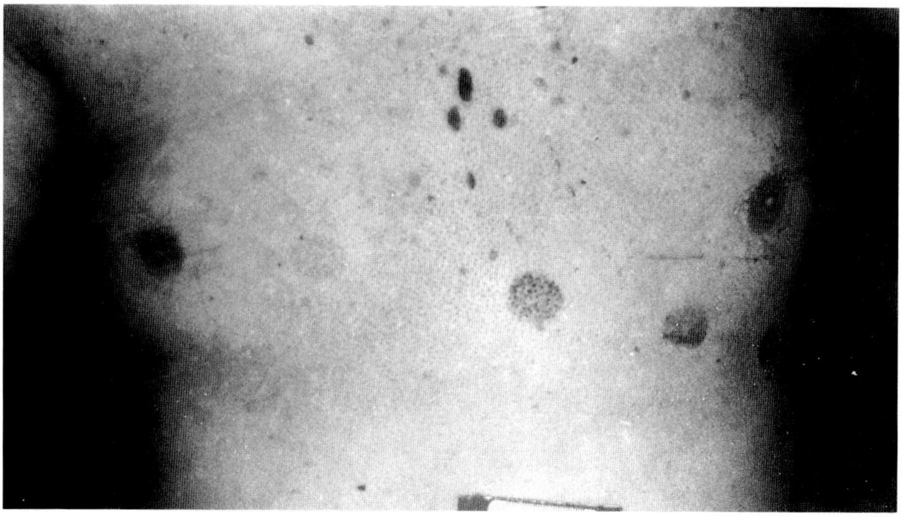

FIGURE 3.7 Suction contusions noted on the chest from the application of suction cup electrocardiogram leads. Small oval contusions similar to these can be seen on the neck or the breast area from "love bites".

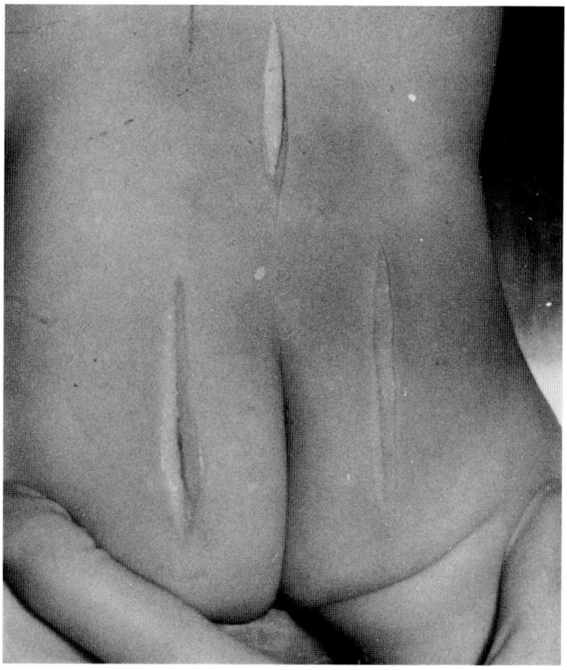

FIGURE 3.8 Incisions have been made through multiple mongolian spots, or birth marks, found on the buttocks and sacral area of a victim of child abuse to demonstrate the lack of hemorrhage in the underlying soft tissue. The infant survived for several days before dying from massive head injury. The medical records indicated numerous bruises over the victim's buttocks and back, which were the mongolian spots shown. At autopsy, the injuries were confined to the head.

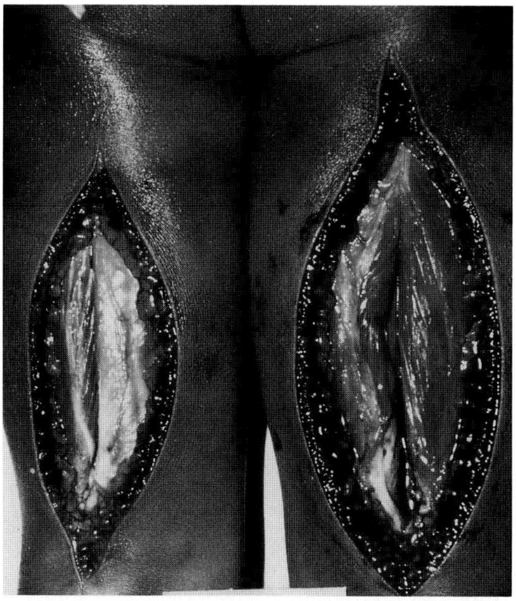

FIGURE 3.9 Incisions have been made into large bruises found on the posterior thighs of a 5-year-old African-American male child who had been beaten with hands, a stick, and a belt. The incisions demonstrate the amount of blood loss into the subcutaneous tissue in the areas of bruising.

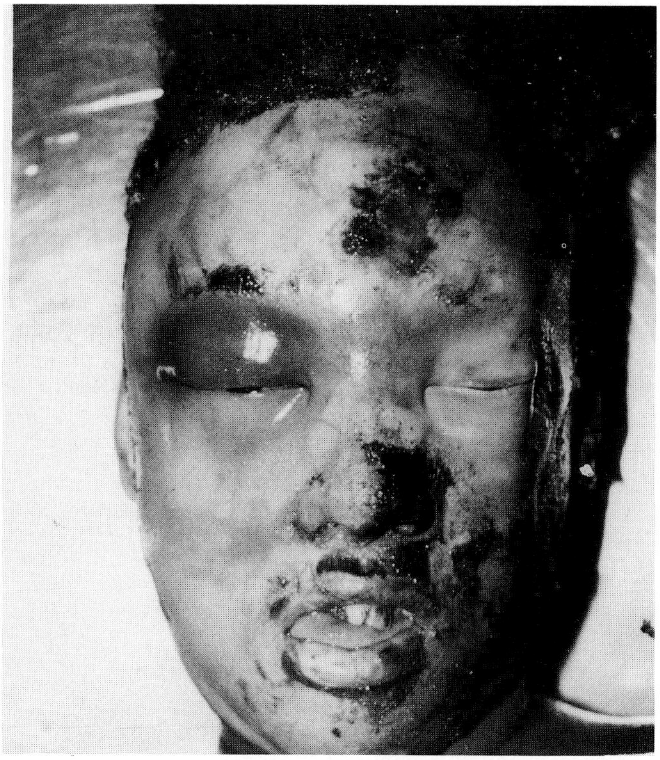

FIGURE 3.10 There are many decomposition artifacts which can be misinterpreted as antemortem injury. True antemortem injury can be identified and differentiated from artifact in decomposed bodies. The bruising of the right eye of this teenage African-American male, pulled from a sewer drain, can still be clearly identified even though the epidermis has sloughed. The death resulted from a linear skull fracture and brain injury sustained from a blow with a golf club. The body was placed in the sewer drain in an effort to conceal the crime. The very dark discoloration of the nose and forehead is from materials within the sewer staining the body.

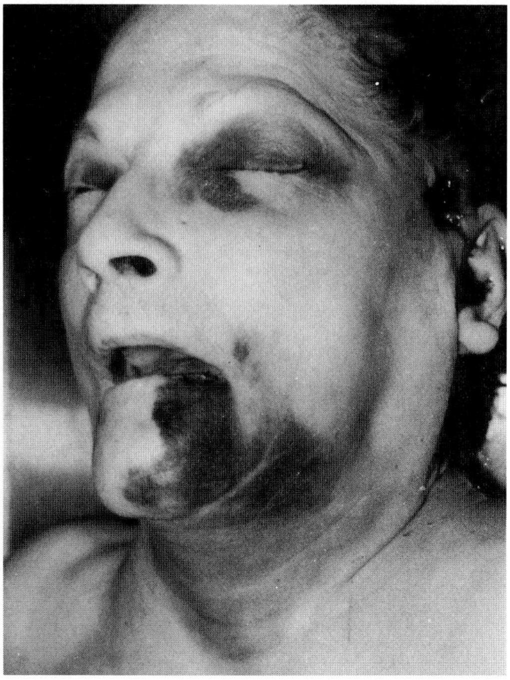

FIGURE 3.11 This elderly white female was first thought to be the victim of spousal abuse because of the extensive bruising about the eyes and jaw. A stellate, contact-range gunshot wound of entry was found on the left temple. The bruising of the eyes resulted from fractures of the orbital plates on the base of the skull from the gunshot wound to the head. Examination of the mouth showed sutures in the left lower gum. Investigation revealed that the subject had several teeth removed the afternoon before her death with the resultant bruises on the jaw and neck. Based on the investigation and the physical examination, the death was ruled a suicide.

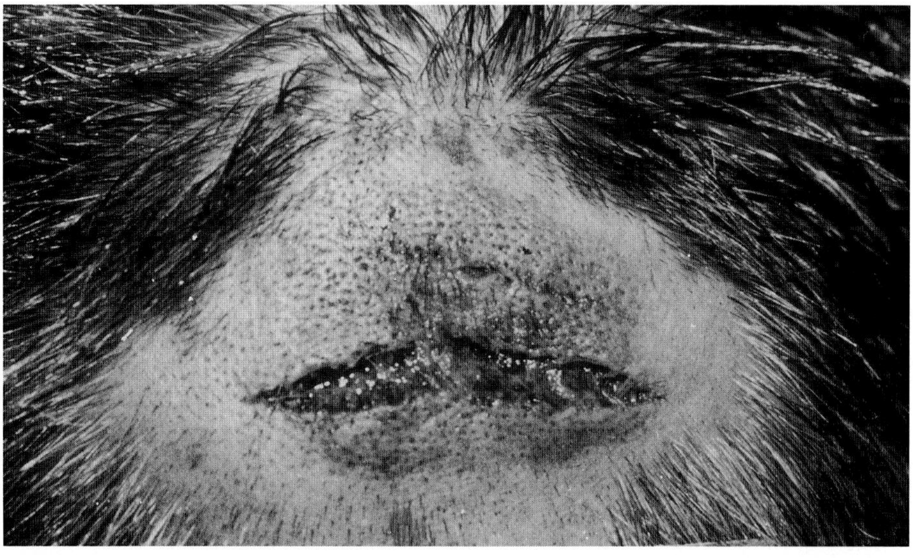

FIGURE 3.12 This middle-aged white male was found unresponsive on the street. Examination of the body revealed this abraded laceration on the occipital region of the head. The upper margin of the wound was undermined, indicating an upward direction to the force causing the injury. This is consistent with the injury occurring as the subject collapsed and struck the back of his head on the curb. There was no underlying subgaleal hemorrhage, indicating that the heart had stopped prior to collapse.

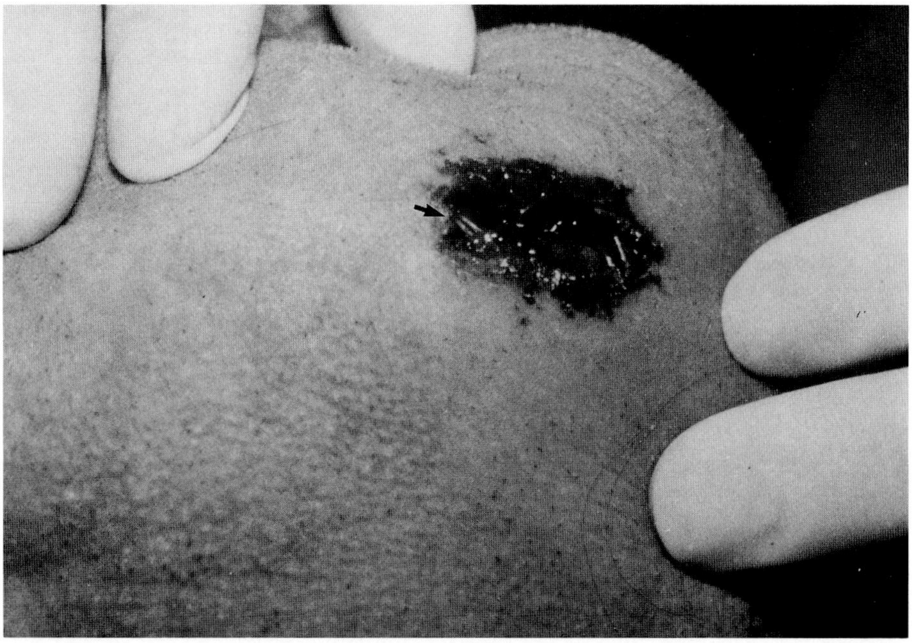

FIGURE 3.13 This laceration on the undersurface of the chin of an elderly man who sustained a single stab wound to the precordium was thought to be a second stab wound by hospital personnel. Note the irregular abraded margin and the presence of fine tissue bridges (*arrow*) on either side of the wound which identify this injury as a laceration due to blunt trauma. The injury occurred when the victim collapsed and struck his chin on a step as he fell.

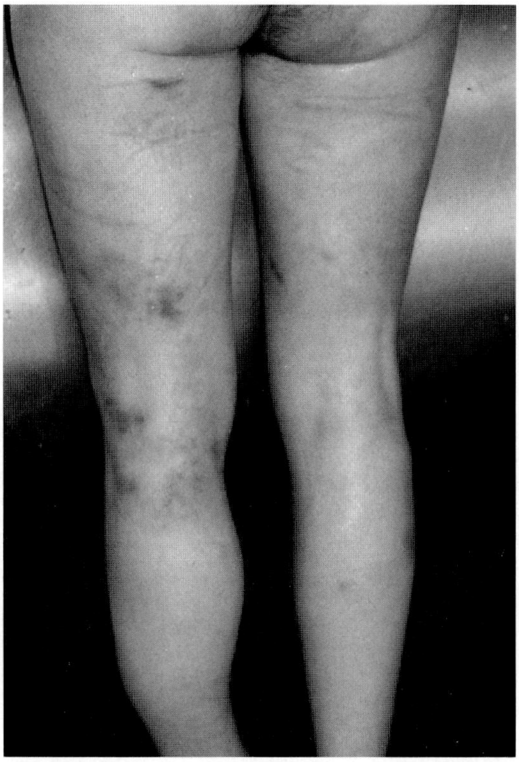

FIGURE 3.14 Fracture of the lower leg sustained by a pedestrian while walking across the street. The distance that a leg injury is above the heel is an indication of the height of the point of the vehicle which struck the victim. In vehicles without antilock brakes, the front end will dip when the brakes are applied, causing the injury to be lower down on the leg. In pedestrian versus motor vehicle cases, the lack of leg injury may be an indication that the pedestrian was lying, not standing, in the roadway at the time of impact. Crushing injury to the head, chest, or abdomen is found in such cases.

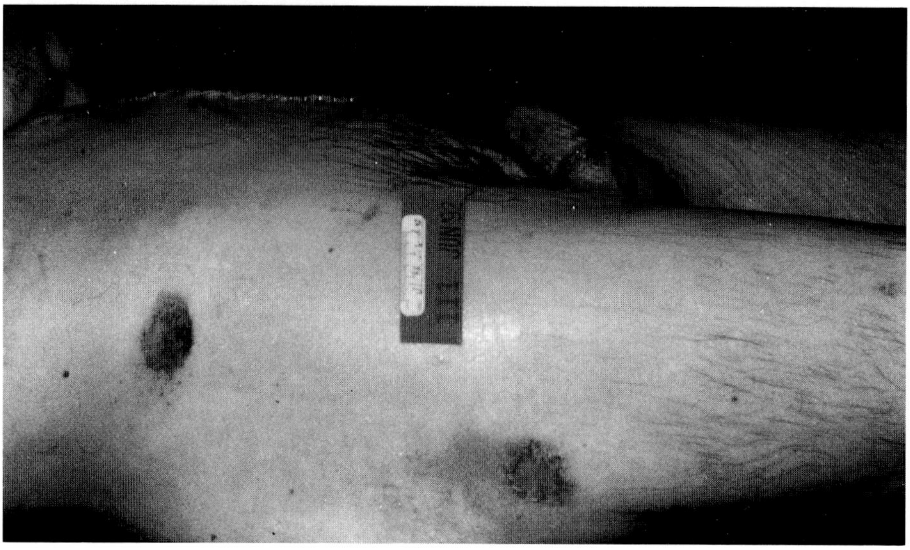

FIGURE 3.15 Abrasions and contusions on the right hip of a pedestrian struck by a motor vehicle. Pedestrian injury is primary, that which occurs when the vehicle strikes the body, secondary, when the body is lifted by the impact and strikes the hood, windshield, or roof of the vehicle, or, tertiary, those that occur when the body falls from the vehicle to the ground. These are primary injuries, from the impact of the vehicle with the subject. In hit-and-run incidents, the clothing, head hair samples, and blood from the victim should be given to the police. Any glass fragments, paint chips, plastic or metal fragments found on the clothing or the body of the victim should also be submitted to assist in identifying the vehicle involved in the incident.

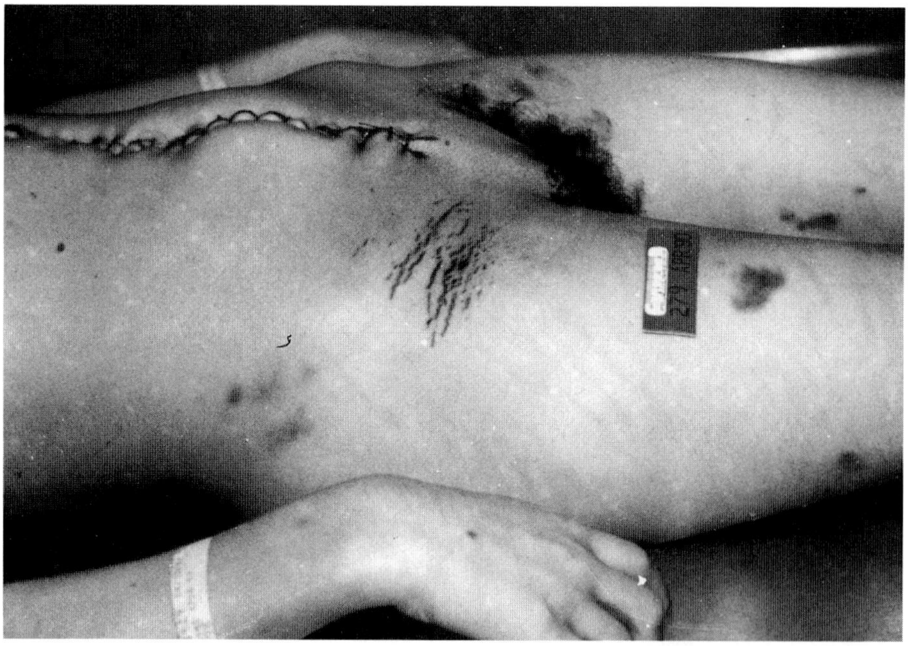

FIGURE 3.16 Note the superficial wavy lacerations of the skin of the right lower abdomen and groin. These result from overstretching of the skin in a pedestrian struck from the rear. The victim was taken from the scene to a local hospital where an exploratory laparotomy and thoracotomy were attempted. She sustained a complete separation of the spine at the level of the twelfth thoracic and first lumbar vertebrae. She was the victim of a hit-and-run driver. The height of the fracture in the body is consistent with being struck by a vehicle with a high front end such as a van or a truck. Witnesses to the incident described a dark, late model van fleeing the scene.

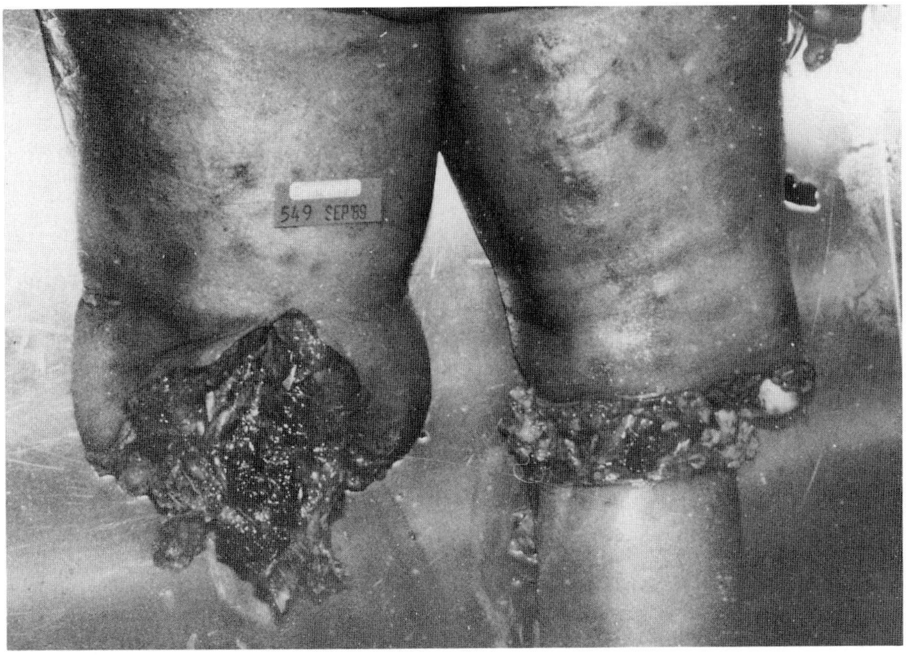

FIGURE 3.17 Massive pedestrian injury with complete traumatic amputation of the lower legs of an elderly crossing guard struck by an automobile traveling at very high speed. Similar injuries are seen when pedestrians are crushed between the striking vehicle and another fixed object.

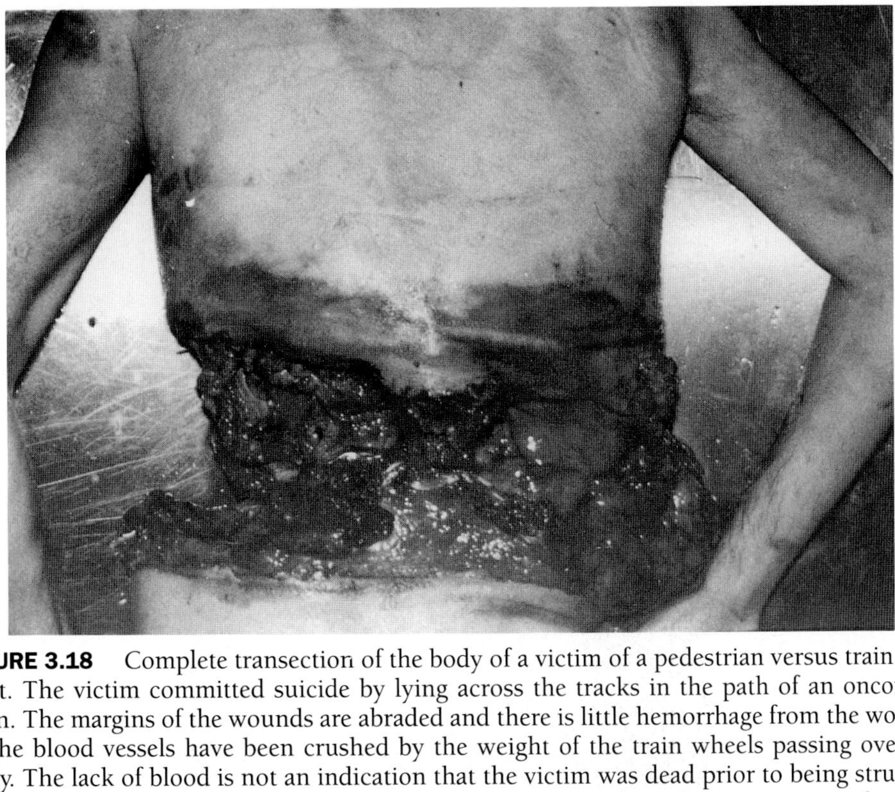

FIGURE 3.18 Complete transection of the body of a victim of a pedestrian versus train incident. The victim committed suicide by lying across the tracks in the path of an oncoming train. The margins of the wounds are abraded and there is little hemorrhage from the wounds as the blood vessels have been crushed by the weight of the train wheels passing over the body. The lack of blood is not an indication that the victim was dead prior to being struck in cases such as this. In most pedestrian versus train incidents, where the victim is upright, massive dismemberment occurs and the bodies frequently contain no blood due to marked blood loss.

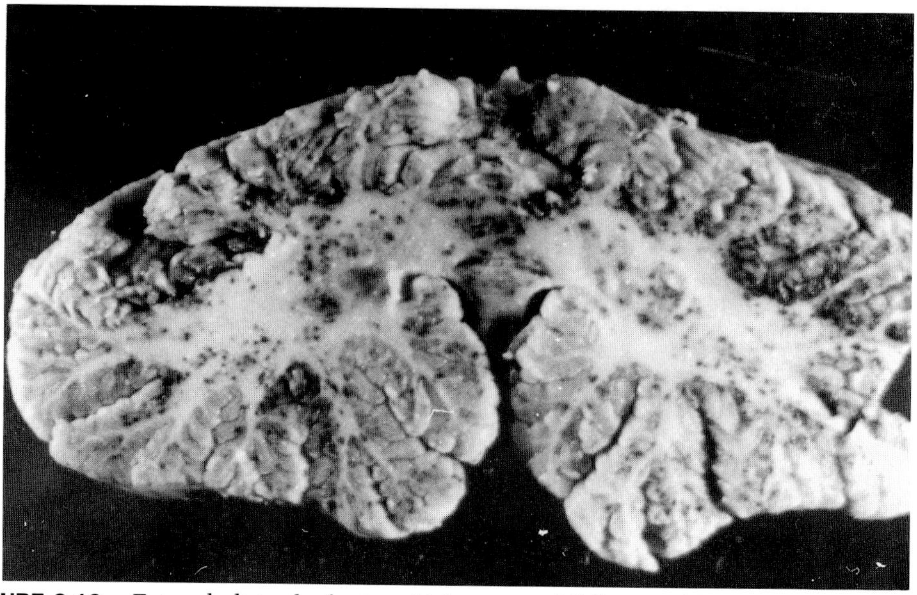

FIGURE 3.19 Fat emboli to the brain which occurred following blunt trauma to the body with crushing injuries of the subcutaneous fat and long bone fractures of the lower extremities. Death due to fat embolism in trauma cases can be delayed for two or more days after the injury is sustained.

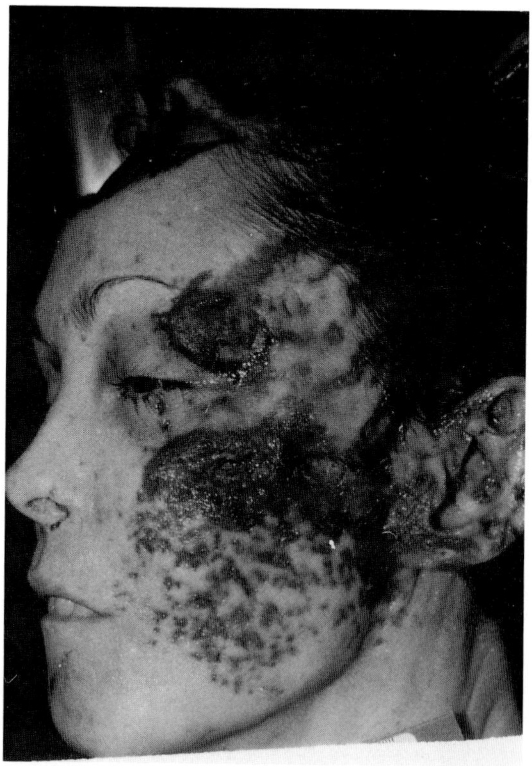

FIGURE 3.20 Dicing abrasions of the left side of the face and the ear in an automobile driver caused by fragments of the broken driver's side window striking the body.

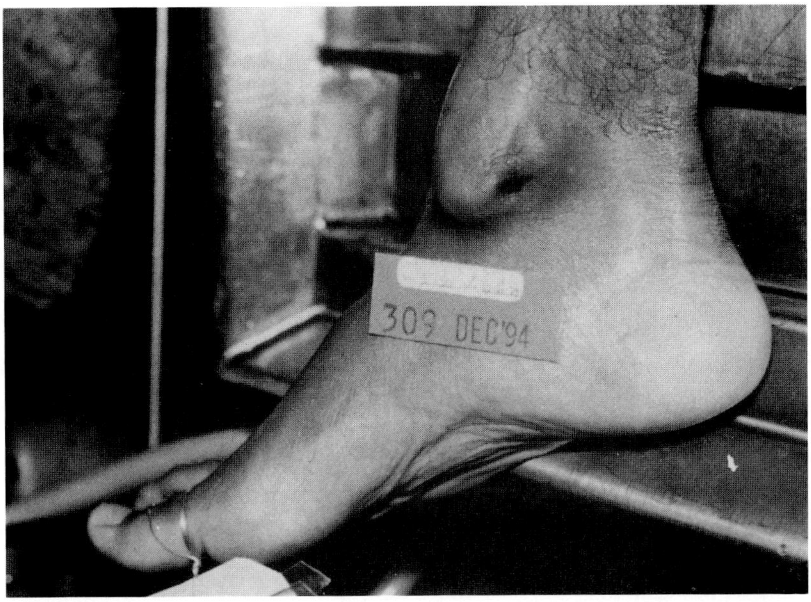

FIGURE 3.21 Pedal fracture of the ankle of a driver of a motor vehicle. This injury occurs when the feet are caught between or under the gas, brake, or clutch pedals in a collision.

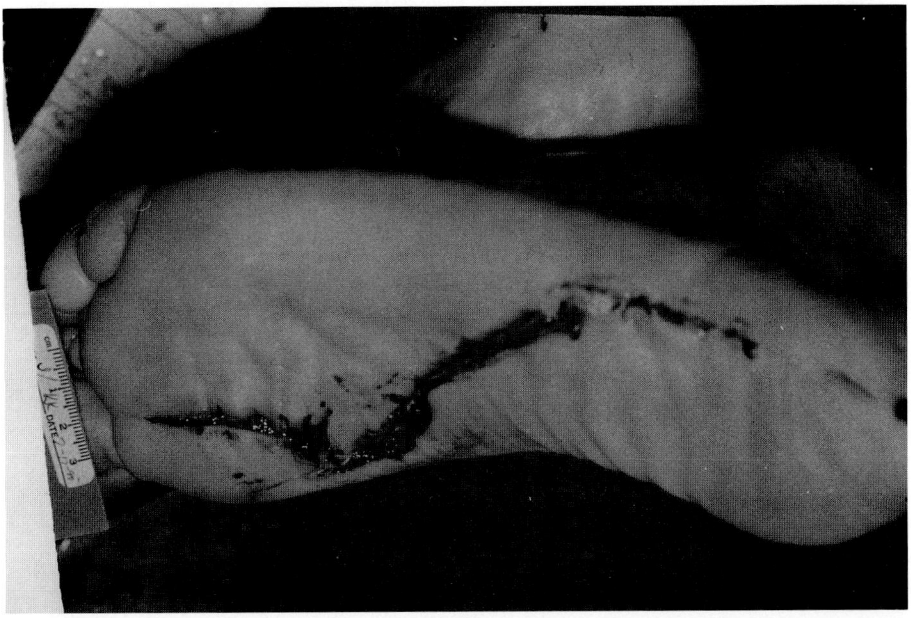

FIGURE 3.22 Laceration of the left sole found on a driver of an automobile who lost control of the vehicle and left the roadway before striking a tree head-on. The shoes of drivers involved in collisions should be examined for any sign of pedal impressions on the soles to indicate if the brake or accelerator was being depressed at the time of the accident.

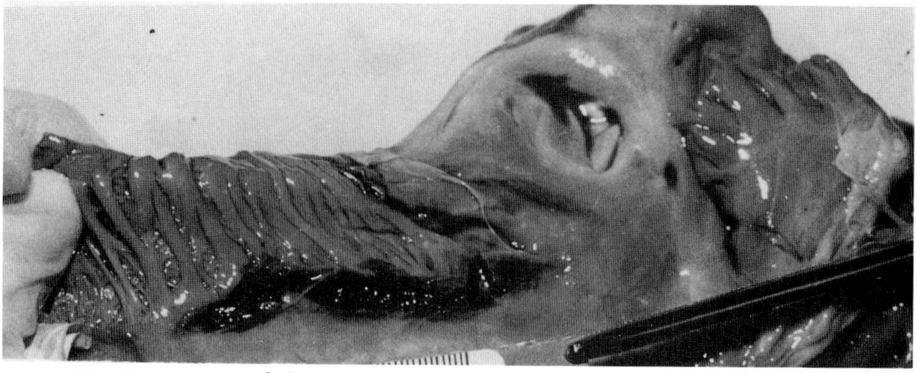

FIGURE 3.23 Laceration of the endocardium in the right atrium found in a driver of an automobile involved in a collision. The subject was not wearing a seat belt and struck the steering wheel with his chest. There was minimal bruising on the skin of the chest noted on external examination. Cardiac lacerations and contusions result from this type of impact. Lacerations of the aorta, usually at or just above the ligamentum arteriosus are found in head-on collisions, even in drivers and passengers wearing seat belts. These injuries occur because of the abrupt cessation of forward movement of the body, while the heart and other organs of the chest continue with their forward momentum. The tear occurs near the ligamentum because the aorta is firmly tethered at this point and relatively mobile above the ligamentum.

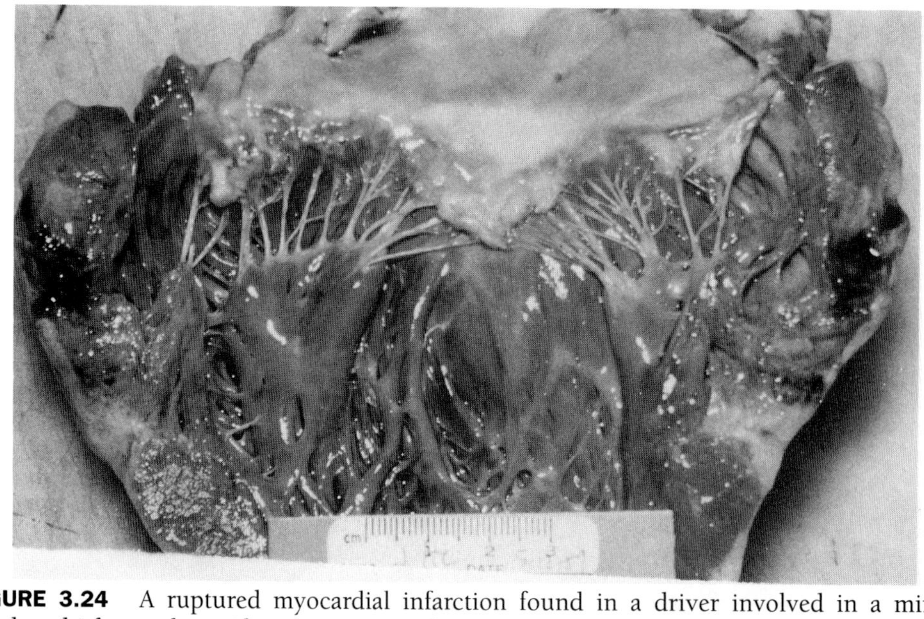

FIGURE 3.24 A ruptured myocardial infarction found in a driver involved in a minor single-vehicle accident. There was minimal damage to the vehicle and witnesses indicated that the driver appeared to collapse before the incident. This type of natural phenomenon, due to rupture of a preexisting infarction, must be differentiated from cardiac lacerations which can occur as a result of the blunt impact sustained in motor vehicle accidents.

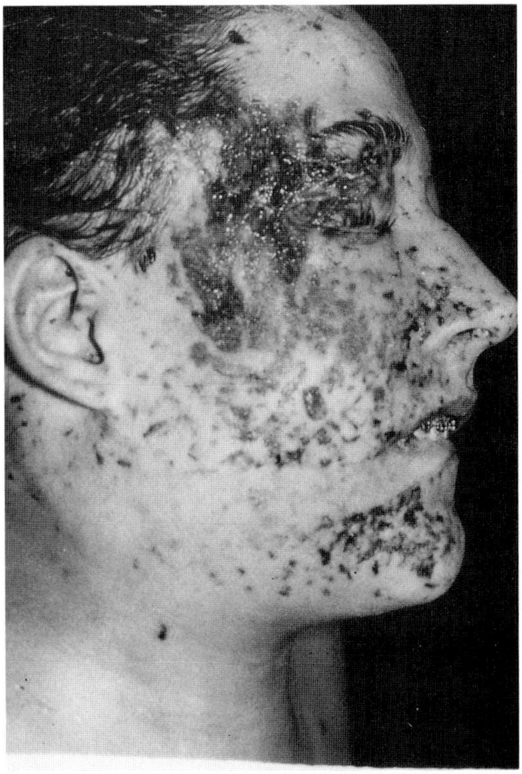

FIGURE 3.25 Dicing abrasions from window glass found on the right side of the face of a passenger in a motor vehicle. Both the driver and this passenger were ejected from the motor vehicle. Identification of driver and passenger is important in incidents where alcohol is involved, especially if one victim dies and another survives.

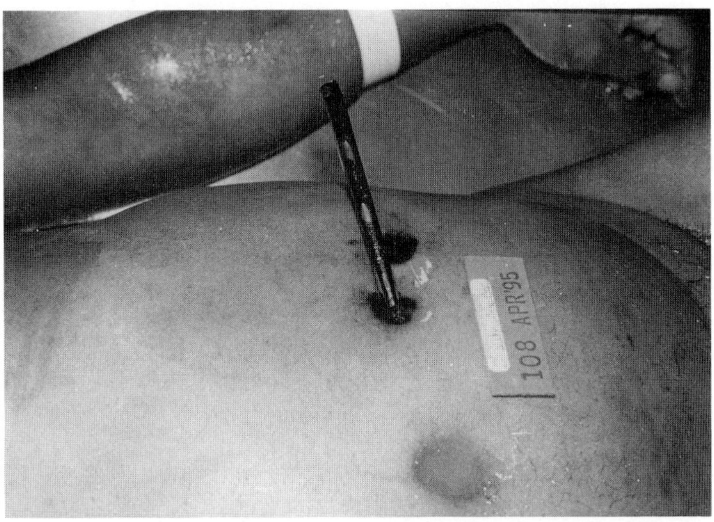

FIGURE 3.26 Impalement by a gear shift. This was the unrestrained passenger in a motor vehicle being driven at a high speed which was struck on the passenger side as it went through an intersection against the traffic signal. The injury lateral to the area of impalement is a round deep abrasion. Both driver and passenger in this vehicle were killed.

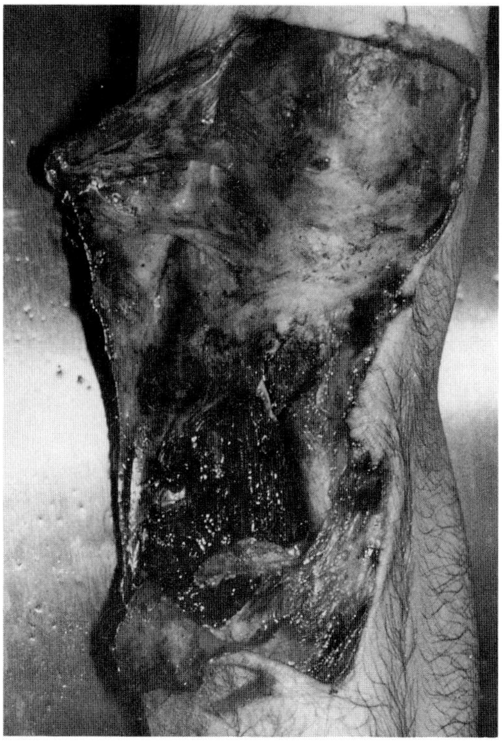

FIGURE 3.27 A large flap or avulsion laceration of the lower leg of a motorcycle rider involved in a collision. Similar avulsion type injuries can be seen in pedestrians where an extremity is run over by the wheels of the vehicle and the soft tissue is pulled away from the underlying bone.

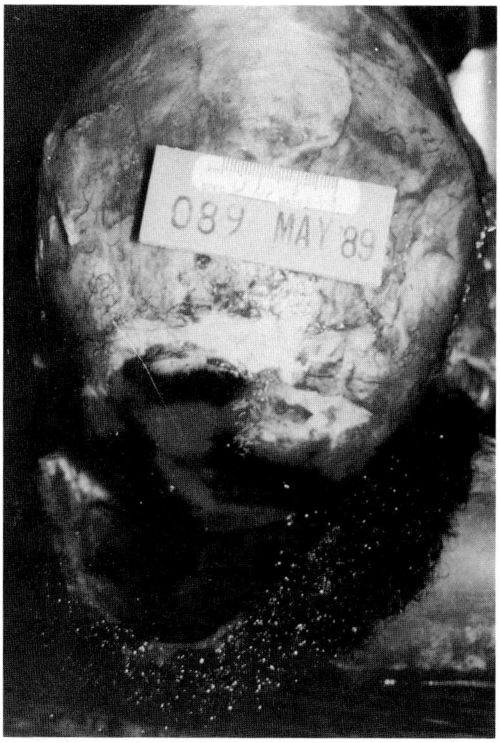

FIGURE 3.28 An occipital subgaleal hemorrhage, without injury to the external scalp, in a man found unresponsive on the street. Subgaleal hemorrhages are blunt trauma injuries due to blows to the head. They may also be caused by violent pulling of the hair. No bruising was obvious on the external surface of the scalp.

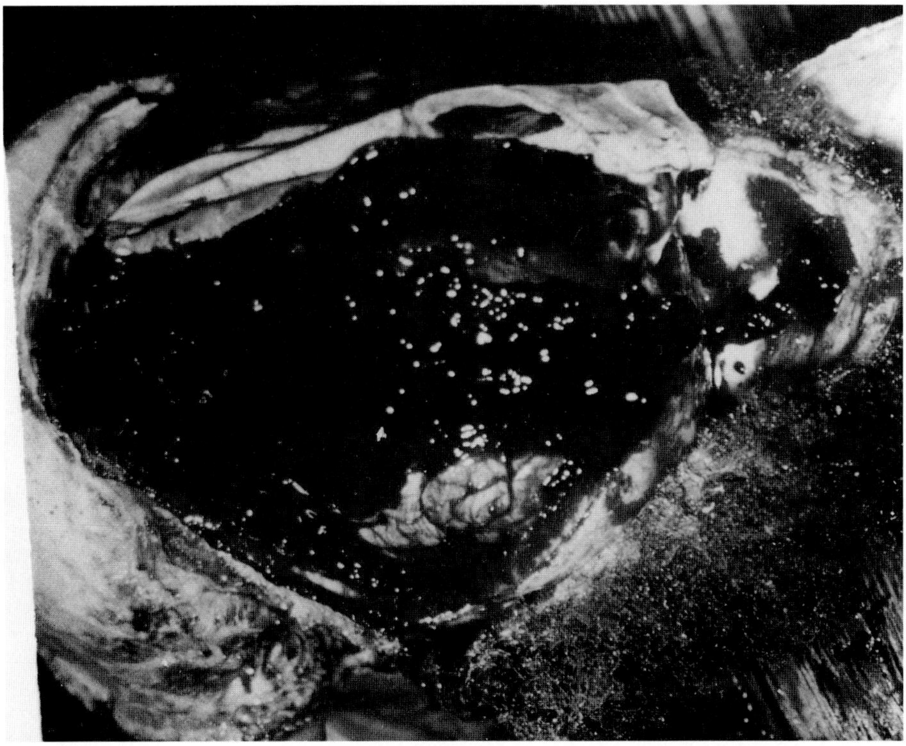

FIGURE 3.29 Large, soft, clotted, fresh subdural hematoma found in the same man. This type of injury commonly occurs in falls, especially in the elderly or in alcoholics and may be unilateral or bilateral. The location of the subdural hematoma, whether on the right or the left, is not an indication of the direction of force. Subdural hematomas can occur from violent shaking or compression of the heads of infants and young children (Table 3.4).

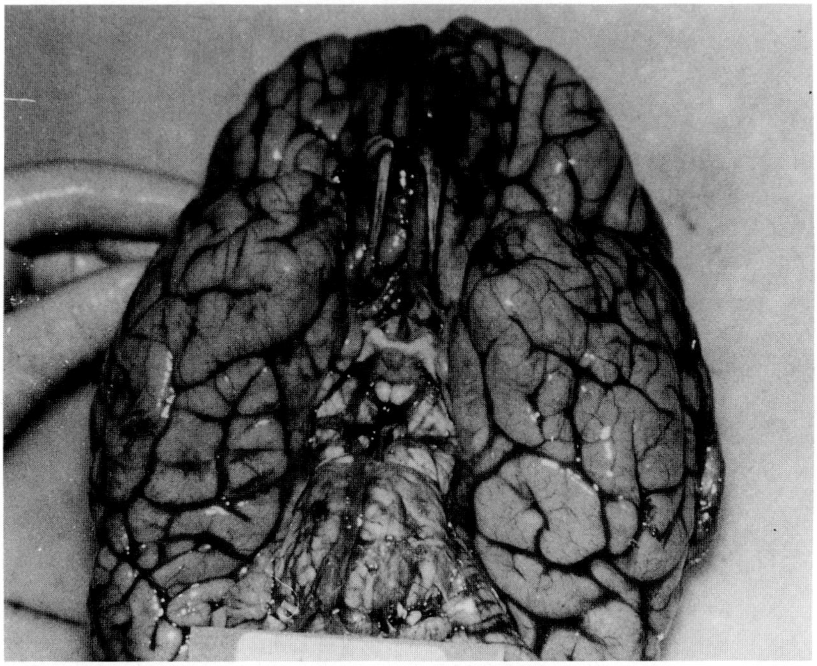

FIGURE 3.30 Gliding contusions on the base of the brain on the orbital surfaces of the frontal lobes and the tips of the temporal lobes. These occur as the brain moves across the base of the skull in falls. Similar contusions can be seen on the superior gyri of the cerebral hemispheres adjacent to the longitudinal fissure. There is cerebral edema with flattening of the gyri, especially on the base of the left temporal lobe.

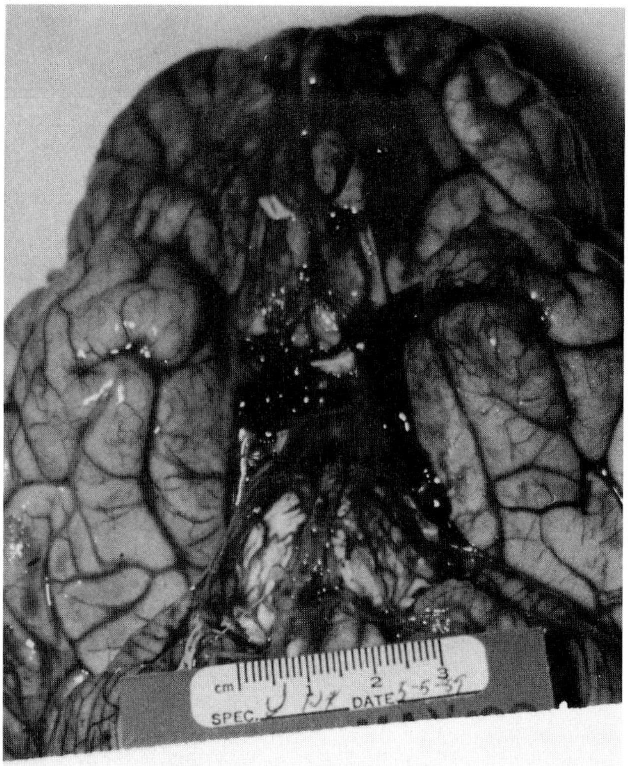

FIGURE 3.31 Gliding contusions of the orbital surface of the frontal lobes and the tips of the temporal lobes with soft clotted blood over the area of the optic chiasm from an associated subdural hematoma. The injuries occurred when the victim was punched during an altercation and fell back, striking the pavement with his head. The manner of death in this circumstance was ruled homicide.

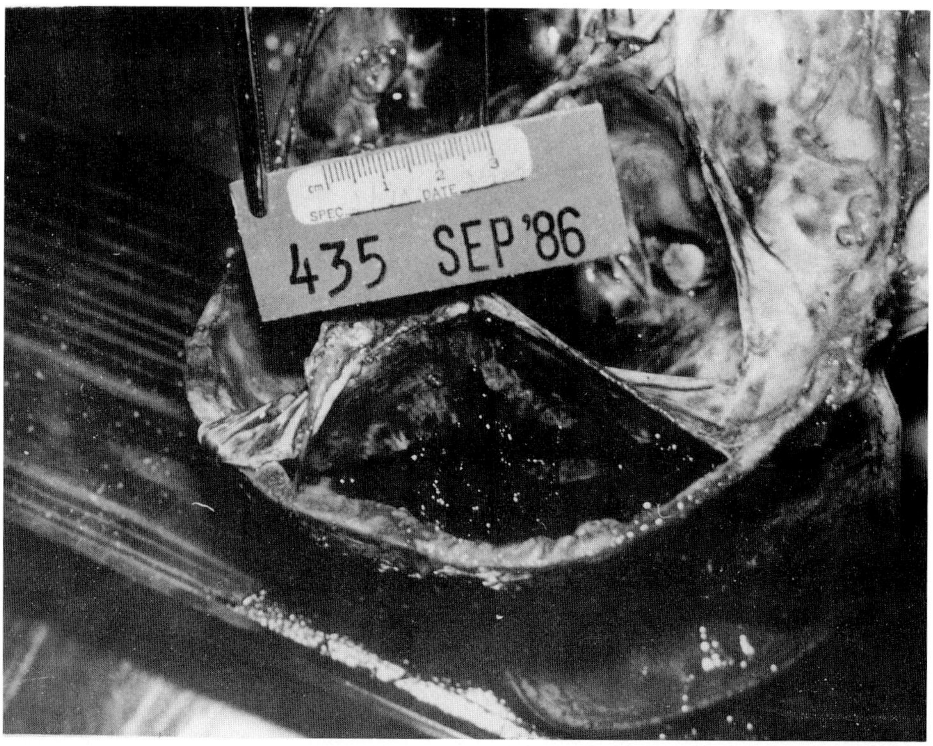

FIGURE 3.32 Clotted epidural hematoma which caused the death of a young boy who fell from a top bunk bed onto a bare concrete floor. This lesion is usually associated with fractures of the occipital bone. The hemorrhage is due to tears of the outer wall of the transverse or sigmoid sinus or the torcular herophili.

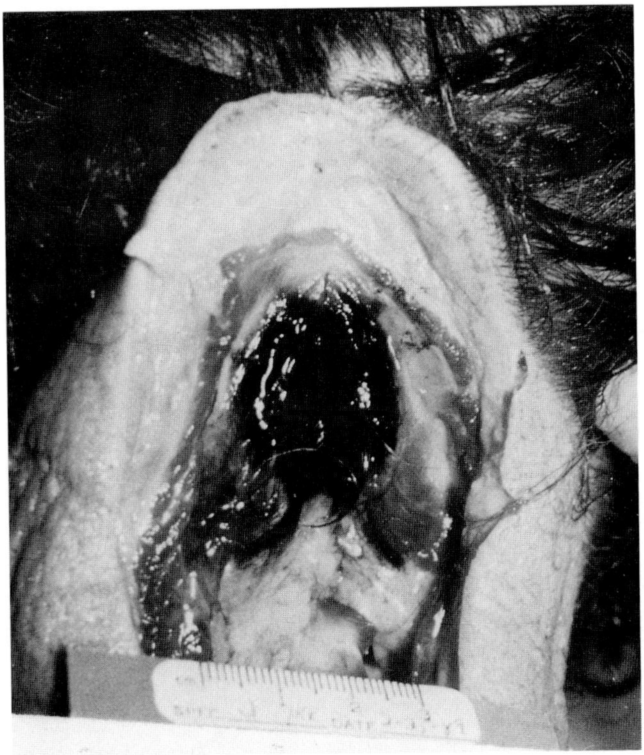

FIGURE 3.33 Posterior dissection of the neck done to demonstrate hemorrhage in the muscle and soft tissue adjacent to the upper cervical spine due to a fracture sustained in a fall down stairs. Fractures and dislocations may not be apparent on postmortem radiographs as rigor mortis makes it difficult to place the body in the proper position. Any unusual movement of the neck found during the autopsy should be investigated by doing this type of dissection to look for evidence of a fracture.

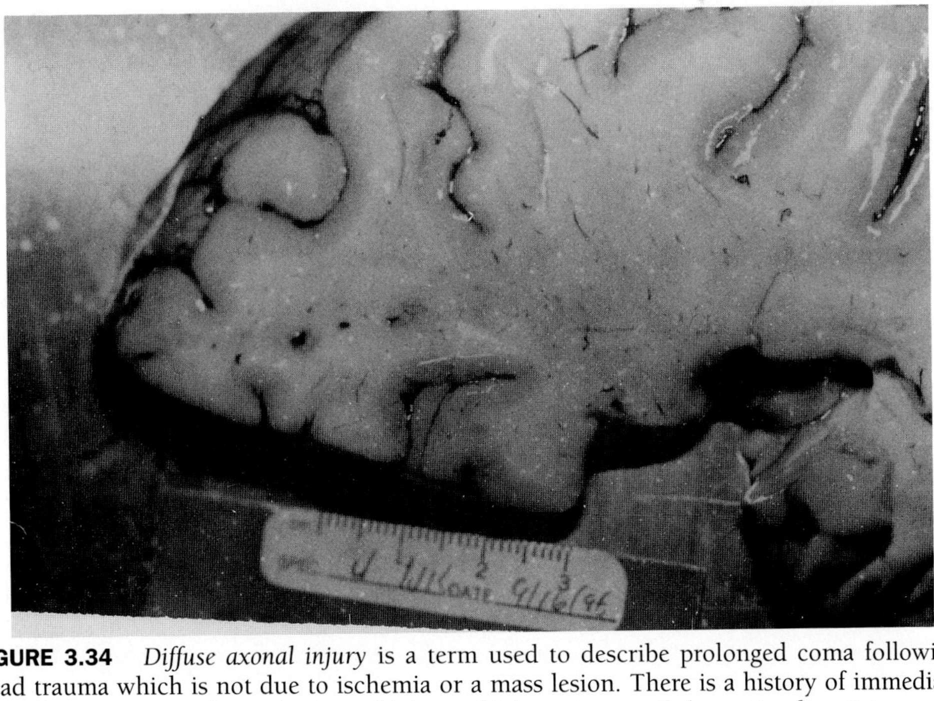

FIGURE 3.34 *Diffuse axonal injury* is a term used to describe prolonged coma following head trauma which is not due to ischemia or a mass lesion. There is a history of immediate loss of consciousness from the time of injury which persists until the victim dies. It is caused by severe shearing injuries with tearing of axons throughout the brain. Grossly, small hemorrhages are seen throughout the brain and in the corpus callosum.

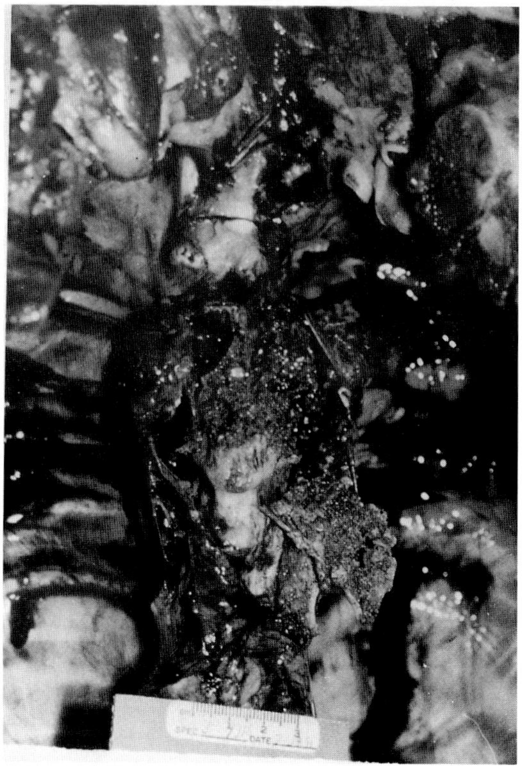

FIGURE 3.35 Burst fracture of the thoracic spine. This was sustained in a fall from a ladder onto a beam which was lying on the floor. The fracture is located at the point of initial impact, where there is the greatest expenditure of kinetic energy.

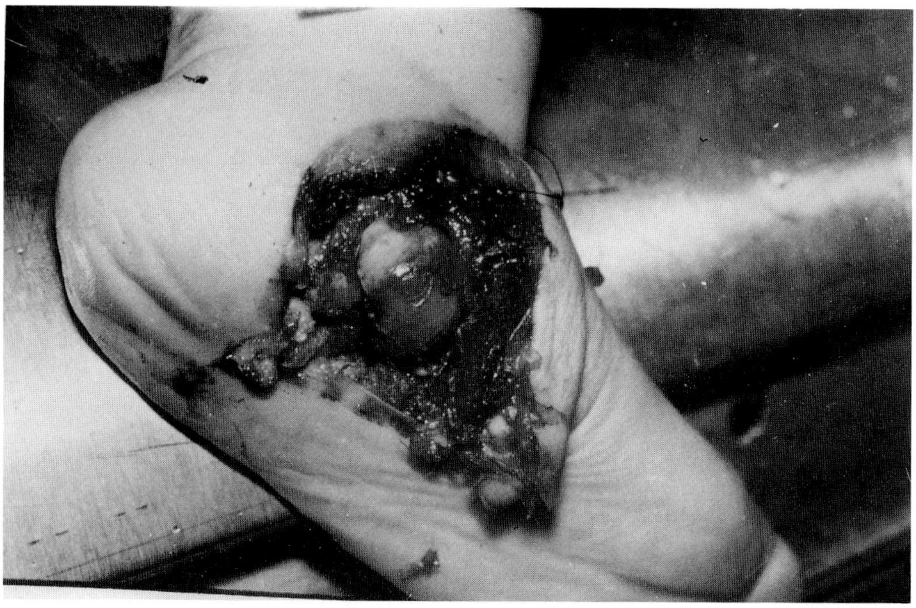

FIGURE 3.36 Laceration with protrusion of the tibia through the sole of the foot sustained in a fall from a height with the victim landing on the feet. A ring fracture may be seen in the base of the skull around the foramen magnum if the force of the impact is transmitted up the spinal column to the skull. Injuries sustained in falls will vary depending on the distance of the fall, the weight of the victim, the position of the victim during the fall, and whether the victim was stationary at the time of the fall or took a running start. The most severe trauma will be found at the point of initial impact with additional, less severe injury if the body then bounces and rolls. Injury can also occur if the body strikes objects on the way down.

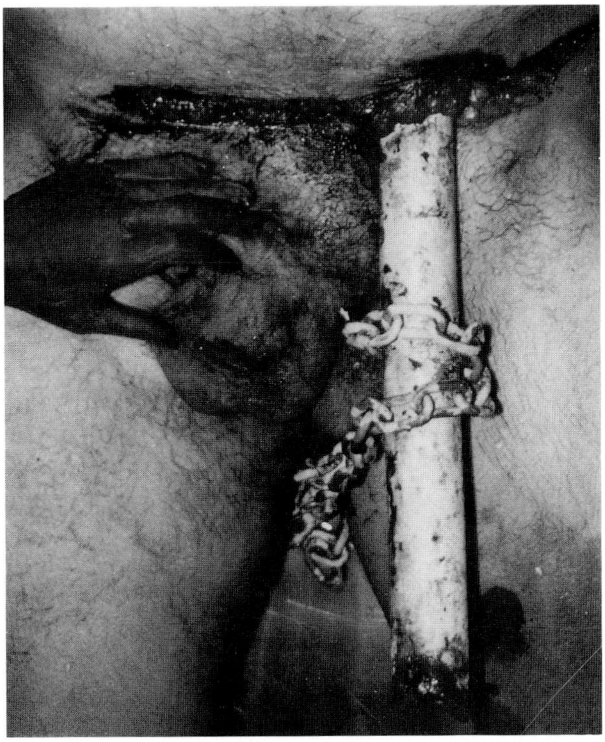

a

FIGURE 3.37a A construction worker who fell from a ladder was impaled on an upright pole adjacent to the ladder. There is a large laceration of the abdomen extending on either side of the point of impact and an abrasion on the skin above the entry point which occurred at the time of penetration. There are postmortem full-thickness thermal burns on the inner thigh caused by an acetylene torch used to cut the pipe so that the body could be moved.

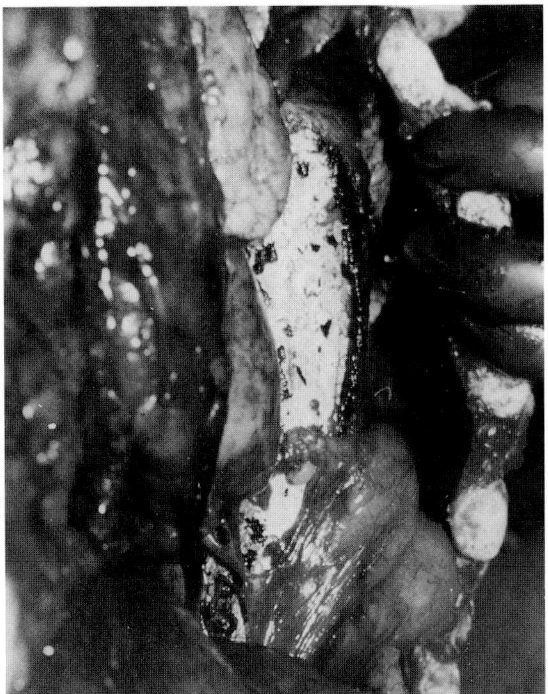

b

FIGURE 3.37b A view of the pipe within the left pleural cavity. The left hemidiaphragm was lacerated. The thoracic contents were shifted to the right and there was a large left hemothorax.

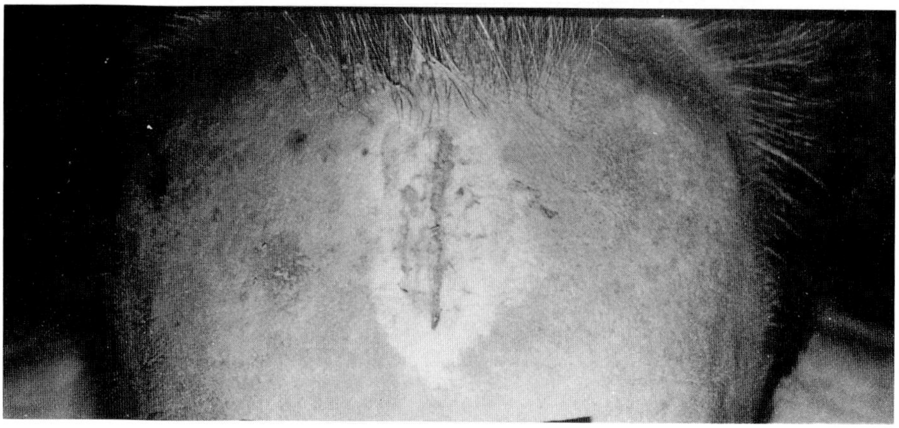

FIGURE 3.38 Laceration on the forehead which has been sealed and masked by the funeral director. The heavy makeup has been washed from the injury so that measurements and photographs could be done. Care must be taken when examining embalmed bodies so that injuries are not overlooked when they have been concealed with makeup.

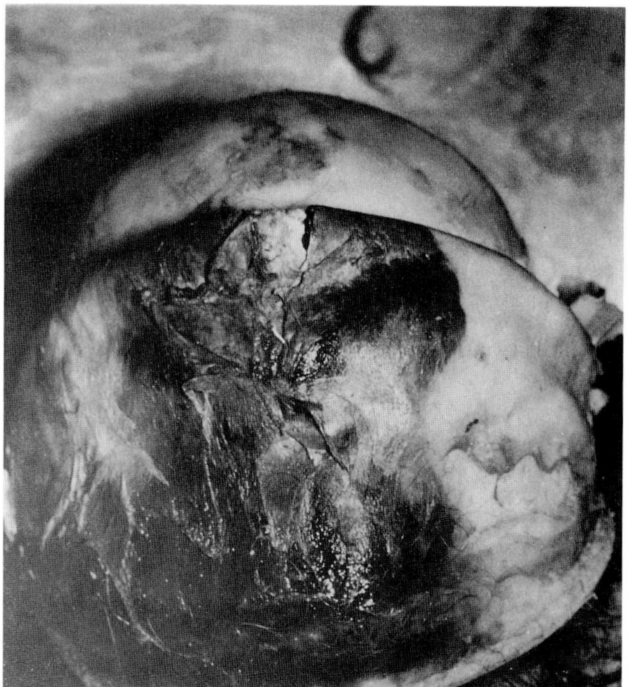

FIGURE 3.39 Large frontal subgaleal hemorrhage found under the laceration noted above. The laceration had penetrated through the full thickness of the scalp as can be seen from the tear in the periosteal layer of the scalp.

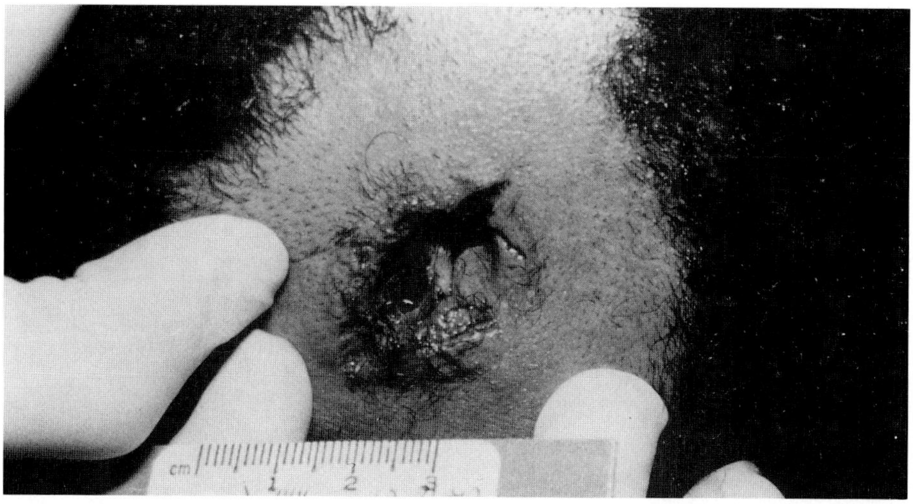

FIGURE 3.40 Large circular laceration of the vertex of the head caused by a blow from a hammer. Though the wound has a strong resemblance to a contact-range gunshot wound of entry with an irregular rim of abrasion, there is no evidence of charring and no gunpowder within the wound. A round, coin-shaped depressed fracture was found in the skull directly beneath the laceration. The margins of fractures caused by hammers have a scalloped or rounded appearance. Hammer blows that do not completely fracture the skull may leave a rounded dimple or depression in the outer table of the skull.

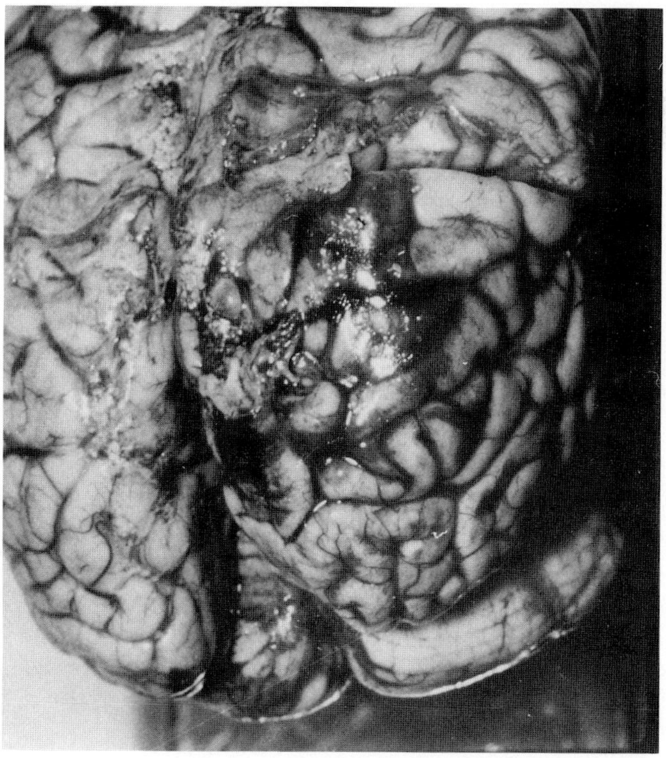

FIGURE 3.41 Fracture laceration and contusion (coup type) of the brain caused by the hammer blow to the head. The surface of the brain adjacent to a skull fracture can show lacerations and contusions which are a result of the same impact that caused the fracture.

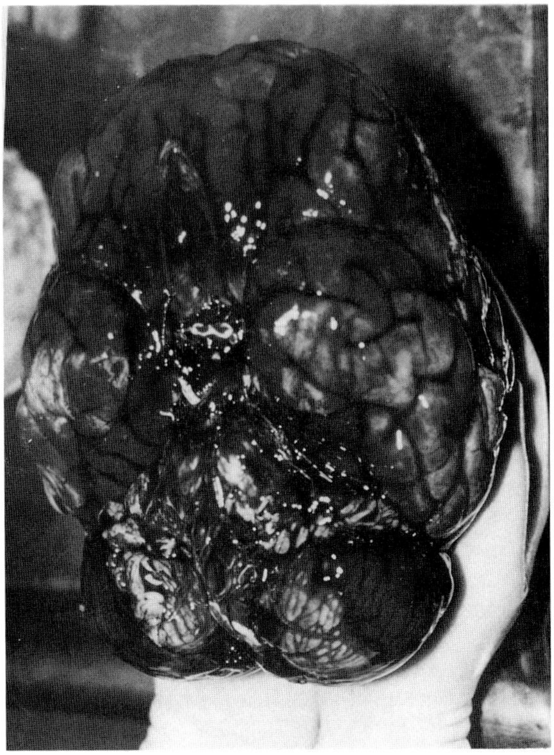

FIGURE 3.42 Traumatic basal subarachnoid hemorrhage sustained in an assault. This injury results in rapid loss of consciousness with death following shortly after. There is typically only minimal injury found on the face or head, and a history of only one or two blows, with a fist, a foot, or an object. The source of the blood may be a torn vessel in the circle of Willis at the base of the brain or one of the vertebral arteries.

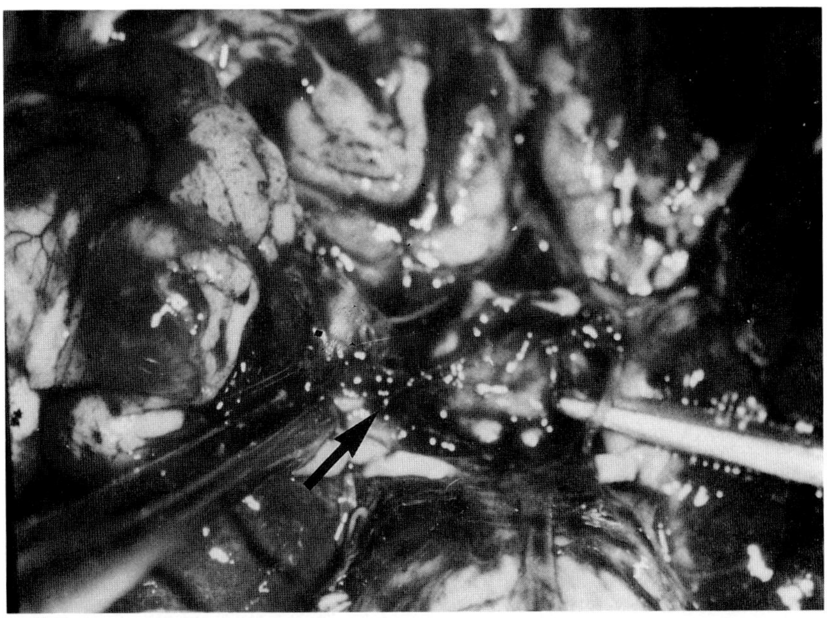

FIGURE 3.43 Torn blood vessel (*arrow*) in the circle of Willis leading to the traumatic basal subarachnoid hemorrhage. These tears result from rotation and hyperextension of the head leading to stretching of the blood vessels or the vessel being dragged across bones on the base of the skull.

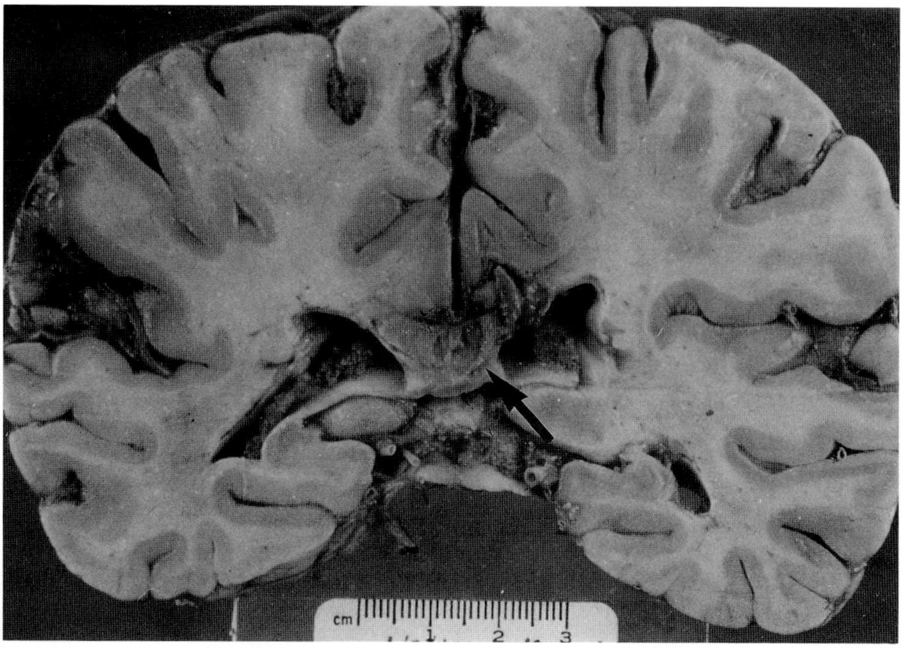

FIGURE 3.44 Brain section from an Alzheimer's patient who survived for 4 months following an assault where she sustained significant head trauma. She remained comatose from the time of the injury until her death. There is generalized cerebral atrophy as found in Alzheimer's disease but there is also an organizing hemorrhagic infarction of the splenium of the corpus callosum (*arrow*).

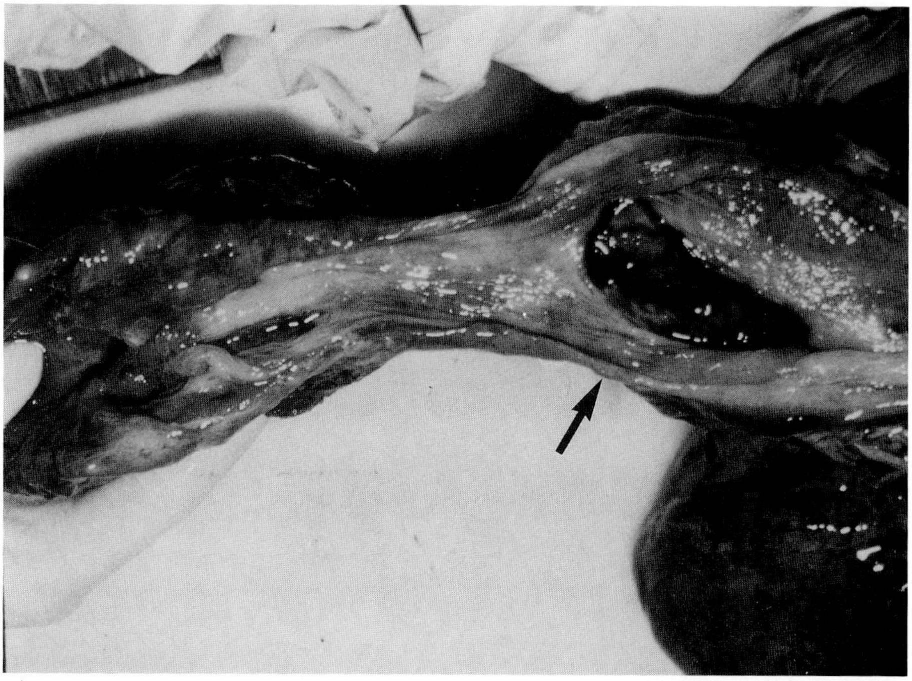

FIGURE 3.45 Tracheal–esophageal fistula (*arrow*) which caused the death of a young adult African-American male several months after an assault. He sustained a fracture of the cervical spine when he was shoved down during a strong-arm robbery. He developed quadriplegia and required long-term intubation leading to the formation of the fistula. The death was ruled a homicide.

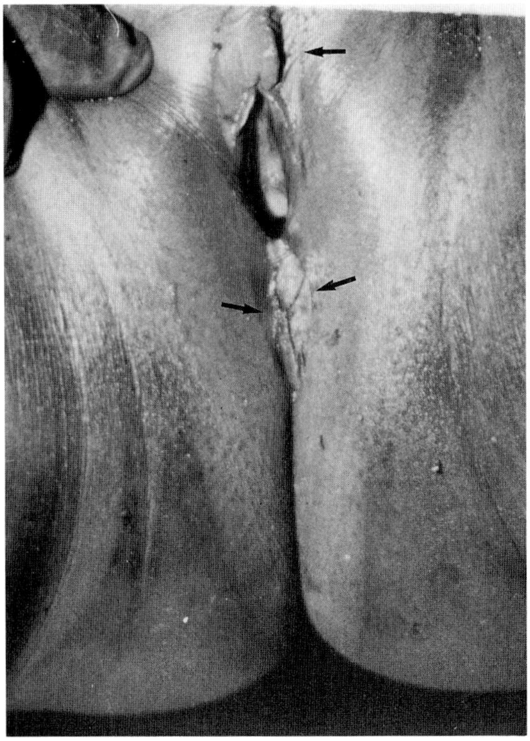

FIGURE 3.46 Six-year-old victim of sexual assault with lacerations (*arrows*) of the perineum and tissues adjacent to the clitoris and labia minora. Significant injury to the genitalia is common in the very young and very old victim of sexual assault. Adult females in the reproductive years, especially those who are normally sexually active, may have only minor abrasions or erythema of the vagina or no injury visible at all. Injury may result from penetration by a penis or a foreign object.

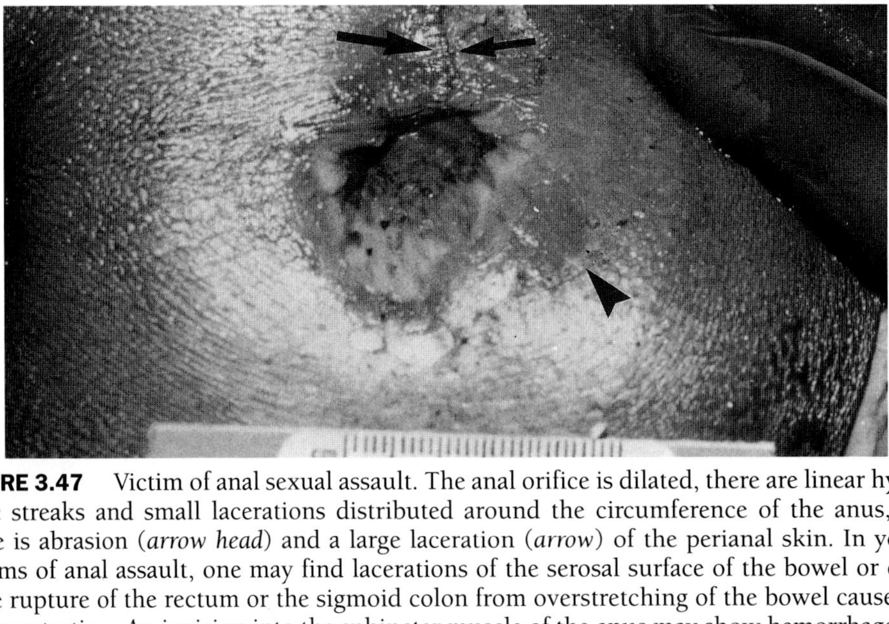

FIGURE 3.47 Victim of anal sexual assault. The anal orifice is dilated, there are linear hyperemic streaks and small lacerations distributed around the circumference of the anus, and there is abrasion (*arrow head*) and a large laceration (*arrow*) of the perianal skin. In young victims of anal assault, one may find lacerations of the serosal surface of the bowel or complete rupture of the rectum or the sigmoid colon from overstretching of the bowel caused by the penetration. An incision into the sphincter muscle of the anus may show hemorrhage due to laceration of the muscle from the penetration.

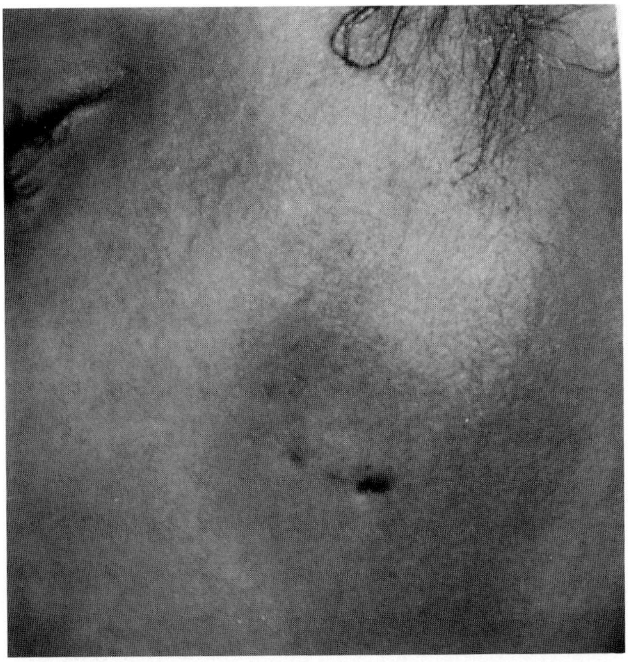

FIGURE 3.48 Bite mark found on the cheek of a victim of sexual assault. Swabs can be taken from the area before washing the body, to be tested for ABO blood type or for DNA studies. A forensic odontologist should be contacted to make impressions of the wound for later comparison with the dentition of possible offenders. If a forensic odontologist is not immediately available, good photographs using a rule and color scale should be taken. These photographs can also be used for comparison studies, though impressions are preferred.

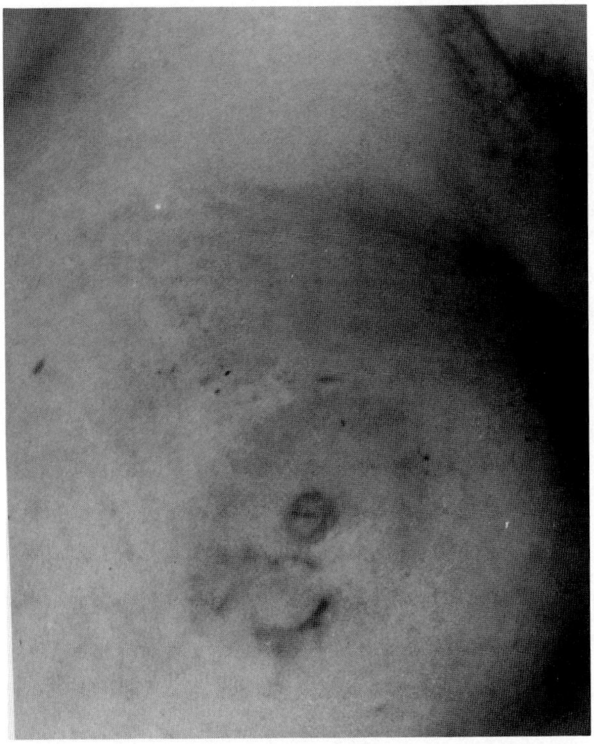

FIGURE 3.49 Bite mark on the areola of another victim of sexual assault. Bite marks are frequently found in cases of sexual assault on the face, breasts, genitalia, and inner thigh. They are also seen in cases of child abuse where they can be anywhere on the body. Adult human bite marks are normally over 2 centimeters in size while those of children are smaller. A bite mark found on a body may have been self-inflicted, so the victim's own teeth should also be examined.

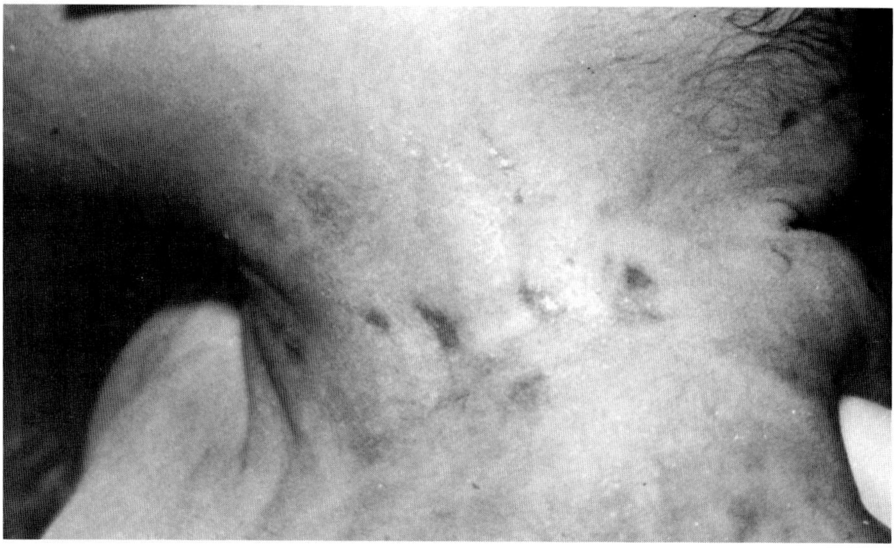

FIGURE 3.50 Numerous fingernail abrasions found on the neck of a stillborn infant delivered at home by the mother. Such injury occurs from attempts to deliver an infant by the mother. They are not seen in cases of infanticide where the infant is strangled. Radiographs of this infant showed no air in the lungs, airways, or the gastrointestinal tract. The lungs did not float when placed in water, but rather sank rapidly. The mother indicated that the child never moved or cried after she delivered it. All of these are consistent with the child having died in utero.

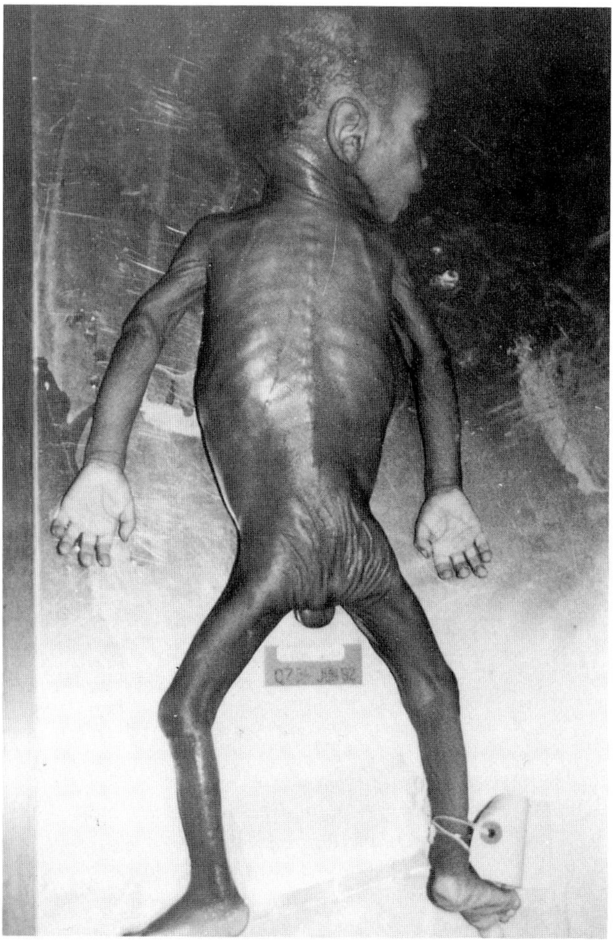

FIGURE 3.51 Victim of child abuse due to neglect. Note the marked emaciation with loss of subcutaneous fat in the arms, legs, and buttocks with resultant loose skin folds. The ribs and vertebral column are prominent. The stomach and intestinal contents should be examined and listed and if empty this should also be noted. Hydration can be evaluated by obtaining vitreous humor and sending it for electrolytes. One cubic centimeter of fluid is the minimum required. If only a small amount is obtained, then blood urea nitrogen (BUN), creatinine, and sodium should be ordered.

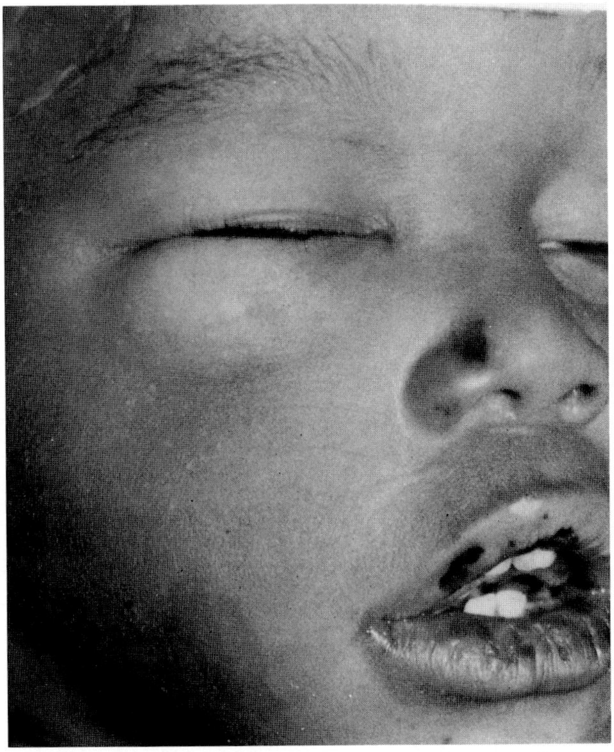

FIGURE 3.52 The injuries to this child's face are from abuse and are not consistent with accidental injury. There is swelling of the eye and bruising beginning on the inner corner of the eyelids. There are abrasions of the right nasal ala and multiple abrasions and bruises on the lips, and the lips are swollen. A café au lait spot is present on the right lower cheek which must not be mistaken for additional injury.

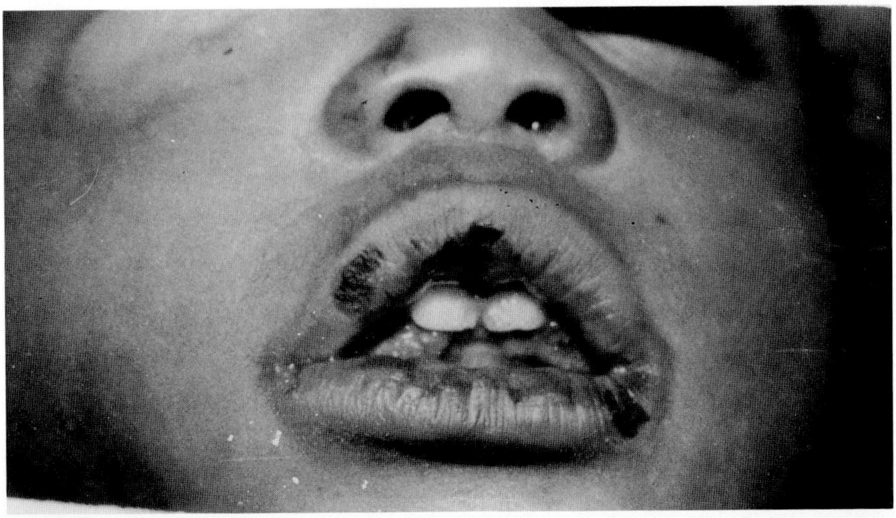

FIGURE 3.53 Close-up view of the injuries to the mouth. They are found on both sides of the mouth and on both the upper and lower lip which is inconsistent with the injuries occurring as part of normal childhood play or the usual childhood injuries from falls or running into things.

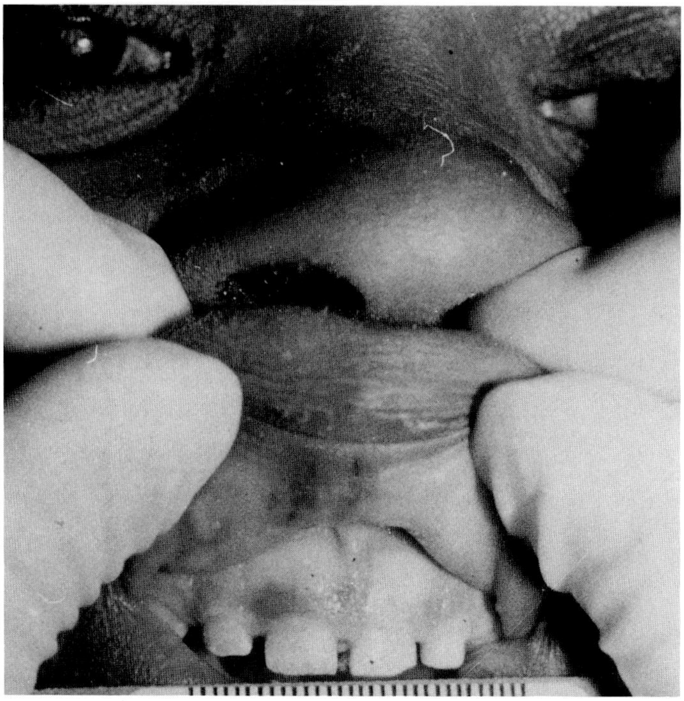

FIGURE 3.54 Contusions found on the mucosal surface of the upper lip and on the gingiva lateral and above the right upper central incisor caused by a blow to the mouth. They can also occur in smothering. It is important to remember to examine the inside of the mouth in all autopsy examinations, but this is vital in cases of assault or child abuse. Bruises on the lips and the inside of the mouth, or loose teeth can be seen in blows to the face or mouth and in cases of sexual abuse where the victim has been forced to perform fellatio.

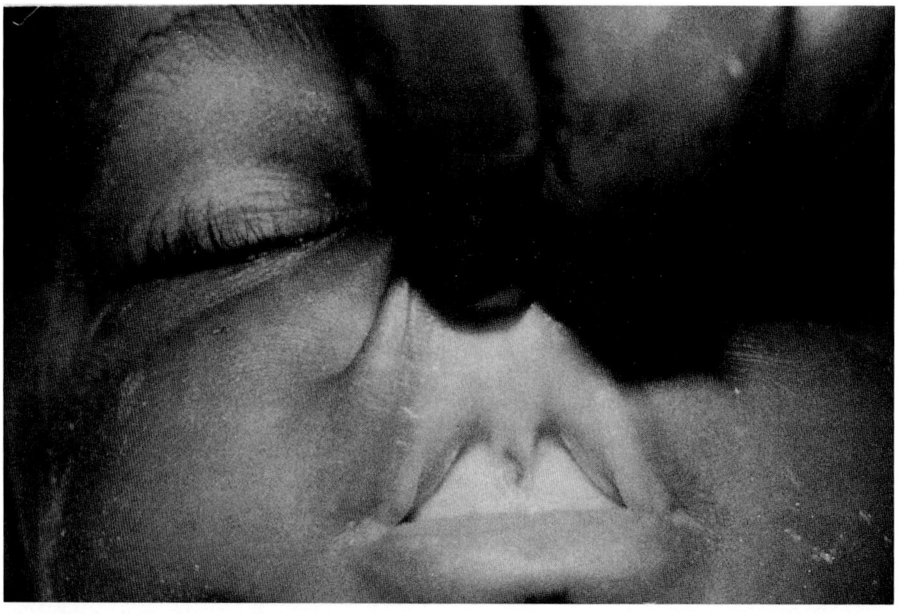

FIGURE 3.55 Laceration of the frenulum of the upper lip. This type of injury can occur from a blow to mouth or by forcing the nipple of a bottle or pacifier into the mouth of a crying child.

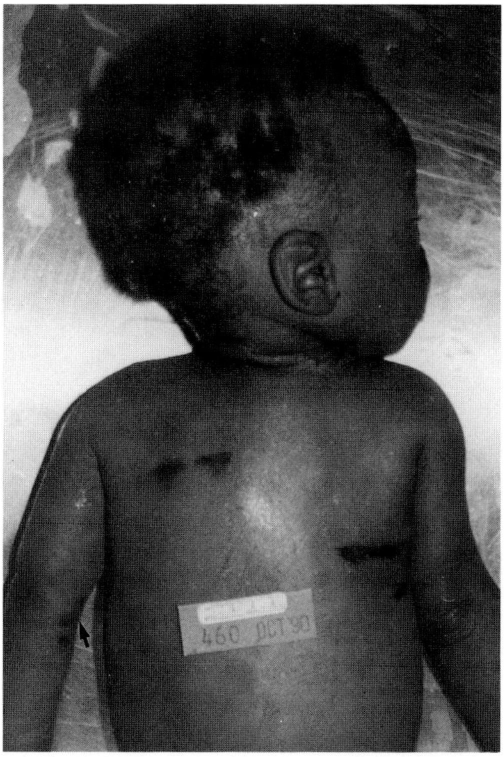

FIGURE 3.56 Abrasions and bruises on the back of a victim of abuse. Children sustain blunt trauma injury in many innocent ways, such as falls, which are usually found on the head, arms, and legs, especially on the knees and elbows. Injuries to the back are highly suspicious of abuse, and injuries such as these, on both sides and multiple are inconsistent with a fall, even a fall down a flight of stairs. Note fingerprint bruises due to grabbing, on the left arm (*arrow*).

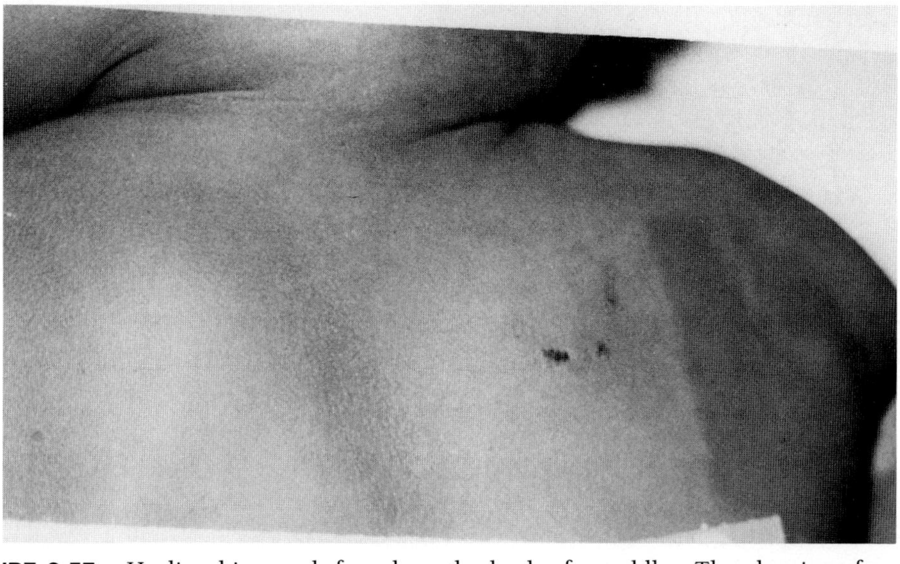

FIGURE 3.57 Healing bite mark found on the back of a toddler. The abrasions from the incisors have well-formed scabs. The wound measured 1.5 cm and is consistent with a bite mark from another child.

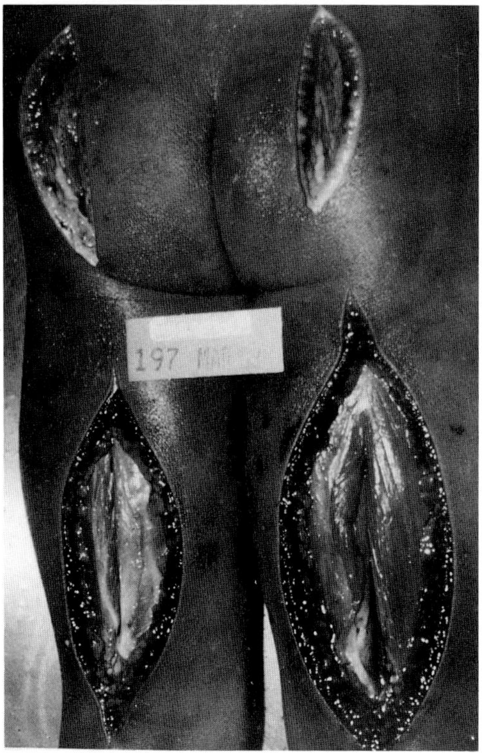

FIGURE 3.58 Five-year-old child who was beaten to death for not being able to recite his ABCs. The back, buttocks, and thighs showed near confluent purple red bruises and areas of abrasion. Incisions into those areas show the hemorrhage into the soft tissue. This child died from hypovolemic shock as he lost a significant amount of his blood volume into the soft tissues of the thighs. No injury was found to the internal organs during autopsy.

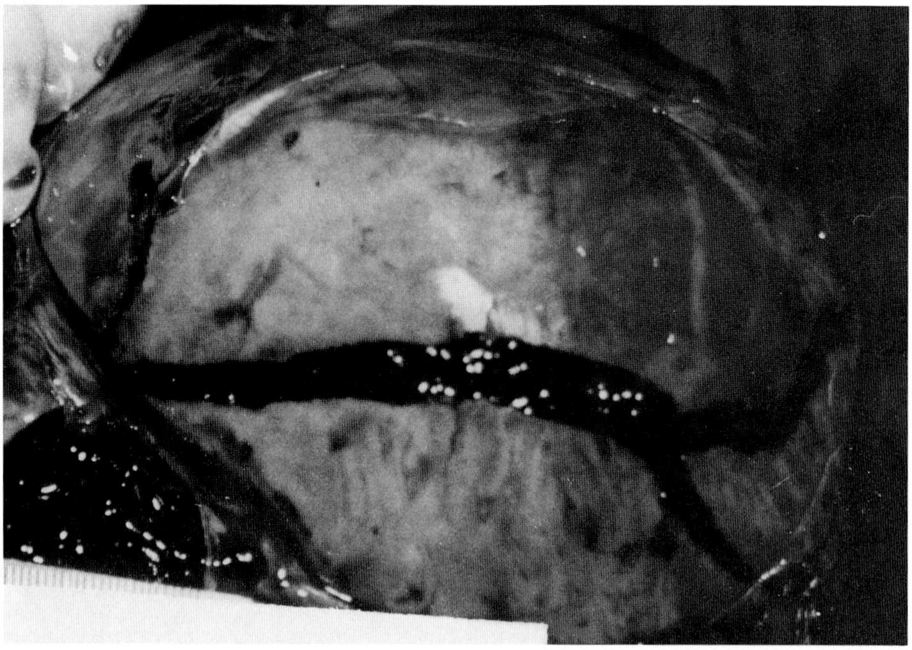

FIGURE 3.59 Complex skull fracture found in a child abuse victim. Children can sustain skull fractures from falls, even falls from short distances. Most such fractures are simple, linear, and nondisplaced. They heal well with no sequelae. Large, displaced, arborizing fractures that cross suture lines, or involve suture lines such as seen here are the result of deliberate trauma. To sustain a skull fracture such as this from a fall would require a distance of several stories.

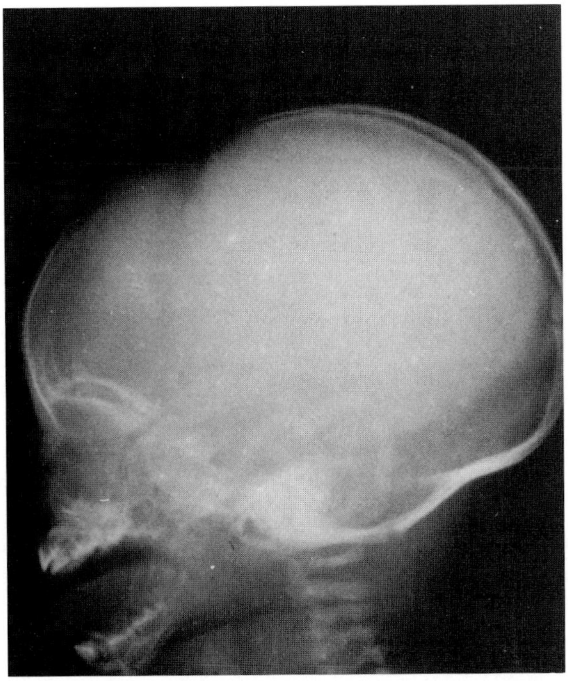

FIGURE 3.60 Total body radiographs with cone down views of the joints should be done in all cases of child abuse or suspected abuse. This lateral head and neck film shows slight diasteal fractures (widening) of the cranial sutures and basal skull fractures in the area of the orbital plates.

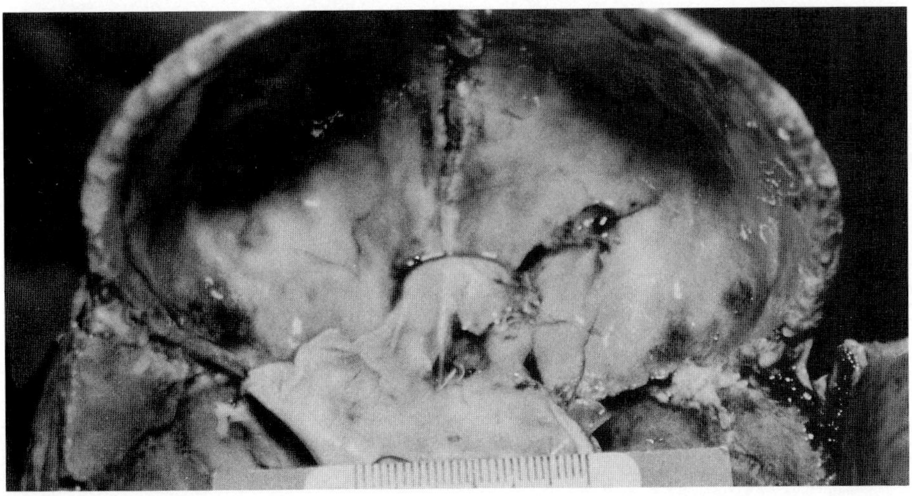

FIGURE 3.61 Fractures of the orbital plate in an infant from a blow to the eye with a fist. The eyes should always be removed and examined for retinal hemorrhages in cases of child abuse, especially cases with head trauma.

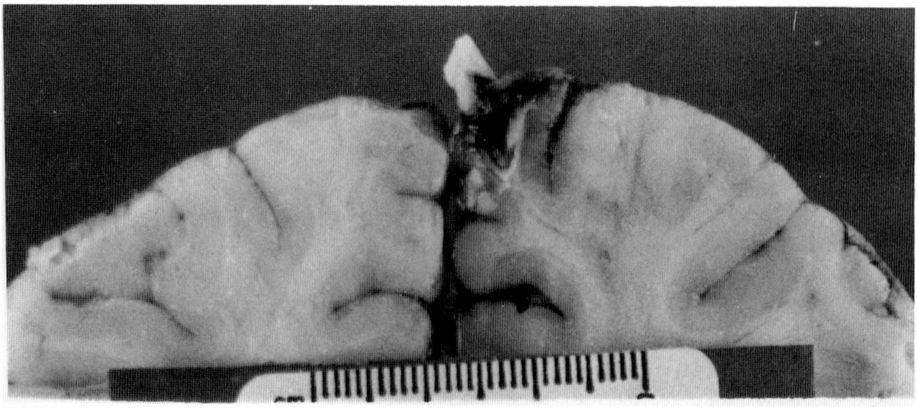

FIGURE 3.62 A healed gliding contusion found in the right frontal lobe of a 7-month-old female infant who died from bilateral acute subdural hematomas consistent with "shaken baby syndrome". This finding is evidence of prior episodes of abuse which the child survived. Shaken baby syndrome is defined as the presence of subdural hematoma, with or without retinal hemorrhages, in the absence of external signs of trauma. Rib fractures, especially in the posterior aspect, or metaphyseal fractures of the long bones, corner, or bucket handle fractures may be seen.

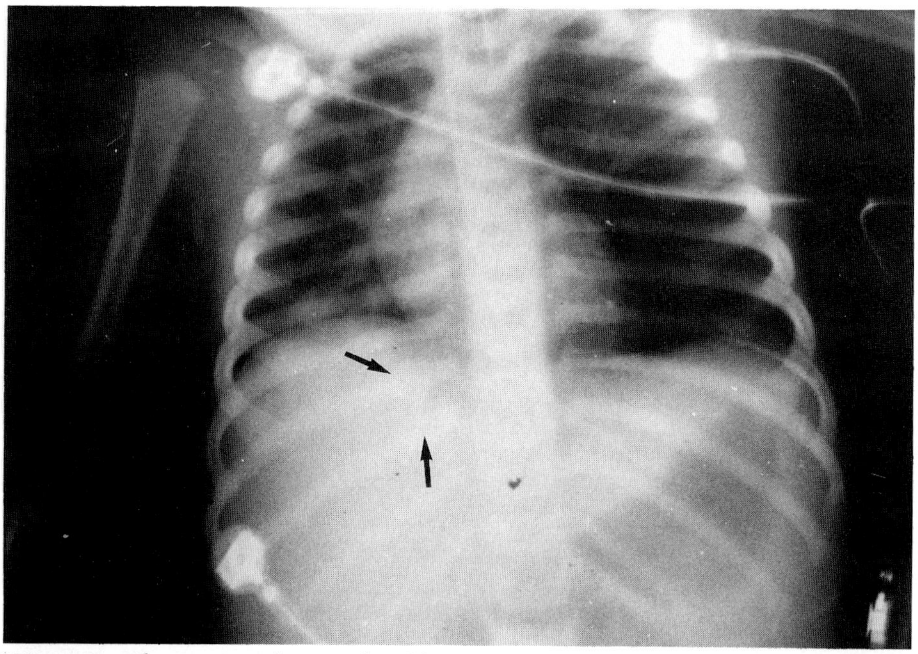

FIGURE 3.63 Chest x-ray taken at a local hospital when the infant described in Figure 3.62 was hospitalized for a spiral fracture of her right femur 3 months prior to her death. The mother indicated that the fracture happened when the 4-month-old infant had put her leg through the crib slats and then rolled over. The injury is not consistent with that story, but the hospital personnel accepted the explanation. Routine skeletal survey was done because of the leg fracture to rule out child abuse. The radiologist who read the films missed healing fractures of the posterior aspects of the right ninth and tenth ribs (*arrows*) and the infant was released to the home where she was fatally injured 3 months later.

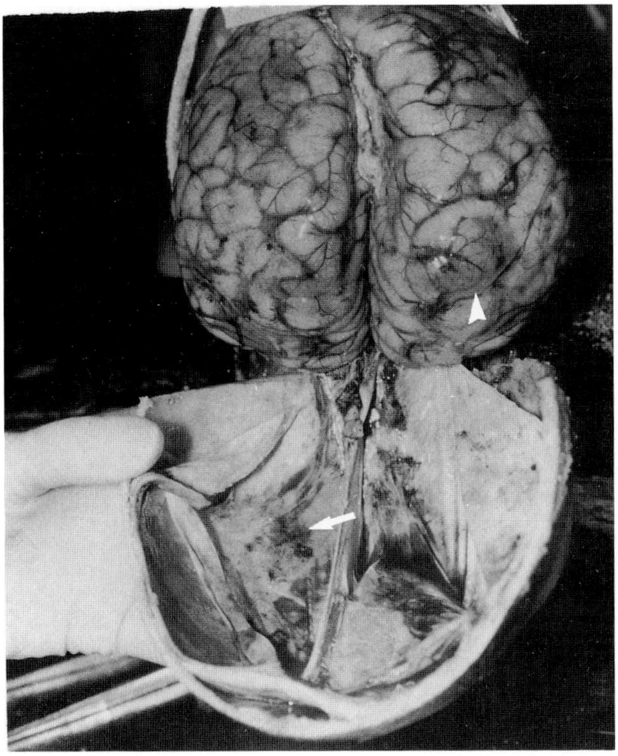

FIGURE 3.64 Extensive old healed subdural hematoma with well-formed inner and outer membranes. The lesion contained xanthochromic fluid. Note small areas of organizing hemorrhage (*arrow*) on the surface of the inner membrane. There is marked cerebral edema and areas of cortical contusion (*arrow heads*) from recent head trauma. This 3-year-old child had been violently shaken and sustained subdural hematomas when she was 1 month old.

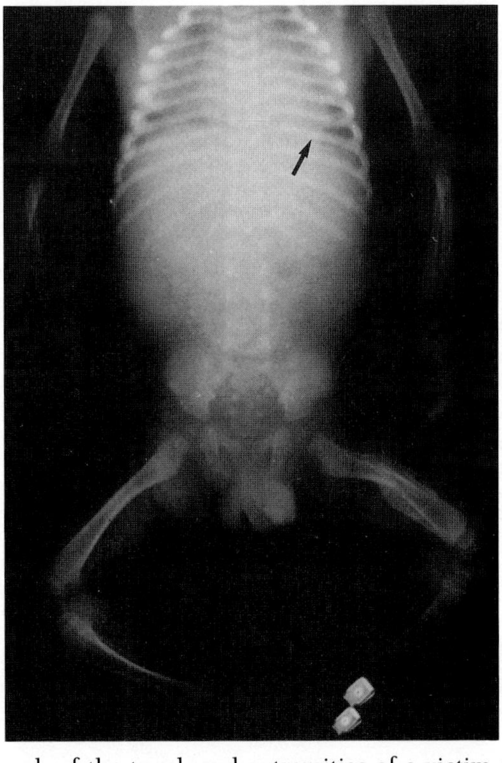

FIGURE 3.65 Radiograph of the trunk and extremities of a victim of child abuse showing healed misaligned fracture of the left femur and healing rib fractures (*arrow*) on the left.

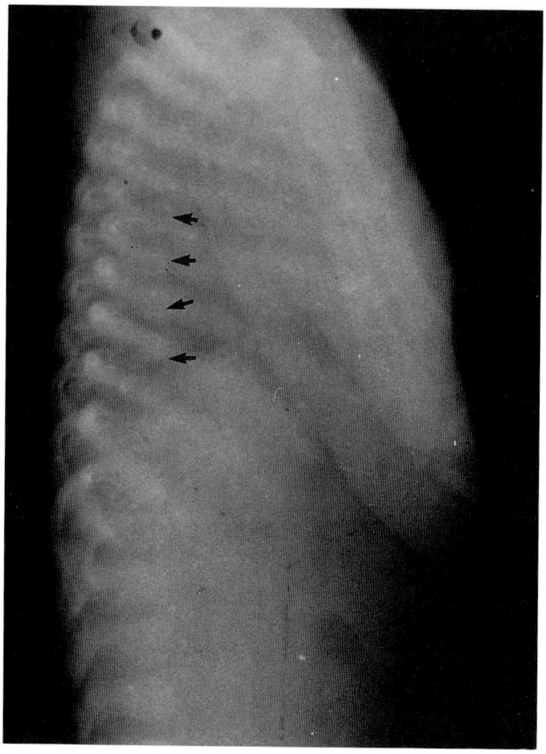

FIGURE 3.66 Lateral chest film from the same infant shows multiple healing rib fractures (*arrows*). They appear as round, pearl-shaped defects on the ribs. It is very difficult to identify acute rib fractures on plain radiographs. In the living child, rib fractures can be identified by performing bone scans. The nucleotides will aggregate at the site of fractures, as well as at sites of inflammation. Unfortunately, this can not be done in the dead.

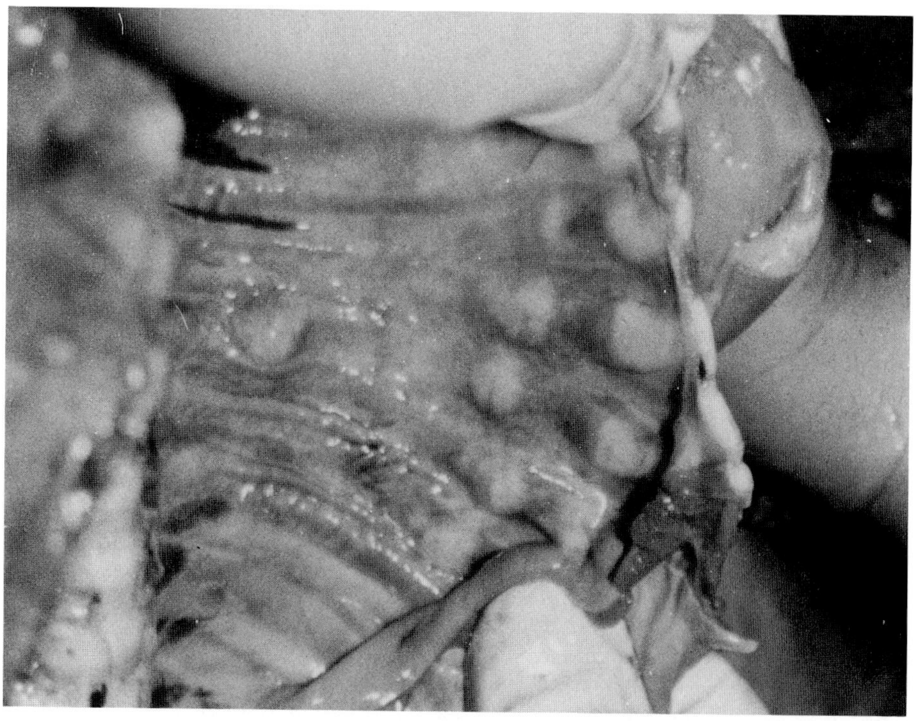

FIGURE 3.67 There are numerous healing rib fractures found in this infant. Healing fractures appear as round, white nodules on the rib due to callous formation.

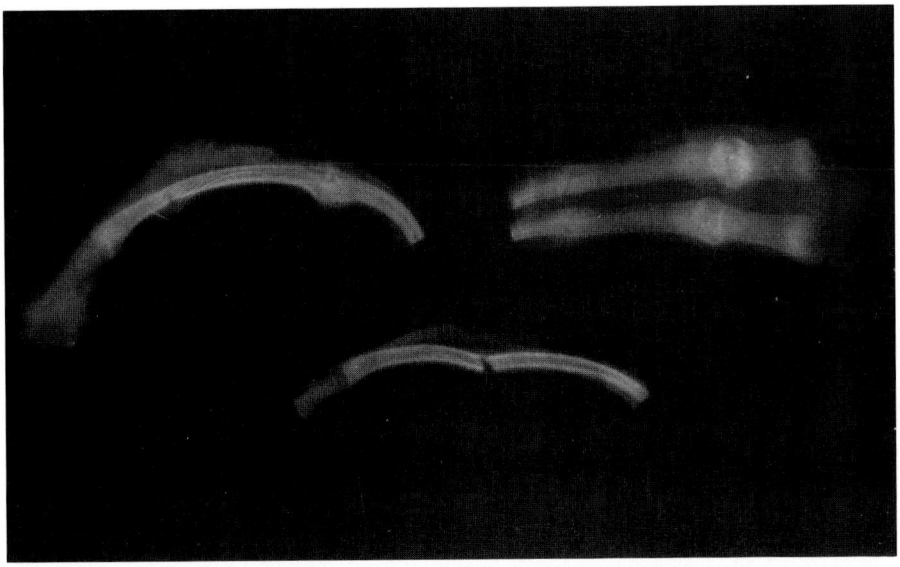

FIGURE 3.68 Several individual ribs have been removed and radiographed. This was done to document the number of healing rib fractures and acute fractures that were present. Rib fractures in children do not occur from cardiopulmonary resuscitation as they do in adults. Fractures occur from direct blows to the chest or from compressing the chest by squeezing which causes fractures to occur on the lateral aspect of the ribs or just lateral to the costovertebral joints.

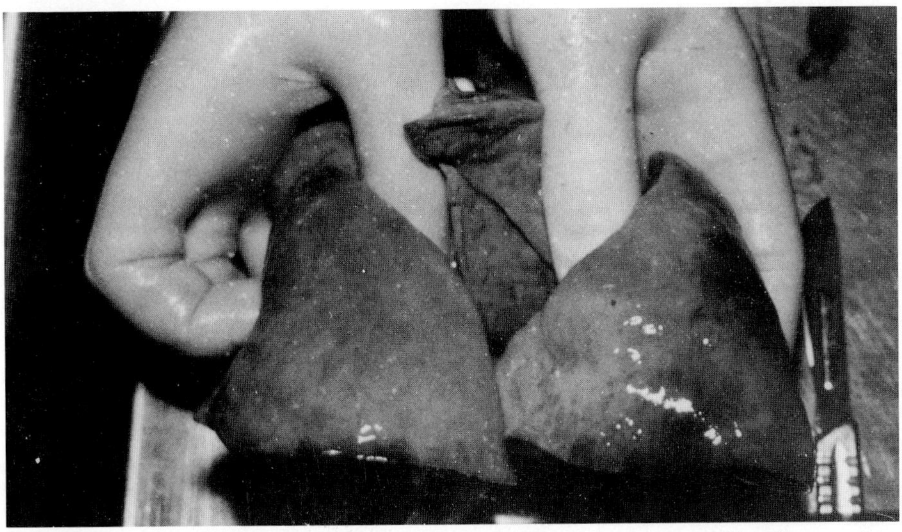

FIGURE 3.69 Multiple contusions of the lungs from blunt trauma to the chest and back of a victim of abuse. The contusions are most prominent on the inferior border of the lower lobes and at the apical segment of the left lower lobe.

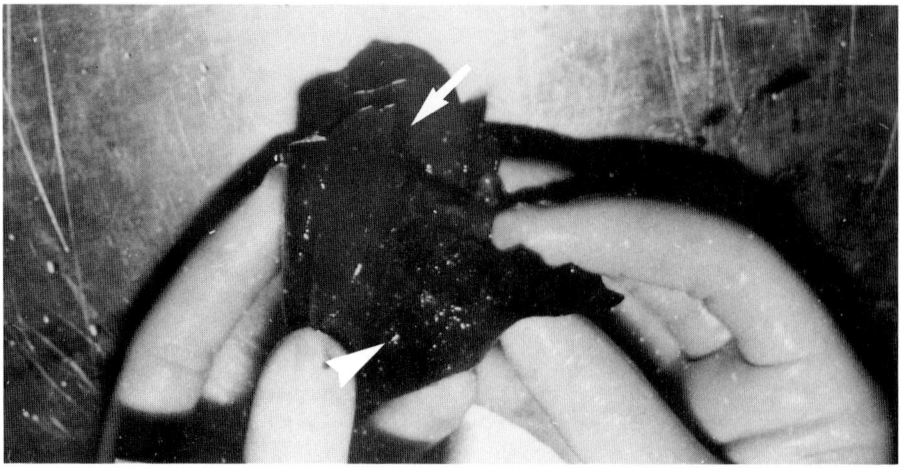

FIGURE 3.70 Lacerations (*arrow*) and contusions (*arrow head*) found within the spleen due to blows to the abdomen in a victim of abuse. Similar injury can be seen in victims of motor vehicle accidents, an indication of the degree of force involved.

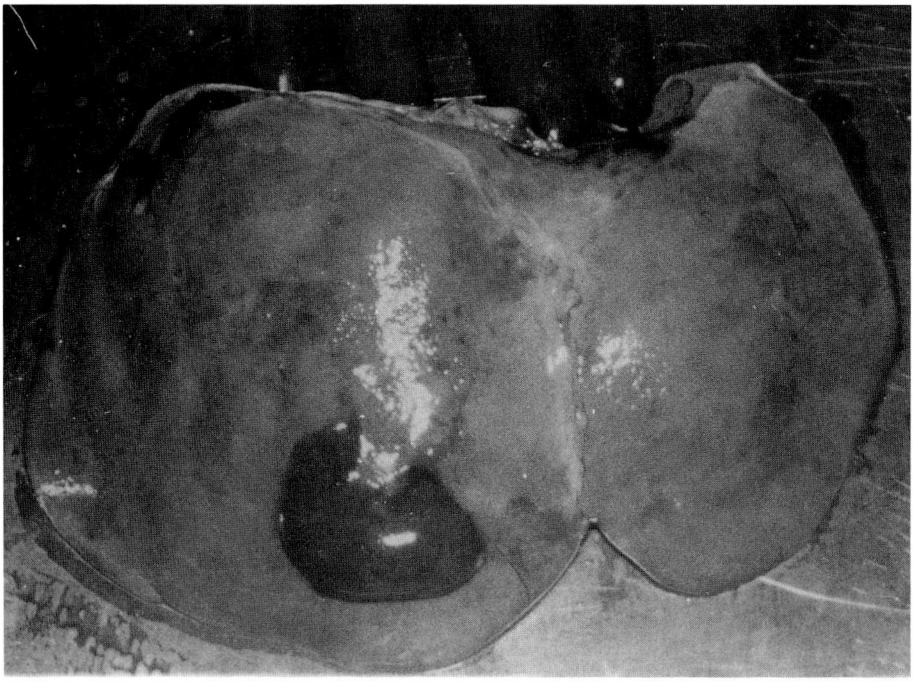

FIGURE 3.71 Subcapsular hematoma of the liver. If this is an isolated finding, and there have been extensive resuscitation efforts, this injury must be evaluated carefully as such an injury can be caused by chest compression during cardiopulmonary resuscitation. There are also several small contusions over the dome of the right lobe and small contusions on the left lobe.

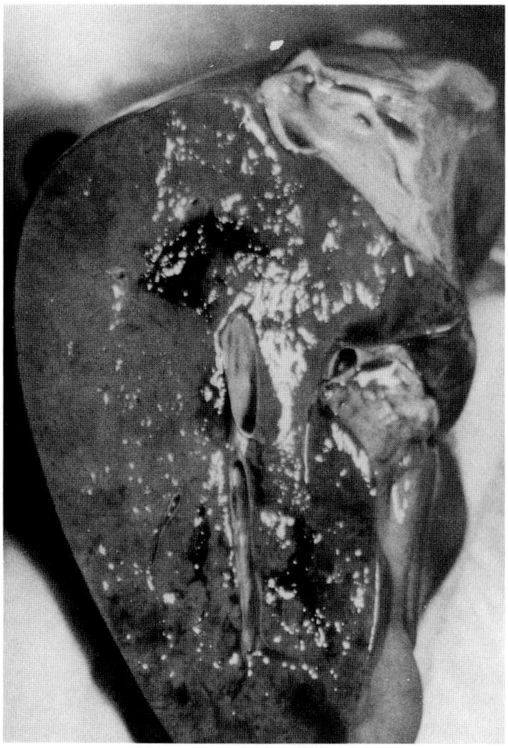

FIGURE 3.72 Cut section of a liver which shows multiple contusions as well as several lacerations from a 6-month-old female who had been left with her father. Autopsy examination revealed bilateral subdural hematomas as well as blunt injury to the abdominal organs.

FIGURE 3.73 Close-up photograph of faint contusions and fine linear abrasions found on the abdomen of a 2-year-old girl who collapsed in a grocery store after reportedly bumping into a rack holding bags of potato chips. The emergency room personnel reported finding no injuries on the body.

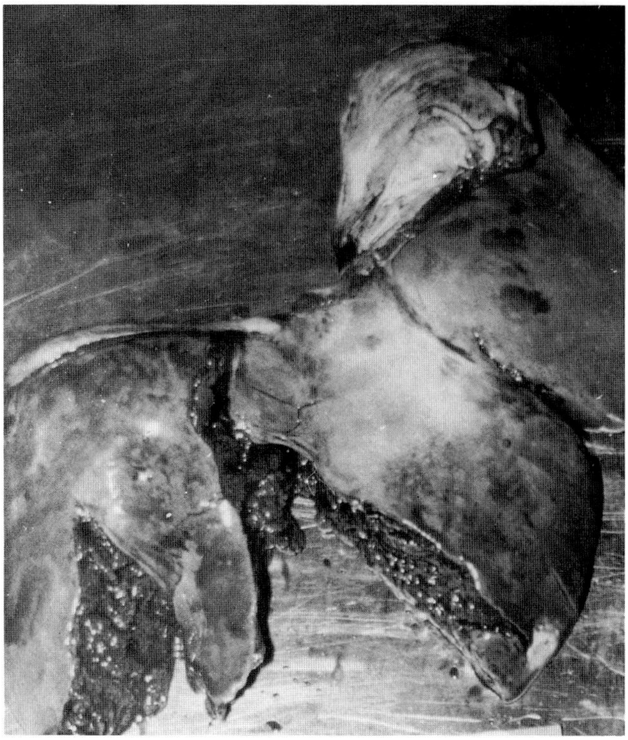

FIGURE 3.74 This is the liver of the 2-year-old described in Figure 3.73. There are multiple deep lacerations which extend nearly through the organ. The abdomen contained several hundred milliliters of fresh blood. Investigation showed that the child had been beaten about 15 minutes prior to her collapse. With such extensive injury to the liver, one would expect the child to have collapsed much sooner from hypovolemic shock. With injuries to organs such as the liver, which has a thick capsule, rupture and blood loss may be delayed for a time if the capsule remains intact, serving as a type of pressure bandage over the organ for a period of time. This is the most likely explanation for the delay in this child's collapse.

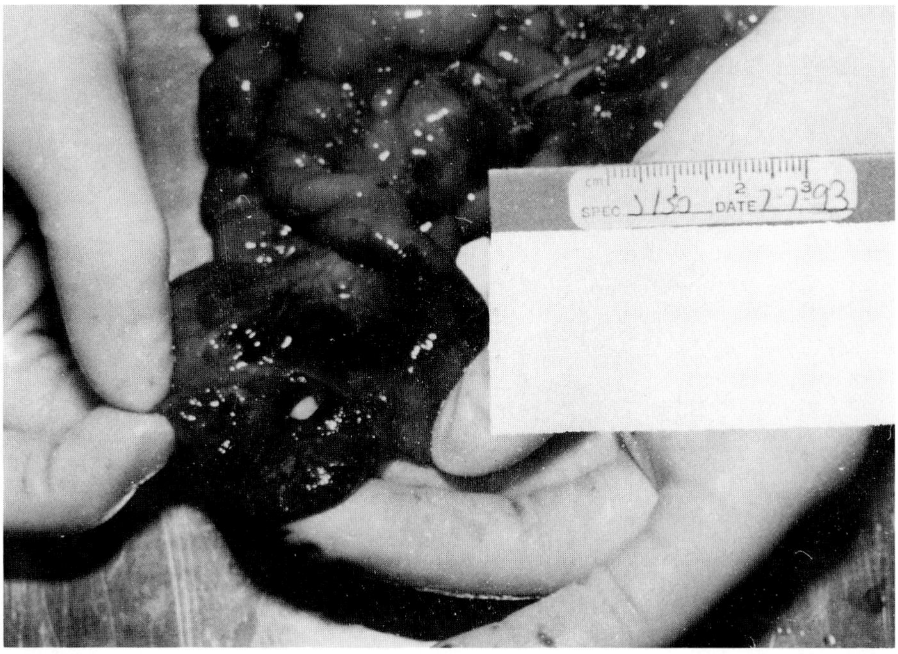

FIGURE 3.75 Multiple contusions with focal serosal and mesenteric lacerations of the small bowel found in a child victim of blunt abdominal trauma. Lacerations of the mesentery require considerable force. Not all victims of this type of injury die immediately. Death may occur several days later as a result of chemical or bacterial peritonitis.

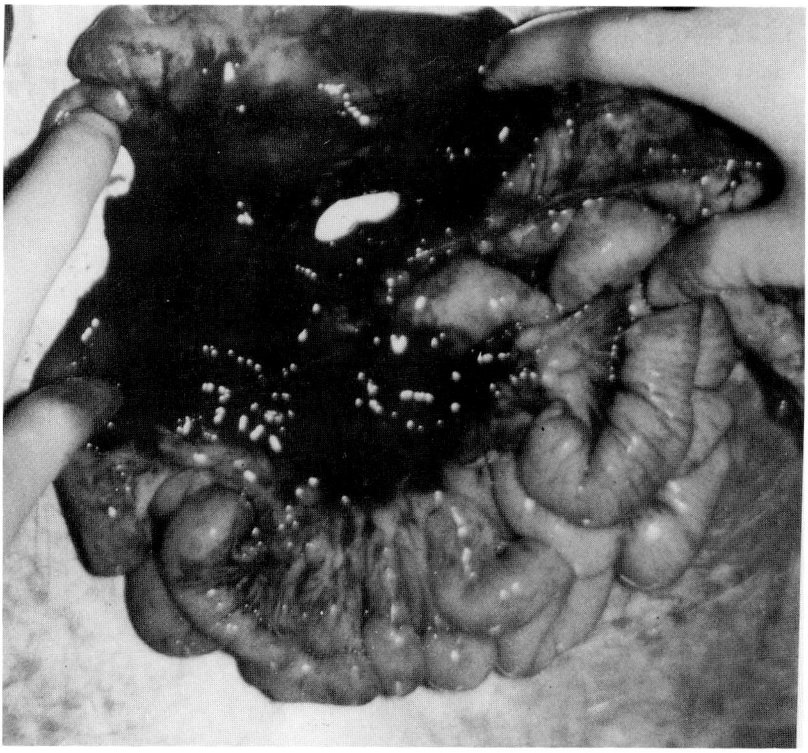

FIGURE 3.76 Large hemorrhage involving nearly the entire mesentery and a large laceration of the mesentery in another child abuse victim which led to rapid exsanguination and death.

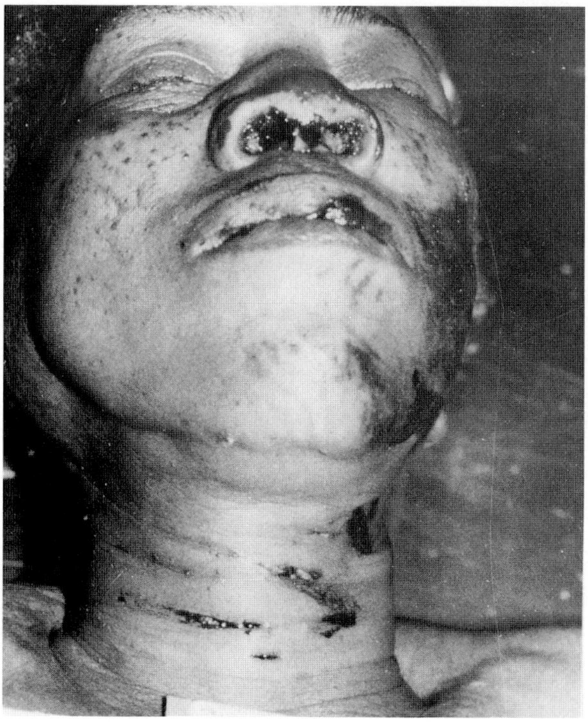

a

FIGURE 3.77a, b Footwear impressions found on the cheek and chin of an elderly woman who was beaten, stomped, and stabbed during a home invasion. Note the stab wounds on the neck. Comparisons can be made between the injuries of the face and the soles of the shoes of an alleged offender. Victims of assaults should be examined as is, that is, before the body is washed, as some patterns on the body may be dirt or blood imprints which will be lost when the body is washed. The impressions seen here are actual abrasions.

b

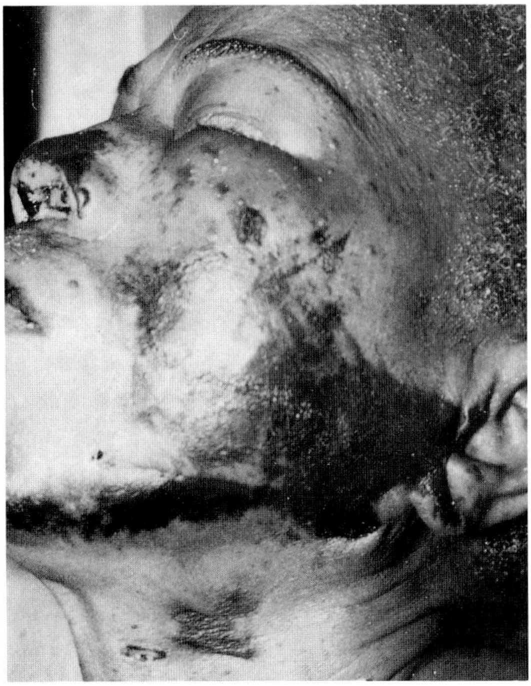

FIGURE 3.77b (continued)

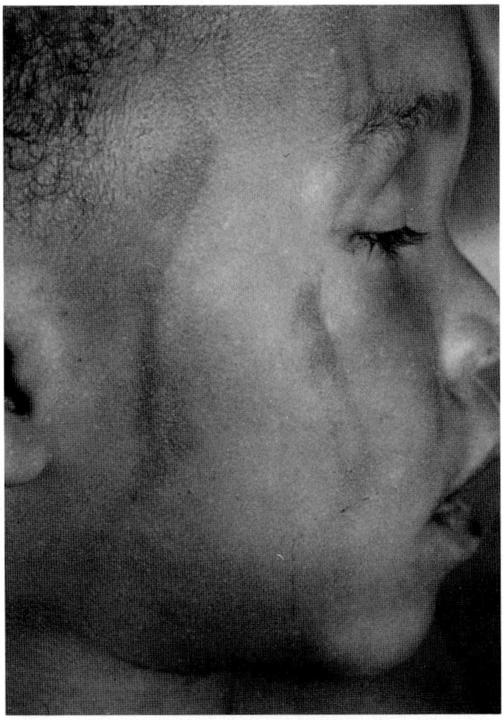

FIGURE 3.78 Tire tread impressions on the face of a 3-year-old found unresponsive in an alley. These patterned bruises are the result of the tissues being squeezed into the tire tread as the wheel of the vehicle ran over the child's head. Again, comparisons can be made between the patterned injury on the face and the tires of a suspect vehicle.

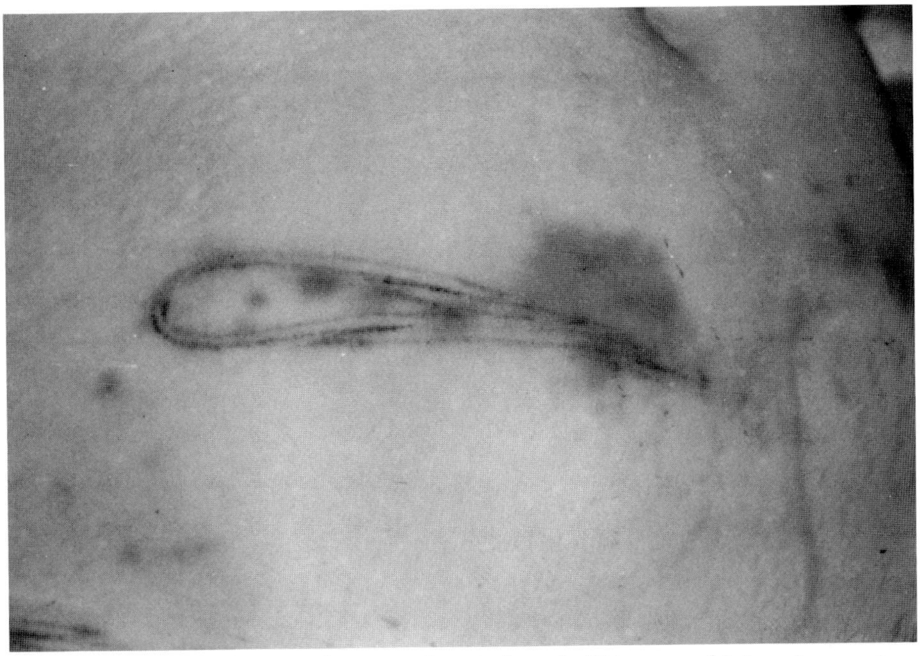

FIGURE 3.79 Patterned bruise from an electrical cord. This type of injury is seen in cases of child abuse, both fatal and nonfatal. This injury was on an adult female victim of domestic abuse.

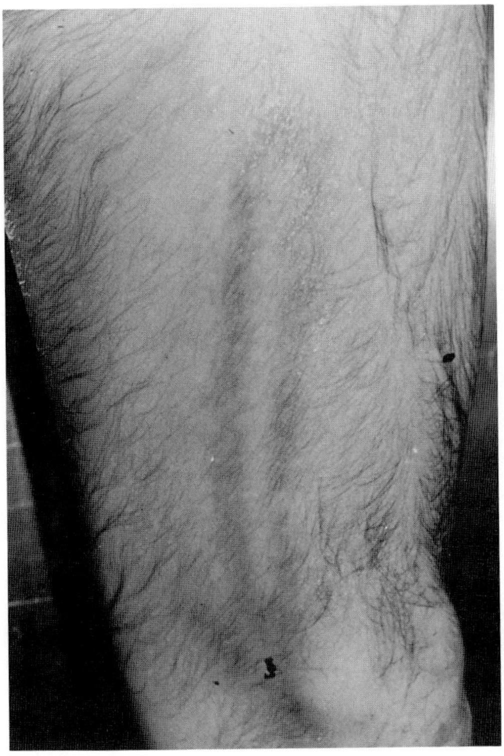

FIGURE 3.80 Patterned bruise caused by a blow from a baseball bat. Similar injury can be seen in blows from any cylindrical object such as a flashlight or night stick. As the object strikes and crushes the skin, the blood is pushed towards the sides leaving a pale central area with bruising on either side.

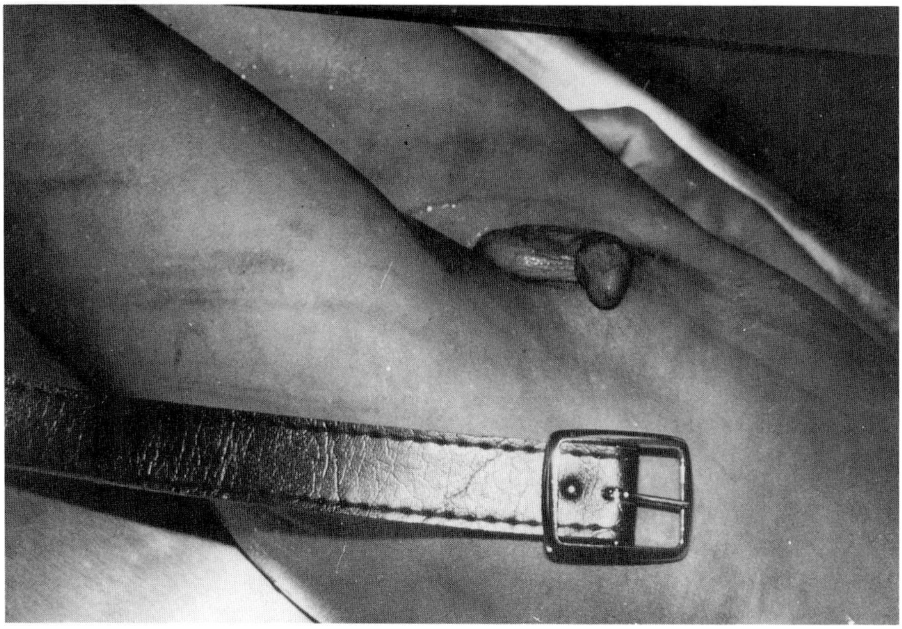

FIGURE 3.81 Patterned bruises caused by a belt. The belt has been placed next to one of the bruises to demonstrate the corresponding size of the bruise to the belt.

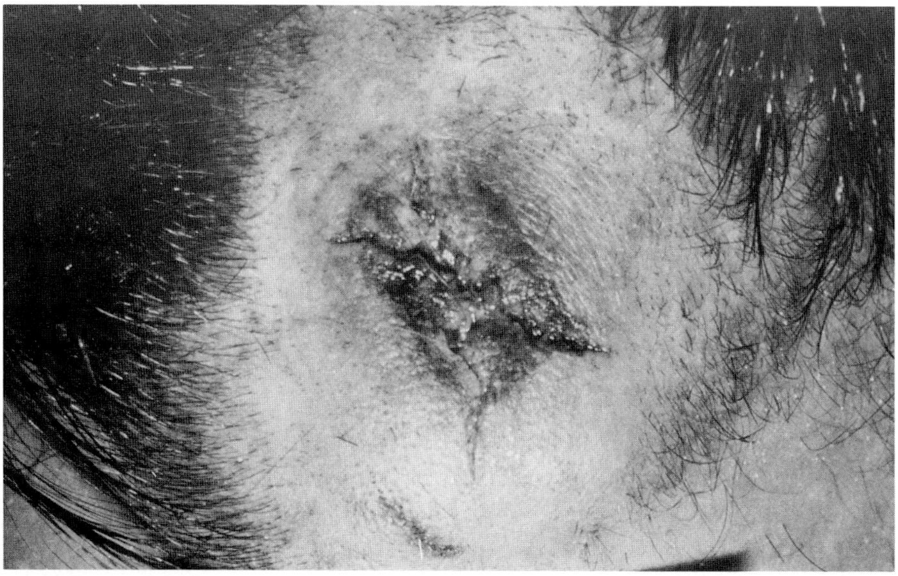

FIGURE 3.82 Patterned injury on the head due to a blow from the butt of a handgun. Note the rectangular appearance of the injury. There is a central arborizing laceration with surrounding abrasions and contusion.

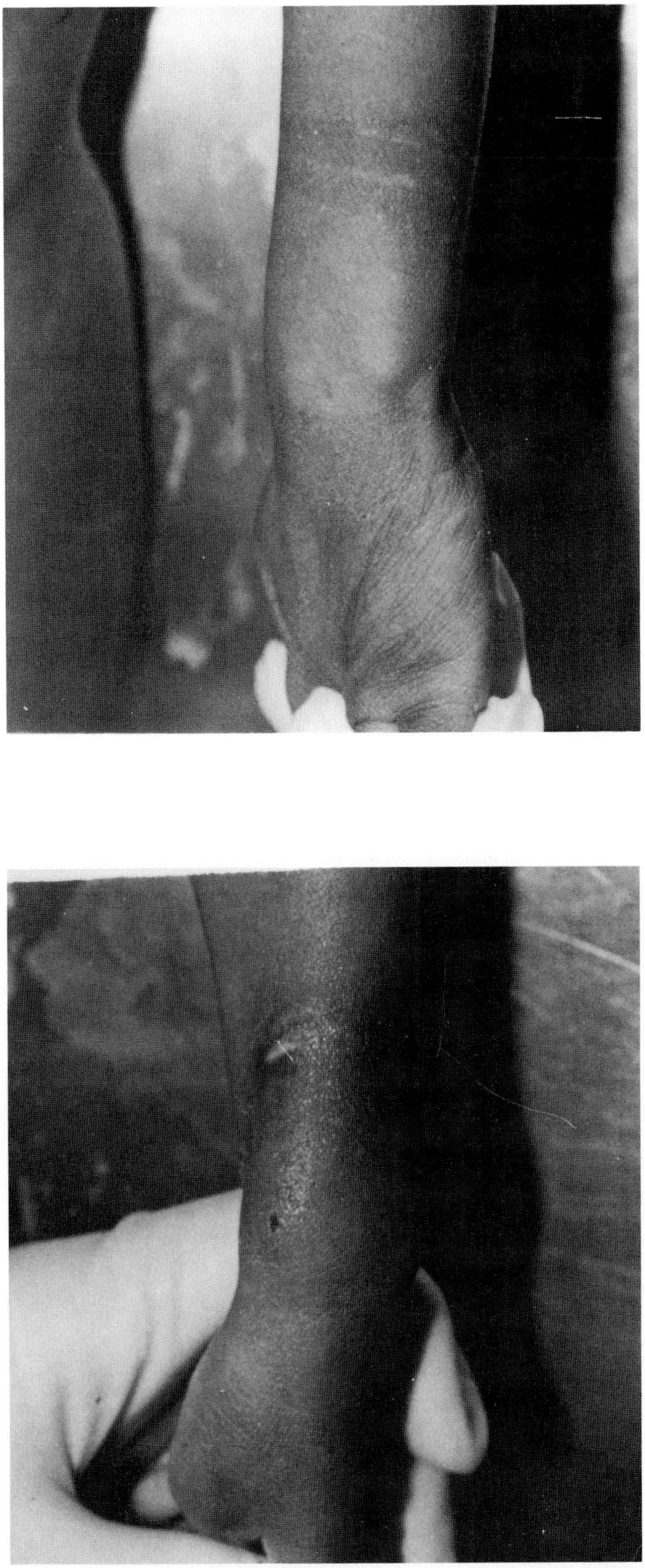

a

b

FIGURE 3.83a, b Ligature abrasions found on the arms of a 2-year-old child abuse victim. There are depigmented scars as well as fresh friction abrasions present indicating multiple episodes. Similar wounds were found on both ankles. The child had been tied in her bed with cords on several occasions so that her mother could go out and party. Her body was covered with new and healing injuries with numerous scars.

4

Injury Due to Firearms

HANDGUNS AND RIFLES

Deaths and injuries due to firearms have become all too common in our society. The majority of these wounds are caused by handguns and so these will be discussed in detail. Rifle wounds are similar in appearance to those caused by handguns, but due to the increased kinetic energy, a result of the higher muzzle velocities of rifles, they do show an increased amount of tissue destruction.

Gunshot wounds of entry are characterized by a round or oval central defect with a surrounding collar of abrasion. The shape of the central defect results from the rounded shape of the nose of the bullet. The size of the central defect should not be used to determine the caliber of bullet. There is some correlation between the size of the defect and the caliber of the bullet, but the amount of skin elasticity also affects the size of the hole which remains. Generally speaking, the smaller the caliber of the bullet, the smaller will be the size of the central defect. However, small- and medium-caliber bullets do frequently leave wounds of the same diameter. It is also important not to try to determine the caliber of the bullet used on the basis of radiographs. If the bullet found on x-ray is close to the x-ray tube, then the bullet will appear larger on the resulting radiograph. Conversely, a bullet further away from the tube will appear smaller than the actual size. There is also a degree of magnification or reduction which occurs as a result of the distance between the bullet within the body and the x-ray film cartridge.

The abrasion collar around entry wounds is the result of the bullet scraping away the epithelium as it penetrates through the skin.

The abrasion collar may be concentric, if the bullet strikes the body on the perpendicular, or it may be eccentric, that is, wider at one point, if the bullet strikes the body at an angle, or strikes a curved portion of the body. Abrasion collars are not an indication of range of fire. Nearly all gunshot wounds of entry will show an abrasion collar, whether the weapon is fired at contact, close or distant range. The abrasion may be the same width as the central defect, larger than the central defect, or just a very fine rim. It may have a pink fleshy appearance, or if drying occurs, a reddish black or black leathery appearance.

Range of fire may be determined by careful examination of the skin about the wound of entry or the clothing that was covering the site of the wound for physical evidence of contact or close range fire. When a weapon is fired, the bullet, hot gases from the exploding gunpowder, unburned particles of gunpowder, and metal fragments from the bullet and from the barrel of the weapon are propelled out of the muzzle at the same time. In contact-range wounds, the hot gases and the particulate matter are blasted into the body at the same time as the bullet. The hot gases char the tissues around the entrance defect and the gunpowder and metal fragments will be deposited in the soft tissues along the wound track or on the surface of the skin, depending on how tightly the weapon is in contact with the body. The skin and soft tissues around the wound may also have a cherry red hue similar to that seen in cases of carbon monoxide intoxication. If the weapon is pressed tightly against skin overlying a bone, like the skull, the wound may have a starred, stellate, or lacerated appearance due to the expansion and tearing of the tissues by the gases being blown into the wound. If the weapon is pressed against skin overlying soft tissue, the wound will usually not be lacerated as the gases can be dispersed more readily into underlying soft tissues. It is not uncommon for a second abrasion to form around a contact-range gunshot wound caused by the gases pushing the skin outward and abrading the tissue against the muzzle of the weapon.

Close-range and near-contact-range gunshot wounds are characterized by the presence of stippling or tattooing around the wound. This is small, dry, reddish orange abrasions caused by unburned powder and small metal fragments striking and abrading the skin about the wound of entry. Occasionally, small gray powder or metal flecks may be found embedded within the skin. The closer the muzzle of the weapon is to the skin, the more likely that charring and gray soot or powder deposition will be seen in association with stippling. The amount of stippling will be affected by the distance the weapon is from the wound. In closer ranges of fire, there will be a very dense, but narrow band of stippling around the central defect, while the further away the weapon is, the wider and less dense the margin of stippling will be.

Evidence of close-range fire, stippling, charring, and powder may be masked by overlying clothing or dense head or body hair. The clothing and hair should be examined for evidence of charring or powder deposition. If no clothing is received with the body to be examined, and if the wound shows no charring, powder deposition, or stippling, then it is best to make no determination of range of fire. The currently available handguns and ammunition allow for deposition of evidence of close range fire, especially stippling, to be apparent if the weapon is held as far away as 18 to 24 inches. In general practice, the weapon has usually been held closer than this if evidence of stippling is found. Accurate determination of range of fire can only be done by obtaining the actual weapon used, loading with the same ammunition, and test firing at several different distances, then comparing the resultant patterns of stippling to that found on the body. Clear, well-focused photographs containing a small scale, and accurate measurements by the pathologist are very important.

Distant or long-range gunshot wounds of entry will show no charring, powder deposition, or stippling. These wounds will have the round or oval central defect and the abrasion collar found in nearly all gunshot wounds of entry.

Gunshot wounds of entry described above are those that are the result of the body being penetrated, or perforated, by a bullet that has not been damaged or deflected by striking or perforating an intervening target. Bullets that are damaged or that strike the body while tumbling or yawing will not create the typical oval or round wound described. They produce wounds that are irregular with a "P" or "D" shape or that have small lacerations around the periphery of the wound, giving the wound the appearance of an exit wound. The abrasion collar may be distorted or absent.

Reentry or ricochet wounds usually do not perforate the body, and the bullet may not penetrate as deeply, as some of the kinetic energy of the bullet is lost at the time it strikes the intervening target. Intermediate targets can be objects far removed from the victim's body, or may be parts of the victim's own body or clothing.

Gunshot exit wounds can be of any size or shape. They are usually irregular, being either slit-shaped, square, or stellate. They may be larger or smaller than the entrance wound. They do not have collars of abrasions which is one of the common ways to distinguish entry wounds from exit wounds. There is a type of exit wound that does show an abrasion collar. This is a shored exit wound. This occurs when the skin at the exit wound is abraded against an overlying object pressed against the body as the skin is pushed outward by the passage of the bullet. This object may be clothing such as tight-fitting T shirts or jeans, or a belt. Or it may be a building or the pavement that the body is pressed against. Shored entrance and shored exit wounds can be found close to one another in the area of the waist, where the bullet pushes clothing against the body as it enters and then pushes the body against the clothing as it exits. The bullet in such cases may bounce off the overlying clothing and reenter the body through the exit wound, and lodge in the superficial tissues between the entrance and exit wounds. It is sometimes difficult to differentiate a shored exit wound from a shored entrance wound, even for an experienced forensic pathologist.

SHOTGUNS

Entrance wounds from shotguns vary in appearance depending on the distance between the target and the muzzle of the weapon. They will also vary depending on the type of ammunition that is loaded in the weapon, the length of the barrel, and the choke of the weapon used.

If a shotgun is loaded with a shell containing a rifled slug, normally used in hunting large game, then no matter the distance, the wound will have a large, round central defect with a surrounding abrasion collar as seen in handgun and rifle gunshot entry wounds.

If the shotgun is loaded with shells containing lead shot, then the appearance of the entrance wound will depend on range of fire. As the lead shot from the shell comes out of the muzzle of the shotgun, the individual lead shot will remain as a tight mass for a short distance before beginning to scatter due to the forces of gravity, friction, and wind resistance. The length of the barrel and the choke influence how long the shot will remain as a tight mass, and care must be taken when making estimations of range of fire in shotgun wounds if the type of shotgun used is not known.

If a shotgun is fired at contact range, the entrance wound will show a round to oval central defect with an abrasion collar. The central defect will have a size comparable to the size of the muzzle opening or the bore of the weapon. As the distance between target and the shotgun increases, the appearance of the entrance wound changes. In near-contact and close-range shotgun wounds, there will be a large central defect which is slightly larger than that of contact-range wounds, and one may observe stippling about the wounds. There may be a petal or rectangular shaped abrasion noted if the plastic shot cup used to hold the lead shot, or the wadding within the shell strikes the skin surrounding the entrance defect before entering the body, or falling away from the body. As the distance increases, the large central defect will begin to show a scalloped margin as the individual shot pellets separate. Increasing the distance further will result in a large central hole with small satellite defects caused by individual shot pellets striking and penetrating the body. The size of the central defect will become smaller as the diameter of satellite wounds becomes larger. In distant shotgun wounds, there is no longer a central defect but numerous scattered individual entry wounds. These small wounds will still show a central defect with surrounding abrasion collar. The size of the individual pellet wounds depends on the size of the pellets. Small lead shot, or bird shot, will leave small wounds, while buck shot and larger shot create holes similar in size to those left by bullets. No matter the range of fire, once within the body, the lead shot scatters over remarkable distances.

Shotgun exit wounds are very rare, though they may be seen in contact and very close-range shotgun wounds or distant wounds caused by rifled slugs. Lead shot is designed to expend its kinetic energy on the internal organs so as to incapacitate the target, making shotgun exit wounds uncommon. The individual exit wounds from lead shot will be irregular in shape and may be stellate or lacerated.

When describing gunshot wounds of entry and exit, it is important for the examiner to measure and record the size of the central defect, to measure and record the appearance of the abrasion collar, and to measure any margin of stippling or gunpowder deposition around the wound (Table 4.1). It is common to use a clock face when describing the location of various features around the wound. The location of the wound should be given by measuring the distance of the wound from landmarks on the body, such as the distance below the top of the head or above the heel, and the distance the wound is found to the right or left of the midline of the front or the back of the body. If the wound is located very near to a landmark, such as the eye, nose, or ear, the distance from that structure can also be given.

When describing gunshot wounds, the terms *penetrating* and *perforating* are used. *Penetrating* gunshot wounds are those where the bullet enters, but does not exit the body. In these cases, the location of the bullet when recovered, should also be given in terms similar to those used in describing the location of the entrance wound. The path of the bullet through the body is also described, such as from front to back, left to right, and downward. All of the organs and tissues affected by the bullet and the order in which they are affected should also be given. *Perforating* gunshot wounds are those with both an entrance wound and an exit wound from the bullet passing completely through the body. The location of both wounds should be given to allow for identification of the path of the bullet through the body.

It must be remembered that the path of the bullet through the body can be significantly altered if the bullet strikes bone or a dense organ on its course. Small-caliber bullets and lead shot may enter blood vessels or the heart and embolize to distant parts of the body far removed from the point of entrance. The path of the bullet through the body may reflect the path of the bullet outside the body, and allow the pathologist to form some opinion as to the location of the weapon in relationship to the victim at the time the weapon was fired, but this is not always the case.

A common request made by police investigators is for the pathologist to place a probe into the entrance wound and along the path of the bullet and to then measure and photograph the angle of the probe to the body in order to try to position the victim in relationship to the offender. This may occasionally accurately reflect the direction from which the bullet came at the time the victim was shot or the actual path of the bullet through the victim's body at the time he was shot. What this procedure always accurately reflects is the path of the bullet through the body as it now lays on the autopsy table. Shooting victims have the inconvenient habit of being in various postures and positions, or may be running, jumping, or leaning one way or the other at the moment of being shot. These movements can affect the path of the bullet through the body. It is impossible to demonstrate this while the body is supine and static on the autopsy table. For example, if a victim is running away from an offender with his head down, a bullet fired in a downward direction by the offender, which travels along a downward path through the body of the victim, will appear to travel in an upward direction when the victim's body is on the autopsy table. If asked to do this by investigating officers, by all means, if time allows, do so. Please explain that the resulting angles may not be a true representation of what actually occurred.

Spent bullets recovered from the bodies of gunshot victims should be handled with care so as to avoid damaging or marking the bullets in any fashion. Jacketed bullets will sometimes separate when they penetrate the body, and it is important to recover both the lead core and the jacketing material. The jacket is the part of the bullet which will have the markings left by the lands and grooves in the barrel of the gun, which allow comparisons to be made between the bullet recovered from the victim and bullets test fired from recovered weapons. Bullets are best recovered by using gloved hands to avoid putting any marks on the soft lead or the jacketing. If it is impossible to recover a bullet with the hands, then instruments that are Teflon-coated can be used. There is a bullet available on the market which is called a "Black Talon". This particular bullet was designed for use by police because the deformation of the bullet which occurs at the time of impact causes the bullet to form talon-like structures which grab and hold on to the tissues within the body of the intended target. This prevents these bullets from perforating, or passing through the target and then striking and injuring an innocent bystander. It also increases the wounding capability or stopping power of the bullet. These talons are very sharp and are extremely dangerous to the person recovering the bullet. It is very helpful to have Teflon-coated hemostats or forceps to recover these bullets. The Teflon coating prevents the instrument from scratching the bullet.

Bullets should never be engraved with the initials of the person recovering the bullet. This includes the pathologist performing the autopsy and trauma surgeons. Bullets should be rinsed, photographed and then placed in evidence envelopes or other suitable containers labeled with the victim's name, the date, the initials or name of the individual who recovered the bullet, and the anatomic site where the bullet was recovered. This last is particularly important when multiple bullets are recovered, as it allows for identification of the bullet at a later date when in the courtroom setting. The bullets should then be turned over to the investigating police agency, along with blood samples and any other evidence recovered from the case, such as clothing. The pieces of clothing that have gunshot defects should also be examined and photographed.

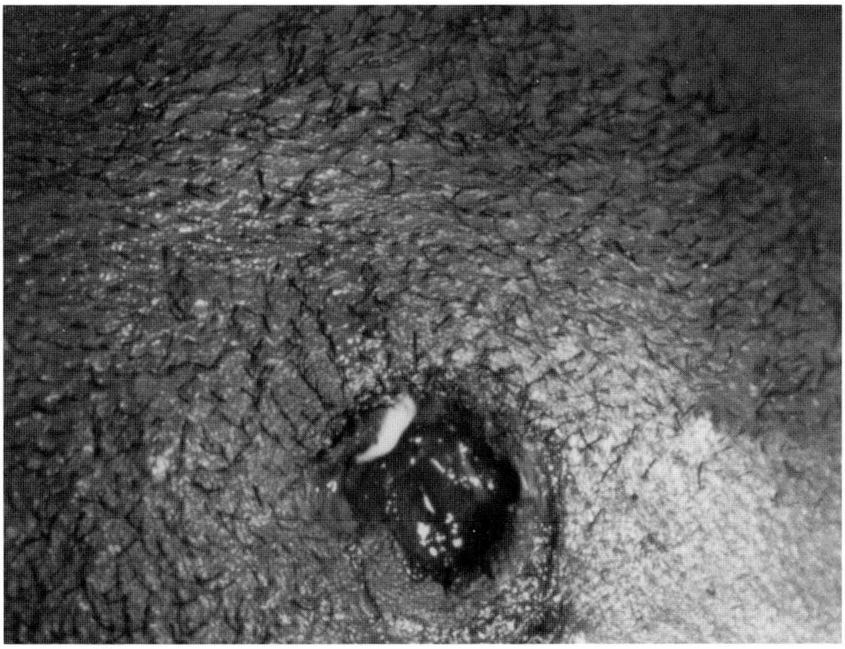

FIGURE 4.1 Contact-range gunshot wound of entrance to the temple. There is a round central defect with fine lacerations at the 5 to 7 o'clock position. There is a muzzle abrasion around the wound which is complete to the point of including the pattern left by the sight on the barrel. The weapon was held upside down at the time it was fired.

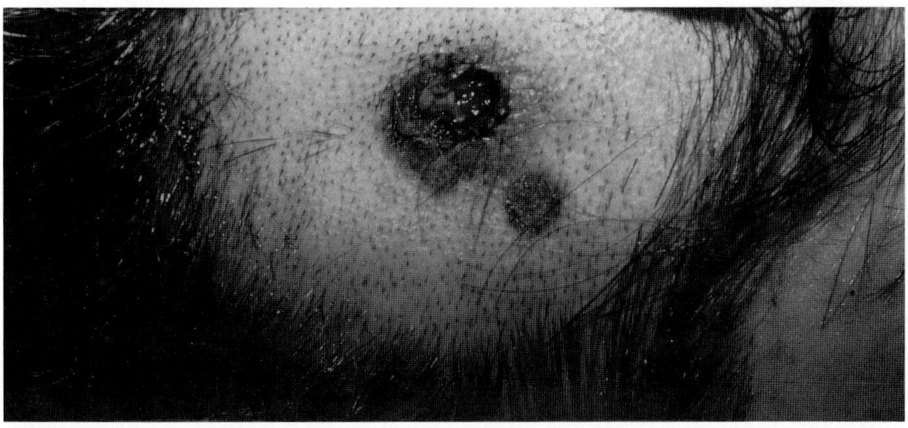

FIGURE 4.2 Contact-range gunshot wound of entrance from a semiautomatic hand gun. The wound shows slight charring of the margins and there is again a muzzle abrasion around the wound complete to a round abrasion from the ejector rod.

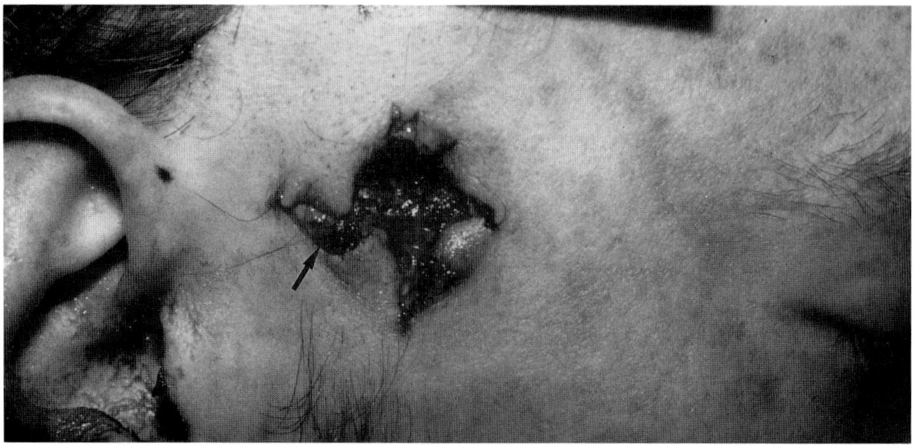

FIGURE 4.3 Hard contact-range handgun wound to the head. The gun had been held against the jacket hood, but was still tight enough to cause extensive lacerations of the wound from the gases blown into the soft tissue when the weapon was discharged. This wound could be mistaken for an exit wound as it lacks any charring or an abrasion collar. There is gunpowder present within the wound track (*arrow*) which identifies this as an entrance wound. Examination of the clothing which showed a charred hole on the right side of the hood would clear up any confusion.

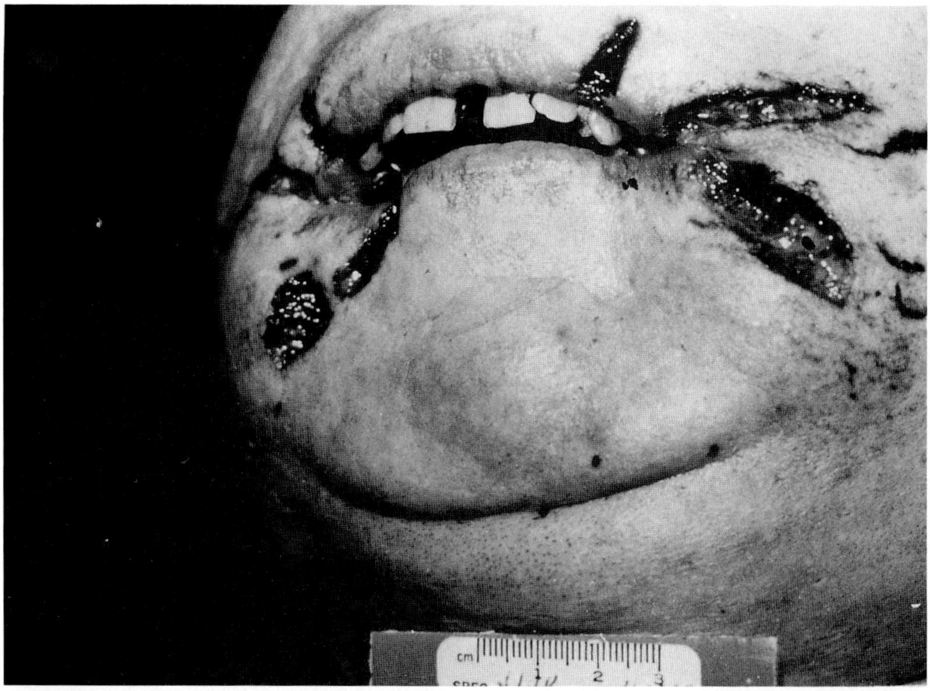

FIGURE 4.4 Hard contact-range gunshot wound to the hard palate using a .357 magnum handgun caused these lacerations around the mouth. They are due to overstretching of the tissue which occurred when the weapon was discharged and the gases expanded within the mouth. The bullet severed the brainstem leading to immediate death.

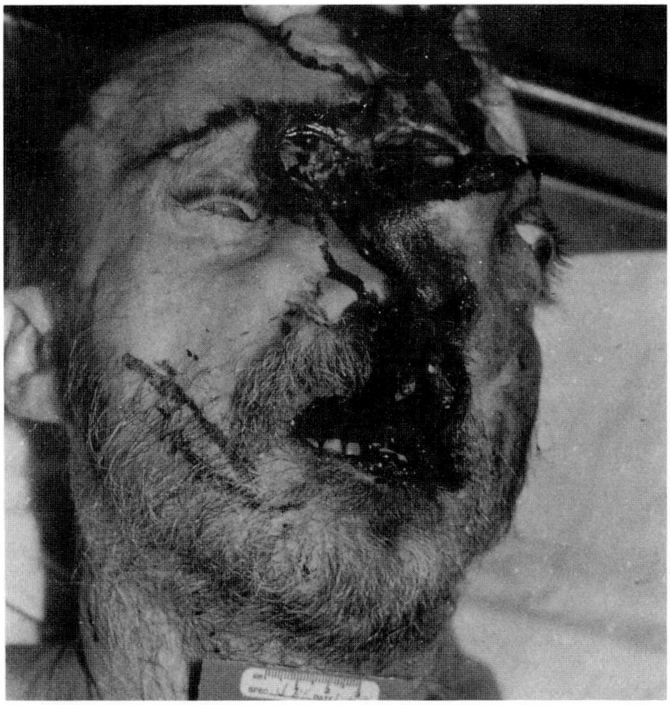

FIGURE 4.5 Extensive lacerations of the face of a man who committed suicide by placing a gun against the hard palate. The angle at which the muzzle was placed caused the bullet to travel upward through the face instead of traveling into the base of the skull and transecting the brainstem. Though the bullet never entered the skull, there were extensive contusions of the brain from the passage of the bullet through the face.

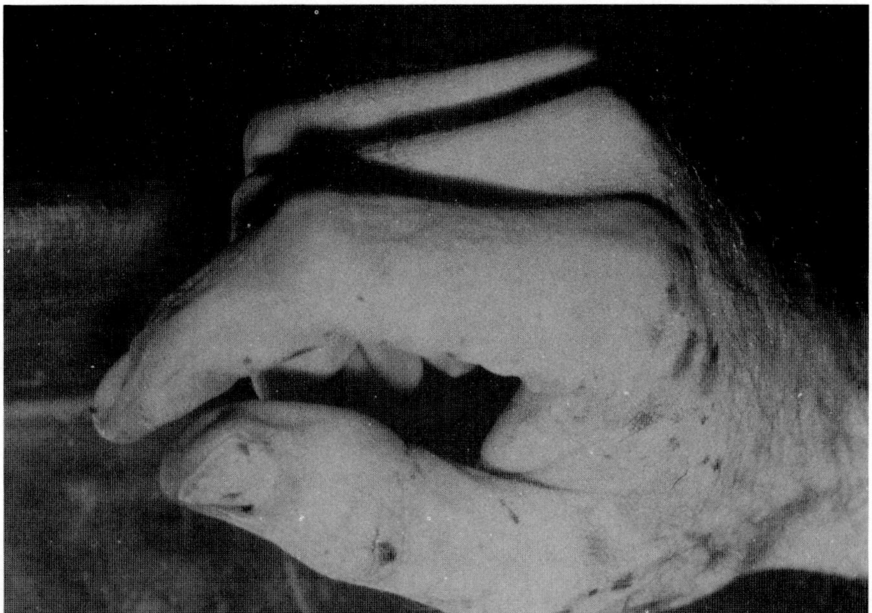

FIGURE 4.6 Blow-back blood splatter on the hand of a suicide victim. This is evidence that the weapon was held in the victim's own hand at the time it was fired.

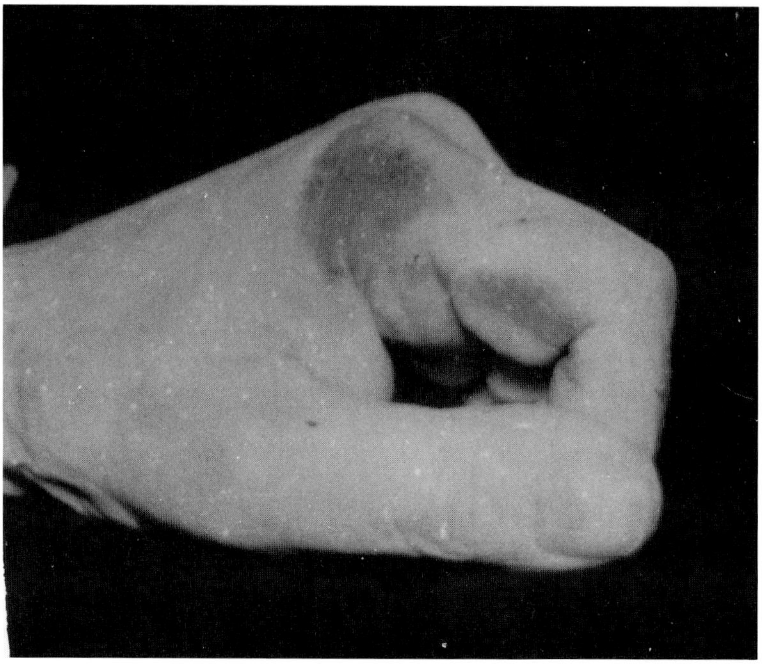

FIGURE 4.7 Soot, or gunshot residue, from the primer deposited on the hand in a case of a self-inflicted gunshot wound to the head. The residue contains lead, barium, and antimony. Tests for gunpowder residue should be done as soon as possible after the body is found. Many police agencies no longer perform these tests as there are many false-negative results in part due to the passage of time as well as the formulations of the newer gunpowders.

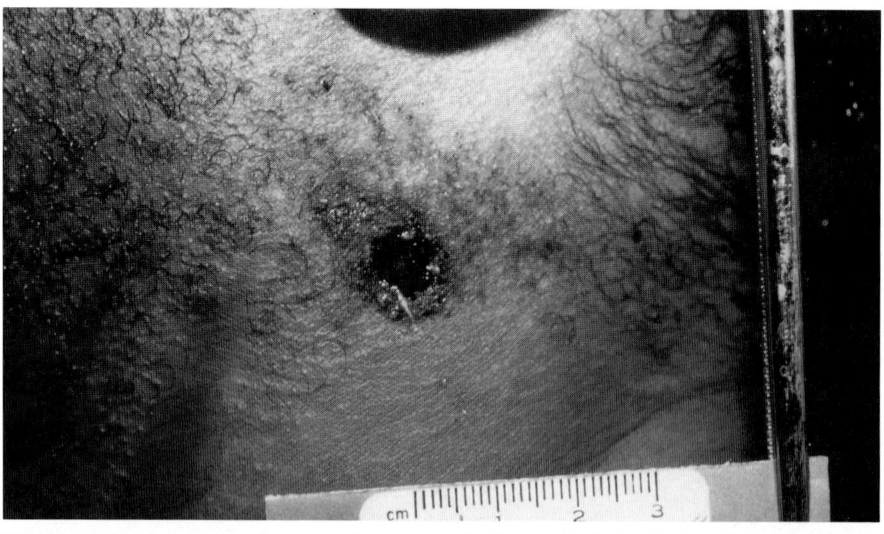

FIGURE 4.8 Near-contact-range gunshot wound of entry which shows slight charring of the wound, an abrasion collar, and an eccentric pattern of stippling which extends from the 8 o'clock position to the 3 o'clock position and is widest at the 11 o'clock position. The pattern of stippling can be a result of the angle the gun was held against the body, or it may be due to the anatomy of the body at that particular site.

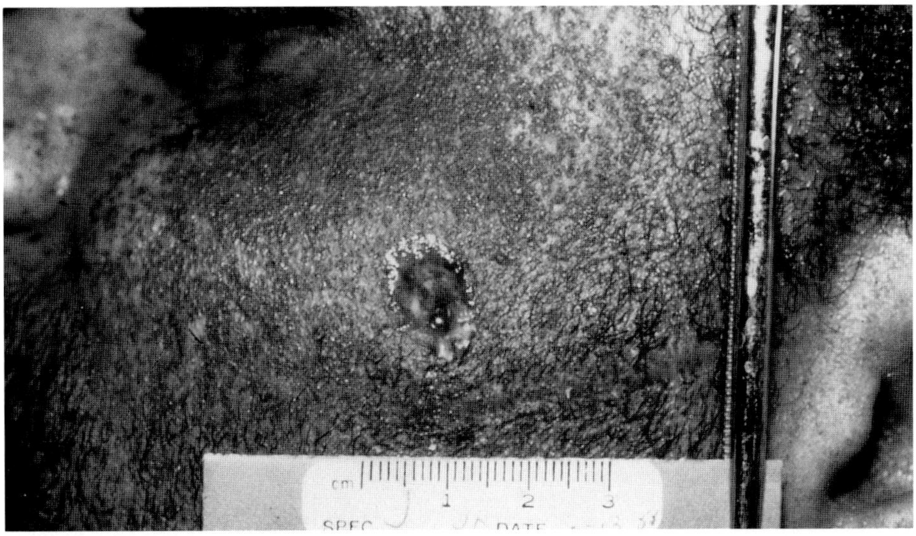

FIGURE 4.9 Close-range gunshot wound of entry with a round central defect, eccentric abrasion collar which is wider at the 11 o'clock position with a dense rim of stippling around the wound.

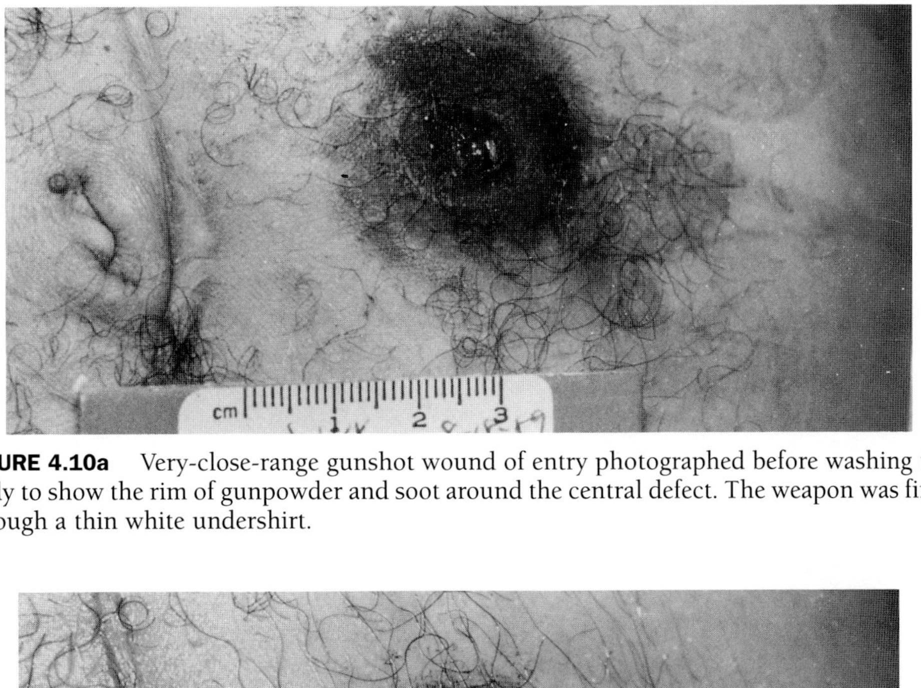

a

FIGURE 4.10a Very-close-range gunshot wound of entry photographed before washing the body to show the rim of gunpowder and soot around the central defect. The weapon was fired through a thin white undershirt.

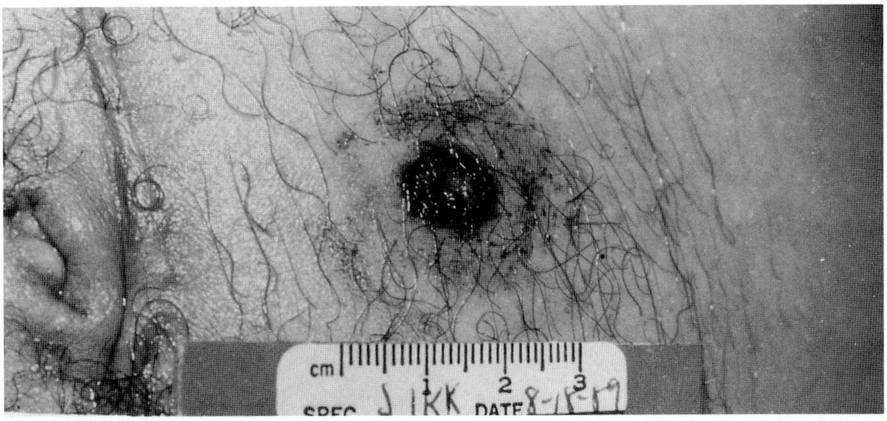

b

FIGURE 4.10b Same wound as seen in Figure 4.10a after the body was washed. Washing removes soot and gunpowder from the skin around entrance wounds making determination of range of fire more difficult. This can happen in gunshot victims who survive long enough to make it to the hospital and into the surgical suite. Stippling, on the other hand, can not be washed away as it consists of small abrasions.

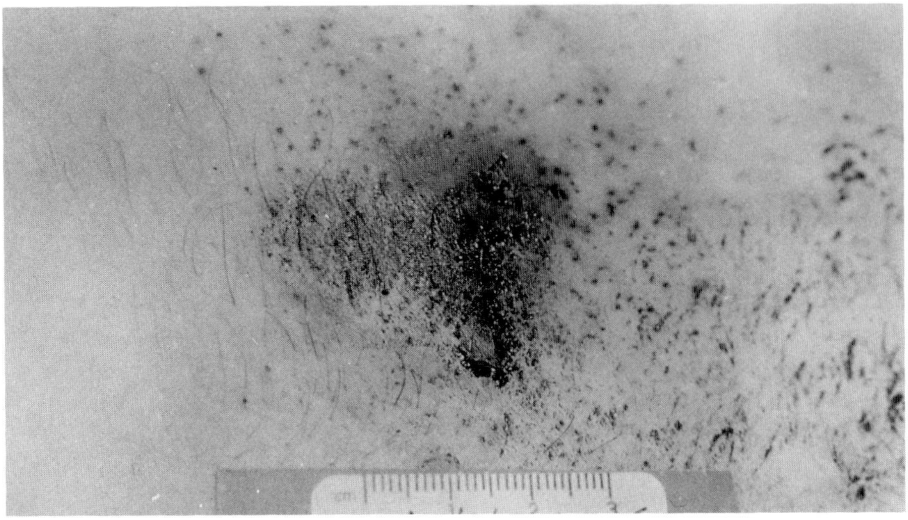

a

FIGURE 4.11a Close-range entrance wound photographed before washing the body to show soot and gunpowder around the entrance defect and a wider and less dense margin of stippling.

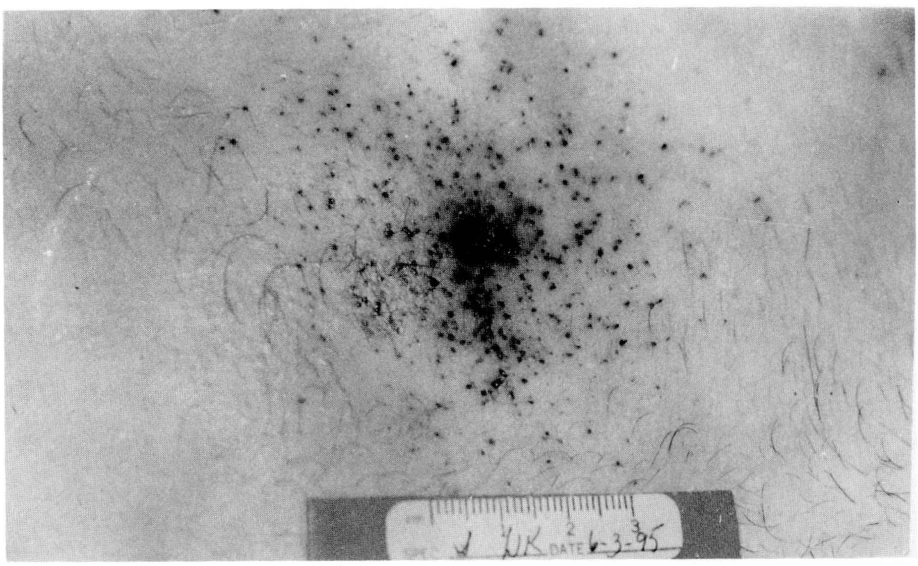

b

FIGURE 4.11b Same wound after washing the body. The small central defect can be more clearly seen. The soot and powder are no longer present, but the margin of stippling still remains.

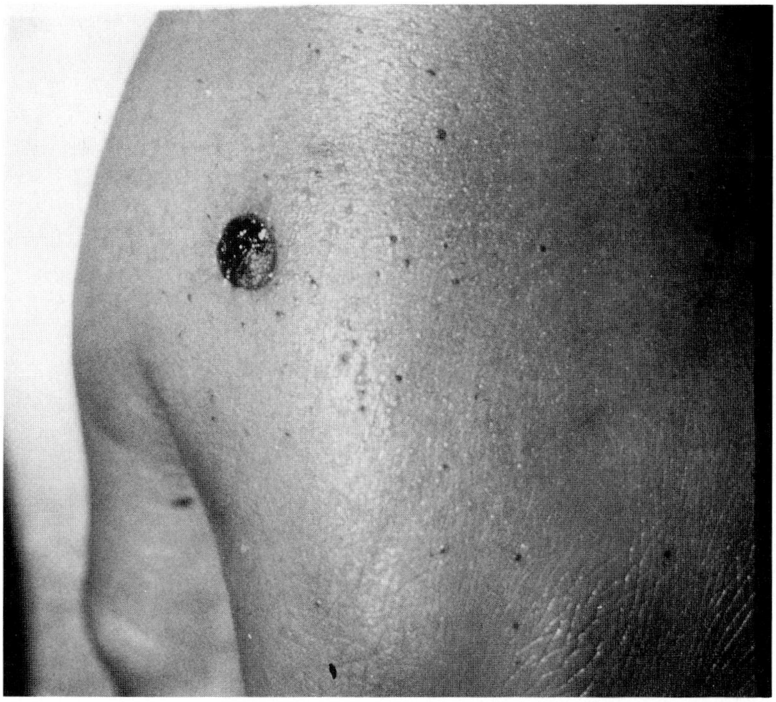

FIGURE 4.12 Healing close-range gunshot wound found on the hand of a victim of multiple gunshot wounds who survived for several days. There is a well-formed scab over the entrance wound and small scabs have also formed on the stippling wounds.

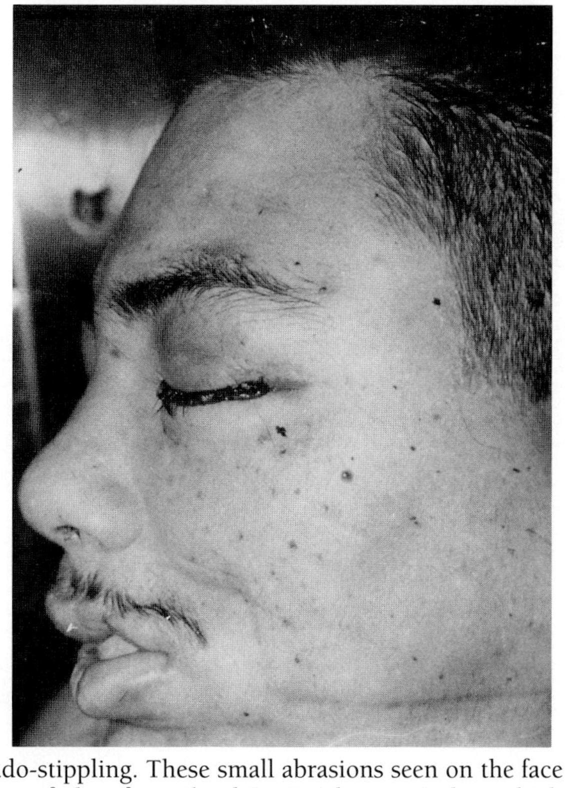

FIGURE 4.13 Pseudo-stippling. These small abrasions seen on the face of a gunshot victim were caused by pieces of glass from the driver's side car window which shattered when the bullet came through the closed window.

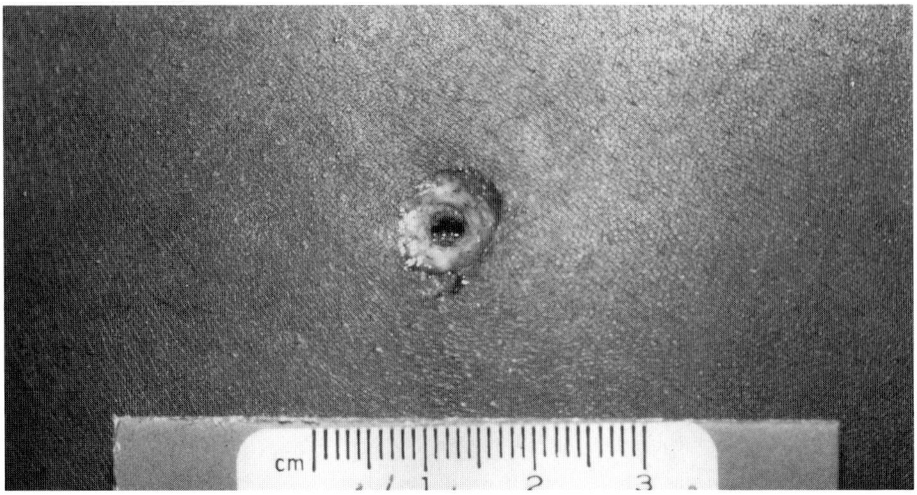

FIGURE 4.14 A distant or indeterminate-range gunshot wound of entry. There is a round to slightly oval central defect surrounded by a concentric abrasion collar. There is no charring, no soot or gunpowder around the wound, and no evidence of stippling. The gun that fired this bullet could have been fired from any distance greater than 2 feet from the victim.

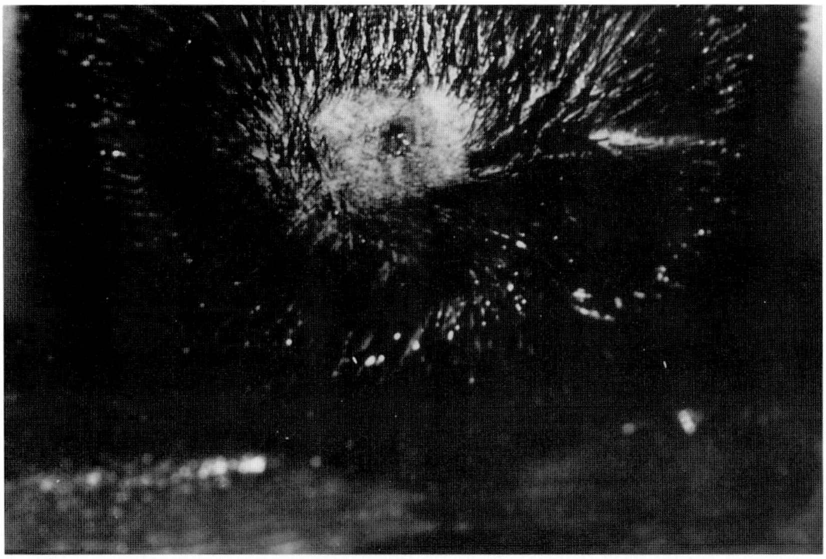

FIGURE 4.15 A gunshot wound of entry found on the top of the head of a victim of multiple gunshot wounds. The bullet that caused this injury was recovered from the soft tissue under the chin at the midline. The path of the bullet through the body is straight downward. This indicates that this wound was inflicted last, while the victim was down on the ground.

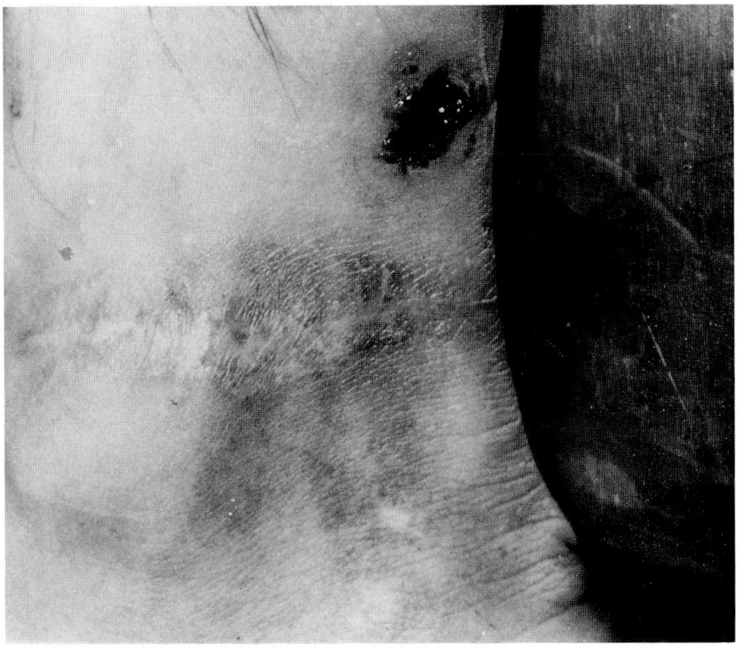

FIGURE 4.16 Atypical gunshot wound of entry found on the medial aspect of the ankle. The wound is irregular and lacerated and has the appearance of an exit wound. It was caused by a bullet that struck the roadway and then ricocheted up into the ankle. The bullet that caused this injury was recovered from the soft tissues a short distance from the entrance wound.

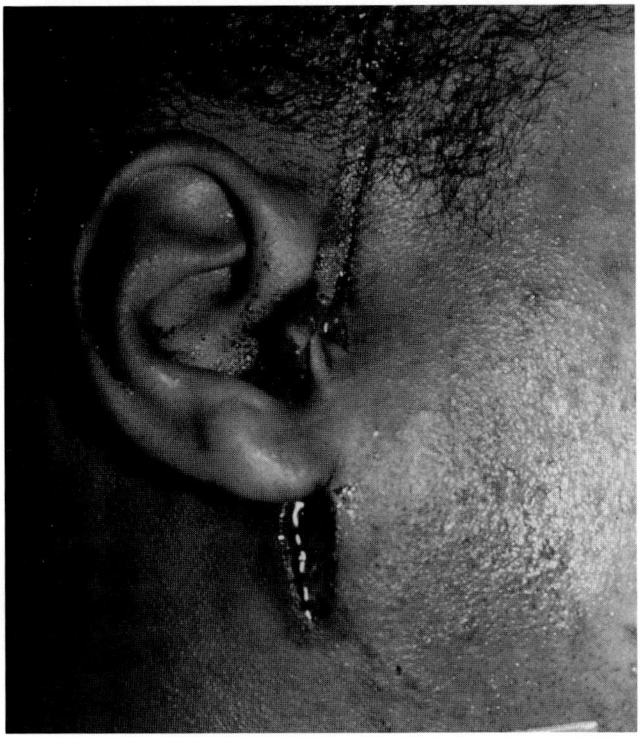

FIGURE 4.17 Graze gunshot wound. The bullet struck the head and traveled along the side of the head in the superficial epidermal tissue, and never penetrated into the body. Direction of fire in graze wounds can be determined by examining the margins of the wound for small triangular skin tags which point back to the direction from which the bullet came.

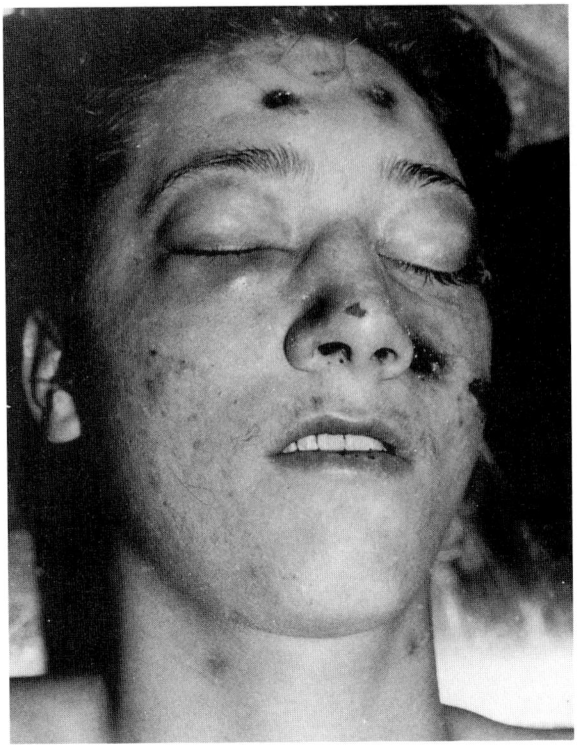

FIGURE 4.18 Multiple distant gunshot wounds to the face. There are two entry wounds to the forehead and a through-and-through wound to the left cheek and nose. This is a single wound which entered the cheek, tunneled a short distance through the subcutaneous tissues, exited next to the nose, then reentered the body on the left side of the nose, then reexited on the right side of the nose. The eyelids are swollen and slightly bruised. Two bullets are lodged in the soft tissues below the right eye which can be recovered by peeling the scalp and facial tissues downward. No iatrogenic damage is then done to the face.

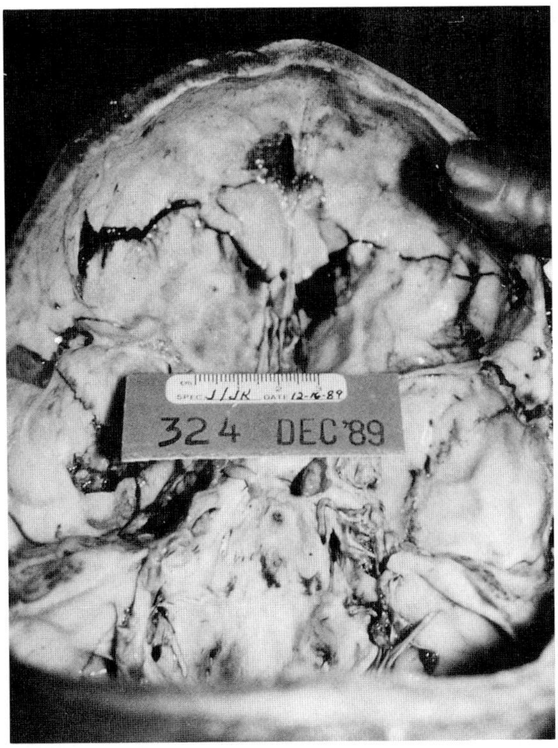

FIGURE 4.19 The dura mater is always striped from the calvarium and the base of the skull in forensic autopsies so that any skull fractures can be identified. There are multiple secondary fractures of the base of this skull due to the multiple gunshot wounds to the face. Secondary fractures are more frequently seen in contact or close-range gunshot wounds, or in wounds from bullets with high kinetic energy.

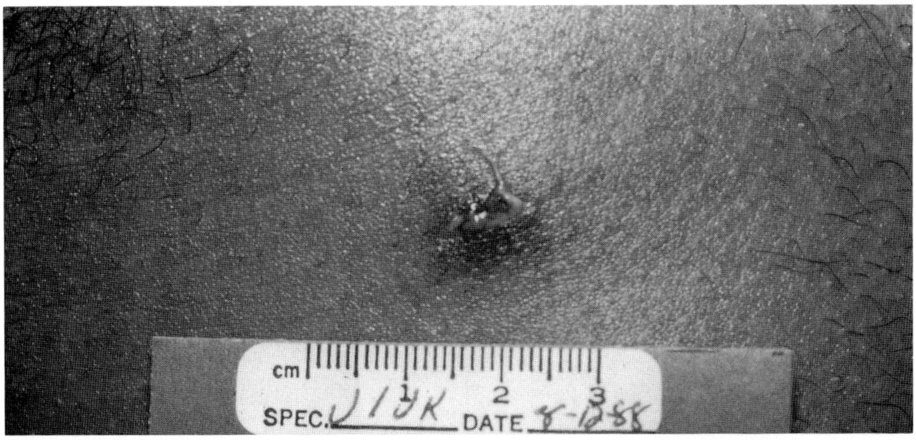

FIGURE 4.20 Typical slit-shaped gunshot wound of exit. There is no abrasion collar around the defect, which helps to identify this as an exit defect. There are small tags of soft tissue protruding from the wound which is frequently seen in exit wounds as tissue and bone fragments are carried out of the body by the bullet. This is not a marker for exit wounds, as tissue can protrude outward from entrance wounds as well.

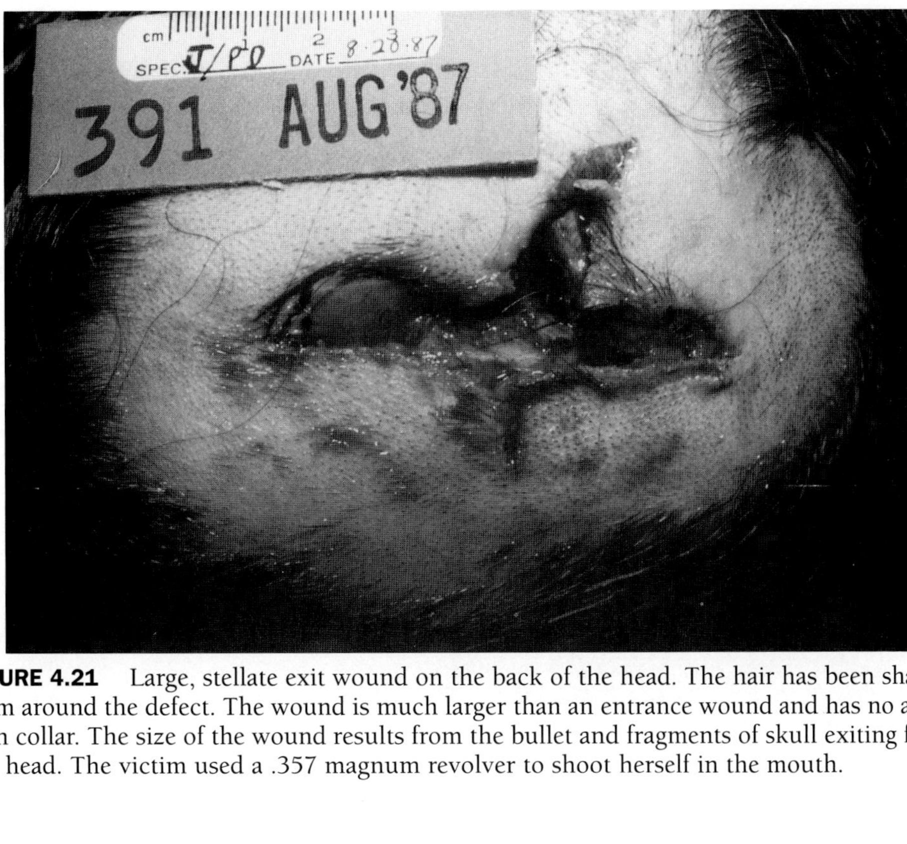

FIGURE 4.21 Large, stellate exit wound on the back of the head. The hair has been shaved from around the defect. The wound is much larger than an entrance wound and has no abrasion collar. The size of the wound results from the bullet and fragments of skull exiting from the head. The victim used a .357 magnum revolver to shoot herself in the mouth.

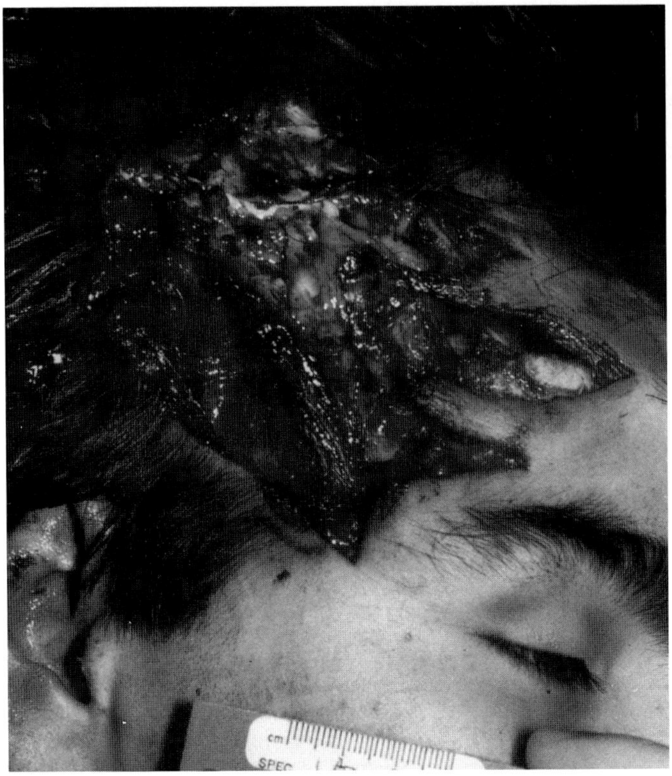

a

FIGURE 4.22a Large, lacerated wound found on the right side of the head of a young Hispanic male. The victim was found on the kitchen floor and a .357 magnum revolver was on the kitchen table next to a partially consumed bottle of beer. This wound was identified as an exit wound by the police officers at the scene. They believed that the victim had shot himself in the mouth.

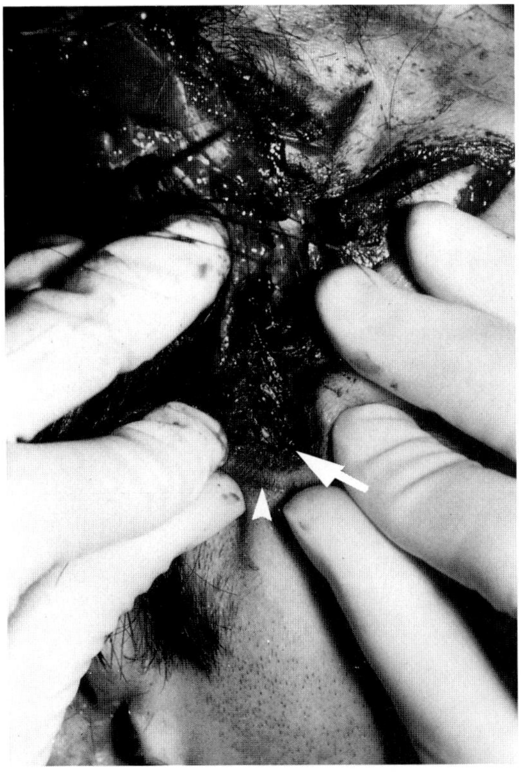

b

FIGURE 4.22b The lacerated defect to the right temple was identified as a contact-range entrance wound. This was done by reapproximating the margins of the wound. This showed a round central defect which is charred (*arrow*), gunpowder in the wound track, and a muzzle abrasion (*arrow head*) a short distance from the central defect.

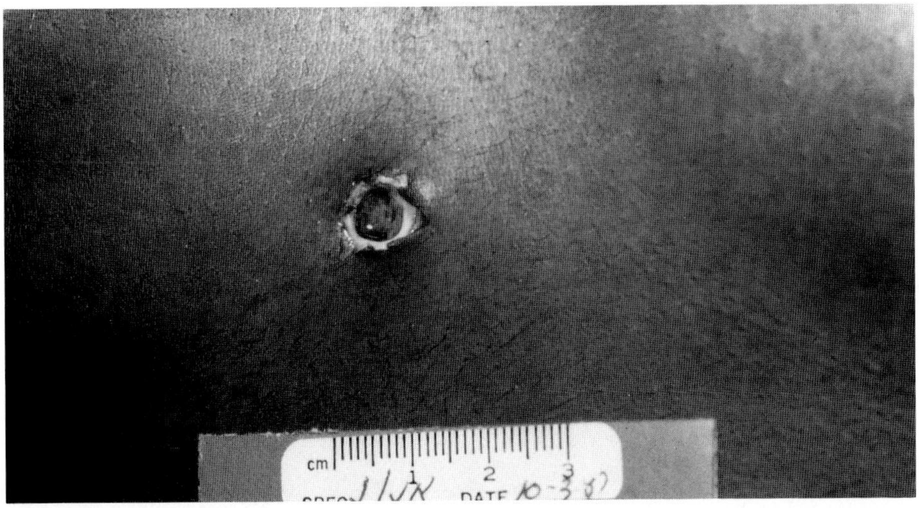

FIGURE 4.23 Shored gunshot exit wound. This wound has a superficial resemblance to a gunshot wound of entry due to the presence of an irregular abrasion collar. The wound is lacerated, suggesting a contact-range wound, but there is no charring, gunpowder, soot, or stippling present. These inconsistencies allow the examiner to accurately identify the wound as a shored exit and not an entrance. The abrasion around the central hole resulted from the bullet abrading the skin against the brassiere as it exited the chest between the breasts. A typical distant gunshot wound of entry was located on the back when the body was turned for the posterior external examination. Gunshot wounds are always identified on the basis of the point of entry. In this case, the cause of death is a through-and-through (perforating) gunshot wound to the back.

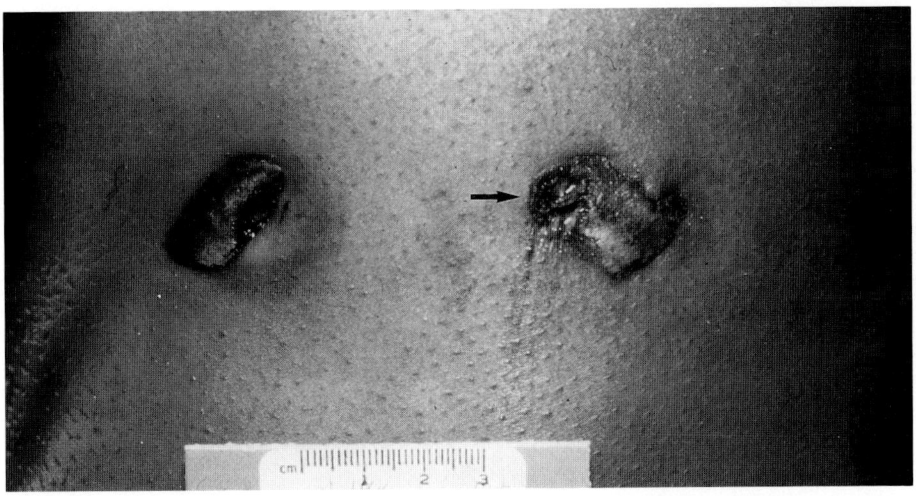

FIGURE 4.24 Perforating, shored gunshot wound to the left side of the waist. The victim was wearing a wide leather belt. The entrance wound (*arrow*) shows a large, irregular abrasion from the 3 to 5 o'clock position with a more normal-appearing abrasion collar from 6 to 12 o'clock. The exit wound shows a large irregular abrasion lateral to the slit-shaped exit defect. The bullet was recovered in the soft tissue between the wounds. The bullet lacked the kinetic energy needed to perforate the belt a second time after exiting the body and rebounded back through the exit wound.

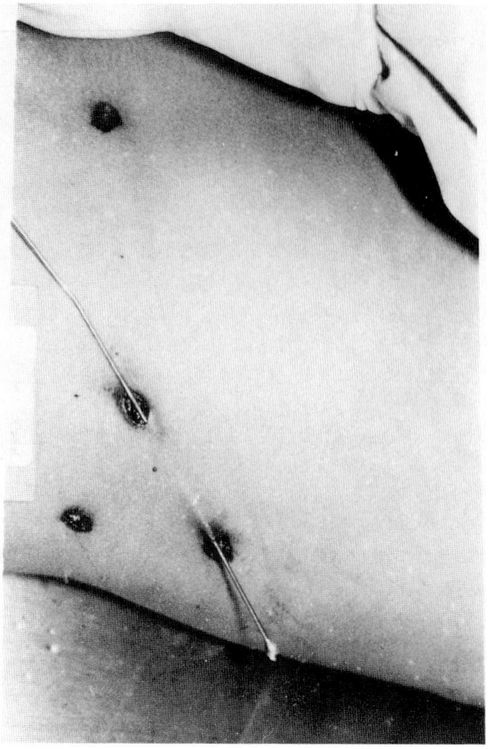

FIGURE 4.25 Demonstration, with a thin bullet probe which will not damage tissue, of the path of a through-and-through superficial gunshot wound to the left flank region. The path is from front to back and upward as the body lays supine on the autopsy table.

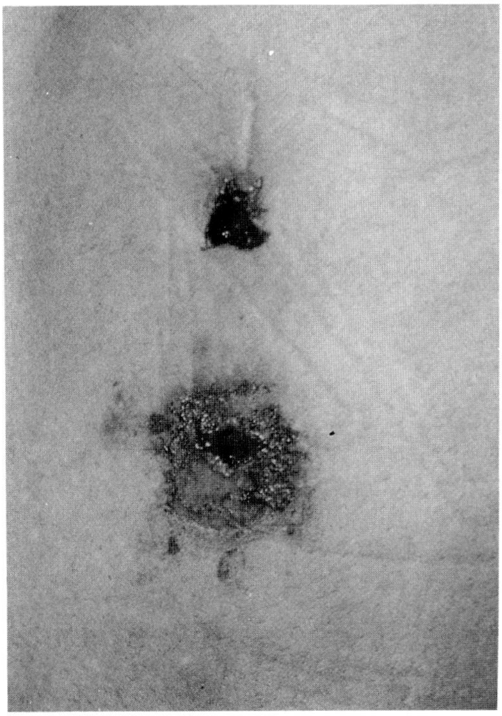

FIGURE 4.26 A young adult African-American female was found stuffed into a steamer trunk. Examination revealed four gunshot wounds on the body, two on the chest between the breasts and two at the midline of the thoracic area of the back. This photograph shows the wounds on the back. The upper wound is a typical, lacerated exit defect, while the lower wound is a near-contact-range entrance wound. There were corresponding holes in the upper clothing, with only one defect found in both the front and the back of the brassiere. The defect in the back of the brassiere showed margins which were singed.

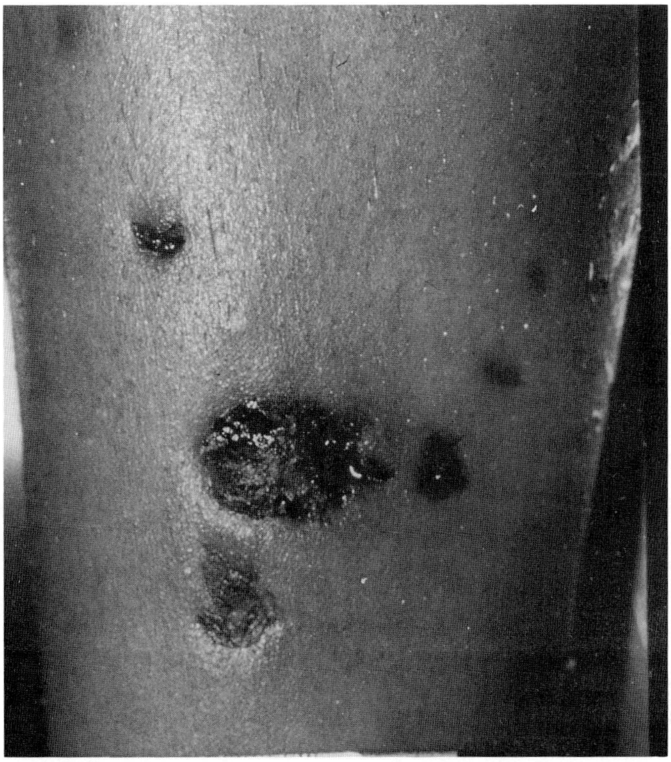

FIGURE 4.27 Shrapnel wounds to the calf of a young victim shot with a semiautomatic handgun. This injury is caused when fragments of jacketing and/or lead from ricochet bullets strike the body. Semiautomatic handguns, such as the Intratec 9 used by gang members in Chicago, can be loaded with clips containing up to 34 rounds.

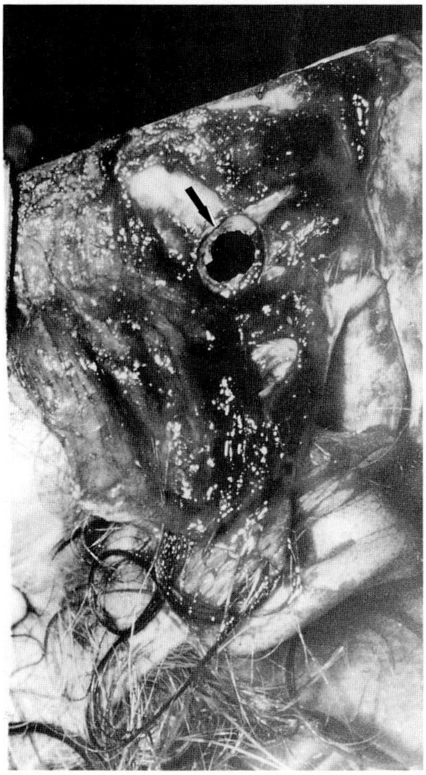

FIGURE 4.28 Gunshot wound of entrance to the skull. The outer table of the skull around the entrance wound is sharply edged. There is a narrow margin of powder deposition around the entrance defect in the bone (*arrow*). When nonjacketed bullets penetrate the skull, they may leave a thin rim of lead around the edges of the hole where the soft lead of the bullet is scraped away by the bone. This fine rim of lead can be seen on skull radiographs.

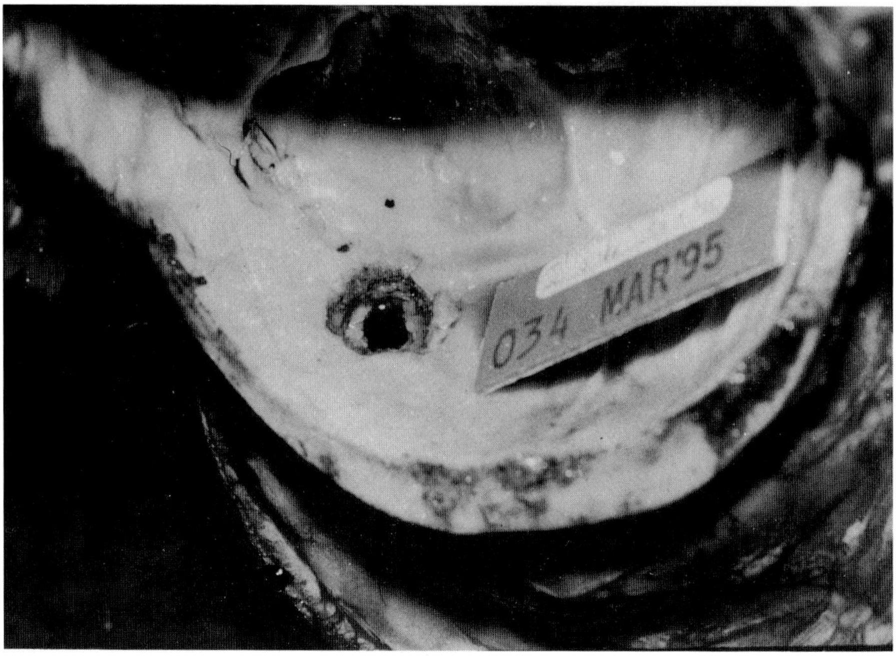

FIGURE 4.29 Gunshot wound of exit in bone. The inner table of the skull is beveled inward. Some of the bone fragments displaced by the bullet are propelled into the brain tissue and act as secondary missiles creating further injury to the brain matter.

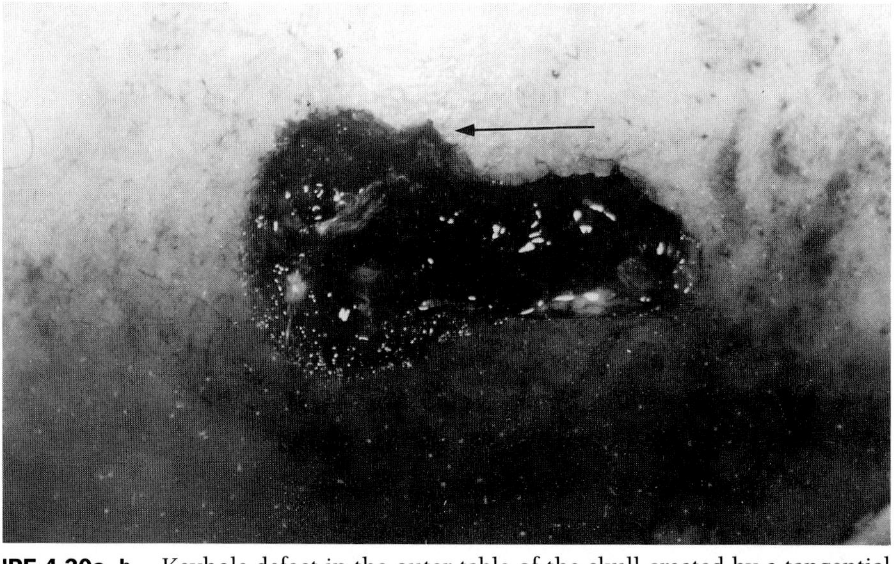

a

FIGURE 4.30a, b Keyhole defect in the outer table of the skull created by a tangential gunshot wound to the head. The direction of the bullet is indicated by the arrow. The bullet struck and fractured the bone, creating a wound which shows a sharp margin on one edge and a beveled margin on the other. The wound on the inner table of the skull also shows one beveled and one sharp edge. The bullet did not penetrate the skull itself, but the bone fragments did, creating extensive damage to the underlying brain tissue.

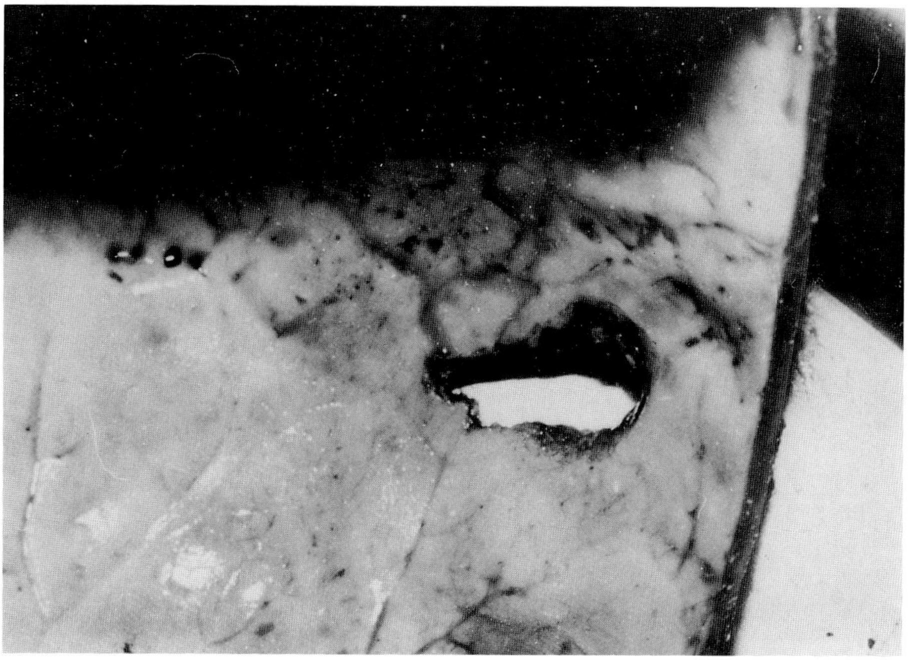

b

FIGURE 4.30b (continued)

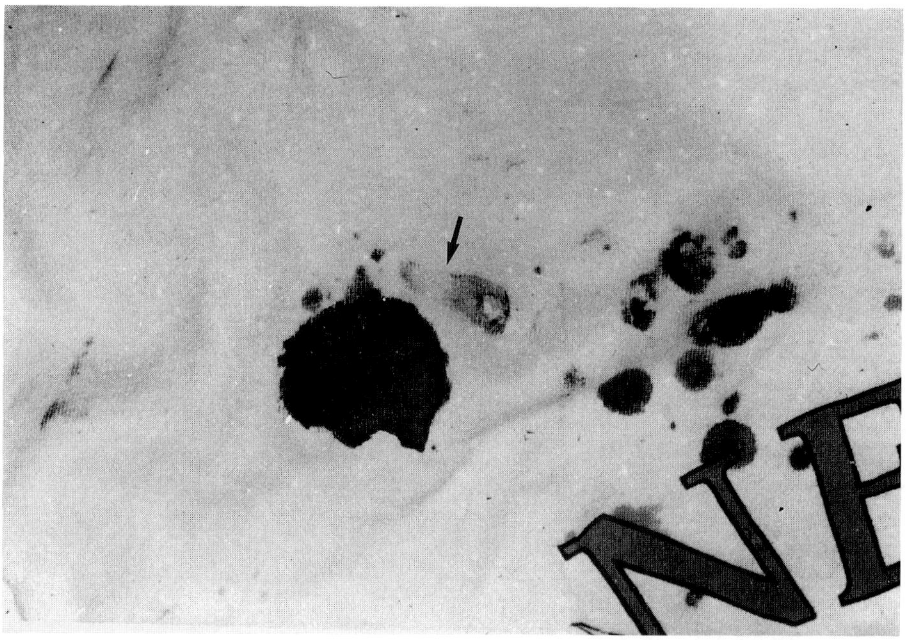

FIGURE 4.31 Direction of fire can sometimes be determined by examining the margin of abrasion about an entrance wound. It can also be determined by examining the clothing. This white sweatshirt shows an eccentric pattern of "bullet wipe" (*arrow*), made up predominantly of soot, with lubricating oil and metallic fragments from the barrel of the gun also present. The wider margin of wipe points back to the direction that the bullet came from.

FIGURE 4.32 Clothing should be removed carefully from gunshot victims, and examined closely. This jacket shows a hole made by a bullet, and a small lead fragment with rifling marks is caught up in the cloth adjacent to the hole. Bullets and fragments of bullets can get caught in the clothing or between layers of clothing when they lack sufficient kinetic energy to continue further.

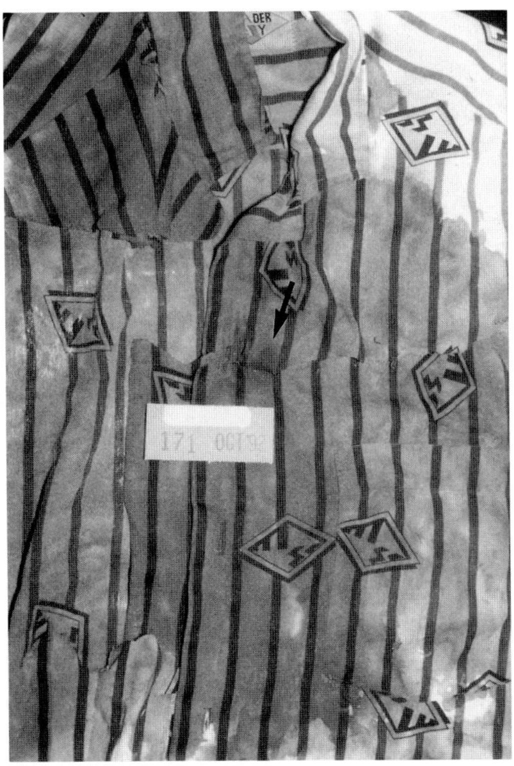

FIGURE 4.33 Clothing should always be examined for soot, powder, or minute metal fragments, evidence of close-range fire. This shirt shows a large amount of blood but there is also a rim of powder and soot (*arrow*) deposited on the shirt around the bullet hole, evidence that the gun was held within inches of the body at the time it was discharged. The body had been washed by emergency medical personnel and there was no powder visible on the skin around the entrance wound.

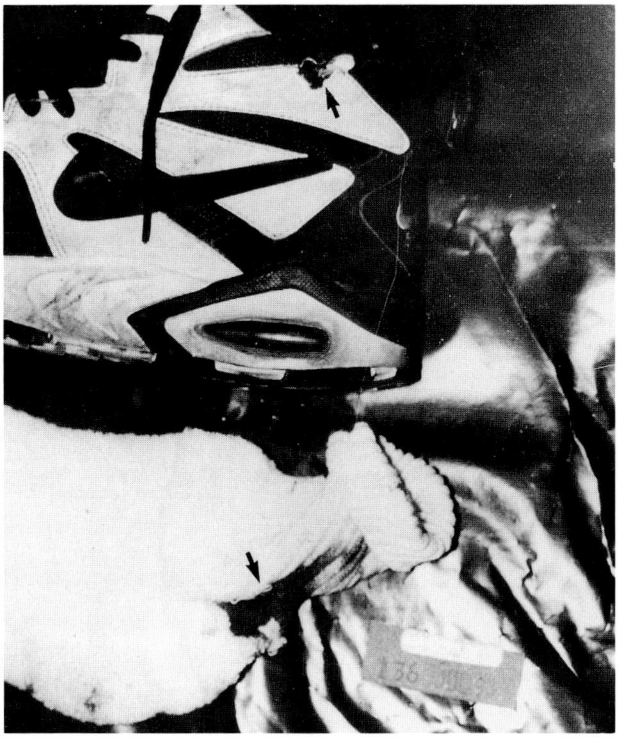

FIGURE 4.34 Shoe and sock from a gunshot victim showing holes (*arrows*) from an entrance wound to the ankle. All clothing from gunshot victims should be turned over to the investigating police agency. Some departments, such as the Chicago Police Department, require that only clothing with gunshot defects be submitted, while other departments, such as the Illinois State Police and the Cook County or Lake County Sheriff's Police, require that all clothing, with or without gunshot defects, be submitted.

a

FIGURE 4.35a, b Not all gunshot victims die immediately from their wounds. Scars from three old, healed gunshot wounds (*arrow heads*) can be seen on the back of this young Hispanic male. One of the three bullets had been recovered during surgery. One lodged in the right musculus rectus abdominis, and the third lodged in the lower cervical spine. The victim was paralyzed. He was found dead in his bed at a rehabilitation center. Autopsy revealed multiple thromboemboli within the right and left pulmonary arteries and the right ventricle outflow tract. Cause of death was determined to be multiple gunshot wounds to the back, manner of death was ruled homicide with pulmonary thromboembolism as the mechanism of death.

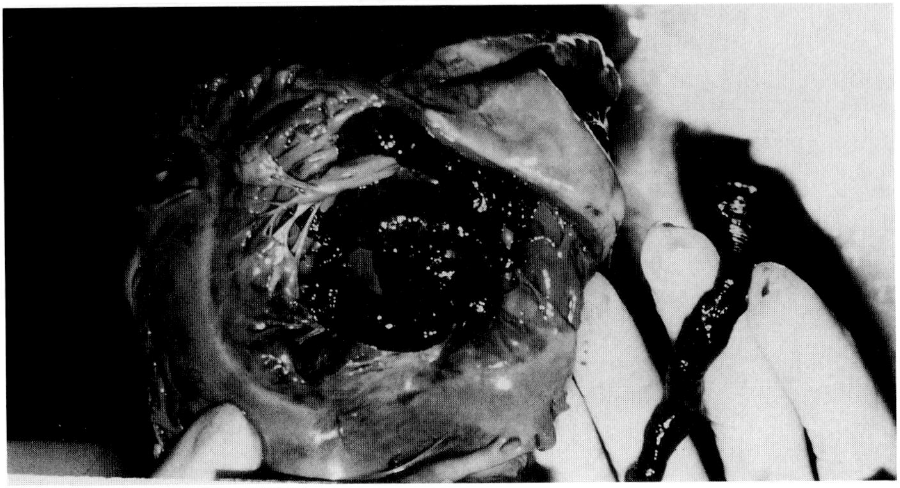

b

FIGURE 4.35b (continued)

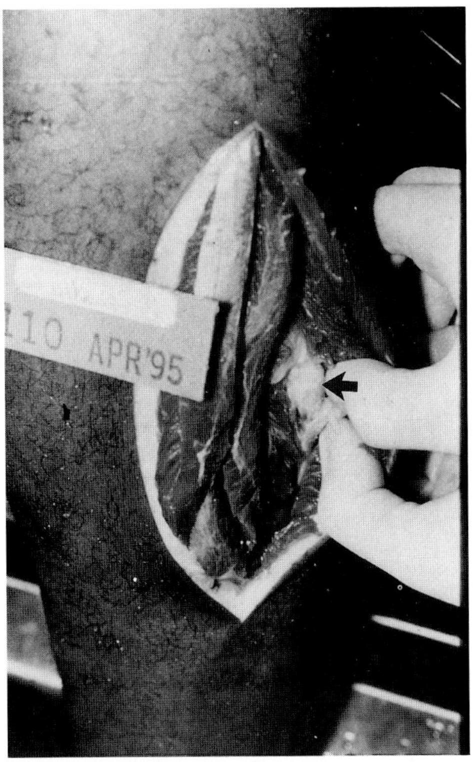

FIGURE 4.36 Old encapsulated bullet (*arrow*) found in the posterior thigh of a gunshot victim. It is not uncommon to find old bullets in the bodies of shooting victims. The old bullets are removed and submitted to the investigating police agency along with any bullets recovered from the current incident. The number of entrance wounds, exit wounds, and recovered bullets should always add up to an even number. If the number of entrance wounds plus the number of exit wounds plus the number of bullets noted on the radiographs do not add up to an even number, always consider the possibility of an old bullet.

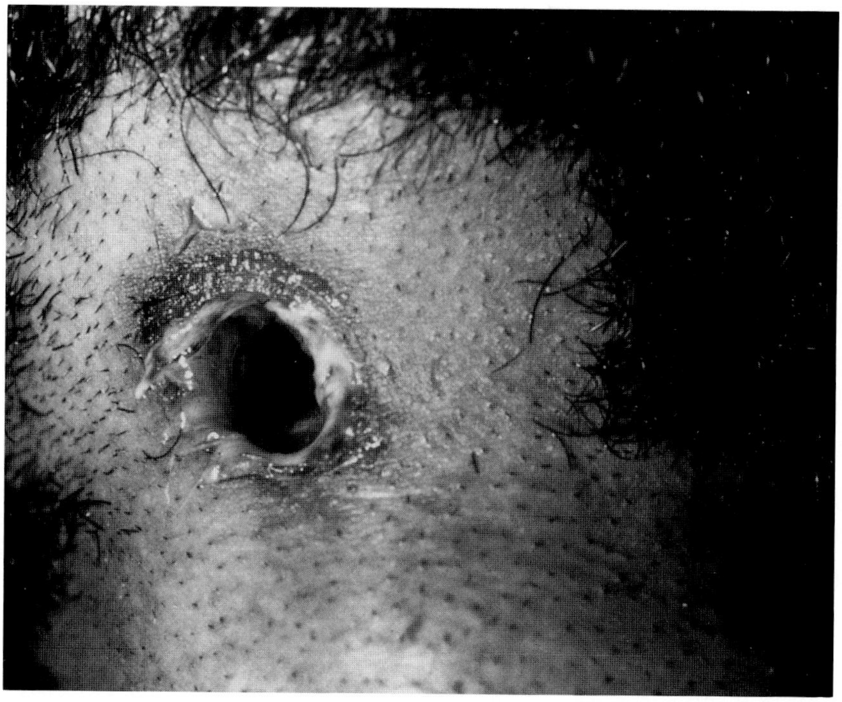

FIGURE 4.37 Contact-range shotgun wound of entry with muzzle abrasion. The entrance wound is the same size as the bore of the shotgun.

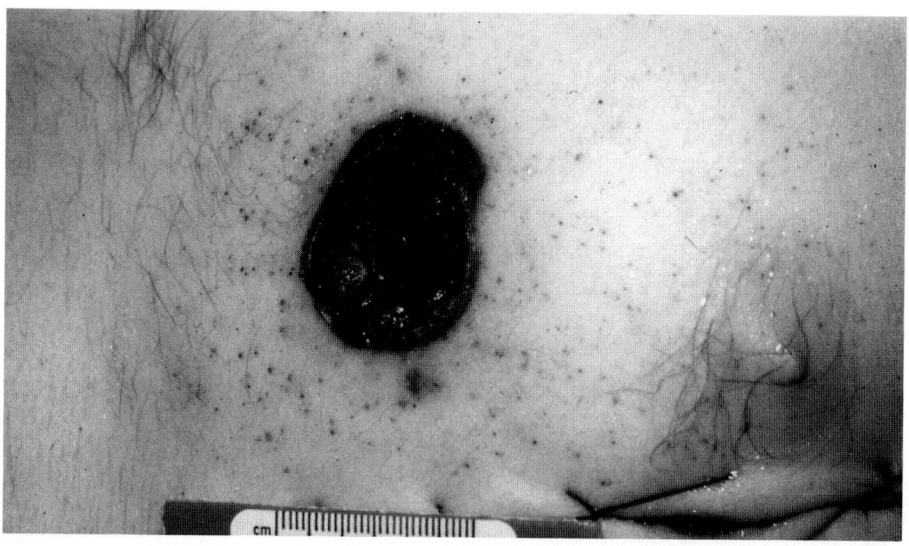

FIGURE 4.38 Very-close-range shotgun wound of entry with an abrasion at 1 o'clock caused by the wadding striking and abrading the skin prior to entering the body with the lead shot. There is stippling around the wound as seen in close-range gunshot wounds.

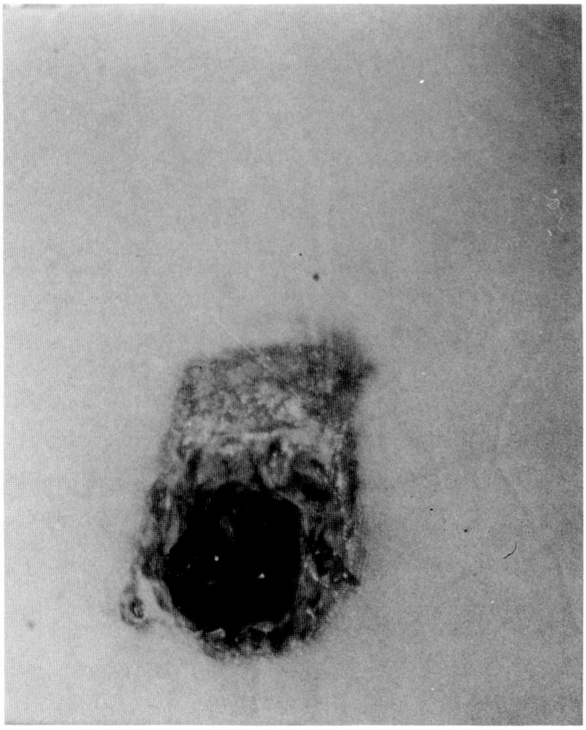

FIGURE 4.39 Close-range shotgun wound of entrance with large rectangular abrasion from the plastic shot cup striking the body prior to penetrating the body. There is a single satellite entrance wound at 7 o'clock. The lead shot is visible in this wound. Note the scalloped margin of the central defect caused by the pellets beginning to separate from the main mass.

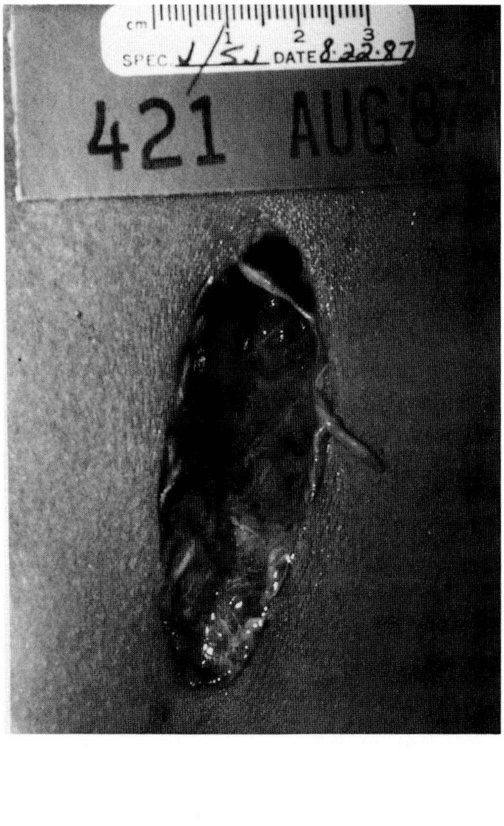

FIGURE 4.40 Large, oval, close-range shotgun wound to the chest just beneath a large pendulous breast which has distorted the wound. Note the scalloped margin of the central defect.

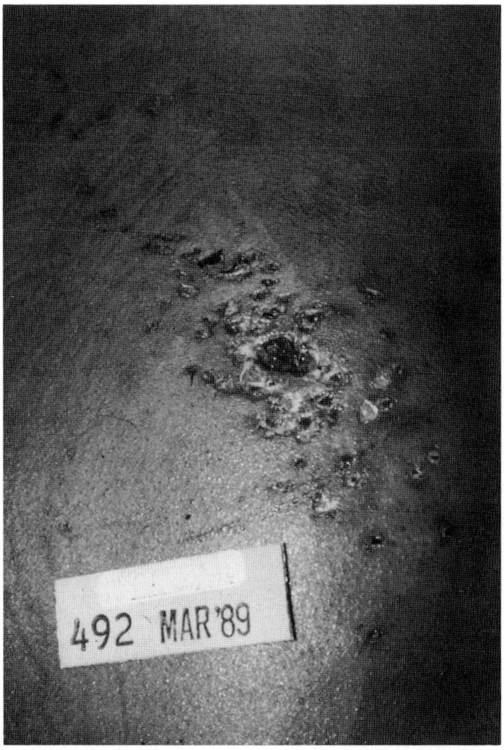

FIGURE 4.41 Intermediate-range shotgun wound of entry with a large defect surrounded by numerous satellite wounds. Fragments of cloth are visible in some of the satellite defects. Secondary missiles such as clothing fragments are carried into the body along with the lead shot.

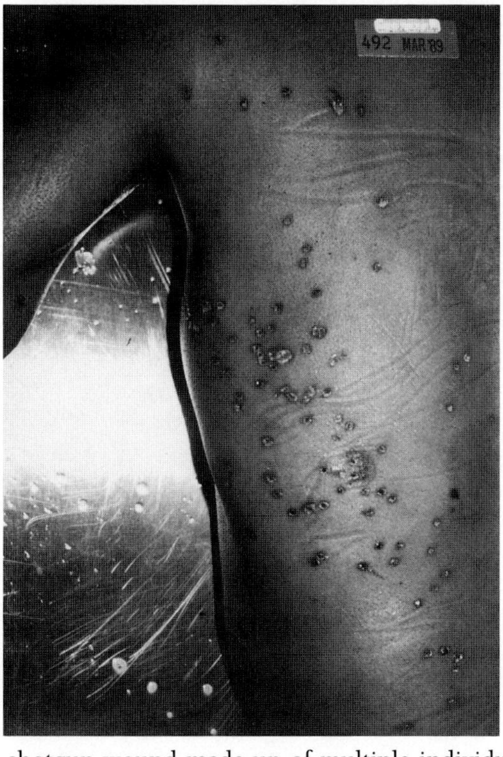

FIGURE 4.42 Distant shotgun wound made up of multiple individual pellet wounds scattered over a wide area of the body.

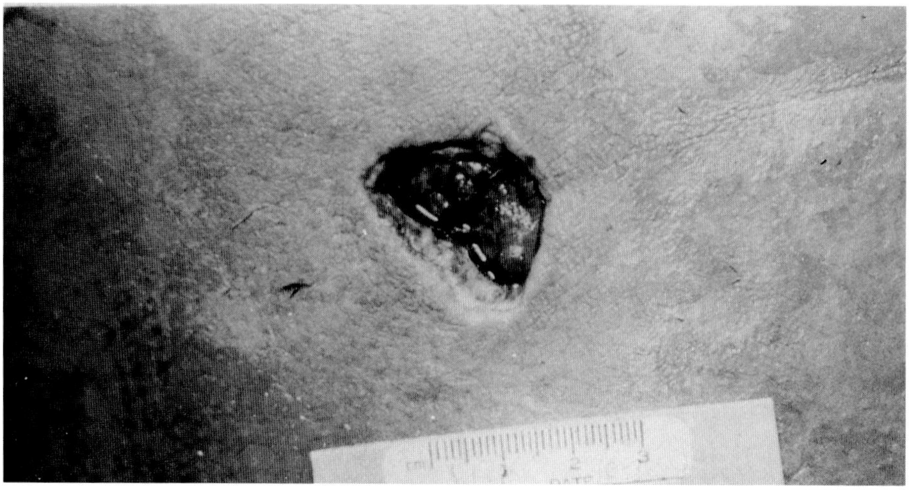

FIGURE 4.43 Distant shotgun wound of entrance from a rifled slug. There is only a single large defect.

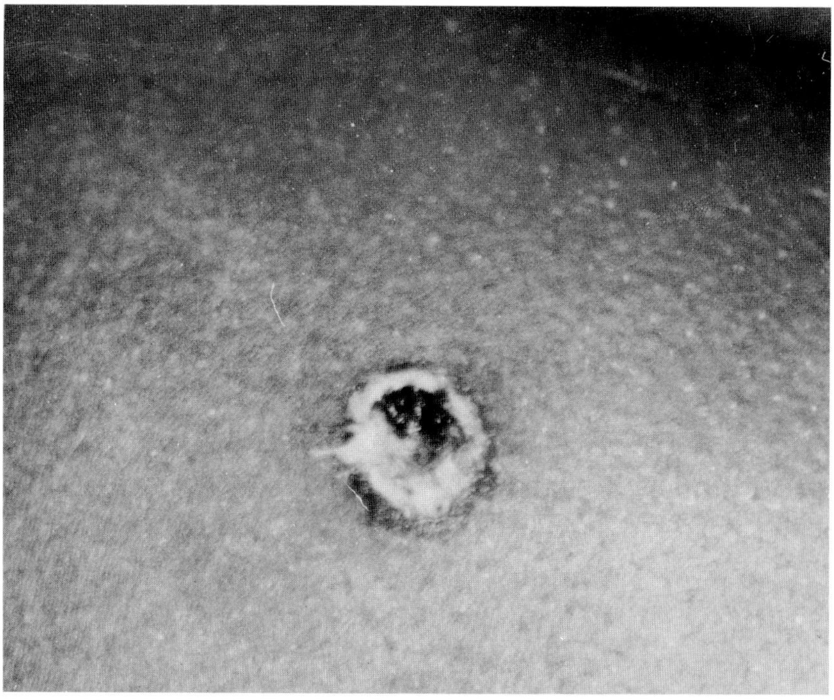

a

FIGURE 4.44a, b Distant shotgun wound of entry. The shotgun shells were loaded with buckshot which created individual pellet defects that can be mistaken for distant gunshot wounds of entry from bullets. The lead shot pellets can deform as seen here when they strike bone. This victim had five individual entry wounds on the back and five pellets were recovered.

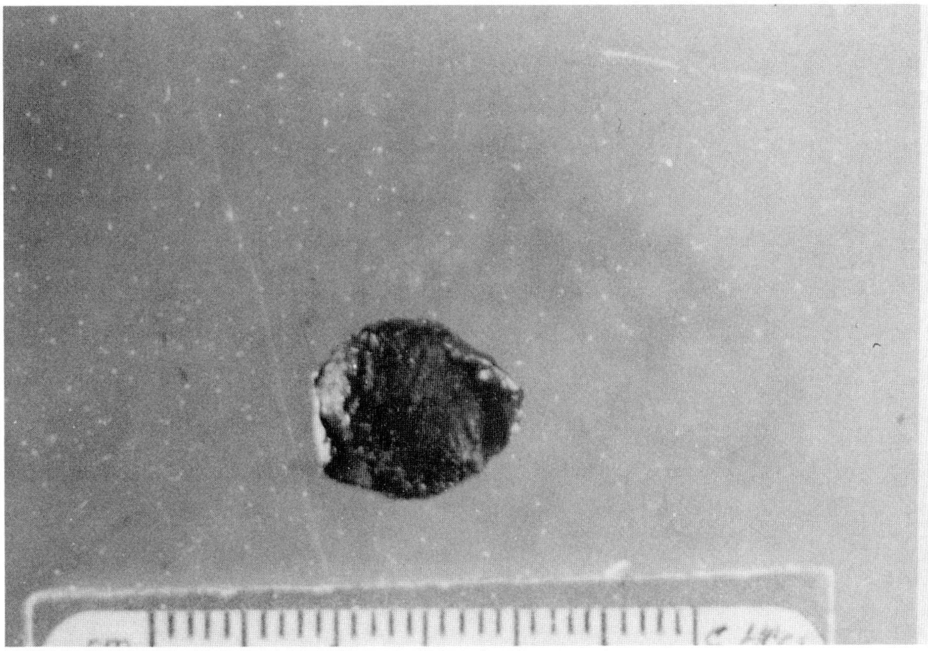

b

FIGURE 4.44 b (continued)

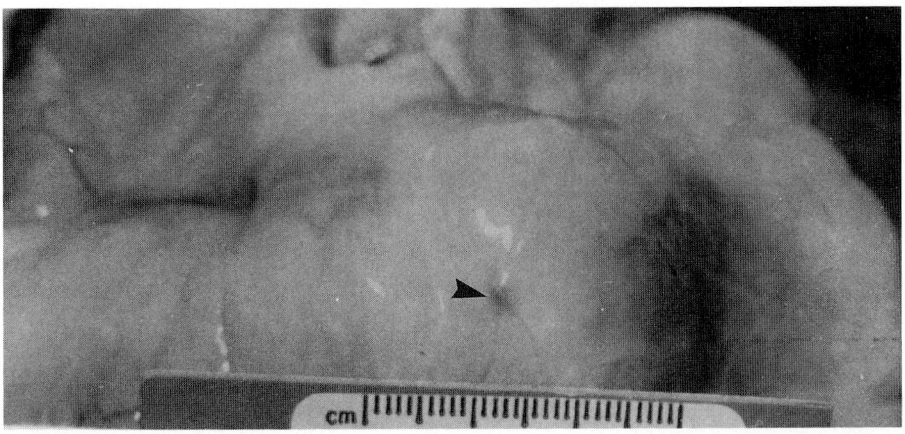

a

FIGURE 4.45a, b Birdshot embolus to right coronary artery. The shot pellet could be seen through the epicardial fat, and was then recovered (*arrowheads*) from the lumen during examination of the artery by serial section.

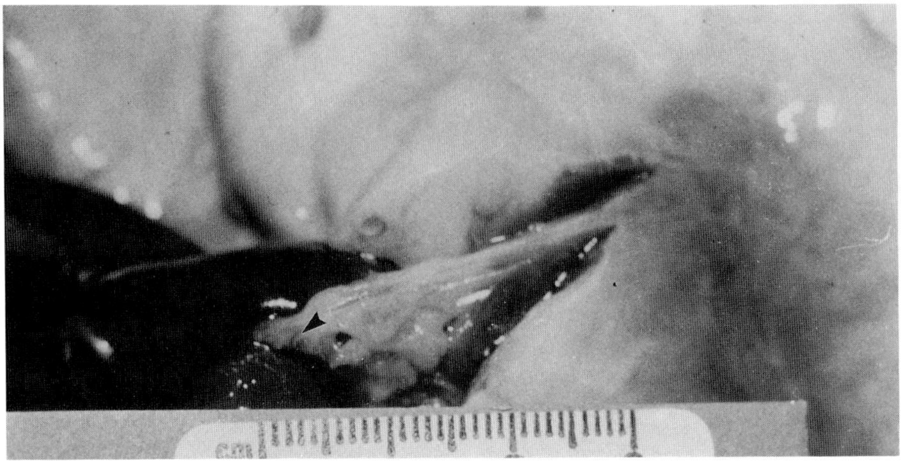

b

FIGURE 4.45b (continued)

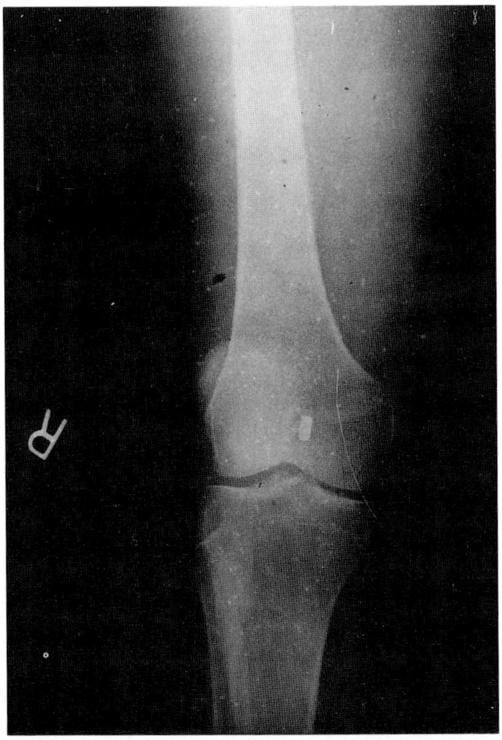

FIGURE 4.46 A radiograph of the right knee showing a small-caliber bullet which embolized to the right popliteal artery from a gunshot wound to the right chest. The bullet penetrated the thoracic aorta and traveled to the back of the knee where it became lodged.

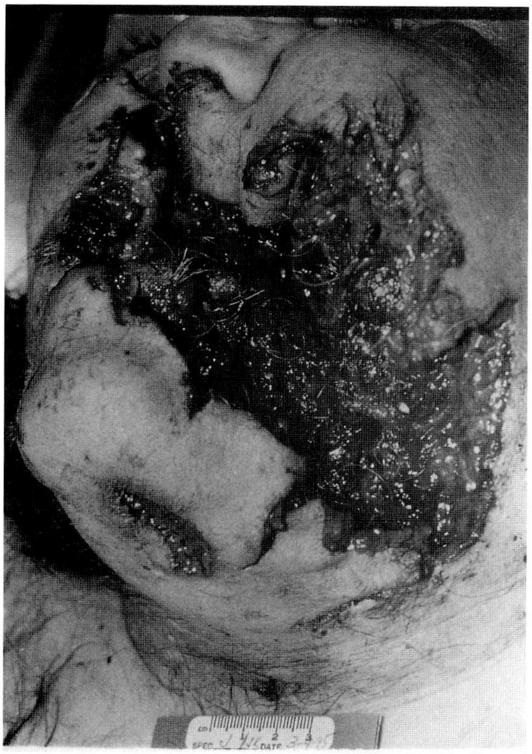

FIGURE 4.47 High-power, intermediate-range entry wound to the face from an M16 assault rifle loaded with .223 cartridges. There is massive destruction of the facial soft tissue and bone due to the large amount of kinetic energy. The kinetic energy or wounding power of a bullet is determined by the mass of the bullet multiplied by the square of the muzzle velocity of the weapon.

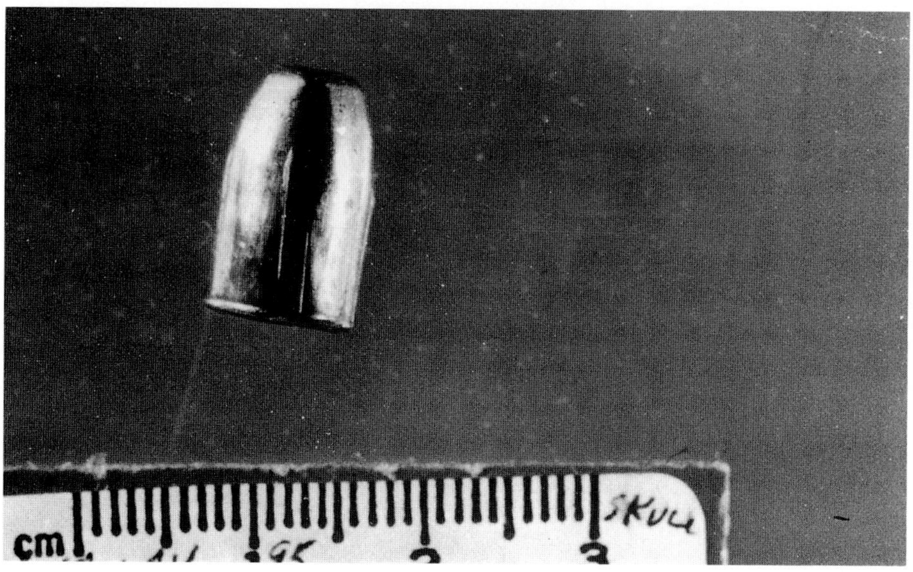

FIGURE 4.48 Close-up of a medium-caliber, fully copper-jacketed lead bullet, a 9-mm. It is best for the examining pathologist to classify bullets as small-, medium-, or large-caliber and to not attempt to identify the exact caliber. The classification of bullets is best left to the firearms experts who will examine the bullet and then testify in court. This bullet was recovered from the skull. There is no deformity of the bullet even though it struck and perforated the bone of the skull. Note the rifling marks which have been left on the jacket material from the lands and grooves within the barrel of the gun.

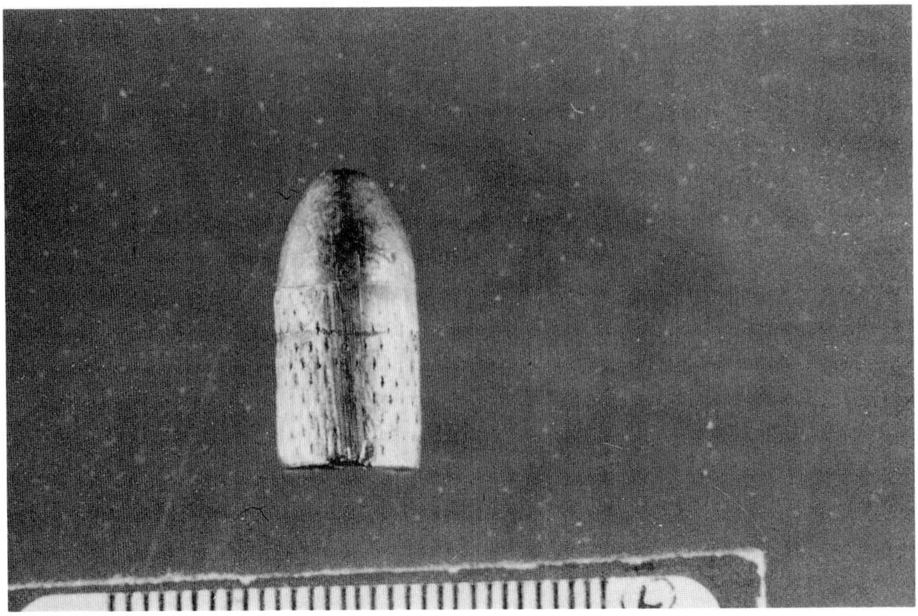

FIGURE 4.49 Close-up of the diamond pattern on the bearing surface of a medium-caliber lead bullet. This type of bullet makes comparison testing very difficult as the pattern on the bullet causes the rifling pattern to be incomplete.

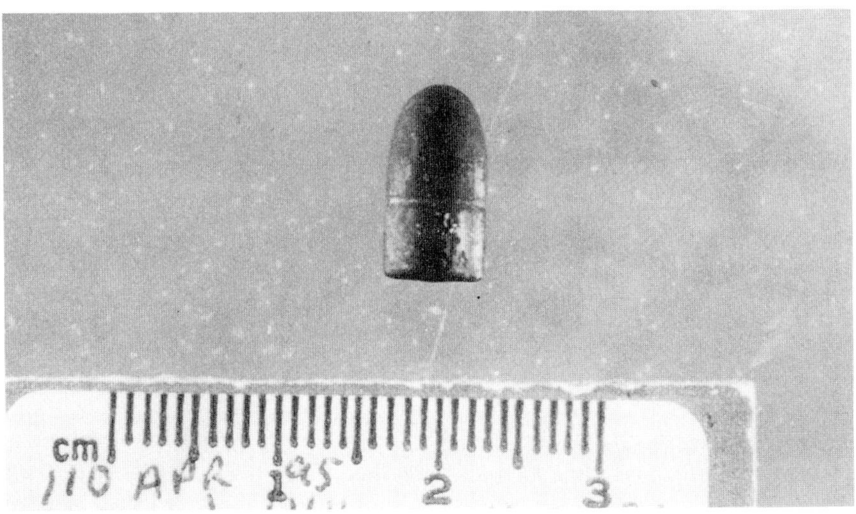

FIGURE 4.50 Old lead bullet recovered from scar tissue in thigh. The bullet has a very dull black appearance due to oxidation.

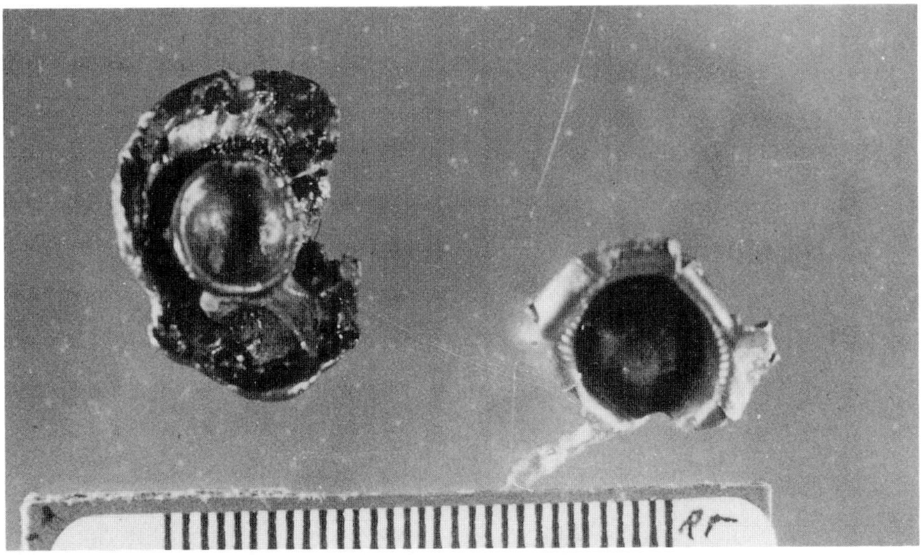

FIGURE 4.51 Lead core and jacket which have separated within the body. It is important to recover both the lead core and the jacket, especially the jacket as it will have the rifling marks necessary for comparison testing.

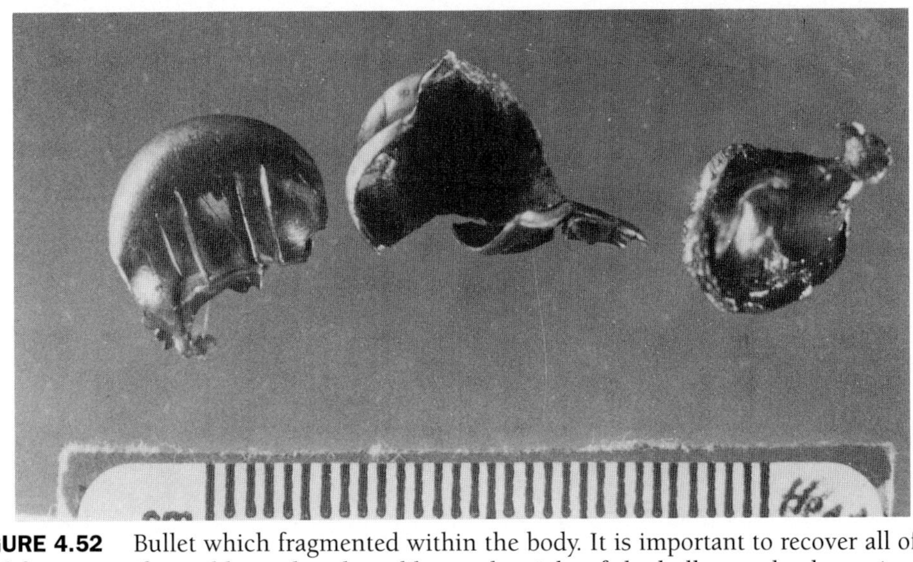

FIGURE 4.52 Bullet which fragmented within the body. It is important to recover all of the lead fragments if possible so that the caliber and weight of the bullet can be determined by the firearms examiner.

FIGURE 4.53 Radiograph of the thigh of a young man shot by the police when he refused to drop the weapon he was holding. The officer was using "Black Talon" ammunition. The opened talons of the bullet can clearly be seen. This type of bullet is dangerous to recover, as the talons are extremely sharp and will easily cut through rubber gloves. A Teflon-coated instrument or the chain-mail autopsy glove are useful in recovering this type of bullet.

a

FIGURE 4.54a, b Photographs of Black Talon bullets recovered from the victim shown in Figure 4.53. One bullet expanded fully upon penetration into the body. The other was deformed upon entry and never expanded.

b

FIGURE 4.54b (continued)

FIGURE 4.55 Ricochet bullet which struck pavement before entering the body. There are linear striations on the flattened surface of the bullet from impact with the ground.

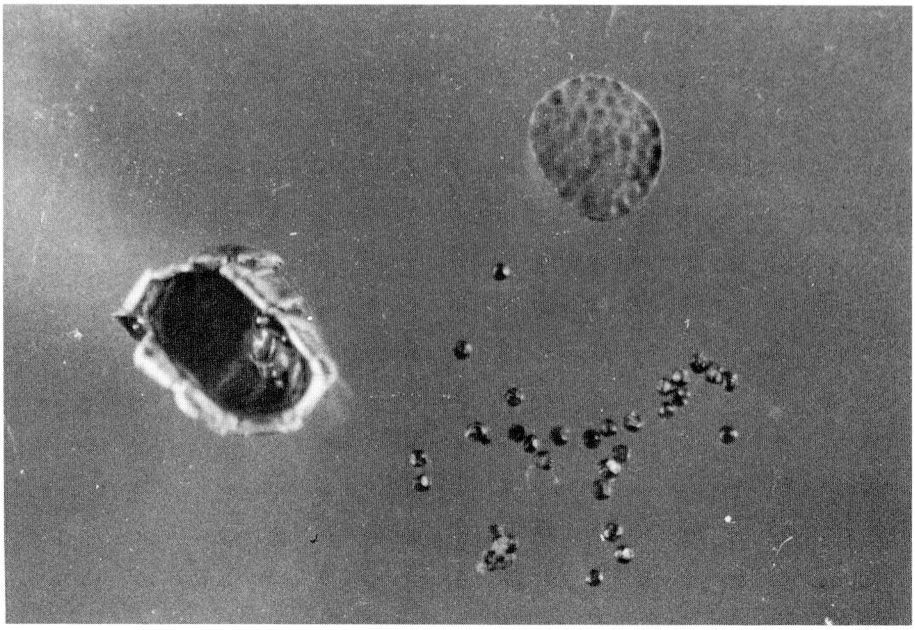

FIGURE 4.56 Glaser Safety Slug. This is a specialty bullet which consists of a metal jacket containing birdshot, sealed with a plastic cap which can be loaded into a handgun. The lead shot disperses in the body after impact. The jacket, plastic cap, and several representative shot pellets have been recovered.

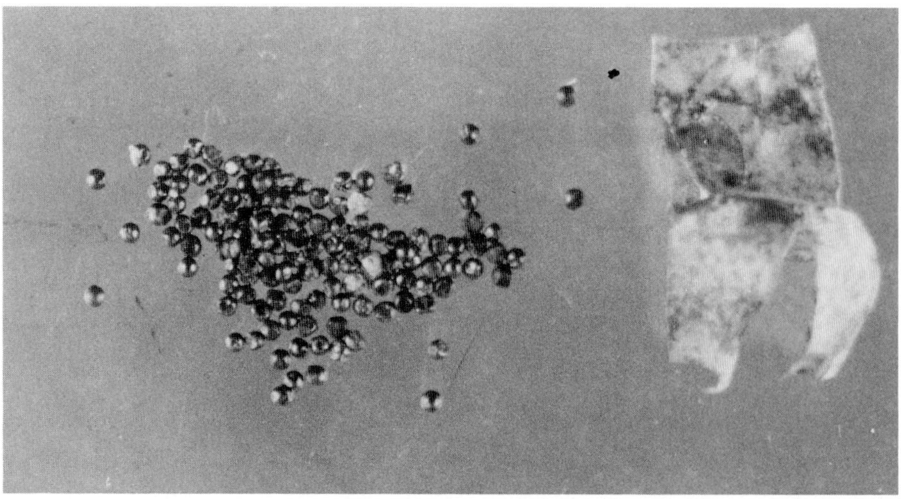

FIGURE 4.57 Lead shot pellets and plastic shot cup recovered from a victim of a close-range shotgun wound. Two of the four plastic petals of the shot cup have peeled back, the other two remained upright.

5

Blast Injury

Not too long ago, deaths due to bomb explosions were uncommon. With the current political environment, these deaths have become more common. Explosions due to natural gas or other fuels and gases have caused deaths and serious injury in the workplace and home. Occasional deaths and serious injury have been caused by tires or batteries exploding in truck and automobile service stations.

Blast injuries can be divided into four groups. The primary group includes those injuries sustained as a direct result of the concussive or blast effect. When an explosion occurs, there is an expanding wave of compressed atmosphere which moves rapidly outward from the epicenter. The force of the blast wave is inversely proportional to the distance from the epicenter. This wave of compressed air causes injury to areas of the body where there is a solid-to-air interface, such as in the ear, lungs, and gastrointestinal tract. In these areas, there is absorption of the wave's energy with resultant injury. The minimum threshold for causing serious injury in humans has been estimated at 100 lb/square inch. The concussive wave is followed by a small wave of rarefied air, causing a second barotrauma to the body.

Explosions occurring in the air and in the water will both cause injury to the gastrointestinal tract with small perforations or lacerations of the bowel. In the lung, the alveoli are ruptured with distortion of the architecture and alveolar hemorrhage. The eardrum is perforated or ruptures. Other injuries due to the blast wave can include lacerations or rupture of blood vessels. Interestingly, the forces of the blast wave can move through solid organs and cause little or no damage. The second group of injury in blast victims is blunt trauma injuries sustained from debris propelled outward at great force by the explosion striking the victim. These injuries include lacerations, amputations, contusions, and abrasions. Dirt, sand, and other fine debris can be blasted into the unprotected skin. The third group of injury, primarily blunt trauma, is due to the victim being lifted and propelled into surrounding objects or buildings. Collapse of buildings in and around the epicenter will cause blunt injury or sharp injury due to shards of glass or metal. The fourth category of injury includes burns and inhalation injury to the airway and the lungs from fires ignited by the explosion.

When examining victims of a bomb explosion, care must be taken to look through the body parts and debris very carefully to find and preserve any foreign material which may be pieces of the explosive device utilized (Table 5.1). It is also important to enumerate and identify all the victims of an explosion. It is not uncommon for a victim very close to the epicenter to be totally dismembered with only small fragments of tissue found.

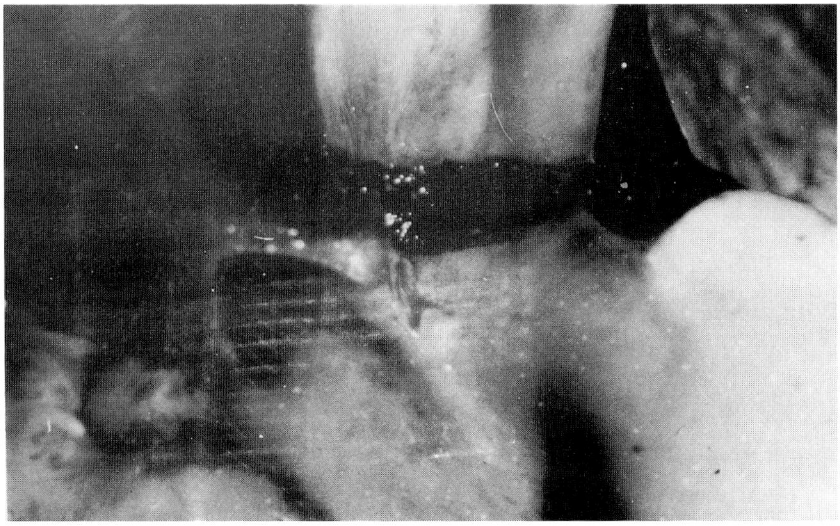

FIGURE 5.1 Laceration of the left subclavian artery at its origin in the arch of the aorta found in the victim of an explosion.

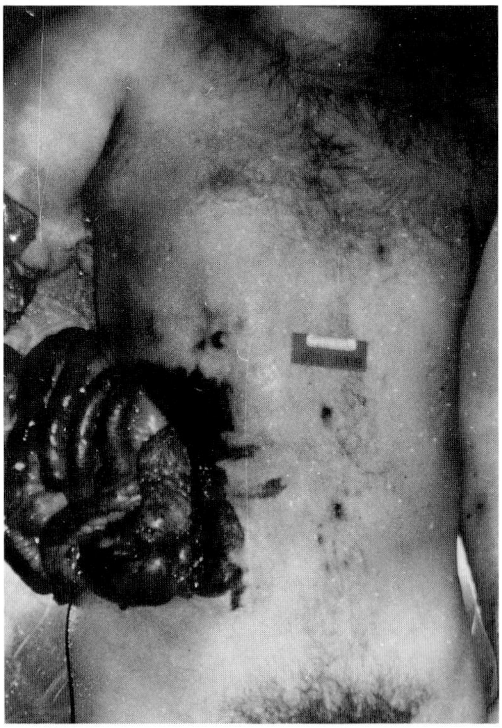

FIGURE 5.2 Blast injury with amputation of the right arm and partial evisceration of the bowel found in a firefighter who was standing close to a metal gas cylinder which exploded during a fire. These injuries are the result of pieces of the cylinder striking the body as they were propelled outward by the explosion.

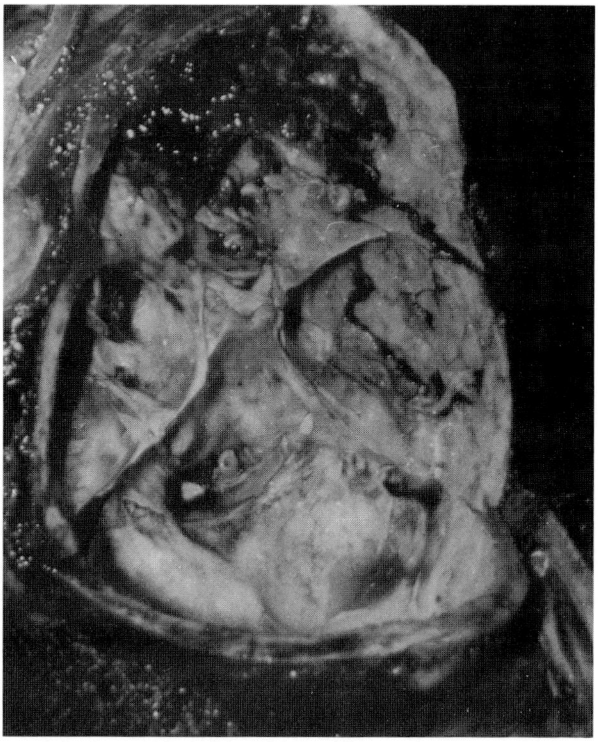

FIGURE 5.3 Fractures of the base of the skull and frontal bones due to a tire explosion in a truck repair shop. The point of impact was the left forehead. The basal skull fractures involve the left and right anterior and middle cranial fossae.

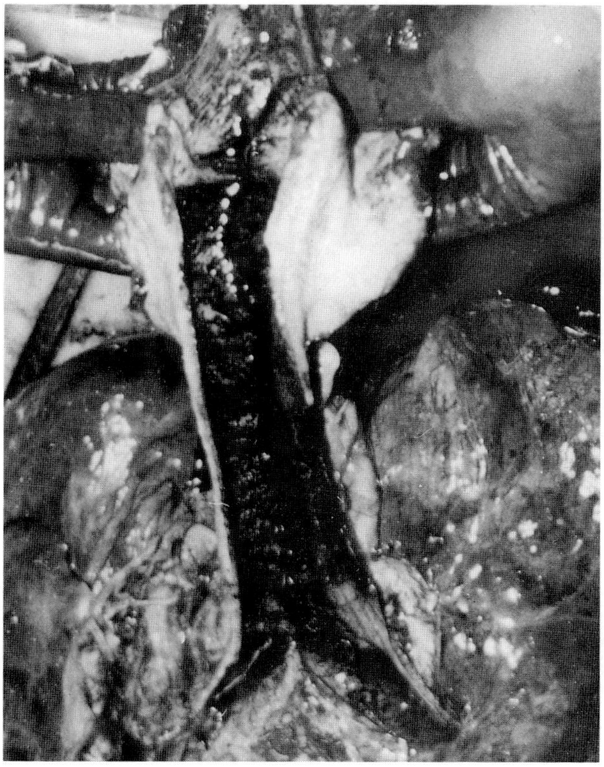

FIGURE 5.4 Fuel oil found in the trachea and lungs of a welder who was working on the roof of a fuel oil storage tank which exploded when the acetylene torch he was using ignited the fumes in the tank. He fell into the tank when the roof was blown off by the resulting explosion.

6

Injury Due to Sharp Instruments

Injuries due to sharp instruments such as knives, razors, and other sharp-edged weapons will show sharp, clean margins which lack the tissue bridges characteristic of lacerations due to blunt trauma. The wounds most commonly encountered include stab wounds, which penetrate deeper into the body than the length of the wound on the surface of the body, and incised wounds, which are longer on the surface of the body than the wound penetrates into the body.

Stab wounds can be the result of knives, screwdrivers, ice picks, awls, scissors, or other instruments that are sharp enough to allow entry through the skin. Stab wounds due to single-edged knives will frequently show one blunt and one sharp margin, whereas wounds from double-edged blades show two sharp margins. The edges of a stab wound may show a fine margin of abrasion, especially if the blade is particularly thick, which leads to increased resistance to the passage of the blade, with increased friction and the resultant margin of abrasion. Stab wounds inflicted by a tapered blade may be larger than the greatest width of the blade, but they can never be smaller than the smallest point on the blade. If a mixture of long and deep, and very short and superficial (shallow) wounds is found, and the wounds are similar in appearance, then it is likely that a single tapered blade was the weapon used. The small injuries are the result of only the tip of the knife blade penetrating the body while the longer, deeper wounds result from the blade penetrating more deeply.

Stab wounds may be linear or they may be "V" or "C" shaped if the blade is twisted in the body after penetration and before withdrawal. Patterned stab wounds are found when items such as scissors or long barbecue forks are used as a weapon. The examining pathologist may find paired injuries with a uniform distance between the wounds if a fork is used, or paired injuries with slightly varying distances between the wounds if a pair of scissors is used.

It is difficult to determine the length of the blade of the knife used in inflicting a particular stab wound based on the depth of penetration of the wound into the body. A rough estimate of knife length is possible, but only an estimate. This is because of the compressibility of the body tissue. That is, the knife may appear to penetrate more deeply, and to have a longer blade than it actually does, because superficial tissues can be compressed inward, sometimes up to several inches, by the force of the thrust used to push the knife into the body. The chest and abdomen are particularly compressible, especially the chest in younger victims, and an overestimation of the length of the blade is very likely to be made.

Incised wounds are the result of the edge of the blade being drawn across a portion of the body. They are frequently found on the palms and dorsal surfaces of the hands, on the arms, and on the legs or feet of stabbing victims. These usually represent defense wounds. They occur when the victim of a knife attack tries to ward off the attacker, either by putting up an arm or a leg to defend themselves, or by trying to grab and take the knife away from the attacker. Defense type incised wounds of the hands can be very deep with partial amputation of the digits. A large sharp wound to the neck with near total decapitation is still an incised wound as the length of the wound on the surface of the skin is greater than the depth of penetration. Single incised wounds of the neck can be found in both homicides and suicides. Incised wounds of the wrists, antecubital fossae, or the ankles are found in suicides. Hesitation marks, more shallow or superficial incisions found in association with deep incisions, are frequently encountered in suicides. They represent practice strokes where the suicide victim is testing to determine the amount of force necessary to produce a lethal incision, or is working through whatever indecision, hesitation, or doubt he or she may still have.

Chop wounds are injuries that show a combination of both sharp and blunt characteristics. These types of injuries are inflicted by heavy objects with a sharp edge such as an axe or meat cleaver. An additional, unusual type of sharp injury is that found when hunting arrows are used. The wounds on the surface of the body at the entry and the exit will show sharp margins similar to those seen in wounds due to knife blades. Most deaths due to arrows are not difficult as the arrow is normally found still within the wound, as the friction of the arrow shaft through the body is sufficient to prevent the arrow from passing completely through the body.

In all cases of sharp injury, the examining pathologist must carefully measure and localize the wounds on the body just as is done in cases of gunshot injuries. Measurements of the length and width of the sharp injuries are taken while the wounds are gaping and then again with the margins of the wound gently reapproximated. This later measurement may be a more accurate approximation of the type of weapon used (Table 6.1).

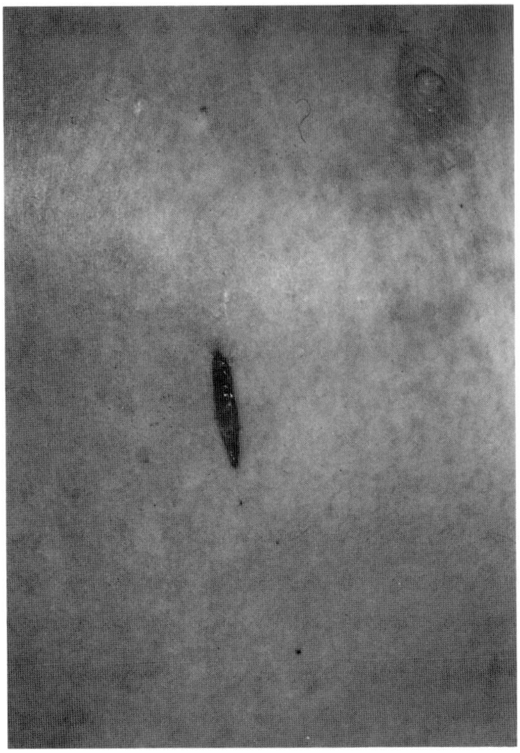

FIGURE 6.1 Stab wound to the left chest from a single-edged knife. There is a slight abrasion at the upper margin of the wound. The wound gapes slightly due to the elastic properties of the skin.

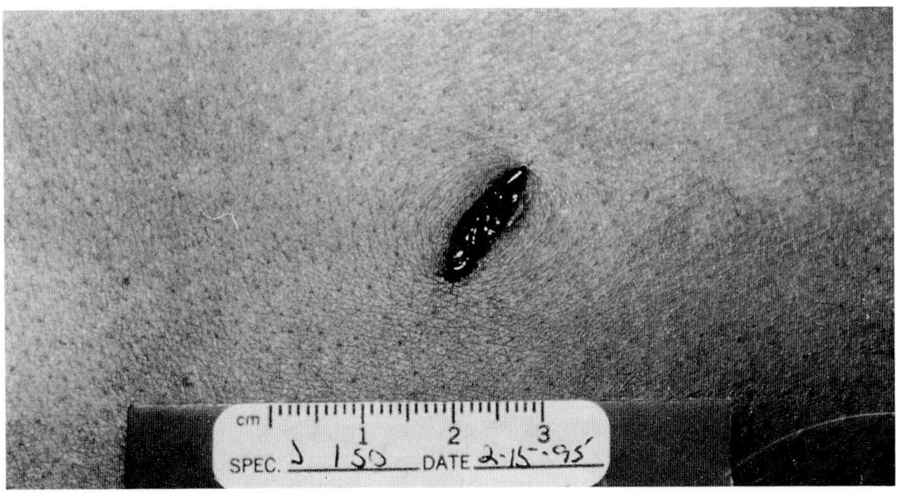

FIGURE 6.2 Gaping stab wound from a single-edged knife which shows a fine abrasion along one margin created by friction as the knife blade penetrated the skin.

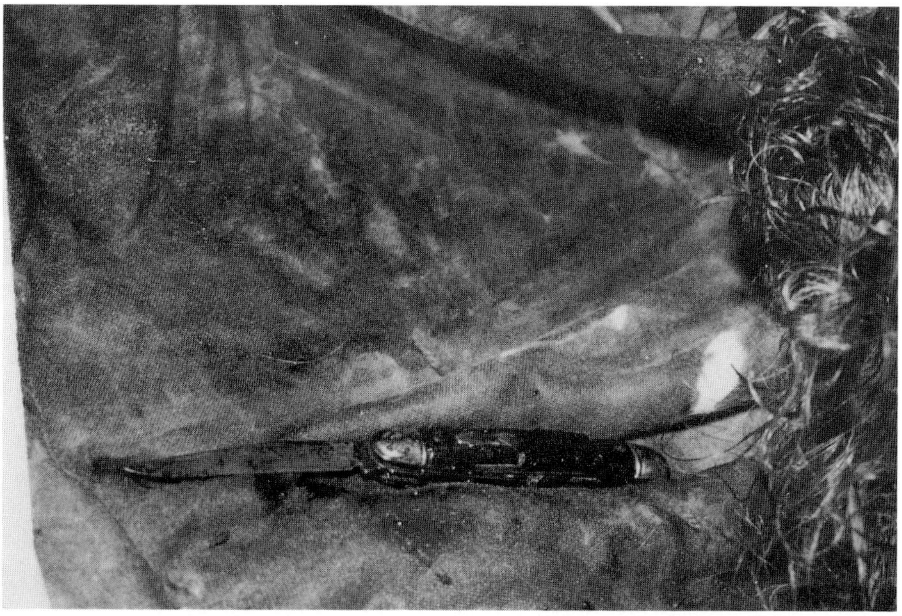

FIGURE 6.3 Single-edged, folding pocket knife recovered from the clothing of a victim of multiple stab wounds.

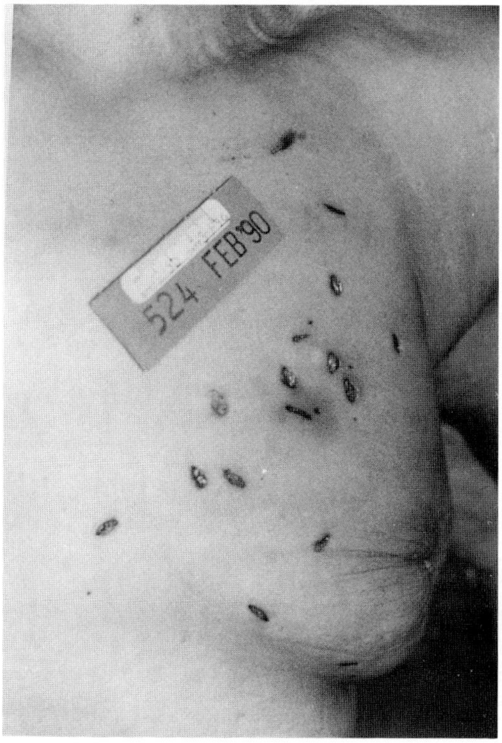

FIGURE 6.4 Multiple stab wounds clustered around the left breast. Bruising is noted around the wounds on the upper inner quadrant of the breast. This may be due to the hand of the assailant striking the body while plunging the knife into the victim. The wounds were created by one single-edged blade. The different lengths of the wounds on the surface of the body are the result of the tapered blade penetrating to different lengths. Some of the wounds show one distinct blunt edge and one distinct sharp edge.

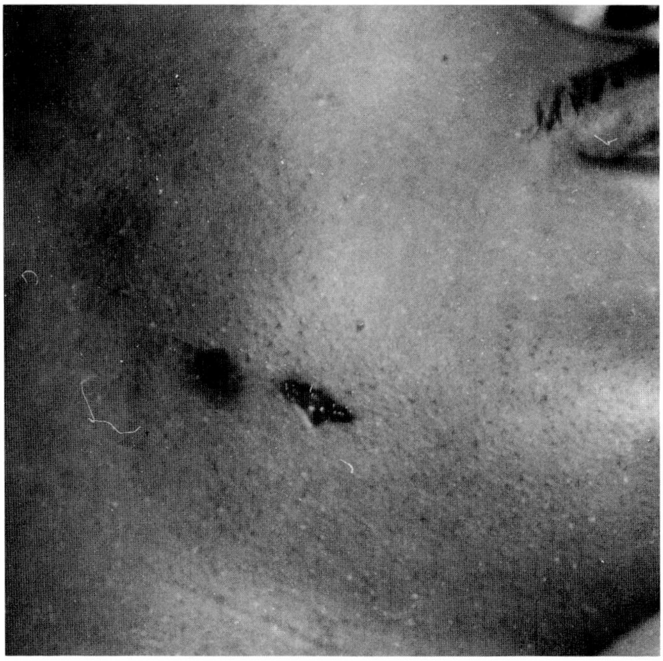

FIGURE 6.5 Paired, heavily abraded stab wounds to the right side of the neck caused by a pair of scissors. There is a small notch in the lower margin of the right wound caused by twisting of the blades in the body before they were withdrawn.

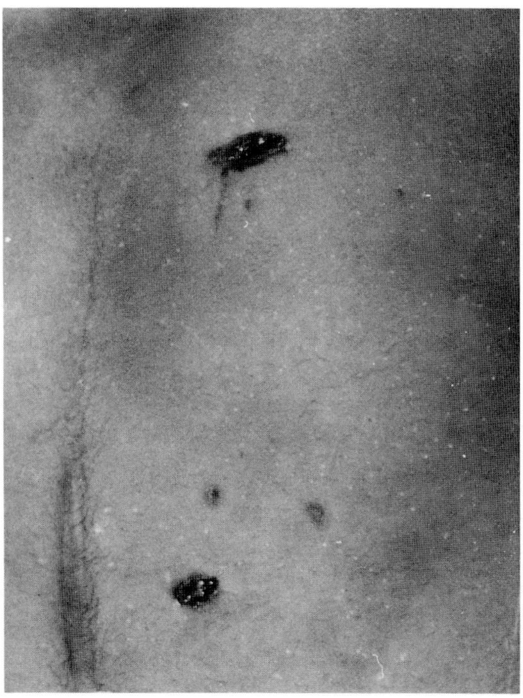

FIGURE 6.6 Stab wounds to the abdomen with very thick abrasions on the margins of the wounds caused by scissors with the blades held together penetrating the body. There are two sets of small paired wounds between the two larger wounds which are the result of the tips of the scissor blades striking, but not penetrating into the body.

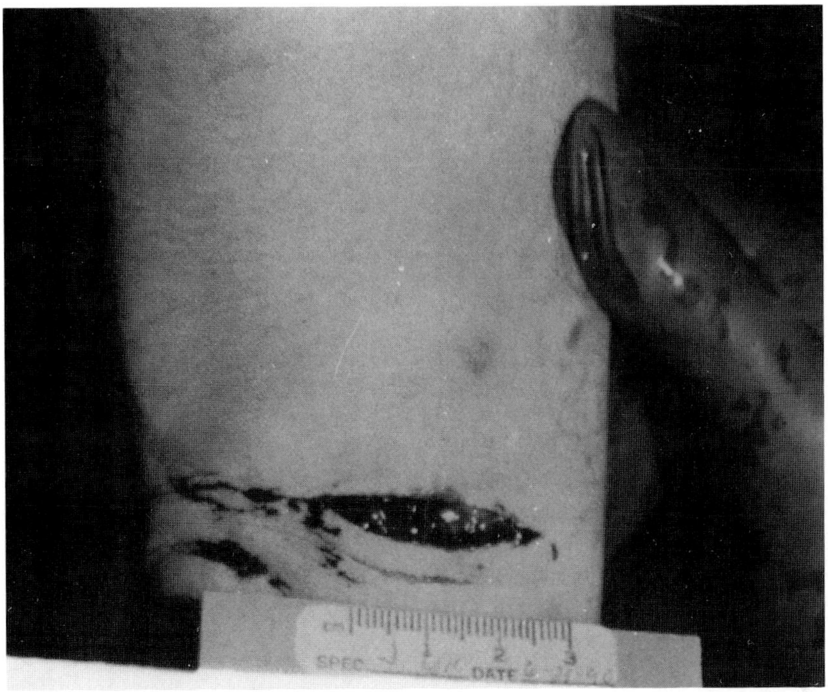

FIGURE 6.7 Multiple incised wounds of the wrist in a suicide. Incised wounds are sharp injuries which are longer on the surface of the body than they penetrate into the body. Suicidal incised wounds are found on the wrists, antecubital fossae, and neck. Suicidal stab wounds are found on the chest and abdomen.

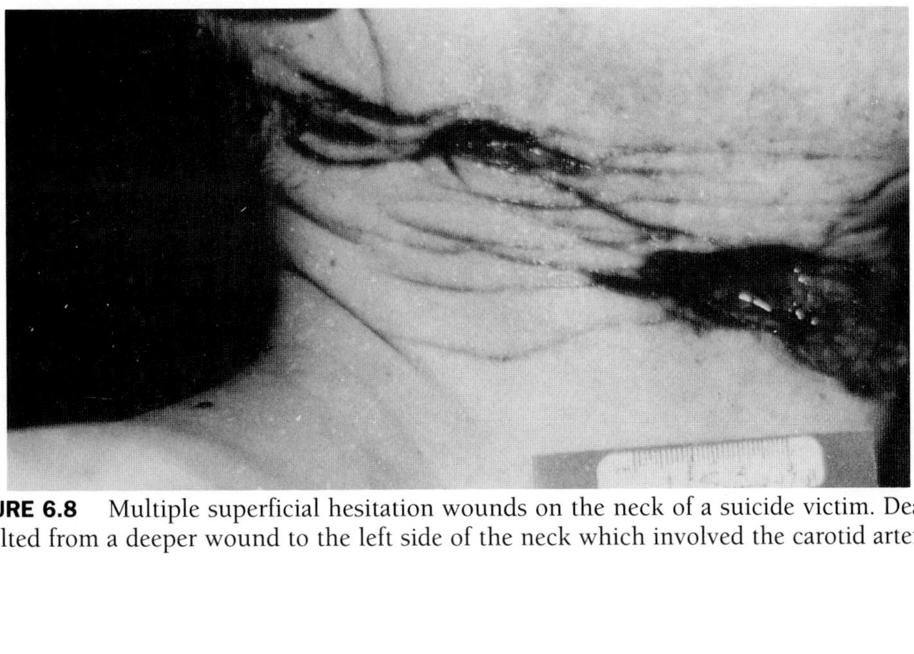

FIGURE 6.8 Multiple superficial hesitation wounds on the neck of a suicide victim. Death resulted from a deeper wound to the left side of the neck which involved the carotid artery.

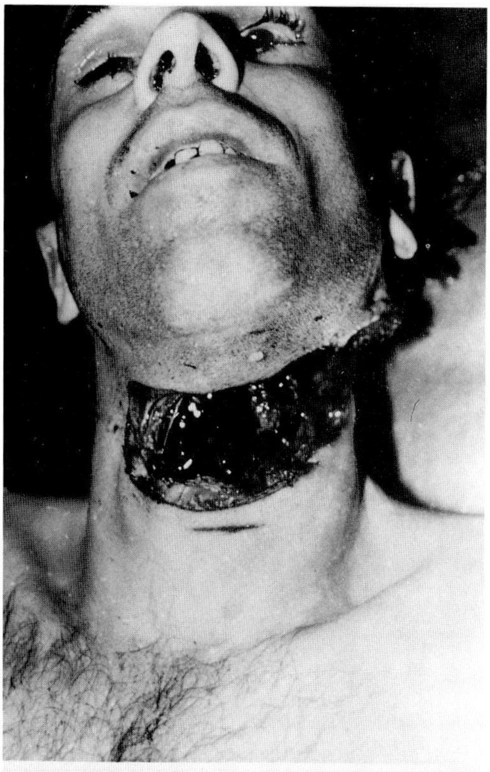

FIGURE 6.9 Large, gaping incised wound of the neck in a suicide. There is a short hesitation wound below the main injury. The victim placed his neck against a circular table saw.

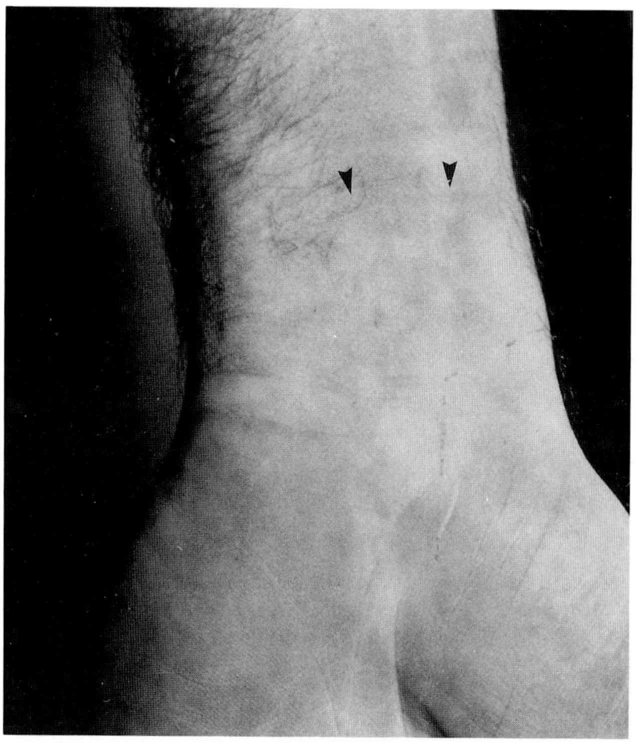

FIGURE 6.10 Faint linear scars (*arrow heads*) on the wrist of a hanging suicide. The scars are from a prior suicide attempt where the wrists were incised.

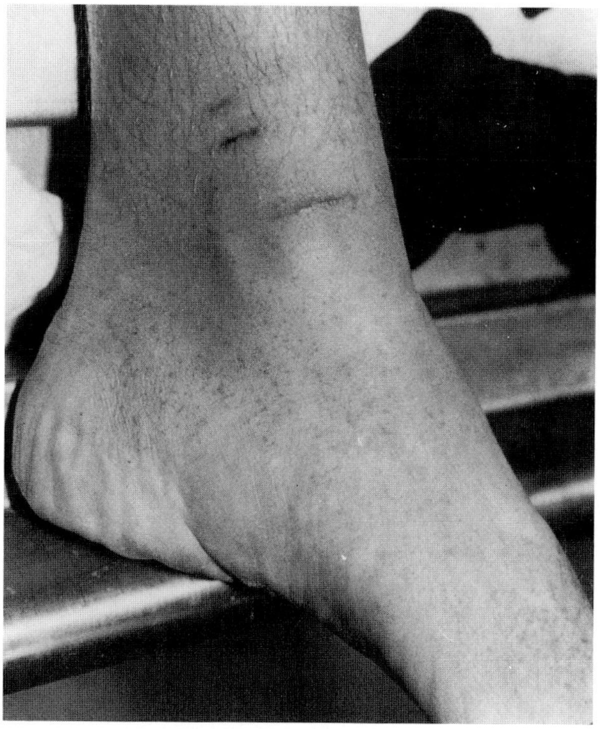

FIGURE 6.11 Recent scars on the ankle of the same hanging suicide. These scars are more recent, and still have a reddish pink color.

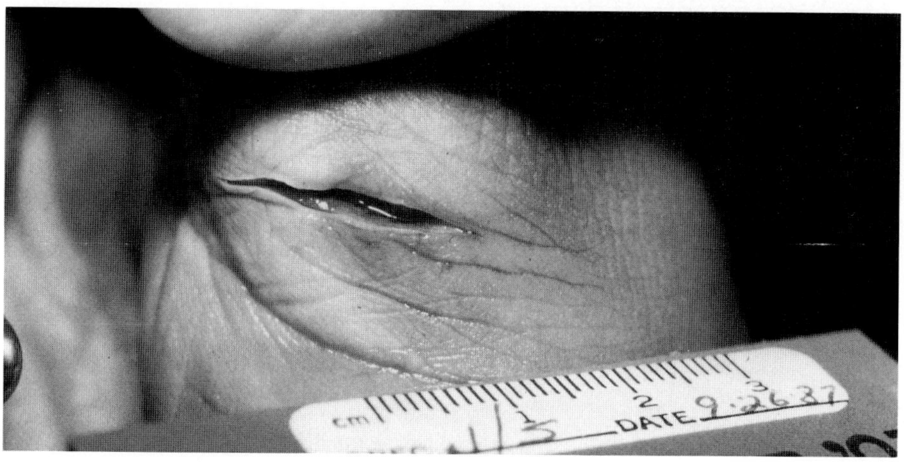

FIGURE 6.12 Incised wound of the thenar eminence of the right hand consistent with a defense wound.

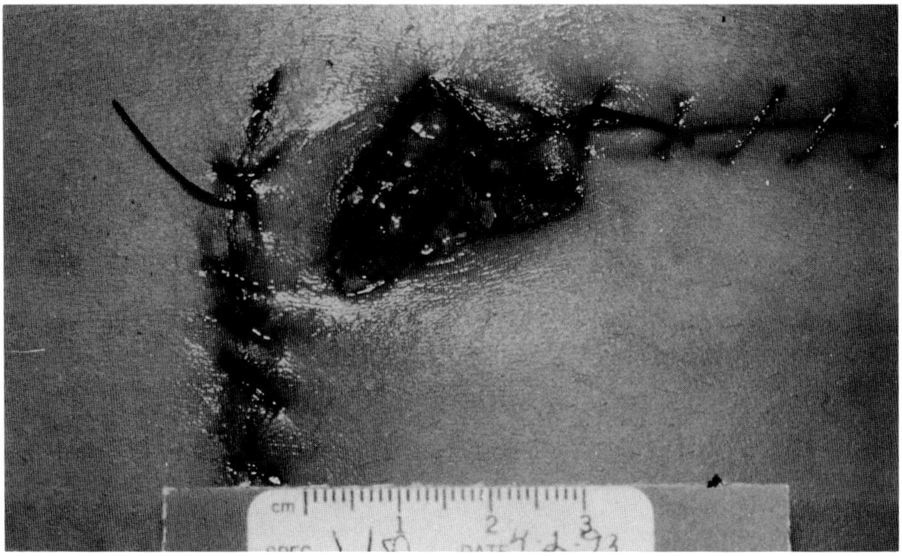

FIGURE 6.13 Triangular-shaped sharp injury due to an arrow. The wound has been distorted by the thoracotomy and laparotomy incisions. The arrow was still in the body, with the arrowhead protruding from the back at the time the victim was found on the street.

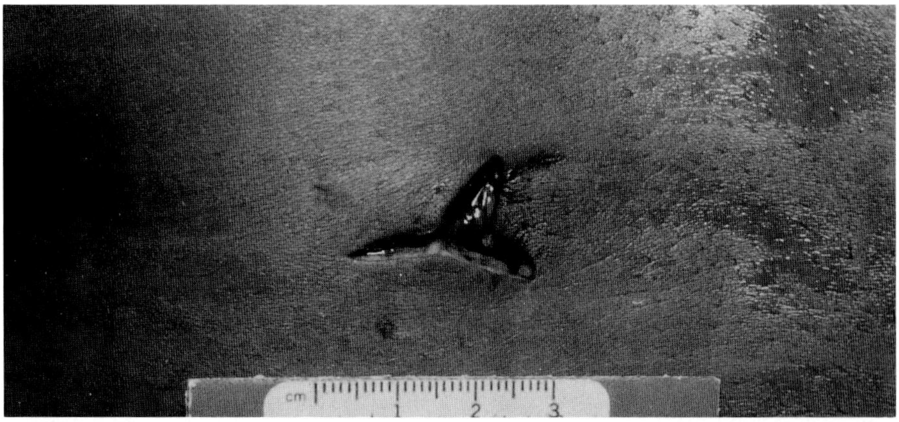

FIGURE 6.14 Wound on the back of the victim shot with an arrow shown in Figure 6.13.

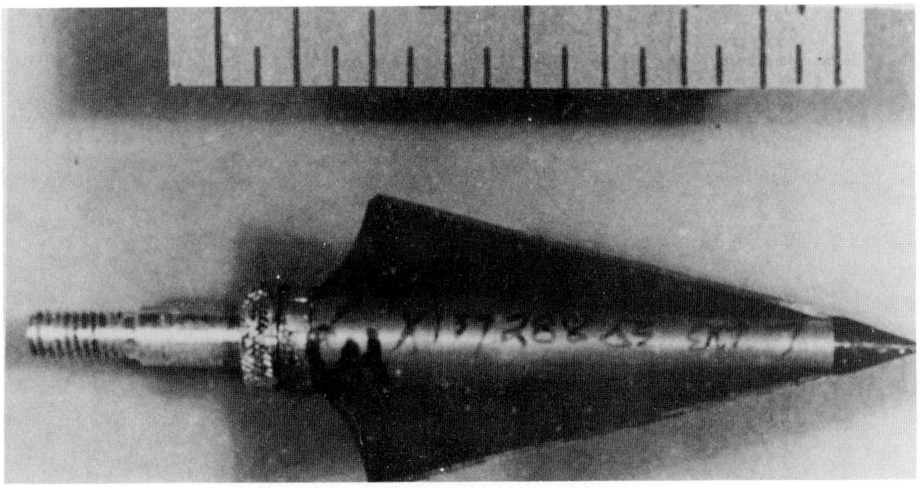

FIGURE 6.15 Arrowhead that caused the wounds shown in Figures 6.13 and 6.14. The numbers on the arrowhead were written by crime laboratory personnel.

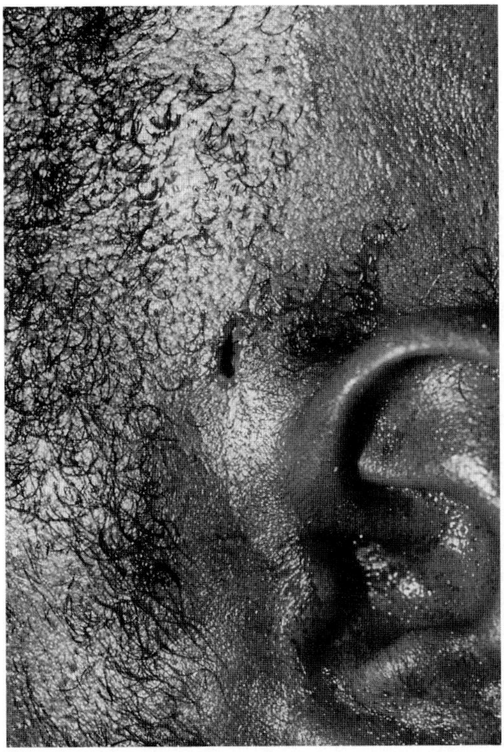

FIGURE 6.16 Stab wound to the left temple caused by a screwdriver. The wound was misidentified as a gunshot wound of entry by hospital personnel.

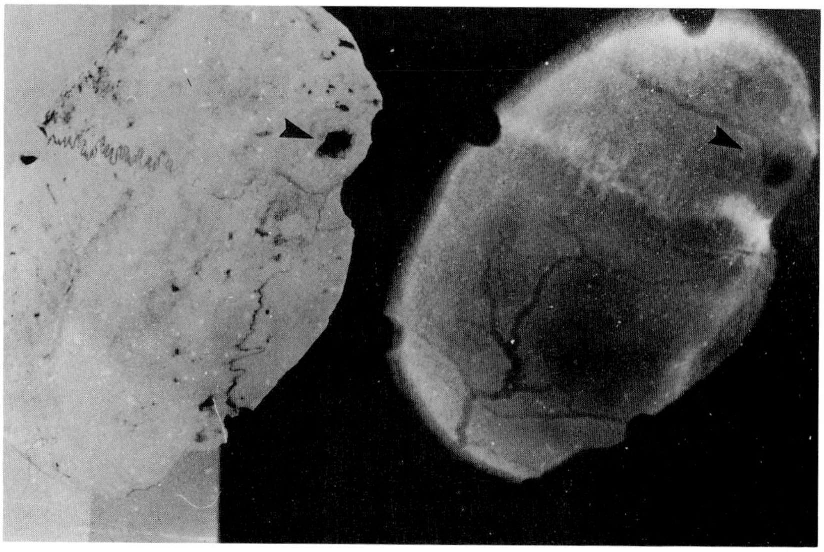

FIGURE 6.17 Bone flap removed at craniotomy in another victim of a screwdriver stab wound to the head. The bone is superimposed over a radiograph of the bone looking for evidence of a lead ring around the defect in the skull (*arrowheads*). The case had been reported as a gunshot wound to the head. No bullet or exit defect was found at autopsy, and hospital records indicated that no foreign object was present in the radiographs of the head taken prior to the craniotomy. The bone flap was obtained from the hospital and radiographed looking for any evidence of a bullet. Investigation revealed that the victim was stabbed in the head with a screwdriver during an argument.

a

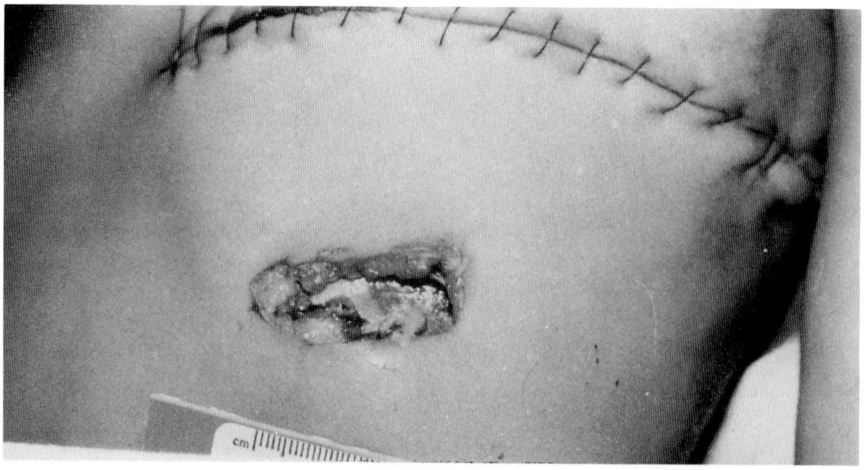

FIGURE 6.18a Large defect in the abdomen with both sharp and blunt trauma characteristics. The wound was caused by shards of glass which penetrated the body when this child fell from a short height onto a discarded aquarium.

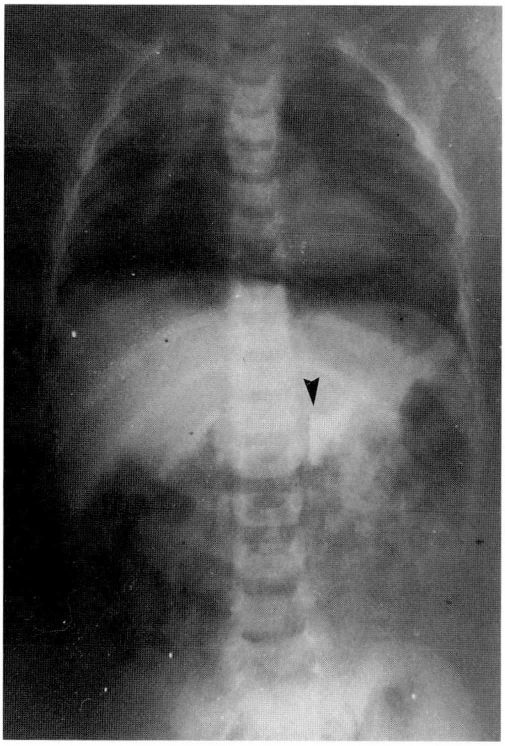

b

FIGURE 6.18b Radiograph of child showing the glass shards (*arrow*) in the left paraspinal region adjacent to the twelfth thoracic and first lumbar vertebrae.

c

FIGURE 6.18c Glass shards recovered from the body.

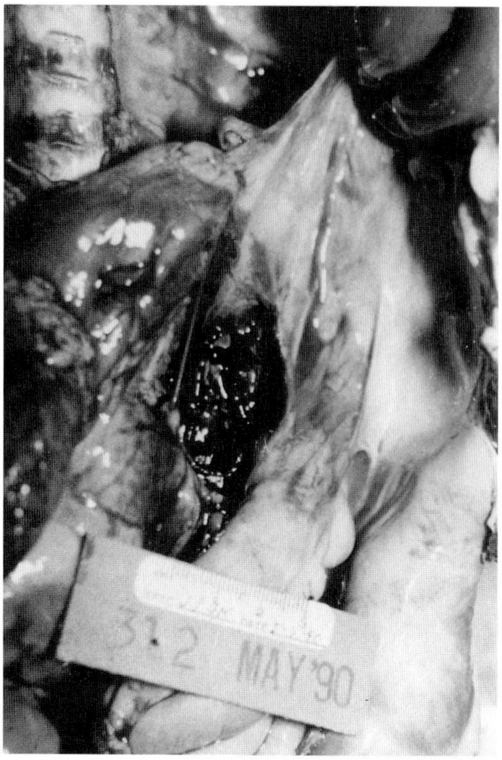

d

FIGURE 6.18d Laceration of the posterior insertion of the diaphragm caused by the glass shards penetrating the body.

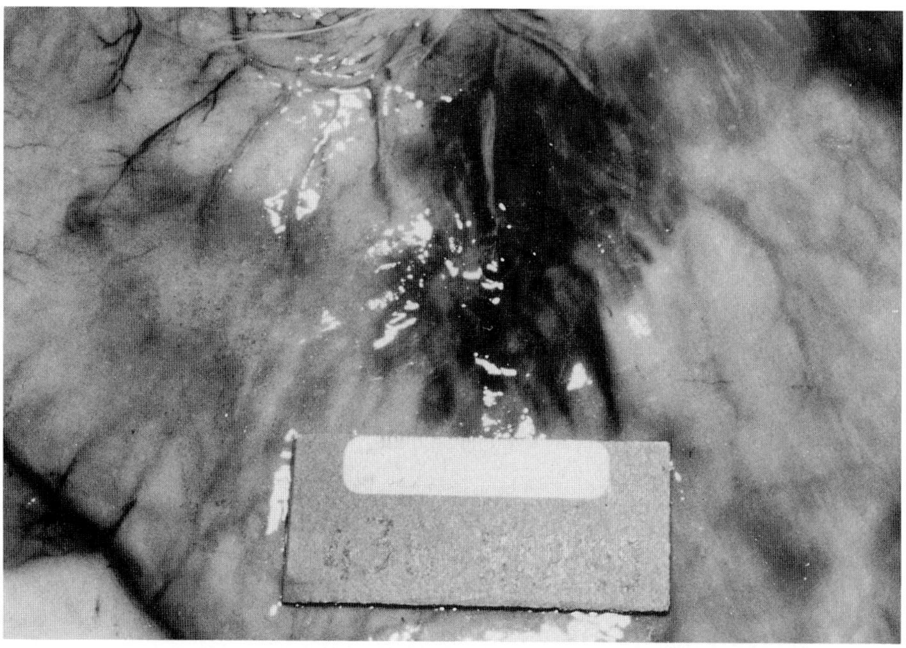

FIGURE 6.19 Close-up of a branch of the gastric artery which was incised during the placement of a gastric feeding tube. The victim died from a hemoperitoneum. Investigation of deaths due to medical malpractice or therapeutic misadventures is a duty of the medical examiner or coroner.

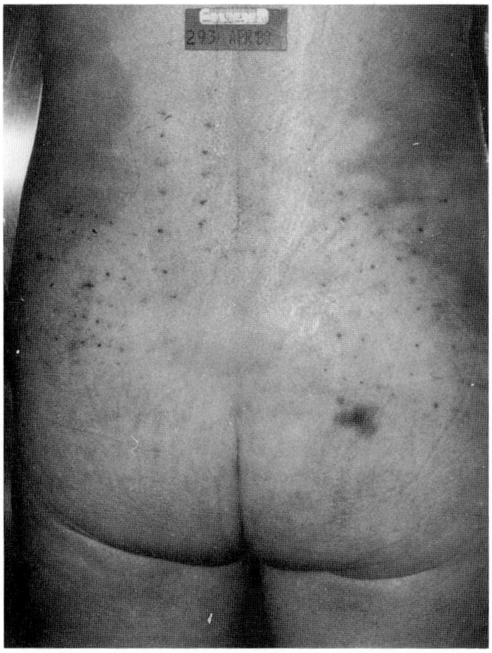

FIGURE 6.20 Multiple patterned needle puncture marks in an acupuncture patient. Death was due to severe atherosclerosis of the coronary arteries. The multiple puncture marks were an incidental finding.

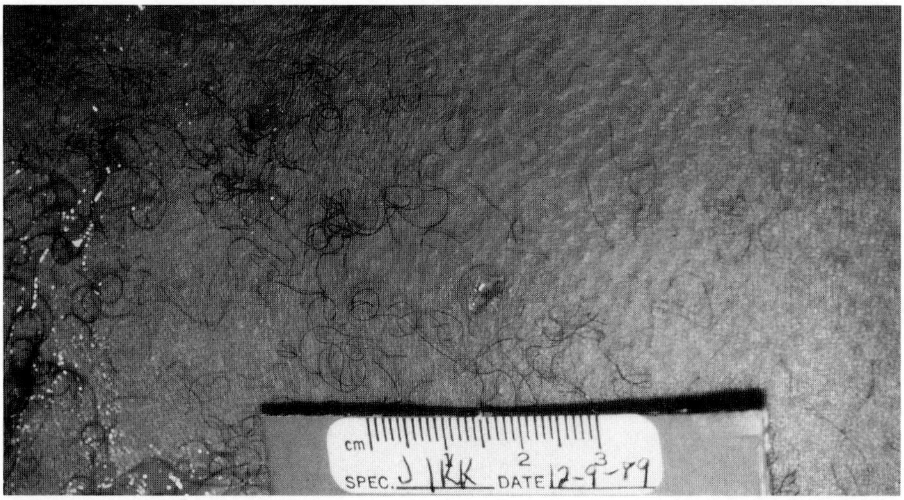

FIGURE 6.21 Stab wound to the left upper chest from an awl. The victim was admitted to a local emergency room while intoxicated with a history of a fall on stairs. The wound was thought to be a laceration. Over a period of time, the victim deteriorated and subsequently arrested and could not be resuscitated.

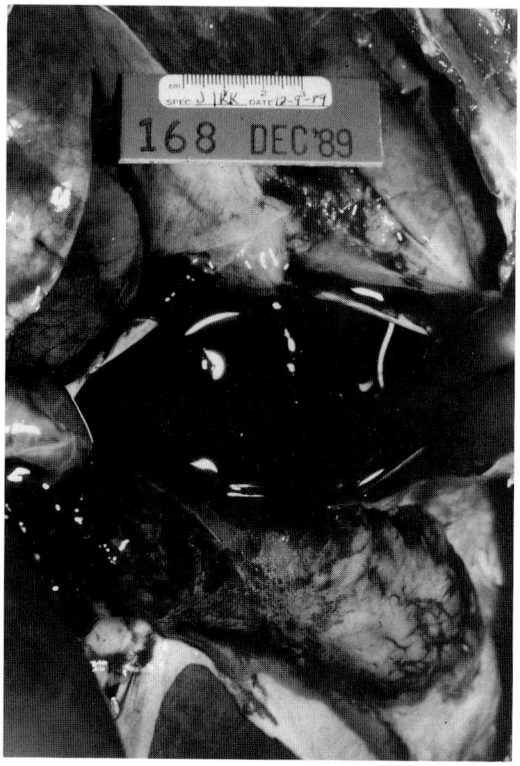

a

b

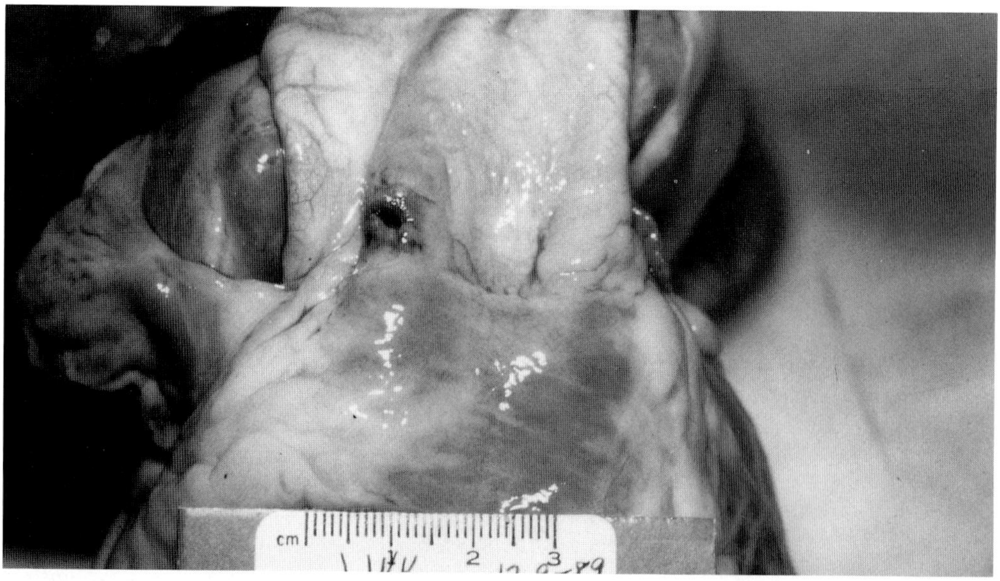

FIGURE 6.22a, b Hemopericardium and stab wound to the pulmonary trunk found at autopsy of the victim described in Figure 6.21.

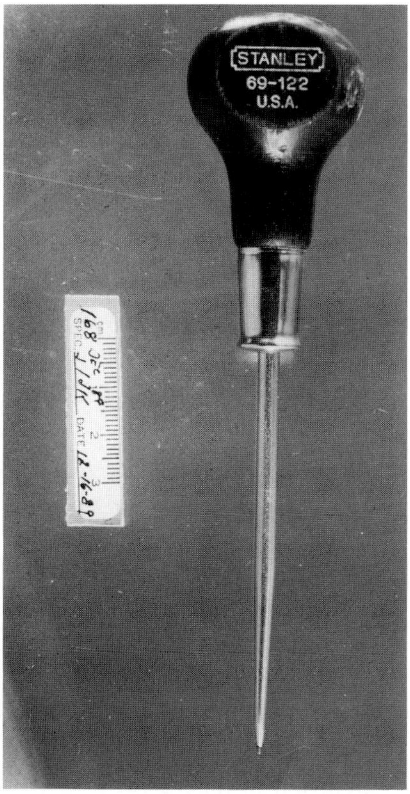

FIGURE 6.22c Awl that was used to stab the victim, recovered from the purse of the offender who was still at the scene. She and the victim lived in the same boarding house and had an argument on the stairway. During the argument, the offender stabbed the victim once in the chest, causing him to fall on the stairs which was the only information relayed to the responding medical personnel.

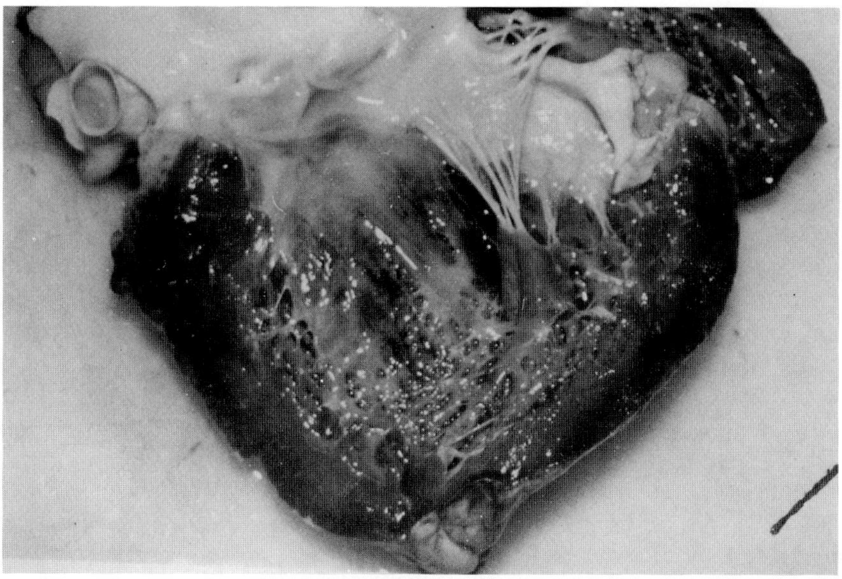

FIGURE 6.23 Subendocardial hemorrhage found in a victim of multiple stab wounds who exsanguinated. Victims of stab wounds do not die immediately from their wounds, but rather will survive until sufficient blood is lost to cause irreversible hypovolemic shock. The hemorrhages in the outflow tract of the heart are a sign of hypovolemic shock and myocardial hypoxia.

7

Asphyxial Deaths

Asphyxia, in common usage, means the lack of oxygen. This can occur due to a reduction or absence of oxygen in the environment; obstruction of the mouth, nose, or the internal airways at any level from the pharynx to the bronchial level; restriction of chest movement from external compression; paralysis due to injury of the spinal cord; or respiratory suppression in the central nervous system due to the ingestion of drugs, diseases or injuries of the lungs that affect normal gas exchange; reduction of cardiac output or of the blood cells' ability to bind, transport, and release oxygen, or the inability of the peripheral tissues to utilize the oxygen delivered.

Some common terms used to describe various mechanisms of asphyxia include *suffocation, smothering, choking,* and *strangulation.* Both *suffocation* and *smothering* refer to the exclusion of oxygen; the former refers to the lack of oxygen in the environment as well as to the obstruction of the airways, while the latter refers to blockage of the mouth and nose by a hand or other object. *Choking* refers to the blockage of the internal airways by foreign bodies; it is also called aspiration of foreign objects. *Strangulation* is the application of external pressure to the neck by means of the hands (called *manual strangulation*) or a ligature. *Hanging* is a form of ligature strangulation. In strangulation, death may be due to reflex cardiac arrest, occlusion of venous blood flow from the brain, occlusion of both arterial and venous blood flow, or to the occlusion of the airways. Compression of the airway requires far more pressure than does the occlusion of arterial or venous blood flow. A reflex cardiac arrest may occur with only minimal pressures. In judicial hangings, the cause of death is fracture of the odontoid process of the second cervical vertebra which then compresses the medulla oblongata affecting the respiratory and cardiac centers. This "hangman's fracture" may also be seen in suicidal hangings involving a long drop from a height.

An unusual type of asphyxial death is confined or closed space asphyxia where the oxygen in an enclosed area, such as a sewer or construction hole, has been depleted or replaced by other gases such as carbon monoxide, carbon dioxide, nitrogen, or methane. Autopsy examination in deaths due to confined space asphyxia rarely, if ever, reveal clues as to the mechanism of death. A cherry red hue to the skin can be seen in deaths due to carbon monoxide, but deaths due to hypercapnia or hypoxia have no such markings. Measuring oxygen or carbon dioxide levels in the dead is useless as oxygen levels fall and carbon dioxide levels rise normally in the postmortem period. It is possible to measure carbon monoxide in the dead by use of a co-oximeter. In deaths due to carbon dioxide, nitrogen, methane, or other noxious gases, taking air samples at the scene is important. Nearly all municipalities have hazardous materials response teams with the equipment necessary to sample air quality readily available (Table 7.1).

Positional or compressional asphyxia is a type of asphyxial death which occurs when the body is in a position that impedes the normal expansion of the chest and the use of the muscles of respiration. This can occur in motor vehicle accidents or when trenches, buildings, or other materials collapse onto workers. A description of the circumstances, with the victim reported as being alive and talking when rescuers first arrive, but gradually losing consciousness during the time needed to free the victim, is common.

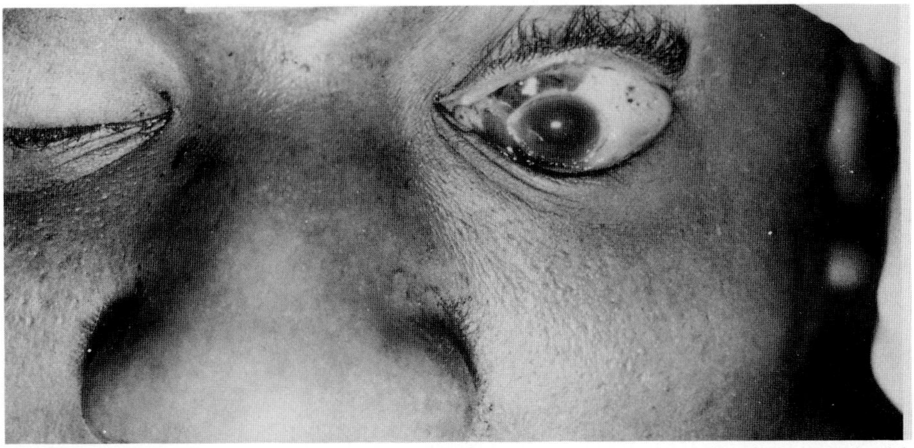

FIGURE 7.1 Scleral hemorrhages are a sign of asphyxia. There are also fine petechial hemorrhages on the bridge of the nose and along the left orbital rim.

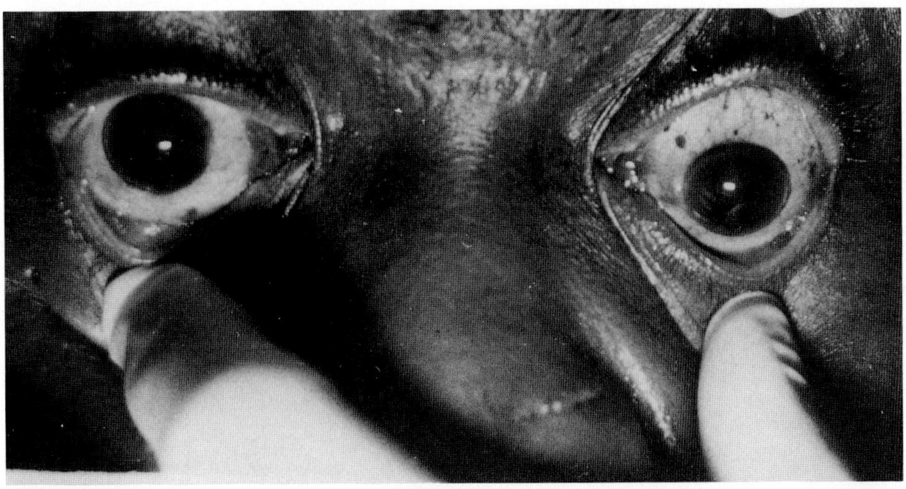

FIGURE 7.2 There are petechial hemorrhages of the sclera in this elderly African-American male who died in a hospital emergency room from severe hypertensive cardiovascular disease. There had been prolonged resuscitation following his cardiac arrest. Though petechiae and scleral hemorrhages are signs of asphyxia, they are not pathognomonic of strangulation, suffocation, or smothering.

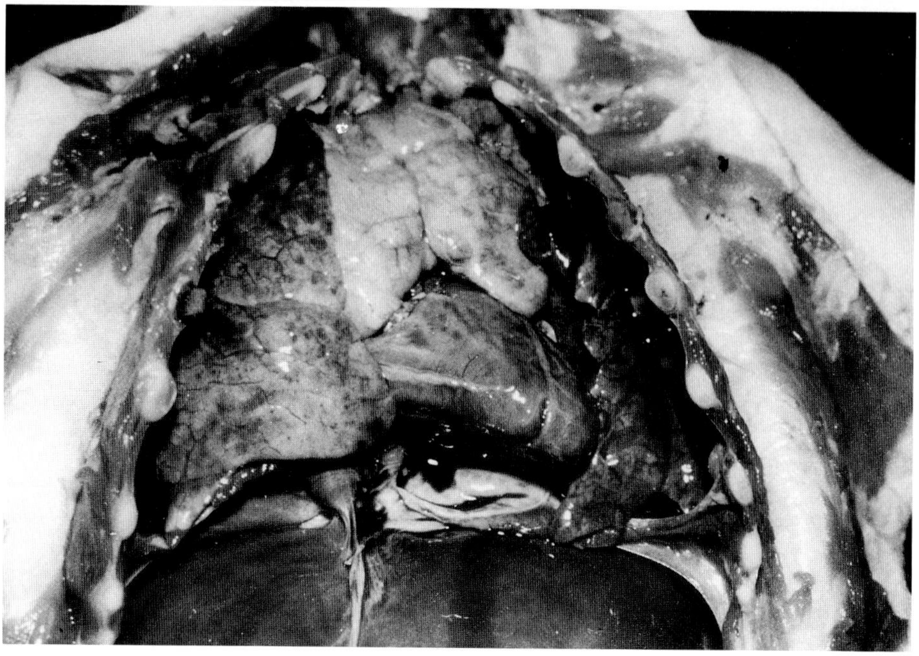

FIGURE 7.3 Numerous petechial hemorrhages of the lungs, thymus, and heart of a victim of sudden infant death syndrome. The diagnosis of SIDS is one of exclusion and is made when there is a negative autopsy, including toxicology and histology, a negative scene investigation, and no suspicion about the death. The findings in a death due to SIDS and a death due to suffocation are the same in infants, that is, there are no findings or the only finding may be the petechiae.

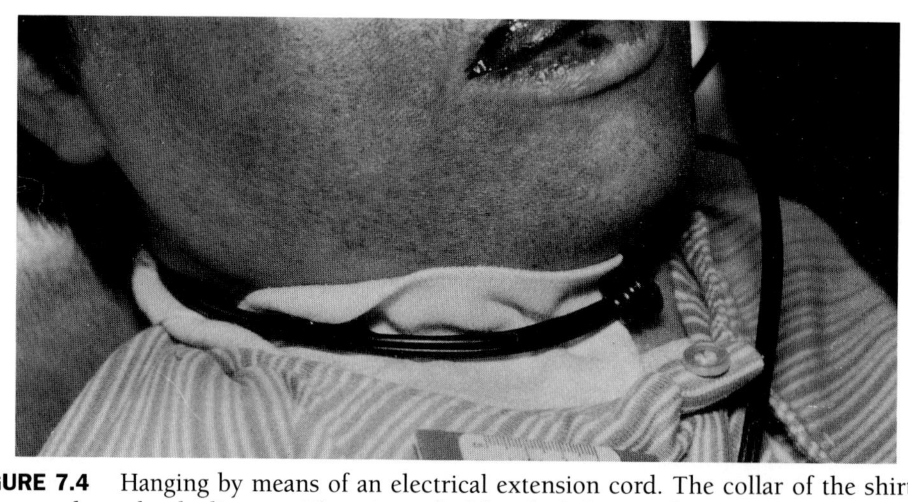

FIGURE 7.4 Hanging by means of an electrical extension cord. The collar of the shirt has been caught under the ligature. There is marked facial plethora and numerous petechiae. The lips and tip of the protruding tongue are very dry.

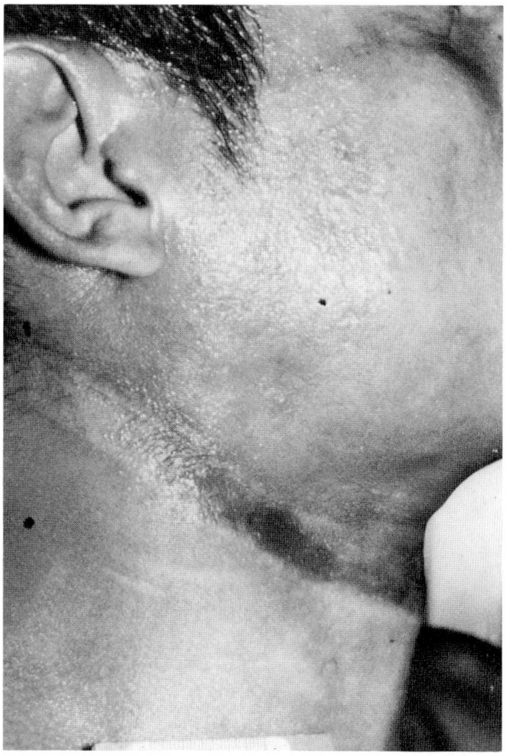

FIGURE 7.5 Suspension type ligature abrasion from a belt. The abrasion passes diagonally down the side of the neck from the suspension point at the back of the neck. This is in contrast to ligature strangulation where the ligature mark is horizontal.

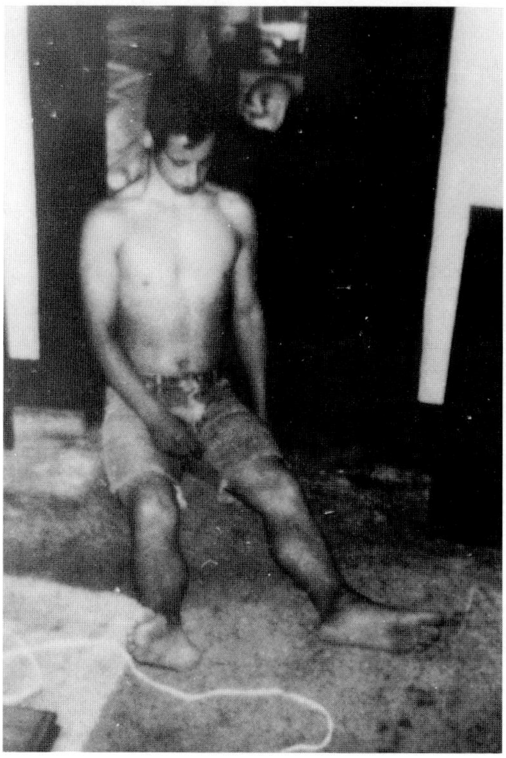

FIGURE 7.6 Scene photographs in a suicidal hanging. The victim is seated on the floor and the belt used as a ligature is attached to the door hinges. It is not necessary for the feet to be suspended above the floor to cause death. Autopsy examination in most hanging deaths reveals very little injury to the internal neck structures. Small hemorrhages of the strap muscles may be seen with congestion of the base of the tongue. The hyoid bone and neck cartilages are usually intact. Fractures of the hyoid bone may be seen in the elderly or in hanging deaths involving a significant drop.

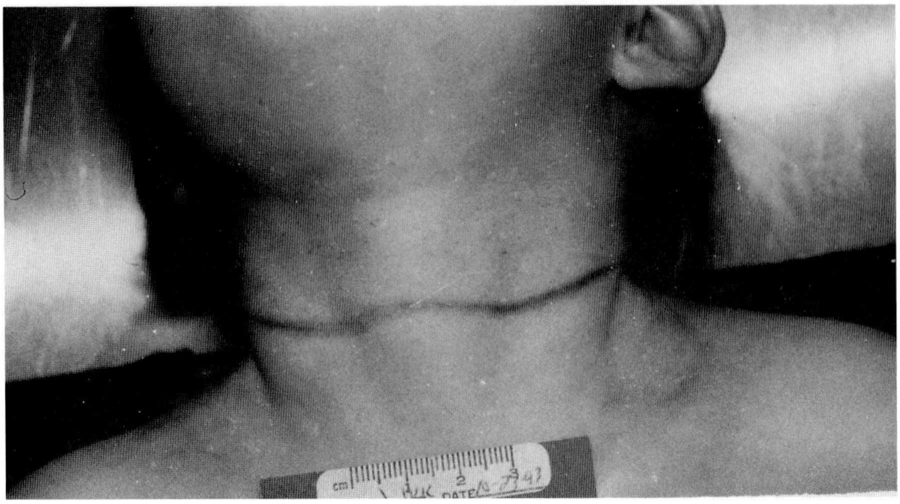

FIGURE 7.7 Thin ligature abrasion on the neck of a toddler who was found hanged from a Venetian blind cord which was adjacent to her crib. There are petechial hemorrhages on the neck above the ligature mark. Deaths due to household products are reported to the Consumer Product Safety Commission. Venetian blinds carry warning labels alerting parents to this danger.

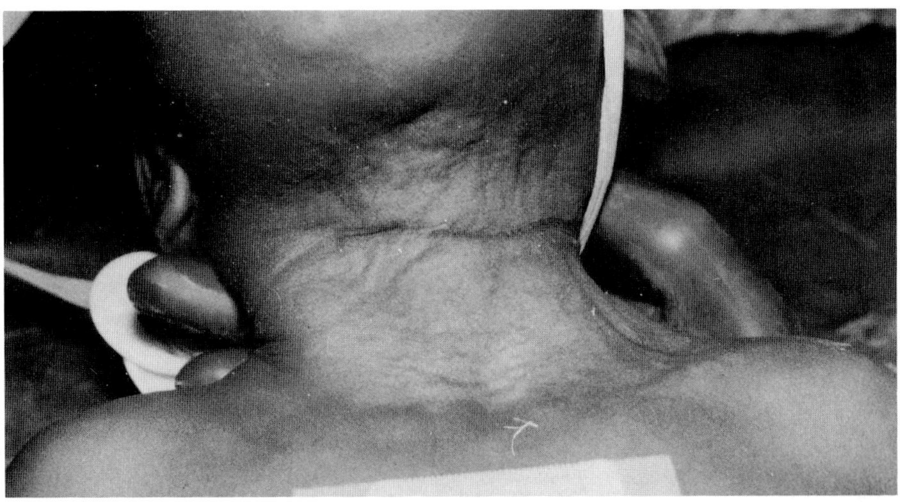

a

FIGURE 7.8a Ligature mark and pacifier cord which created the mark around the neck of an infant who died when the cord caught on a portion of the crib. Parents are warned not to put pacifiers tied to looped cords around the necks of infants and toddlers.

b

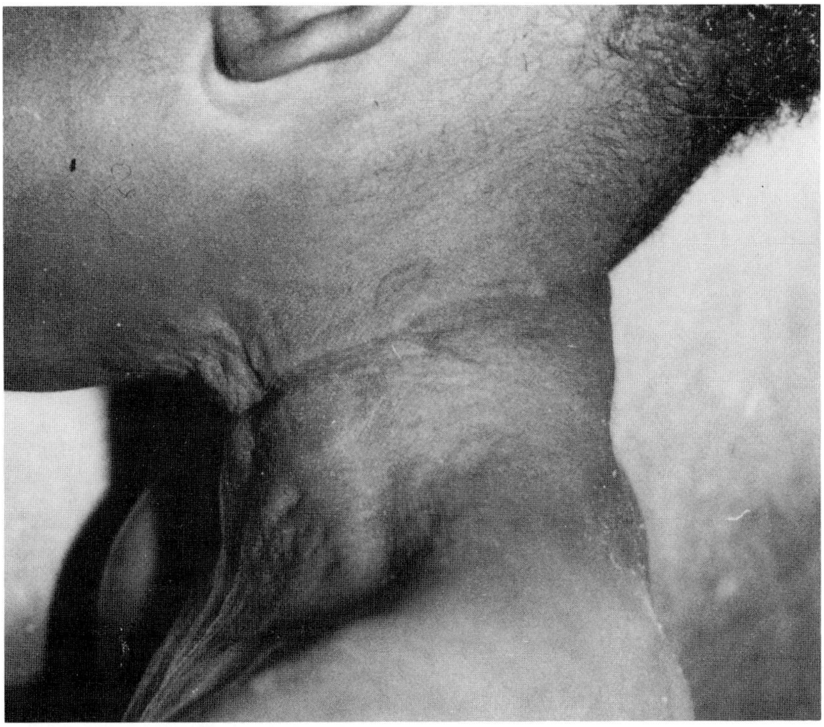

FIGURE 7.8b The ligature abrasion is more prominent on the left side of the neck than on the right as the point of suspension was on the right side of the victim's body.

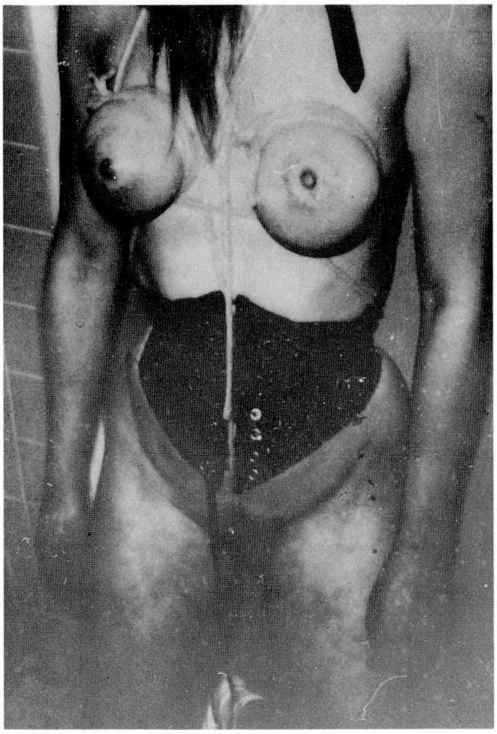

a

FIGURE 7.9a Autoerotic asphyxia in a young adult female. The victim was found in the bathroom of her secure home suspended from the bathroom door. Note the elaborate bindings around the breasts, which was done using soft thick yarn. There was a dog collar on the neck to which the ligature had been secured.

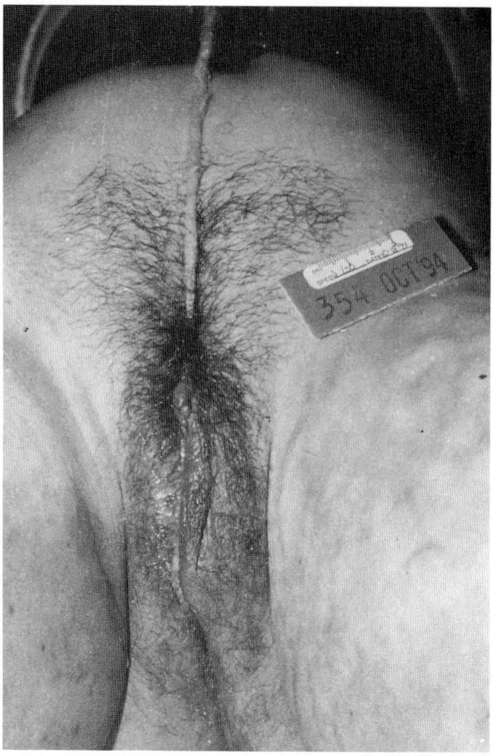

b

FIGURE 7.9b The yarn has been brought up through the labia and against the clitoris as part of the elaborate ritual. Autoerotic asphyxia is unusual in females. It is a dangerous form of self-gratification where cerebral hypoxia is used to enhance sexual pleasure.

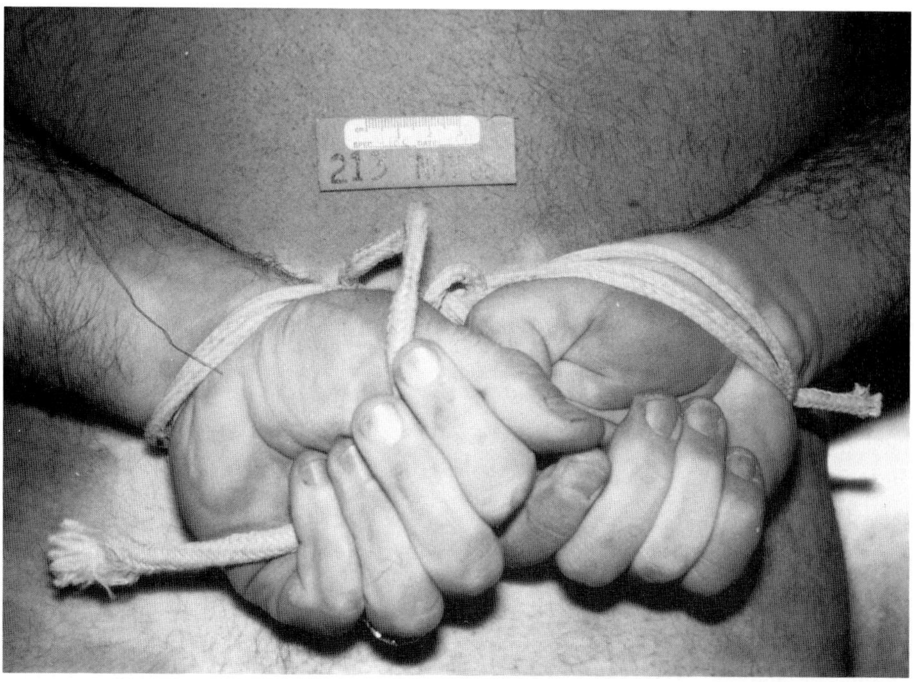

FIGURE 7.10 Close-up of the bindings around the wrists of another victim of autoerotic asphyxia. Note that the release to the bindings is in the left hand. This is to allow the victim to get free before unconsciousness develops, to avoid a fatal outcome.

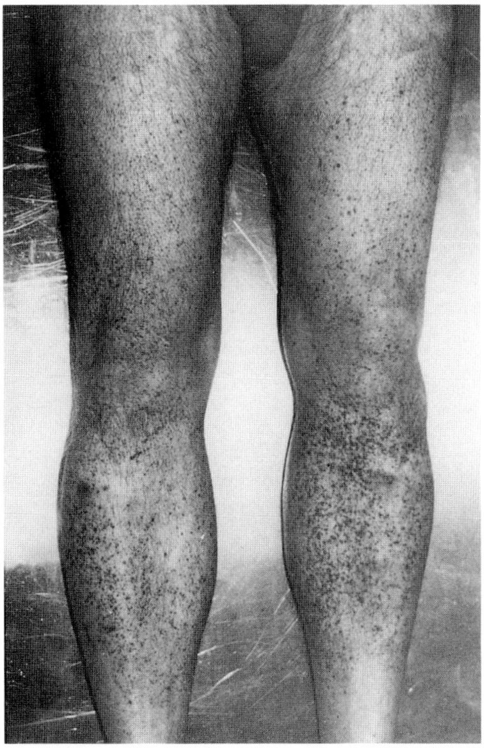

FIGURE 7.11 Numerous Tardieu spots, on the legs of a hanging victim. They are due to the rupture of small venules from hydrostatic pressure releasing the red blood cells into the soft tissues.

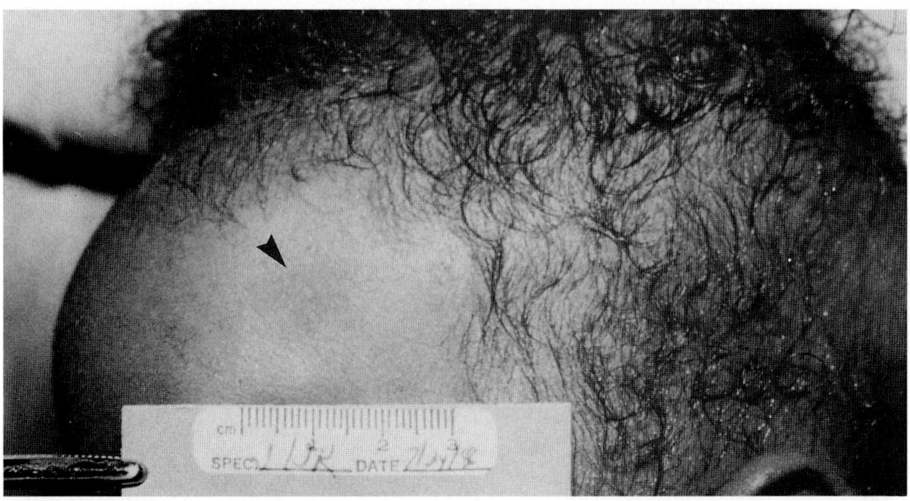

FIGURE 7.12 This 4-month-old infant was found suspended between the wall and mattress of the twin-sized bed where he had been placed for a nap. The feet were not touching the floor. Autopsy examination revealed a small, flattened area of the left forehead (*arrow*) which was due to the head pressing against the wall.

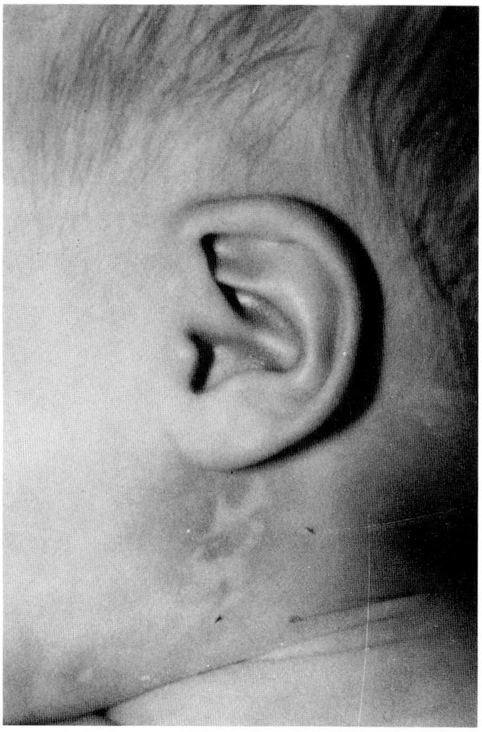

FIGURE 7.13 Note the patterned pressure mark below the ear of this 8-month-old who died after his head and neck became trapped between the mattress and the slats of his crib.

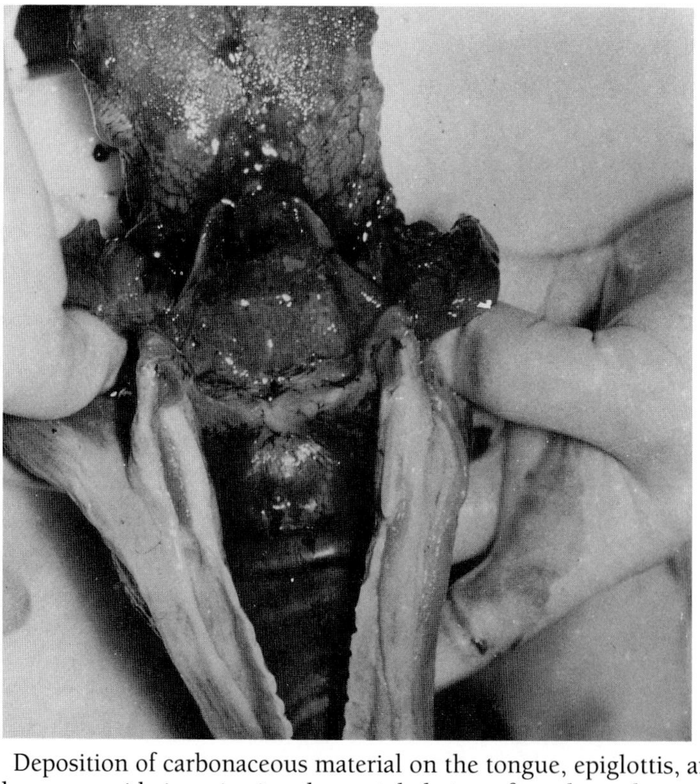

FIGURE 7.14 Deposition of carbonaceous material on the tongue, epiglottis, and trachea of a victim of carbon monoxide intoxication due to inhalation of smoke and soot in a fire. Elevated carbon monoxide levels, soot, or hyperemia in the airways are evidence that a person found in a burned building was alive and breathing during the fire.

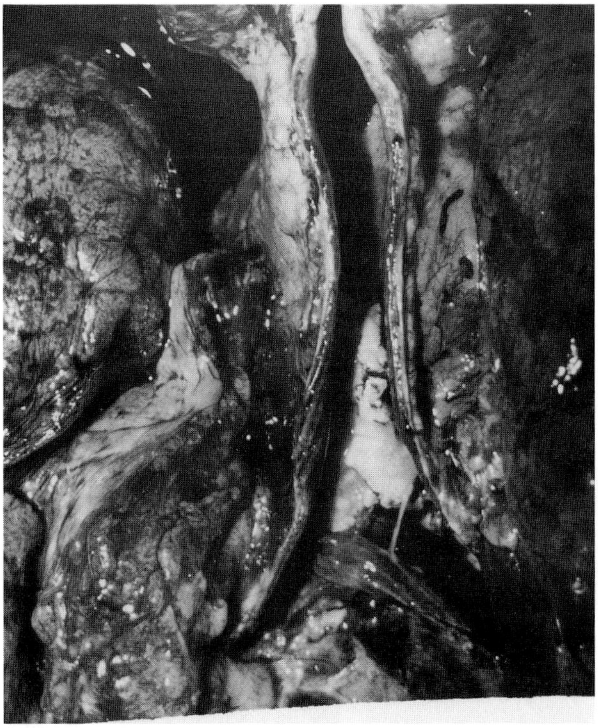

FIGURE 7.15 Food bolus wedged at the carina of the trachea. A smaller bolus had been removed by emergency medical personnel from the laryngeal inlet during resuscitation efforts. It is not uncommon for the adult choking victim to be impaired in some way, such as intoxicated or mentally incompetent. Objects such as balloons, marbles, coins, or food such as grapes, peanuts, or hot dogs are frequently recovered from the airway of infants and children.

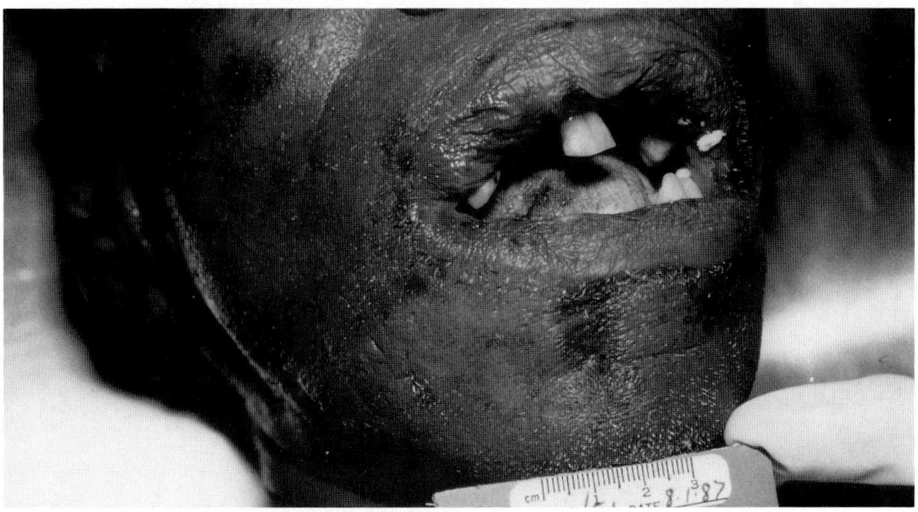

a

FIGURE 7.16a, b Elderly black male found unresponsive in bed. The death was thought to be due to natural causes by investigating police. Autopsy examination revealed several small abrasions around the mouth, and the examination of the mucosal surface of the lips revealed bruises and several patterned, curved abrasions of the upper lip which corresponded to the victim's upper right central incisor. A tooth in the lower right had been forcibly avulsed from the gum (*arrow*). All of these findings are consistent with smothering. The victim's nephew later confessed to smothering the victim with a pillow when he refused to give the nephew money.

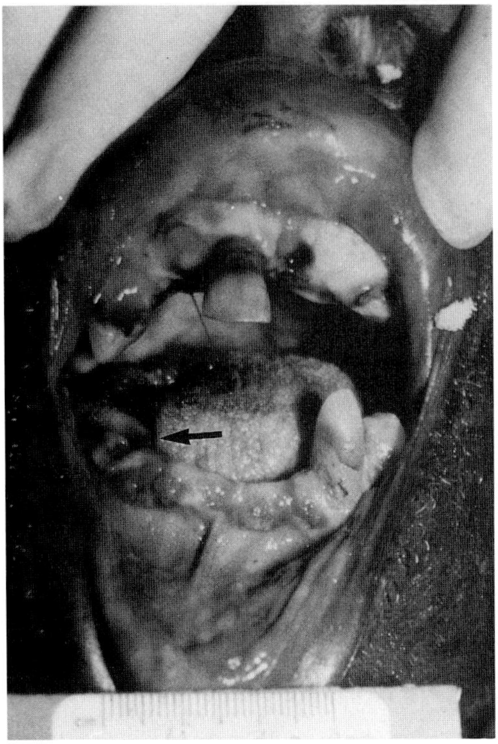

b

FIGURE 7.16b (continued)

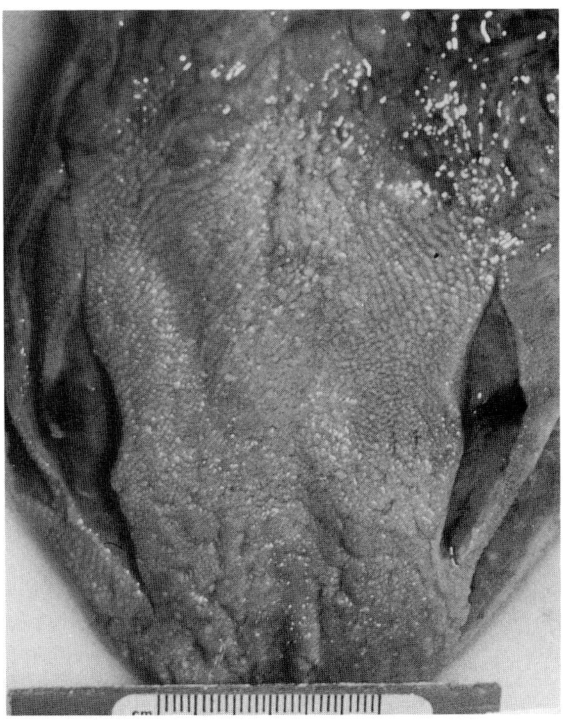

FIGURE 7.17 Incisions in the margins of the tongue to show hemorrhages due to biting the tongue while the victim was being smothered. Similar lesions are found in victims of manual and ligature strangulation. Tongue hemorrhages may also be found in victims who have a terminal seizure.

a

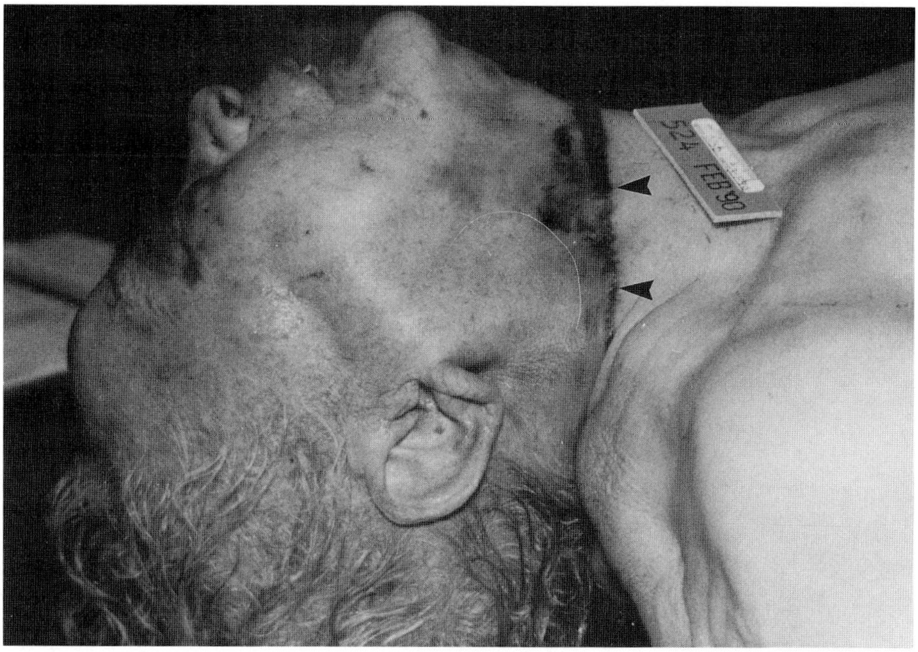

FIGURE 7.18a Horizontal ligature strangulation mark in an elderly victim of a home invasion. There are bruises and abrasions on the undersurface of the chin and above the ligature. Note the pattern to the ligature abrasion at the arrow and compare to the ligature shown in Figure 7.18 b which was recovered still around the victim's neck.

b

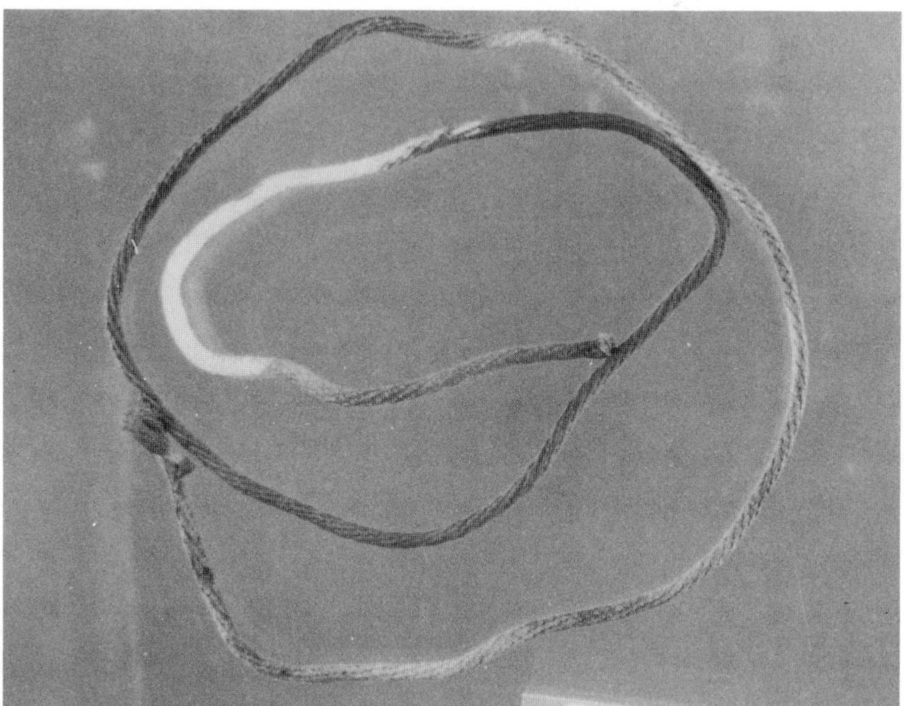

FIGURE 7.18b Ligature removed from victim of home invasion.

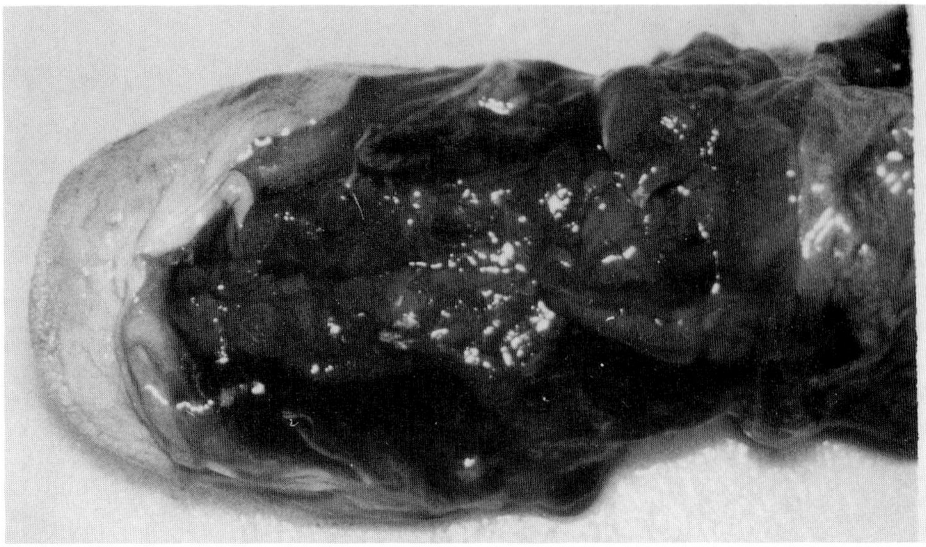

FIGURE 7.19 Tongue and neck organs removed from the body of a victim of manual strangulation showing extensive hemorrhages in the hyoglossus muscles. The hyoid bone and thyroid cartilage were not fractured. It is not unusual for the hyoid bone or the cartilages to remain intact in young victims of strangulation as they are pliable. In older victims, the hyoid bone or the horns of the thyroid cartilage fracture.

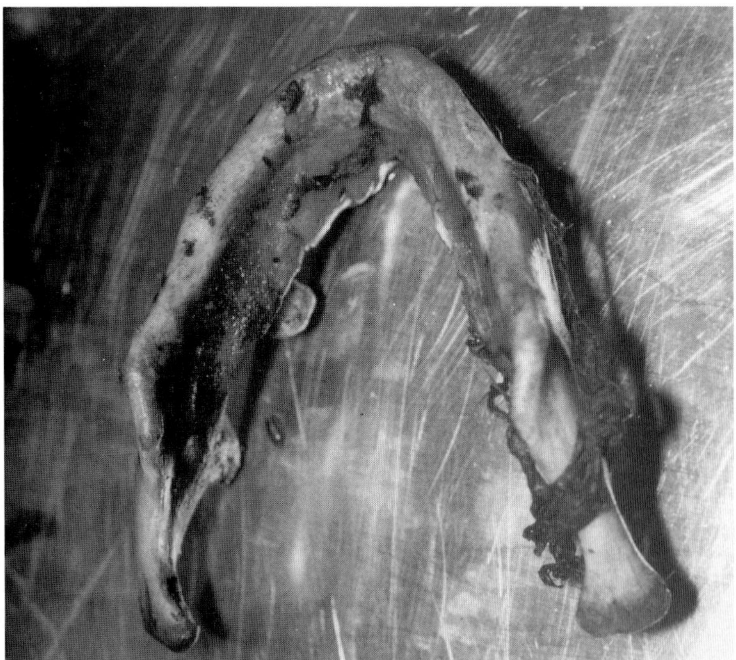

FIGURE 7.20 An intact hyoid bone showing the normal shape of the bone.

a

FIGURE 7.21a One-year-old black child who drowned in a bucket of cleaning water left out by the mother. The infant is suspended over the bucket edge and the bucket, which is empty at the time of this reenactment, still supports the full weight of the victim without tipping over.

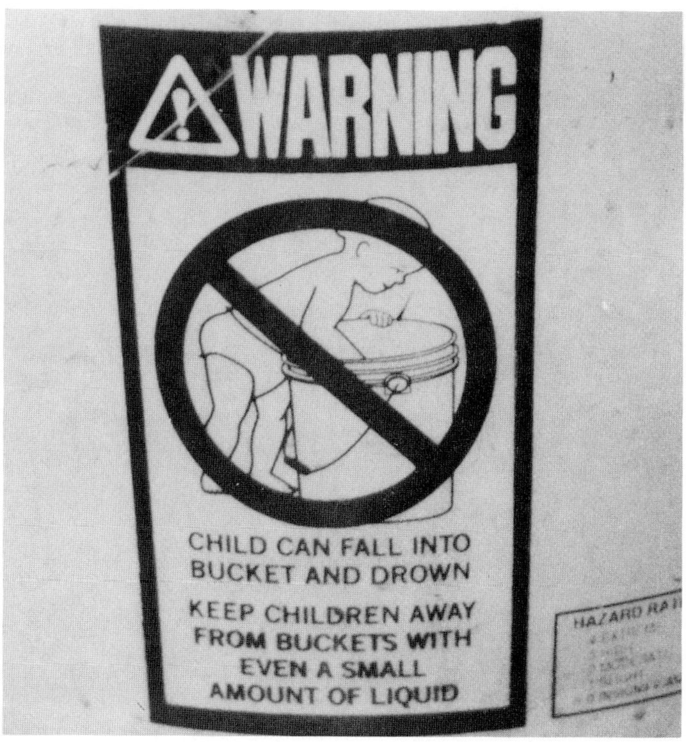

b

FIGURE 7.21b Warning label which has been placed on all such buckets by order of the Consumer Product Safety Commission was clearly visible on the side of the bucket.

c

FIGURE 7.21c Aspiration of the water and cleaning chemicals caused death due to acute respiratory distress syndrome in the 10-month-old child found head down in this bucket. He was still alive at the time he was pulled from the bucket and survived for several days in the hospital. Autopsy showed beefy red, heavy lungs with numerous hyaline membranes and diffuse alveolar damage on histologic section.

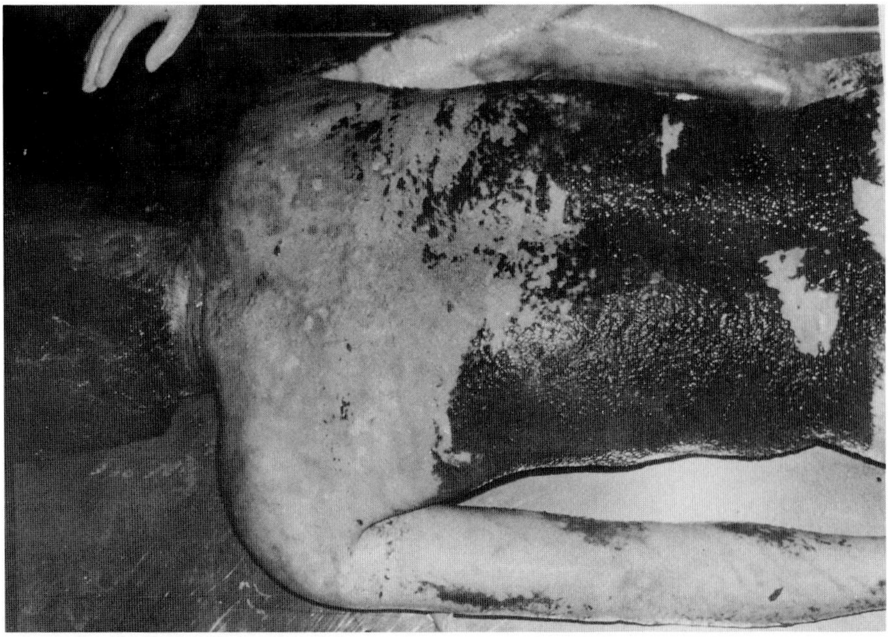

FIGURE 7.22 Young adult white male drowning victim recovered from a river. The victim had been in the water for over a week. There is a fine layer of sand and mud found between the keratin layer and basal layer of the epidermis.

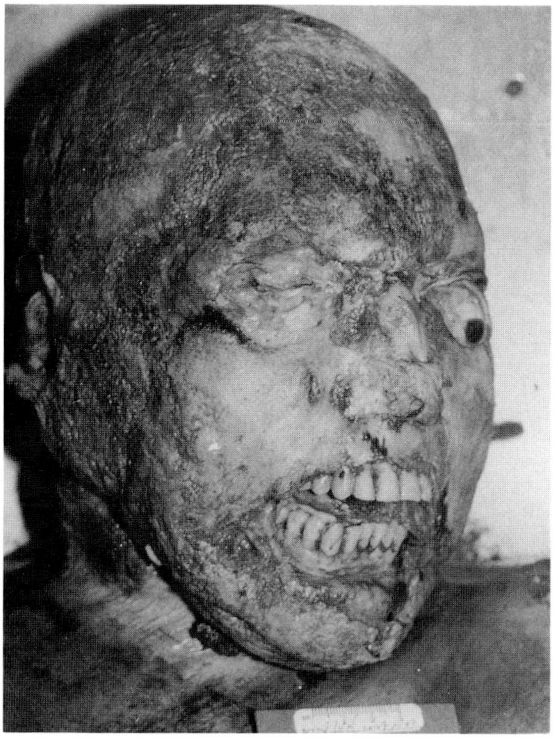

FIGURE 7.23 Adipocere, a waxy, white change of the soft tissues, seen in a drowning victim who had been in the water for several months. Identification of the victim has not been made. The dental chart was placed into the National Crime Information Center (NCIC) files and total body radiographs were taken prior to burial to assist in future identification.

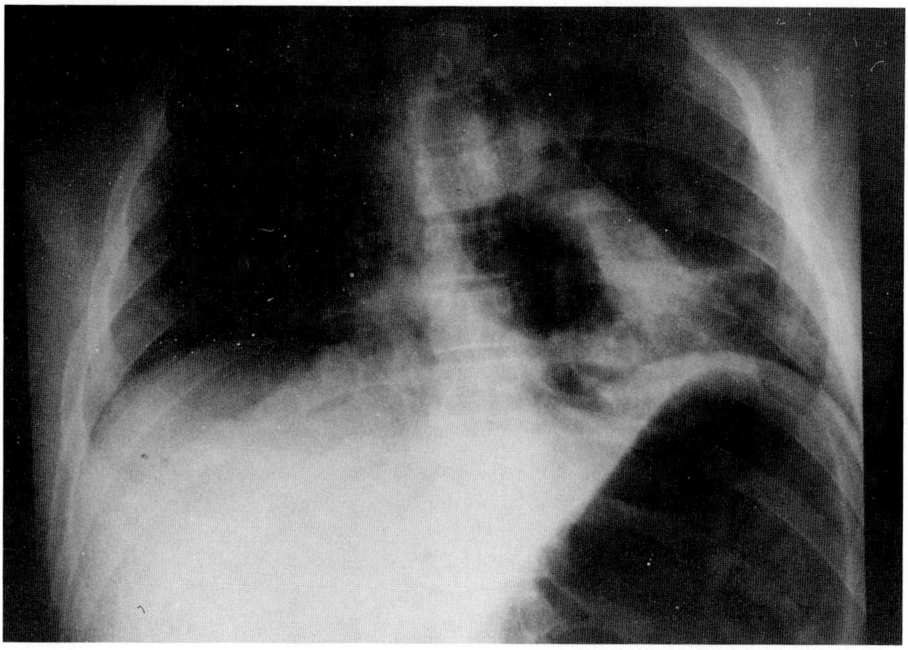

FIGURE 7.24 Lateral decubitus radiograph taken of a scuba diver who died suddenly after surfacing too rapidly from Lake Michigan when his air tanks ran dry. A large air embolus can be seen in the heart and the aorta. The diving equipment should always be examined by a qualified expert in diving accidents to rule out mechanical failure. In this case, the tanks were found to be empty, though they did function properly. Deaths in scuba divers may be due to air embolism, decompression sickness, nitrogen narcosis, drowning, hypothermia, asphyxia, or to natural causes.

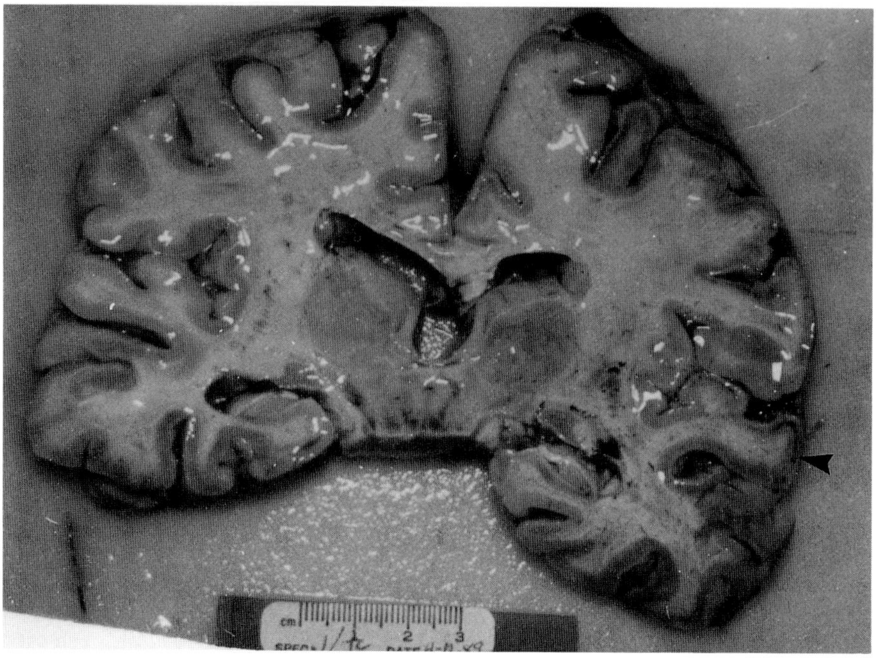

FIGURE 7.25 Laminar necrosis (*arrow*) of the cerebral cortex due to global hypoxia. The neurons are very sensitive to hypoxia and have become necrotic. This change can be seen in all forms of asphyxia when the victim survives for over 24 hours.

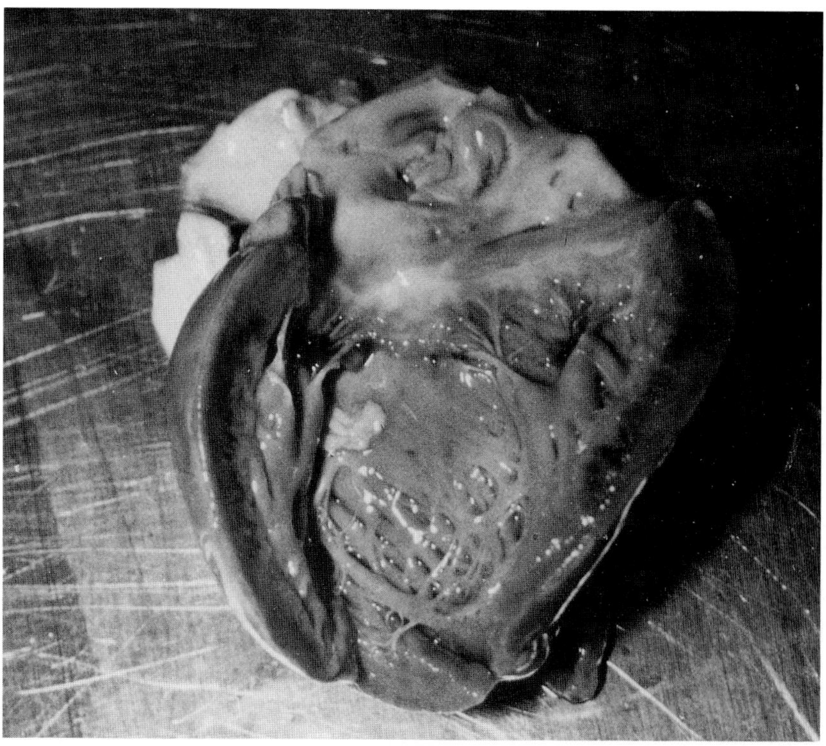

FIGURE 7.26 Subendocardial myocardial ischemia. This infant was resuscitated following a cardiorespiratory arrest due to a subdural hematoma. He then survived for 3 days in an intensive care unit on a respirator before being declared brain dead. The myocardium shows the anoxic injury suffered during the initial arrest.

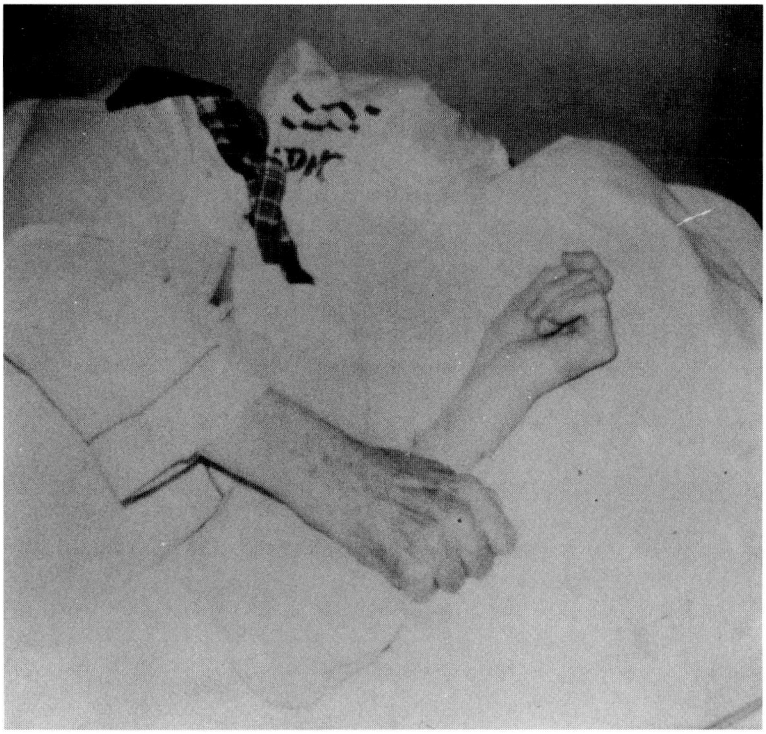

a

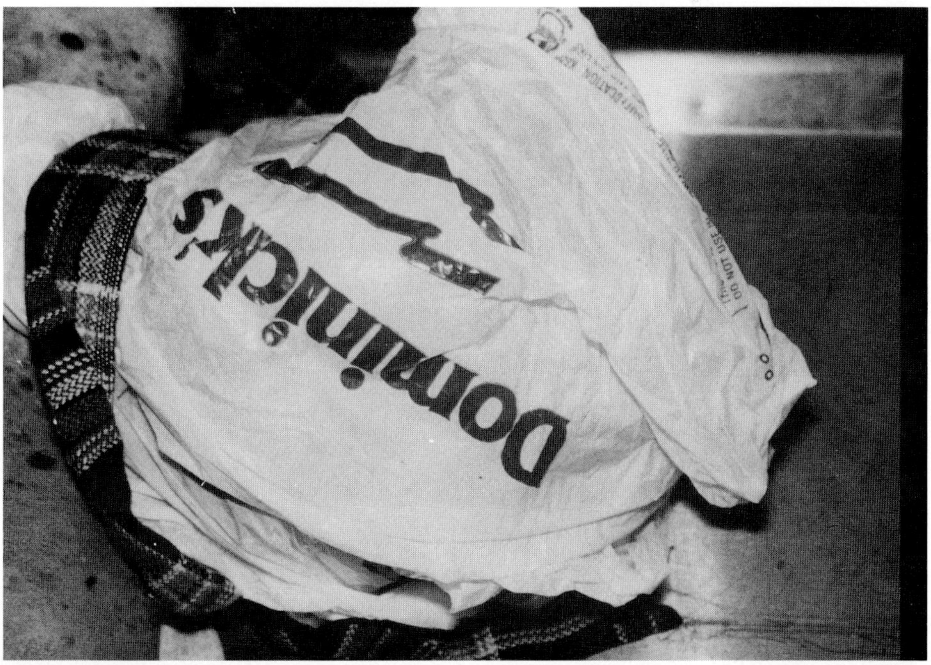

b

FIGURE 7.27a, b Scene photograph and autopsy photograph of an elderly man who committed suicide by tying plastic grocery bags over his head and then lying down in his bed. The bags were secured using the belt from a bathrobe. This form of suicide has become more common since the publication of the book, *Final Exit*.

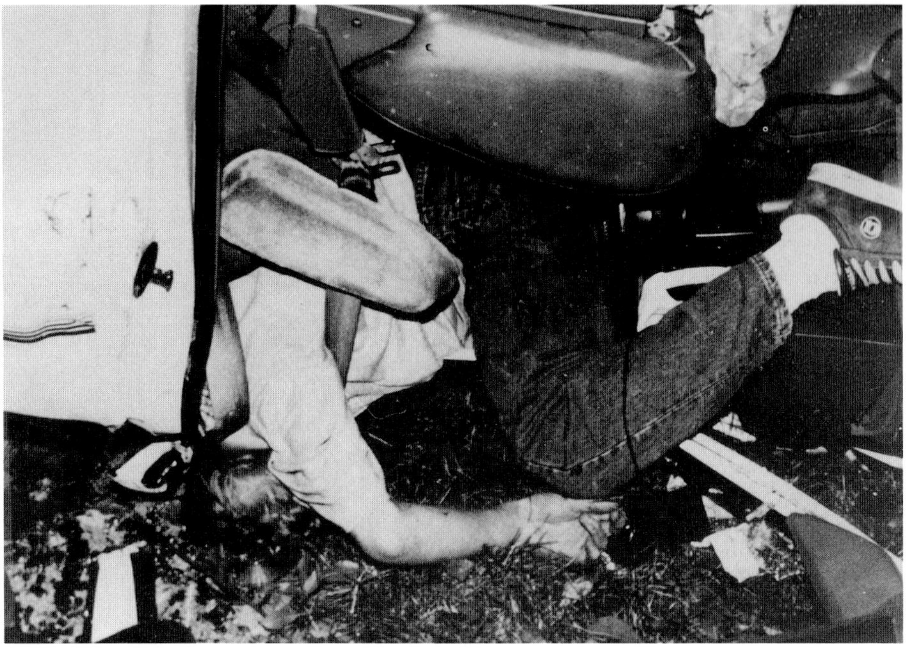

FIGURE 7.28 Positional asphyxia. The victim was the driver of a minivan which flipped over and came to rest on the roof while drag racing. There were no injuries to the body at autopsy. Petechial hemorrhages were noted on the face Scene photographs were requested from the police. They show the victim suspended by the lap belt and shoulder harness with the head hyperflexed causing positional asphyxia.

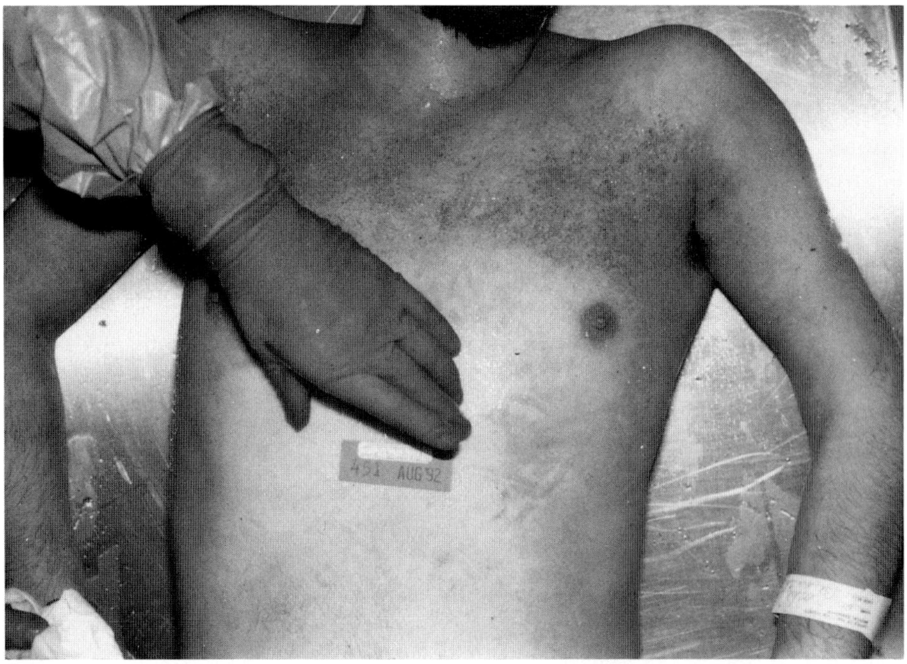

FIGURE 7.29 A section of vaulted sidewalk collapsed on this city worker leading to compressional asphyxia. Note the petechial hemorrhages on the upper chest with blanching of the skin where the sidewalk was pressing against the chest.

8

Thermal Injury

BURNS AND SCALDS

Thermal injuries include flame burns, injury due to contact with hot objects, electrical burns, and scald burns from exposure to hot liquids or steam (Table 8.1, 8.2). Burns were once described as first-, second-, third-, and fourth-degree and are now described as partial thickness (first- and second-degree) and full-thickness (third- and fourth-degree) burns. Partial thickness burns are further divided into superficial and deep and are characterized by sparing of all levels or just the deeper levels of the dermis and the skin appendages. These burns show erythema and some blistering, especially in the more superficial injuries. Full-thickness burns, where the dermis and skin appendages are destroyed, show a waxy white color due to destruction of the blood vessels. If there has been prolonged contact with the heat source, the tissue may have a leathery brown or a black charred appearance with thrombosed blood vessels readily seen. In full-thickness scald burns, there is hemolysis of red blood cells which can give a red appearance to the wound (Table 8.3). This must not be confused with the red appearance of partial thickness burns.

Scald burns are frequently accidental. Home water heaters can be set at unsafe temperatures. The severity of a scald burn depends on the water temperature and the time of exposure. At temperatures of 120° F, it takes 10 minutes to cause a third-degree burn, whereas at temperatures of 150° F, it only takes 2 seconds. The skin of infants and children can burn faster than the skin of adults, requiring less time of exposure. In infants and children, scald burns can occur in the bath or by pulling pans containing hot liquids off the stove, but they may be a form of child abuse. The described circumstances must be evaluated in light of the age of the victim and the pattern and the location of the burns on the body. "Glove and stocking" burns on the hands and feet with a well-defined watermark and no splash marks are highly suspicious for immersion burns.

Patterned thermal burns, or burn scars caused by cigarettes, curling irons, or clothes irons are sometimes found on the bodies of abuse victims. The palms of the hands may show burns or scars from being held against hot pans, electric stove burners, or gas stove flames.

Deaths due to fires are common. Frequently, the victim dies from inhalation of carbon monoxide and other noxious gases before burns are sustained. Blistering is seen in carbon monoxide intoxication and must not be confused with the blistering that occurs in partial thickness burns. To prevent misdiagnosis, the pathologist must be familiar with the numerous artifacts caused by thermal injury. Self-immolation as a form of suicide occurs rarely.

HYPERTHERMIA

Deaths due to hyperthermia from environmental, metabolic, exertional, or chemical causes have no typical gross autopsy findings. Petechial hemorrhages may be found if disseminated intravascular coagulopathy develops. Histologic examination may show rhabdomyolysis and casts within the kidney sections. Determination of hyperthermia as the cause of death can be made where terminal body temperature is known to be greater than 105° F, or based on scene investigation and knowledge of the environmental conditions present at the time of death in the face of an otherwise negative autopsy and chemical examination.

HYPOTHERMIA

Hypothermia may result from exposure to low ambient temperatures or may be the result of metabolic disorders. Deaths due to the latter are not usually the concern of the medical examiner or coroner. In deaths due to hypothermia, there may be paradoxical undressing, where the victim is found naked or only partially clothed in spite of very cold temperatures. As the core body temperature falls, the victim feels paradoxically hot, and may begin to remove clothing in an attempt to cool off. Knowledge of the scene is very important in deaths due to hypothermia. In cold water drowning deaths, the possibility of hypothermia as well as drowning must be considered. Autopsy examination of victims of hypothermia can show a cherry red hue to the body, similar to that seen in deaths due to carbon monoxide. The internal examination may show numerous small erosions of the gastric mucosa or small hemorrhages within or surrounding the pancreas.

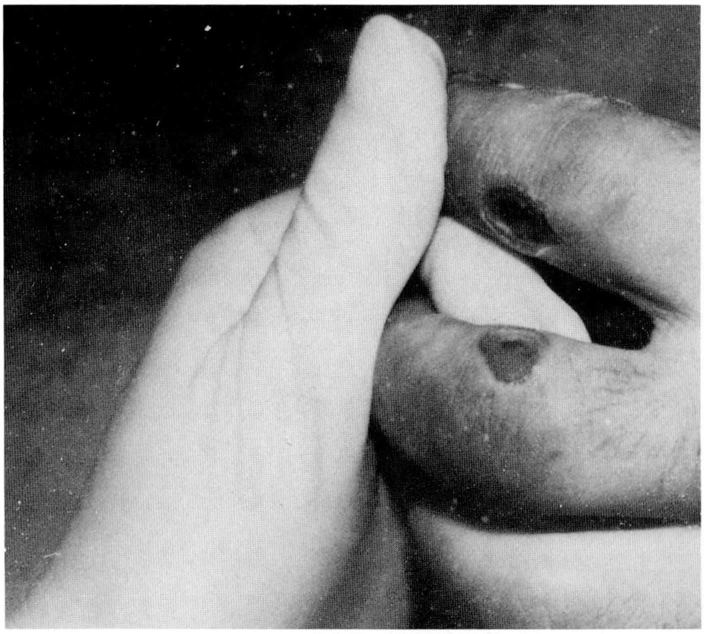

FIGURE 8.1 Postmortem thermal burns from a lighted cigarette found on the index and middle finger at autopsy. There is no evidence of vital reaction about the burns, which are deep partial thickness burns. The victim died from an overdose of codeine and secobarbital.

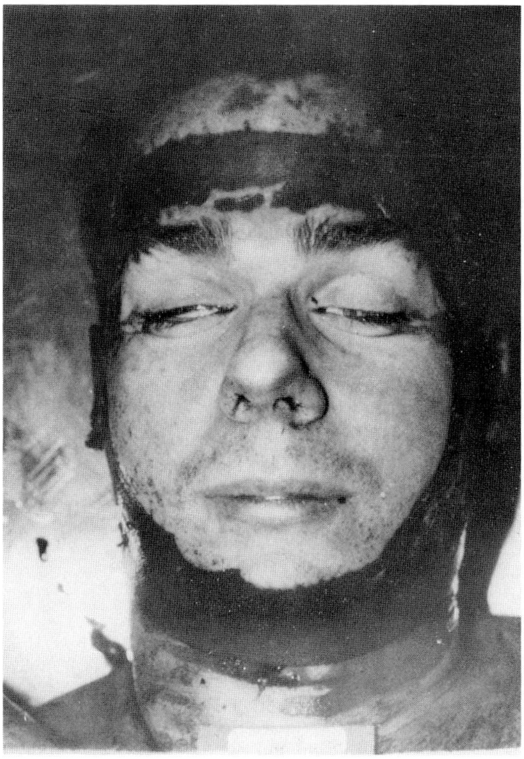

FIGURE 8.2 Patterned burns around the face of a firefighter who died when his air tanks ran out while he was inside a burning building. The pattern is due to the face mask and helmet he was wearing protecting the face and upper forehead.

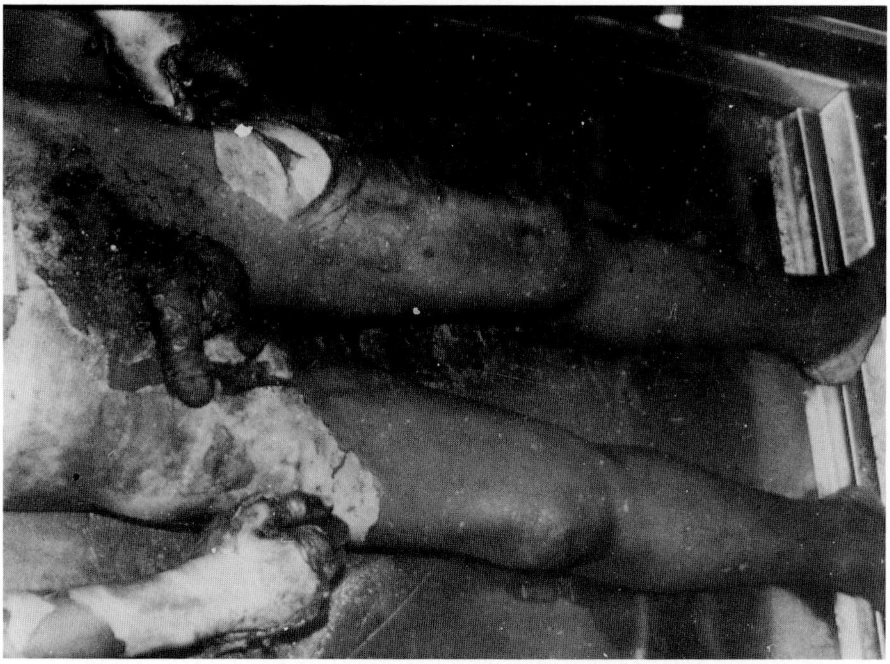

FIGURE 8.3 Full and partial thickness burns on the arms, hands, abdomen, and thighs of a victim of a fire in a service garage. There are large blisters on the left thigh due to burns. The carbon monoxide level was only 5% saturation but soot was found in the trachea indicating that the victim had been alive during the fire. The origin of the fire was never determined and the manner of death was ruled undetermined.

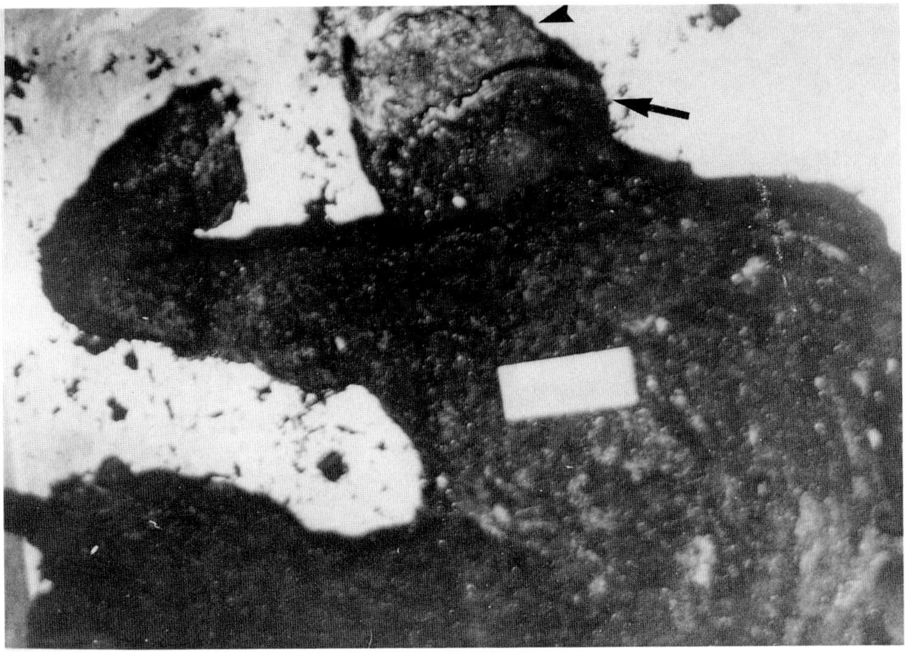

FIGURE 8.4 Pugilistic attitude of left arm and leg in a victim of an apartment building fire. The flexion is caused by heat damage to the tissues. The back of the skull (*arrow*) has been burned away by the intense heat, exposing a thin layer of heat-coagulated blood over the dura mater (*arrow head*). This epidural hematoma is an artifact due to the fire. The loss of the skullcap and the epidural are not evidence of blunt trauma prior to the fire but are the result of the fire. A subdural or subarachnoid hemorrhage found in a fire victim is not an artifact, but is evidence of prior trauma.

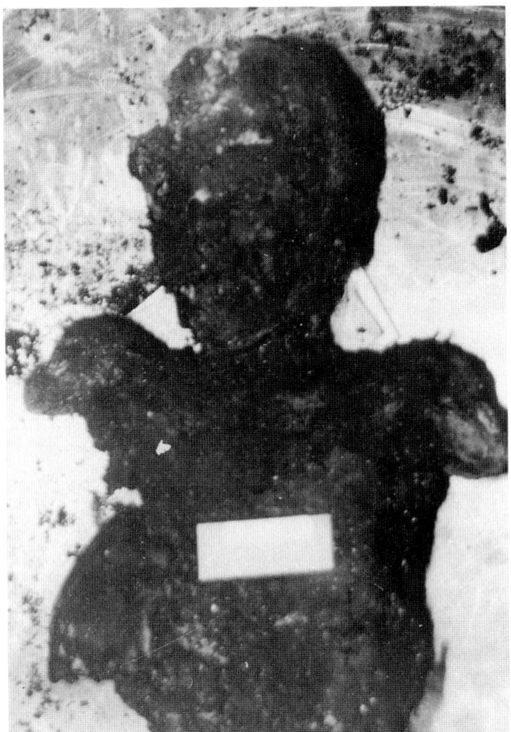

FIGURE 8.5 Five-year-old fire victim. The arms have been burned away leaving only short stumps at the shoulder. The liver is exposed on the right side as the skin, muscle, and rib cage have been completely destroyed. The bodies of infants and small children can be completely consumed in fires. Skin splits are often seen on the bodies of fire victims and are due to the heat.

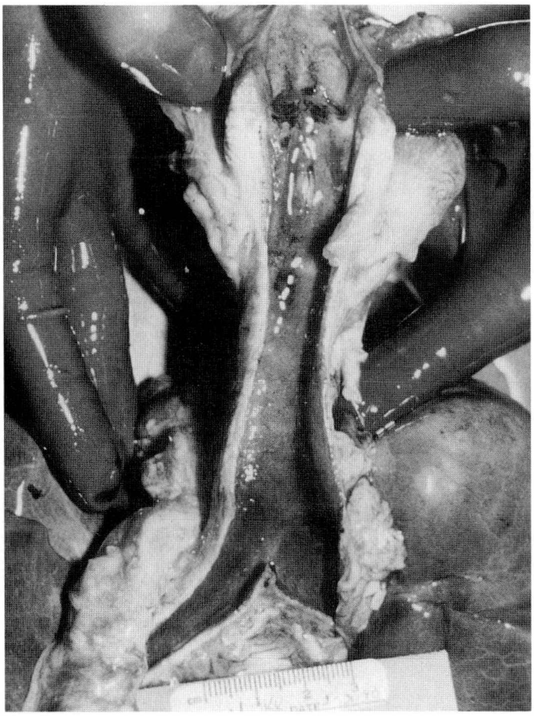

FIGURE 8.6 Small amount of soot and marked hyperemia in the airway due to inhalation of hot gases causing death. Carbon monoxide levels were less than 10% and death was due to the inhalation of the super heated air.

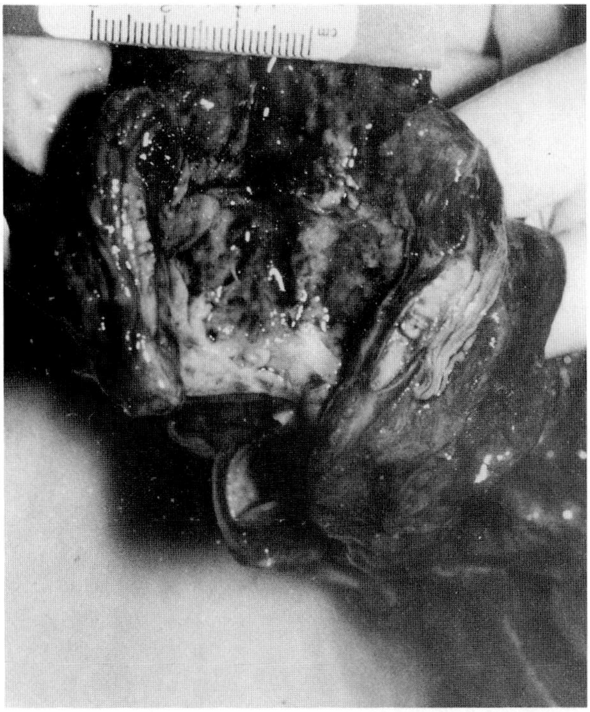

FIGURE 8.7 Severe inflammation and superinfection of the epiglottis and vocal cords following inhalation of smoke and soot in an arson fire. The victim survived for several days following the fire. The death was ruled a homicide.

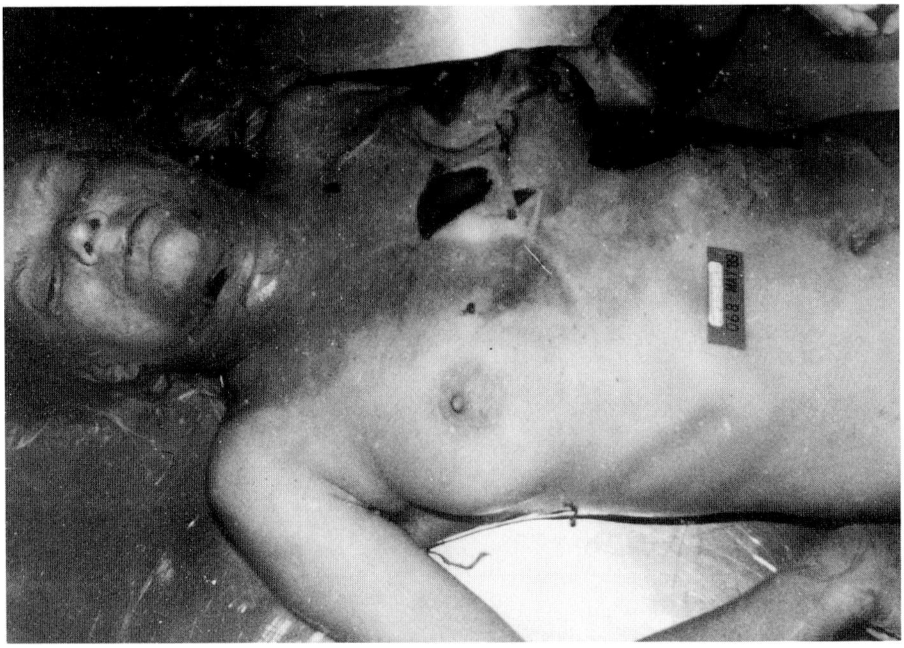

FIGURE 8.8 Scald burns on the body of a 41-year-old woman who suffered from multiple sclerosis. She collapsed into the bathtub while the hot water faucet was still turned on, sustaining partial and focal full-thickness (*arrow*) scald burns.

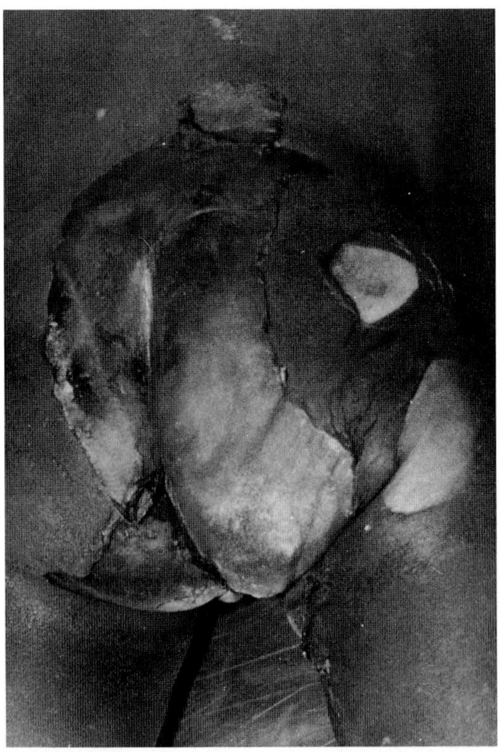

FIGURE 8.9 Full and partial thickness scald burns to the buttocks and the genitalia of a 2-year-old sustained when her mother poured hot water over the area to punish the child for wetting her pants. Immersion burns of the hands, feet, legs, and buttocks are seen in cases of child abuse when the child is forcibly held in hot water. There may be dry burns also found if a hot object, such as an iron, burning cigarette, or curling iron is held against the body.

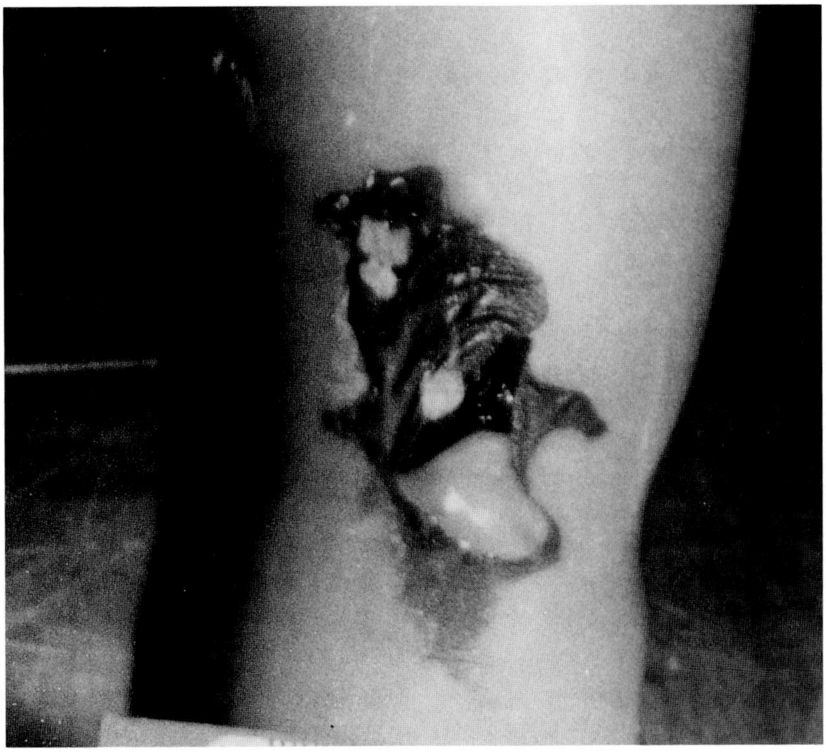

FIGURE 8.10 Chemical burn from sodium bicarbonate which infiltrated the soft tissue around an intravenous catheter.

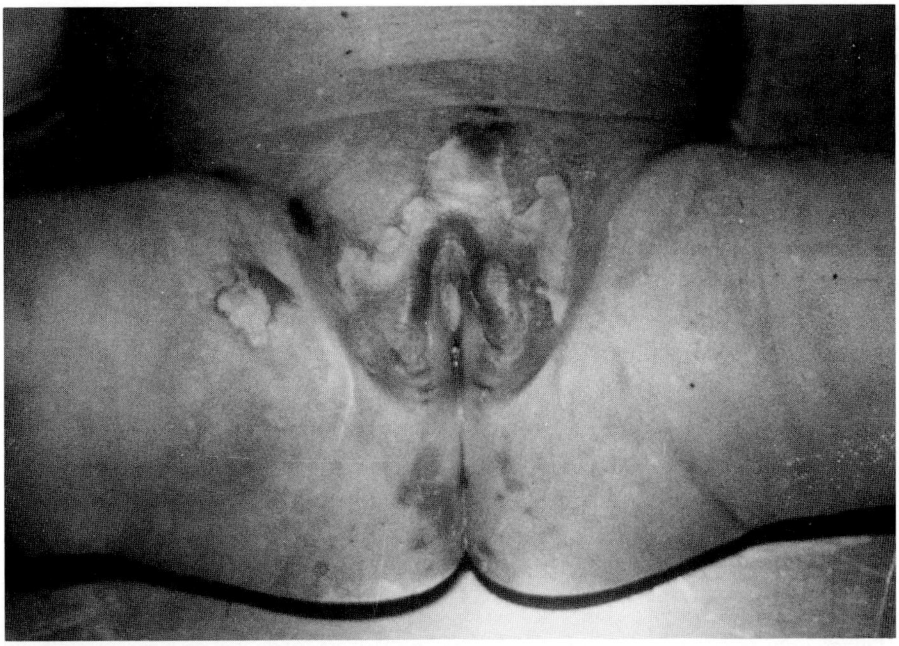

FIGURE 8.11 Postmortem chemical burns from urine which were thought to be antemortem scald burns. There is no reaction around the burns. Note the dark discoloration due to drying of the exposed dermis in the right groin, on the upper labia, and over the mons. Additional chemical burns are present on the right thigh and around the anus.

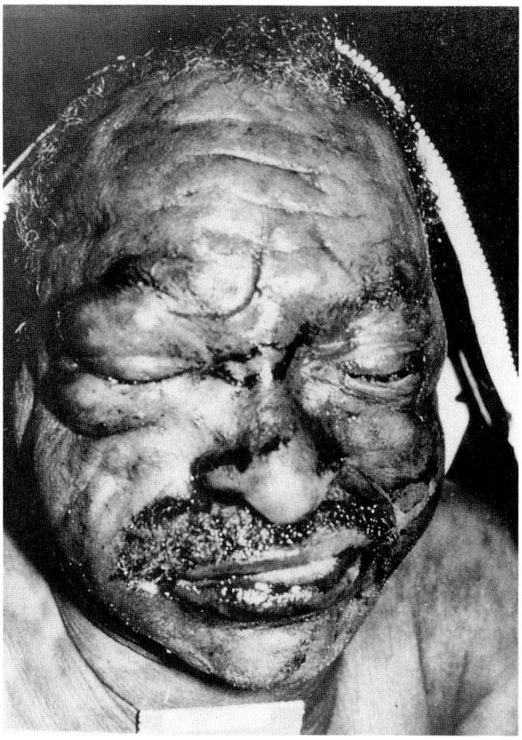

FIGURE 8.12 Elderly victim of hyperthermia in a severe summer heat wave. There are no pathognomonic autopsy findings in deaths due to hyperthermia. This victim had last been seen by neighbors less than 8 hours before the body was found, and the body is already in the early stages of decomposition with gaseous distension of the soft tissues around the eyes and extensive purging.

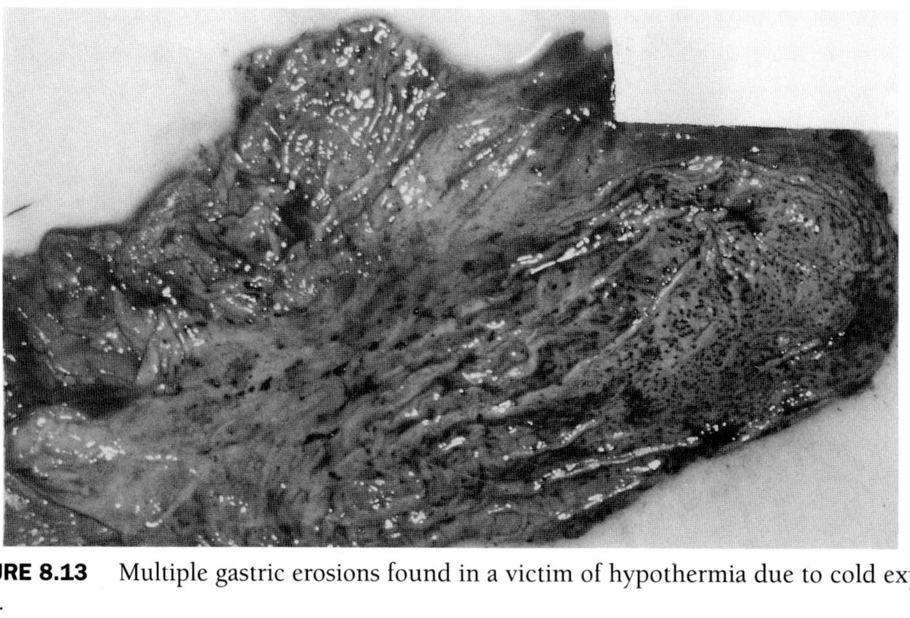

FIGURE 8.13 Multiple gastric erosions found in a victim of hypothermia due to cold exposure.

9

Chemical and Drug Injury

Deaths from recreational and therapeutic drugs result from intentional or unintentional overdose, idiosyncratic allergic reactions such as anaphylaxis, or metabolic sequelae (Table 9.1). Cocaine can cause death from spasms of the coronary arteries, rupture of preexisting cerebral aneurysms, or central nervous system (CNS) hemorrhages due to elevation of blood pressure. Cardiac myocytolysis with fibrosis and small focal aggregates of inflammatory cells in the myocardium can be found on histologic examination of hearts in users of cocaine. These changes can lead to death from cardiac arrhythmia even when cocaine is not present or only present in minute quantities in the blood. There is no well-established fatal level of cocaine as there are for other drugs of abuse (Tables 9.2–9.4).

Ingestion of toxic or caustic substances such as lye, kerosene, or cleaning fluids as a form of suicide is not uncommon. Caustic substance ingestion can lead to rupture of the esophagus or stomach. Perforation of the esophagus and stomach can also occur from the normal autolytic processes that occur following death, and must not be misinterpreted as evidence of a toxic ingestion. Aspiration of these substances into the lungs leads to sloughing of the airway mucosa and hemorrhages within the alveoli. At autopsy, the odor of the gastric contents and the appearance of the gastric mucosa can assist the pathologist in identifying the toxin. Cyanide has an odor of bitter almonds to those who are genetically equipped with the ability to smell cyanide. Cyanide ingestion gives a cherry red hue to the skin of victims and causes a marked hyperemia of the gastric mucosa.

Inhalation of various substances such as cleaning solvents, glue, correction fluid, tape cleaning solutions, or nitrous oxide causes death by actual intoxication or by closed or confined space asphyxia if the fumes are inhaled with a plastic bag over the head or if these chemicals are worked with in small, closed spaces without adequate ventilation. Chemical burns may be seen on the skins of victims overcome by fumes from cleaning solvents in small confined spaces if they collapse into the substance once they are overcome. Paint spatters on the body can also be a clue to a possible inhalation death, as paint thinner is sometimes used recreationally.

Breathing noxious fumes can lead to irritation and hyperemia of the airways with sloughing of the mucosa and lung hemorrhages. Pulmonary edema also occurs from toxic ingestion, especially from opiate use. There may be a "foam cone" found exuding from the mouth and nostrils of victims of opiate intoxication at the time the body is discovered. This same phenomenon occurs in deaths due to drowning and sudden cardiac deaths. The presence of chronic needle track marks, "skin pop" scars, or a fresh needle mark not accounted for in the resuscitation record strongly suggests that the edema is the result of opiate intoxication.

Deaths due to drugs and other toxins require the collection and preservation of proper samples for analysis. Quantitative, not qualitative analysis, is vital and the examining pathologist must ensure that the toxicologic analyses are performed by a qualified, certified forensic laboratory. Collection of the entire gastric contents is mandatory in suspected overdose deaths, as the amount of medication still remaining within the stomach at the time of death can assist the pathologist in determining whether the ingestion was inadvertent or deliberate. It is desirable to have more than one tissue to examine, both to act as quality control and to provide additional drug level information which can be helpful in determining both the cause and manner of death. Tissue from the lung and brain as well as blood can be collected and preserved in head space analysis vials for examination for volatile substances.

Some drugs, such as digoxin, are known to leach from cardiac muscle into the blood and it is recommended that a sample from a peripheral site, such as the femoral artery, be obtained and analyzed. Toxicologic studies can be done on embalmed or decomposed bodies. Alcohol determination is affected by decomposition as alcohol is a product of bacterial and fungal metabolism. Cyanide determination can not be done in embalmed bodies, as cyanides react with the embalming chemicals and can no longer be identified. If toxicologic analysis must be done in an embalmed body, a sample of the embalming compound used should be obtained and analyzed by the laboratory performing the toxicology studies. This is especially important if toxicologic analysis is to be performed on an exhumed body, particularly if one is testing for the heavy metals such as arsenic. In the latter case, it is also important to obtain soil from around the coffin and any water that has seeped into the coffin to test because the heavy metals, such as arsenic, are present in soil and may have contaminated the water that has seeped into the coffin and thereby contaminated the body as well.

Vitreous samples for electrolytes should always be obtained in suspected overdose cases. Dehydration can cause elevated drug levels in the plasma or serum. Also, death due to water intoxication can be diagnosed on the basis of the electrolytes, autopsy findings, and the clinical history. It is important to do histology in all sudden deaths thought to be due to drug intoxication, as the toxicology studies do not always come back with toxic levels. It is also important to remember that some drugs, such as antidepressants or the major tranquilizers, can cause death due to cardiac arrhythmia even at therapeutic levels and the gross and microscopic autopsy will be negative in such cases. Malignant neuroleptic syndrome and other forms of malignant hyperthermia leading to death can occur in individuals on neuroleptic medication or from some anesthetic agents as an idiosyncratic reaction at therapeutic levels.

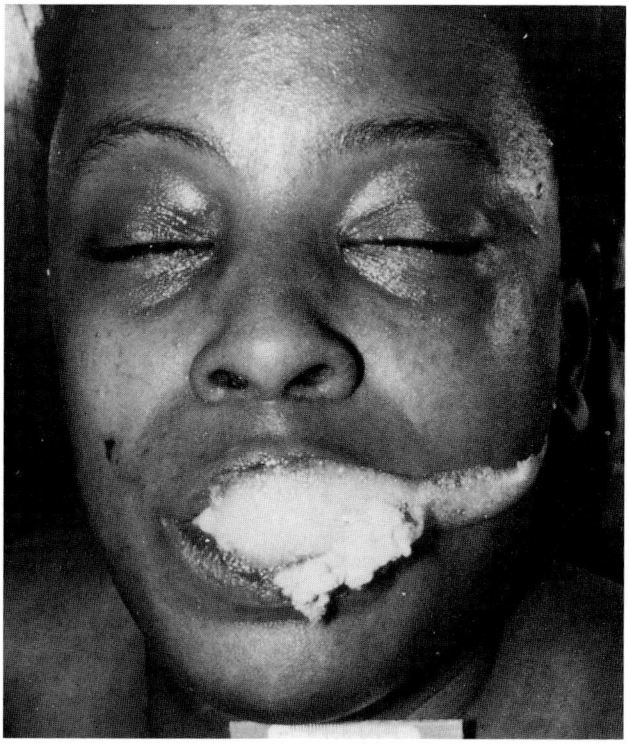

FIGURE 9.1 "Foam cone," a sign of pulmonary edema, in a young woman who died from opiate intoxication. Opiates include heroin, morphine, and codeine.

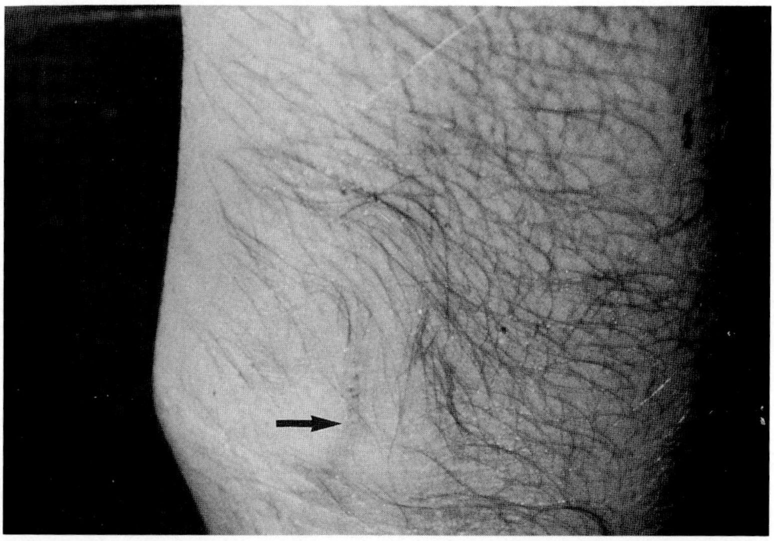

a

FIGURE 9.2a, b Chronic needle track mark scars (*arrow*) in the antecubital fossa. Incision in the area shows scar tissue around the veins, a small hemorrhage from a recent injection, and an abscess. Track marks may be hidden in tattoos on the bodies of addicts, or concealed between the fingers or toes, or in the groin.

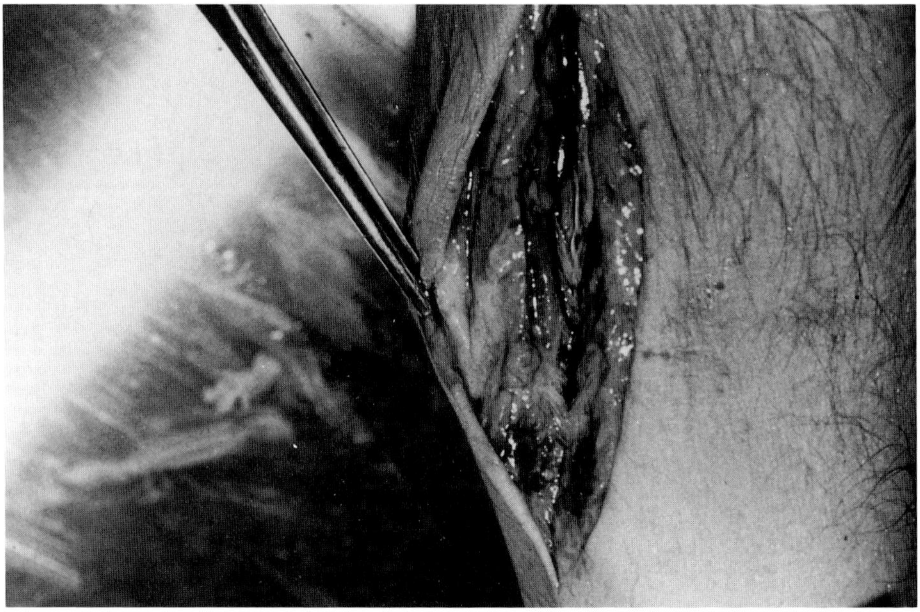

b

FIGURE 9.2 b (continued)

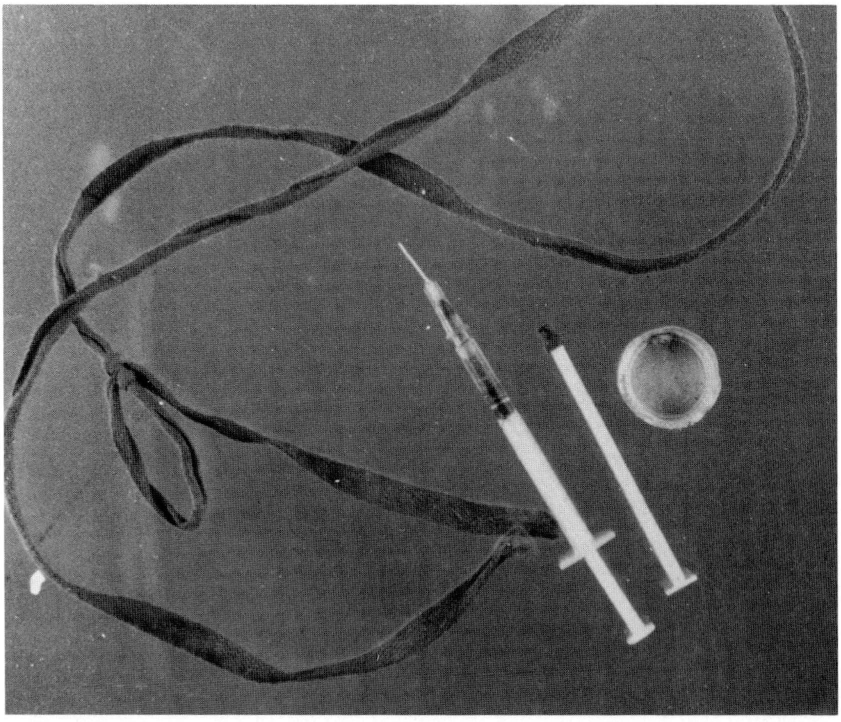

FIGURE 9.3 Shoestring tourniquet, bottle cap for heating and dissolving heroin, needle, syringe, and spare syringe barrel, the "works" found in the pocket of a victim of an acute heroin overdose.

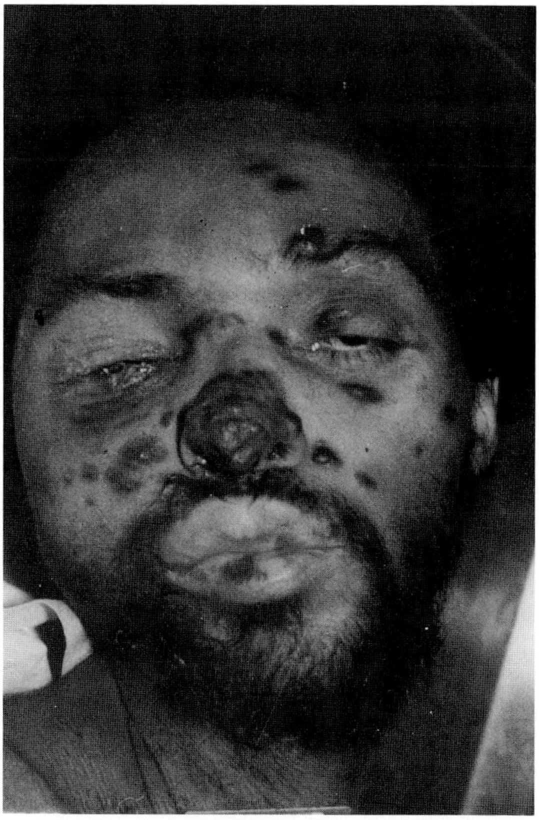

FIGURE 9.4 Kaposi's sarcoma in a young intravenous drug addict who contracted acquired immune deficiency syndrome from sharing needles with other addicts.

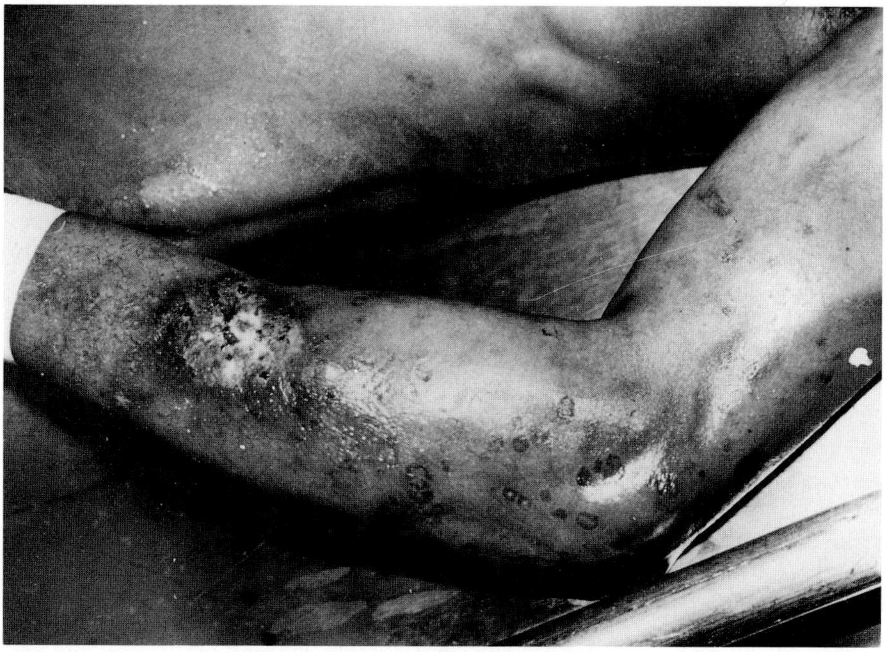

FIGURE 9.5 "Skin pop" scars and a large healed abscess from injecting drugs into the subcutaneous tissues. There were numerous scars on the right arm and on both legs.

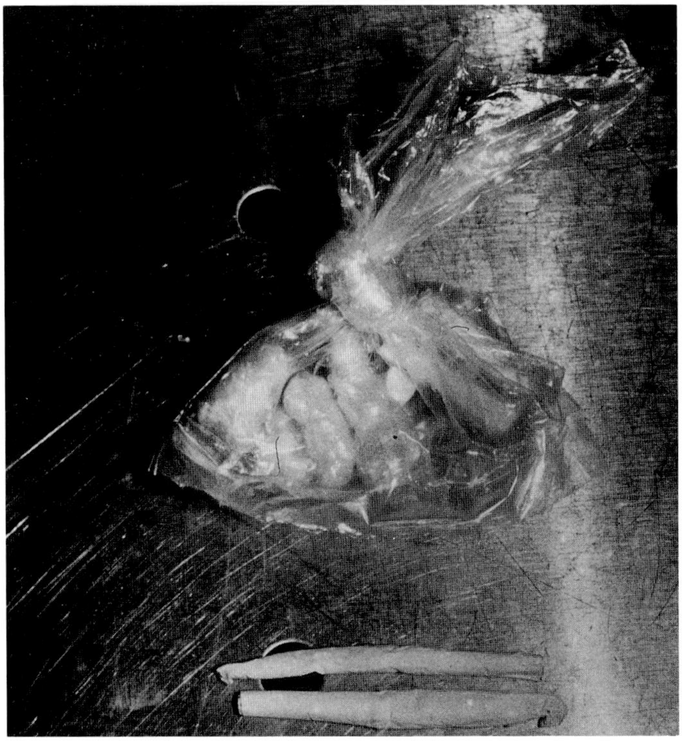

FIGURE 9.6 Plastic bag containing smaller bags of heroin and two marijuana cigarettes recovered from the body of a drug dealer who was shot for trying to deal drugs in someone else's territory.

FIGURE 9.7 Small plastic bag and dollar bill containing cocaine found in the pocket of a victim of cocaine intoxication. Cocaine abusers may also have short segments of plastic drinking straw, small spoons, or glass or metal crack pipes in their possession.

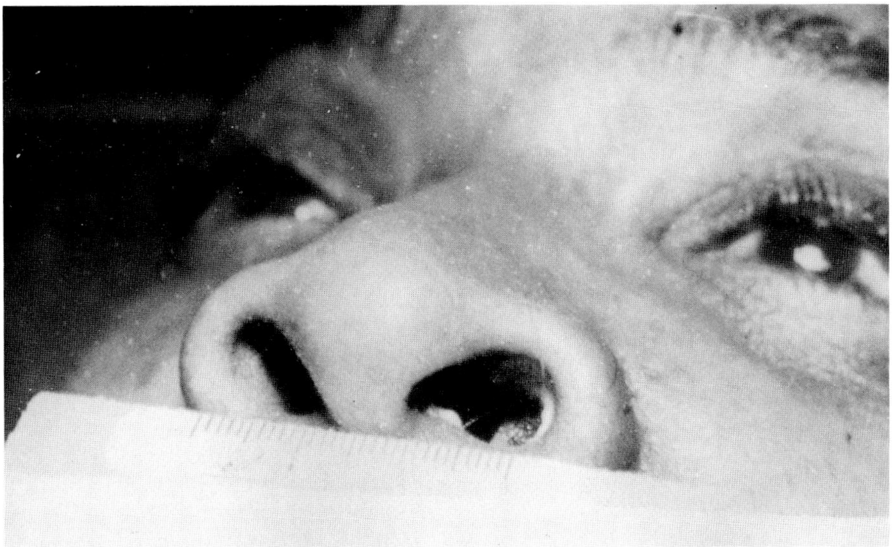

FIGURE 9.8 Cocaine found in the nostril of an overdose victim. Swabs can be taken of the powder which can then be tested to confirm that it is indeed cocaine. Cocaine is known to cause perforations of the nasal septum from chronic long-term abuse. Cocaine is a vasoconstrictor leading to tissue ischemia and necrosis.

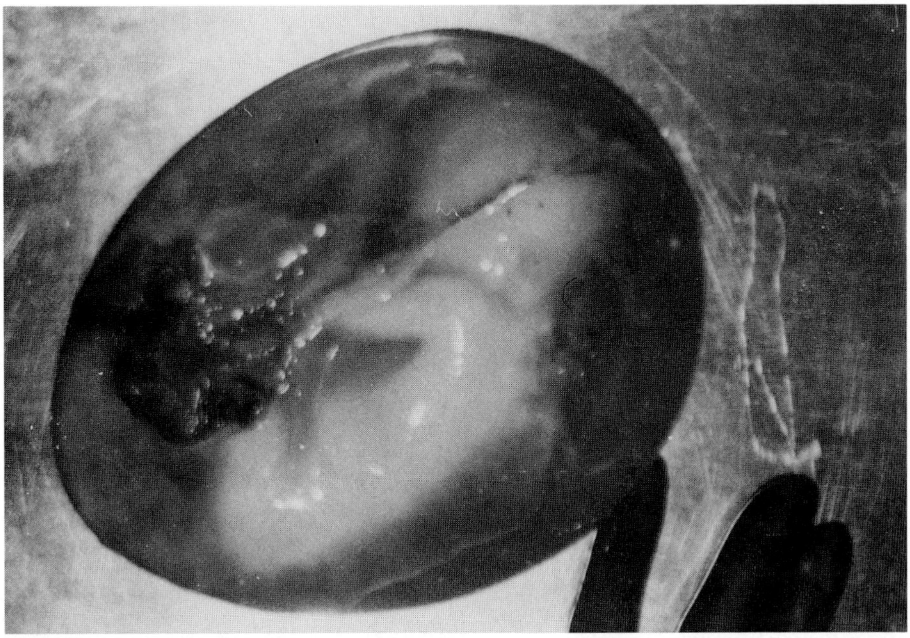

FIGURE 9.9 One of the youngest victims of drug abuse. This 4- to 5-month gestation fetus was expelled precipitously from the mother's uterus while she was high on cocaine. Testing of the amniotic fluid and fetal blood showed cocaine and the metabolite, benzylecgonine. Cocaine metabolism in the fetus is slower than that in the mother.

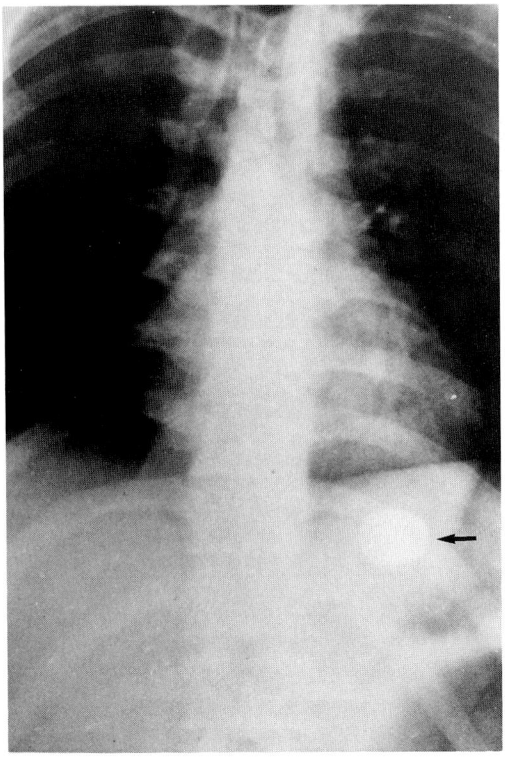

FIGURE 9.10 Radiograph of the chest of a young man arrested for drug dealing who was found unresponsive in the police lockup. Only marijuana was found in his possession at the time of arrest. An interview with the occupant of the cell next to the victim indicated that the victim had seizures prior to becoming unresponsive. There are two round radiopaque objects (*arrow*) in his stomach.

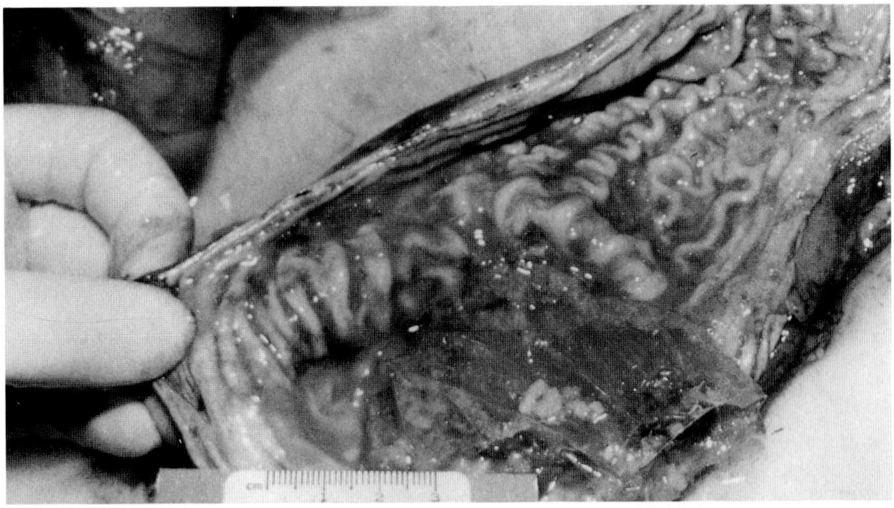

FIGURE 9.11 Stomach of the young man described in Figure 9.10. An open plastic bag was found in addition to one penny and one dime. Toxicology studies were positive for cocaine. The young man had apparently grabbed and swallowed a bag of cocaine which was in his pocket at the time he was arrested. This behavior is referred to as "body stuffing" as opposed to "body packing" which is the transport of drugs in small packages that are swallowed in one place and then defecated out in another place. An occasional "body packer" is found dead from an overdose when one or more of the packets ruptures while in the stomach or intestine.

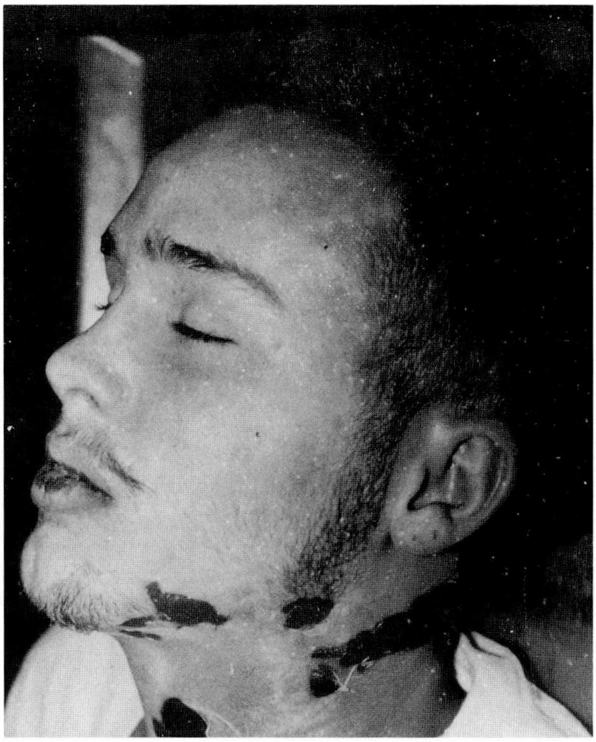

FIGURE 9.12 Young man found dead in his apartment with a plastic bag over his head. The dark areas on the neck are blisters which have ruptured and dried. The cause of the blisters is unclear. He had been inhaling aerosolized tape cleaner which contained a fluorocarbon as the propellant. The mechanism of death in this type of case can be due to intoxication with the toxic substance inhaled, hypercapnia due to passing out and rebreathing the air in the bag, or asphyxia due to the exclusion of oxygen by the plastic bag. In this case, the victim had high levels of 1,1,2-trichloro-1,2,2-trifluoroethane found in his blood and organs.

FIGURE 9.13 Can of tape cleaning fluid recovered from the home of the victim described in Figure 9.12.

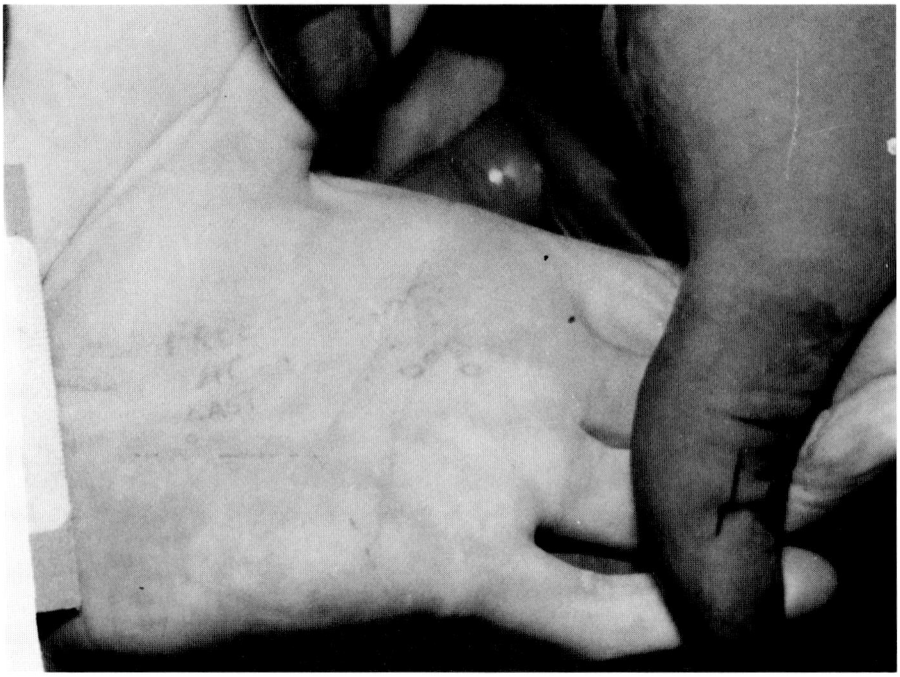

FIGURE 9.14 Suicide note written on the hand in an intentional overdose which reads "free at last" and "LETGO
E O
T D."
The mouth, hands, tongue, and gastrointestinal tract should be examined for discoloration from the dyes used in coloring medication which can occur in drug overdose.

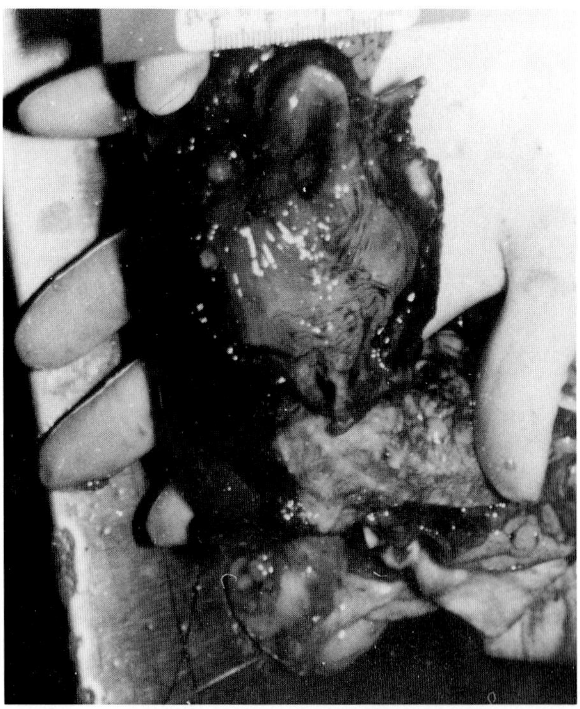

FIGURE 9.15 Death due to anaphylactic reaction to ampicillin. The victim was known to be allergic to penicillin. He took two or three doses of his girlfriend's ampicillin when he developed a sore throat. There is massive edema of the epiglottis and soft tissues of the larynx with near total blockage of the airway.

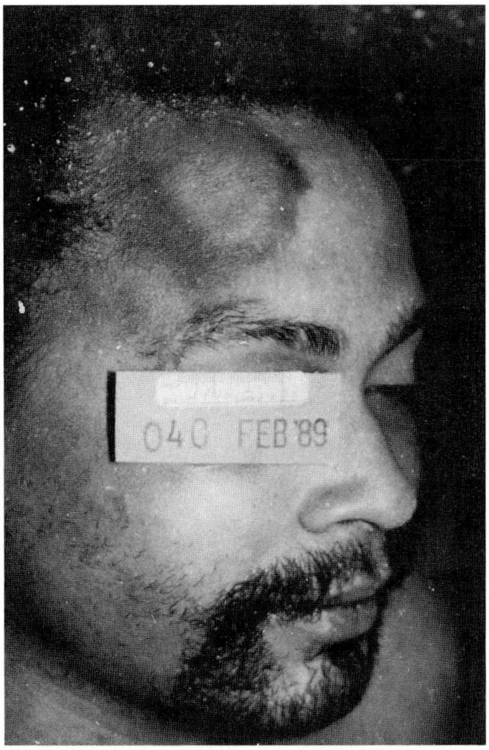

FIGURE 9.16 Chemical burn due to methylene chloride found on a young man who collapsed while using an industrial floor stripper in a small bathroom with inadequate ventilation. The victim and his companion were wearing dust masks instead of chemical masks or self-contained breathing units. Work-related deaths, such as this, require that the Occupational Safety and Health Administration (OSHA) be notified.

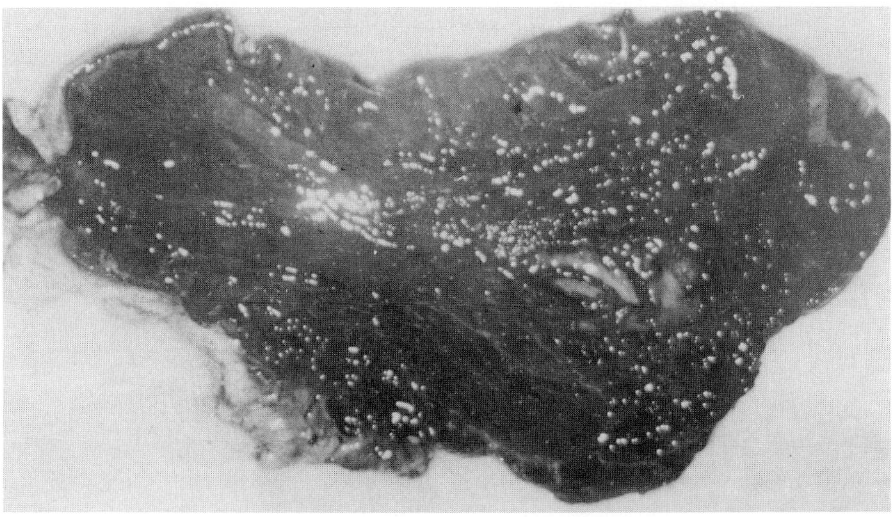

FIGURE 9.17 Congestion and hemorrhage in the stomach mucosa of an elderly woman who committed suicide by drinking a corrosive substance.

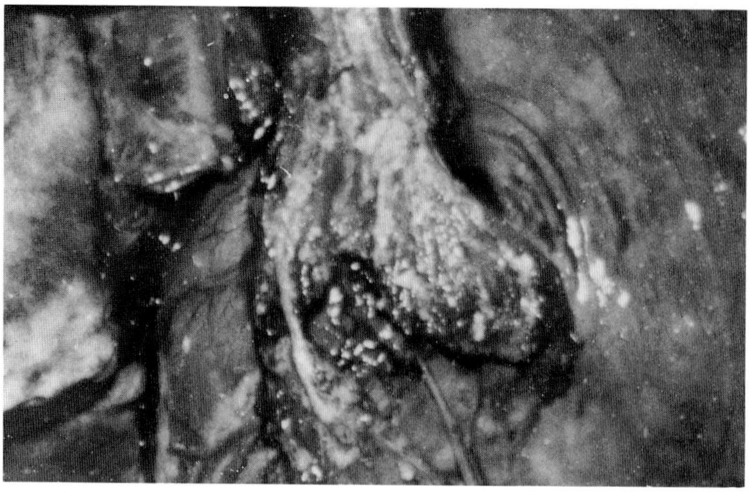

a

FIGURE 9.18a A close-up view of a ruptured esophagus found during autopsy examination of a young man who drank a combination of kerosene and hydrofluoric acid. The kerosene and acid were found within the left pleural cavity.

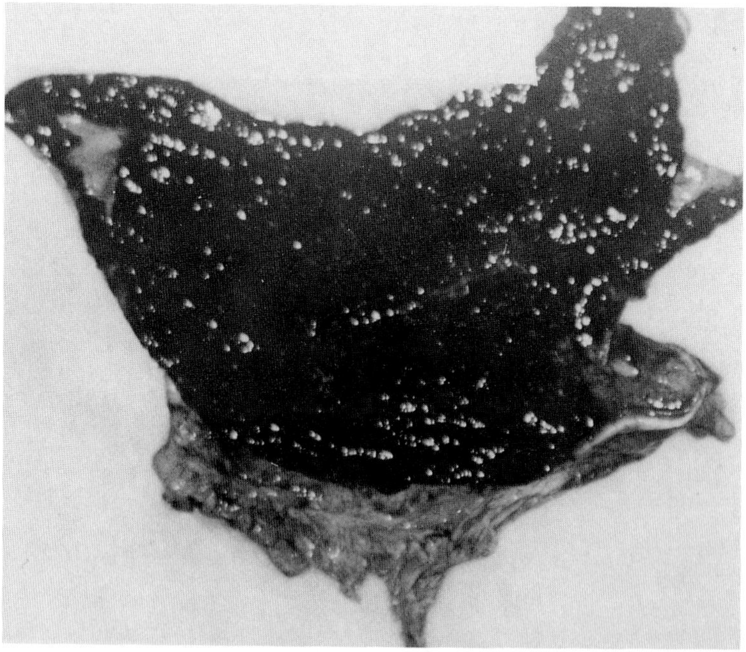

b

FIGURE 9.18b The stomach mucosa of the victim described in Figure 9.18 a was black and edematous. The color change of the mucosa is the result of the chemical ingestion. In cases of toxic ingestion where the victim survives long enough to receive medical treatment, one may find charcoal in the stomach and intestines, coating the mucosa and making it appear black.

10

Environmental Injury

Weather-related injuries are more common than may be realized. Hypothermia due to cold exposure and hyperthermia due to heat waves and times of high humidity, where sweating becomes an ineffective cooling mechanism because of the humidity preventing evaporation of the sweat, have already been discussed. There is also an increase in electrocution deaths in warm weather, possibly due to sweating, which decreases the skin's resistance, or to wearing less protective clothing or footwear. Tornadoes, cyclones and other violent wind storms cause numerous blunt trauma injuries due to collapsed buildings, uprooted trees, debris blown around by the winds, and electrocution because of downed power lines. Flooding causes deaths by drowning, hypothermia, and blunt trauma from debris carried along by the water, and also by the kinetic energy contained in rushing water itself. In cold weather regions, the number of traffic accidents increases with the onset of winter with its ice storms and snow falls causing poor road conditions. In other areas, fog reduces visibility leading to multivehicle chain reaction collisions.

High-altitude sickness occurs due to rapid ascent to elevations above 10,000 feet, not allowing the body to acclimatize to the lower oxygen pressures found at these elevations. The disease is not usually fatal, but two forms, high-altitude pulmonary edema and high-altitude cerebral edema, can be fatal. There are no specific anatomic findings, but autopsy may reveal petechiae, splinter hemorrhages under the fingernails, retinal hemorrhages, cerebral and pulmonary edema, with platelet and fibrin thrombi in the lung and brain on histologic examination.

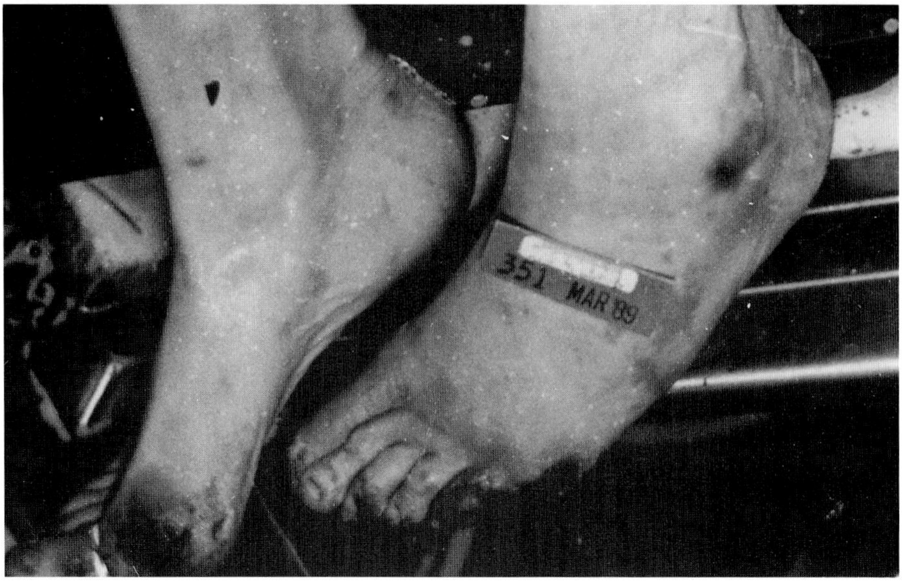

FIGURE 10.1 Homeless man found dead on his mattress on the street. Frostbite damage was found on both feet as seen here. Death was due to hypothermia from cold exposure. The autopsy revealed small hemorrhages in and around the pancreas.

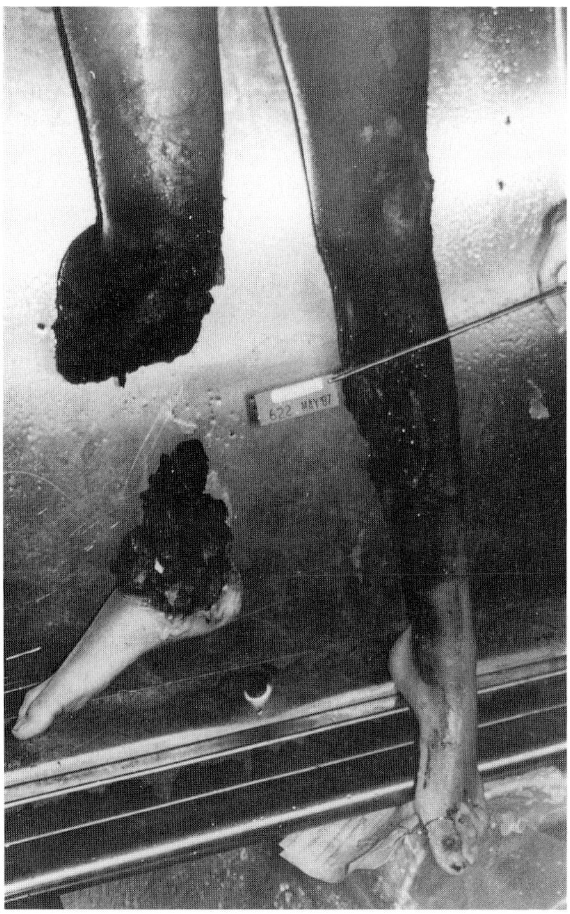

FIGURE 10.2 Severe burns and amputation due to contact with a high-tension power line downed during a severe thunderstorm with high winds.

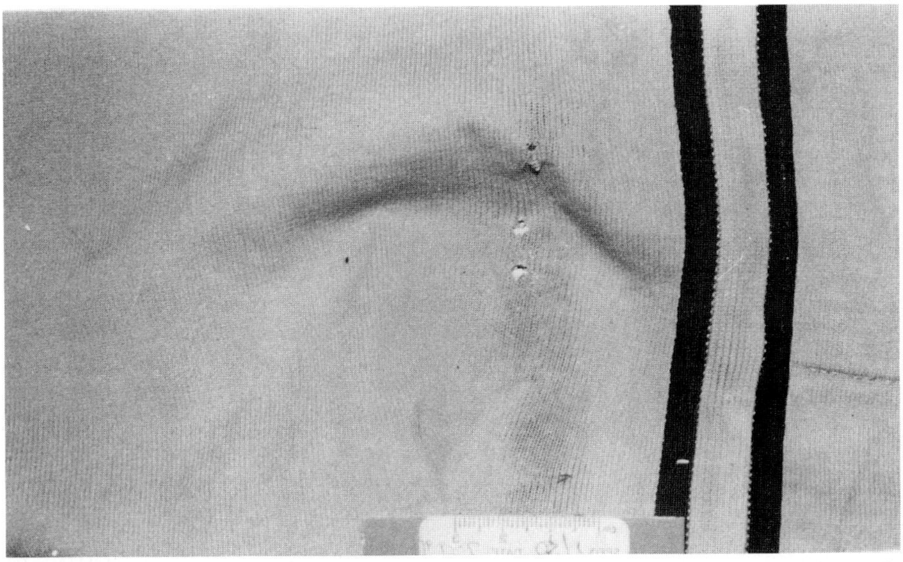

FIGURE 10.3 Uniform of a high school baseball team pitcher who was struck by a bolt of lightning while leaving the field when an electrical storm suddenly blew up. The uniform shows small holes from the electricity exiting the body.

11

Electrical Injury

LOW-VOLTAGE VS HIGH-VOLTAGE

Electrical burns vary in appearance depending on the current, time of exposure, and the resistance of the skin at the area of contact. Death may occur from disruption of neural pathways without marks found on the body surface. This is especially common in low-voltage electrocutions from household current, or from alternating current which is particularly arrhythmogenic. Electrical burns can be crater-like with central charring, blistering, and an erythematous border or may have the appearance of an abrasion or second- or third-degree burn. High-voltage contact results in deep thermal injury with loss of the epidermis and dermis with exposure of deeper soft tissue and muscle. Histologic examination shows nuclear streaming, blister formation, and coagulative changes.

LIGHTNING

Lightning strikes can cause death or only minor injury, depending on the path taken by the bolt through the body. In some instances, the bolt of lightning only flashes over the victim, causing damage or disruption of the clothing and leaving the person untouched. Injuries caused by lightning strikes can be very subtle, with death due to the disruption of normal nerve impulses and only small areas of singed hair found on the surface of the body. At other times, there may be extensive injury on the outside of the body, and sufficient heat from the bolt's passage to fracture bone, rupture organs, or actually char the internal structures (Table 11.1).

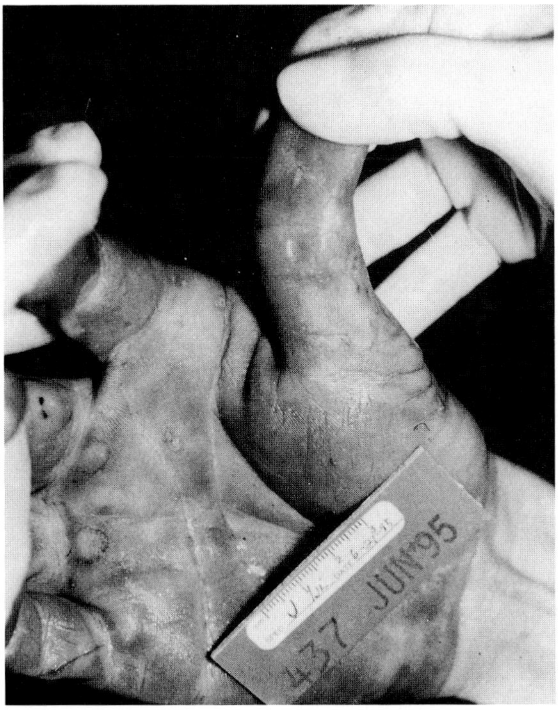

FIGURE 11.1 Low-voltage, household current, electrical burns to the right thumb. The burns appear as small white blisters.

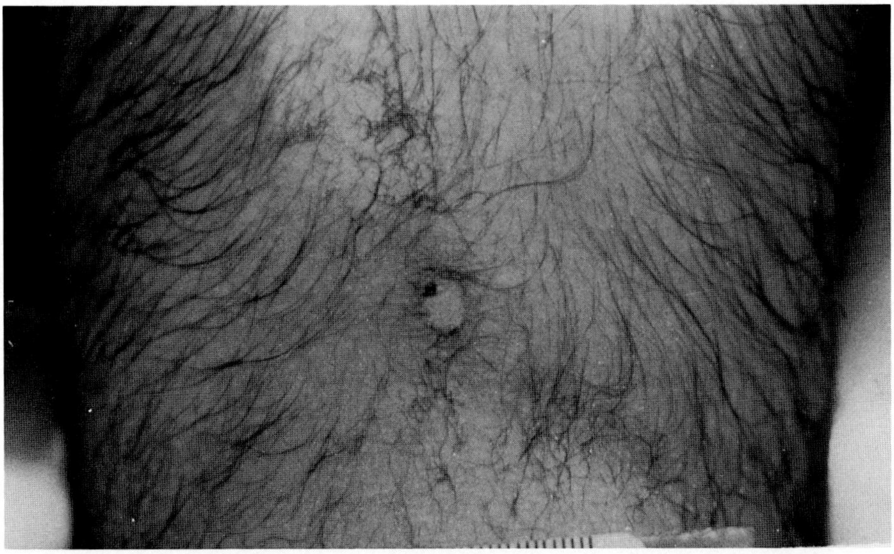

FIGURE 11.2 Electrical burns on the leg of an aluminum siding installer whose ladder came in contact with overhead power lines. There is singed hair and a small superficial burn where the victim's leg was in contact with the aluminum ladder rungs. The victim also sustained massive head injury when he fell from the ladder.

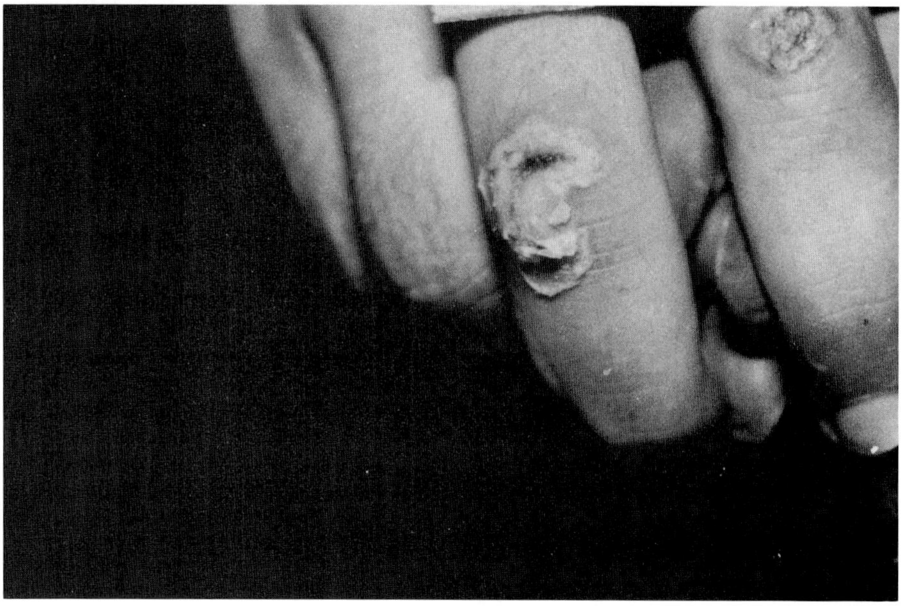

FIGURE 11.3 Crater-like electrical burns on the fingers showing a blister which is focally charred and a fine rim of erythema around the blister.

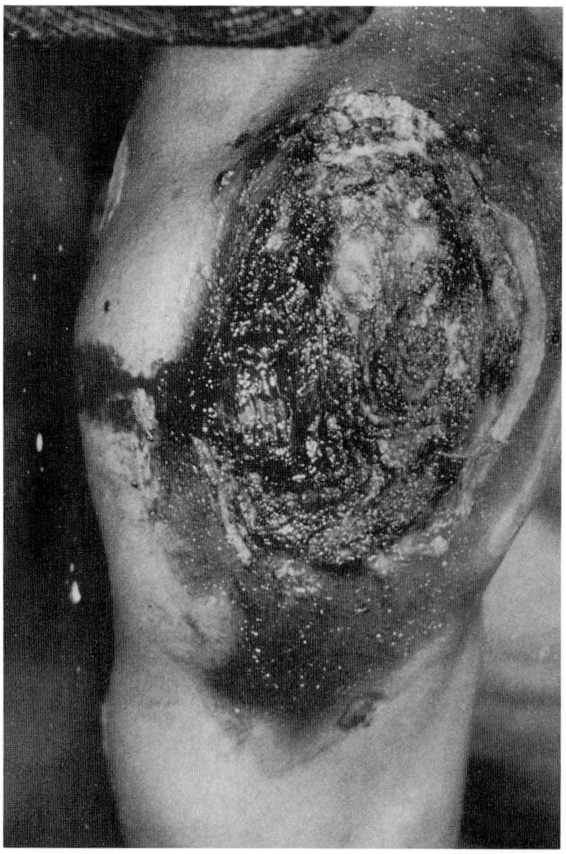

FIGURE 11.4 Severe electrical burn caused by a fall onto the electrified third rail of an urban mass transit subway system. Third-rail electrocution is usually due to physical contact with the rail. There have been cases of individuals being electrocuted while urinating on the rails as urine is an excellent conductor of electricity. The author is personally acquainted with the family of one such victim.

FIGURE 11.5 Exit hole from electricity (*arrow*) found in the shoe of a road construction worker who was electrocuted when the metal pole of the darby he was using to smooth the concrete paving came in contact with the overhead power lines. The electrical current traveled through his hands, down through his body and out his feet. The clothing of electrocution victims should always be closely examined for burns and holes.

FIGURE 11.6 Burns on the metal casing of a window air conditioner. It was a reconditioned unit and testing revealed that the casing became electrified whenever the compressor was running, but was not electrified when only the fan was running. A young man was electrocuted while turning the unit on while his hands were wet and he was in contact with a metal radiator. The victim had been injured in a construction accident 2 days before his death, and the death was thought due to the head injury he had sustained. Electrocution was not considered because the unit was operating at the time the body was found. Electrical burns were found during the external examination, the family was called immediately and told not to touch the air conditioner. It was then removed from the home and sent to an engineering firm to be tested. The unit was not returned to the owner.

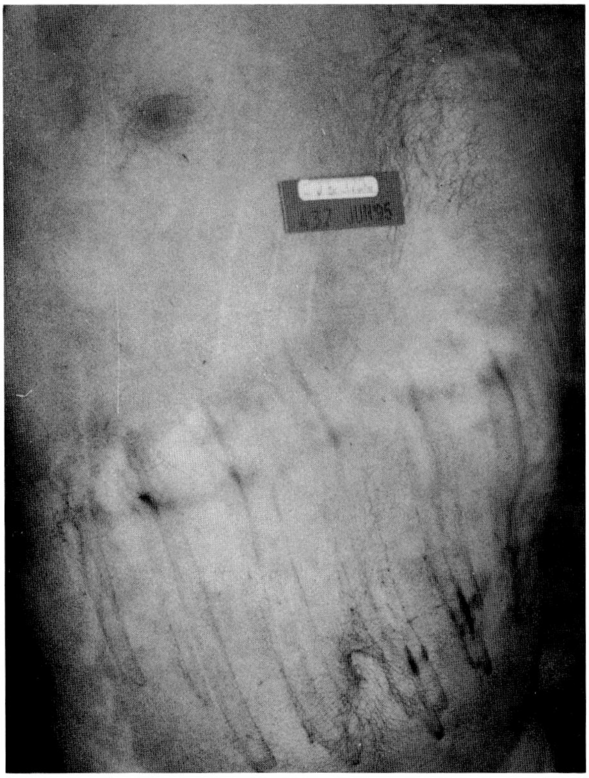

FIGURE 11.7 Patterned burns on the abdomen of the victim described in Figure 11.6 due to contact with the metal radiator.

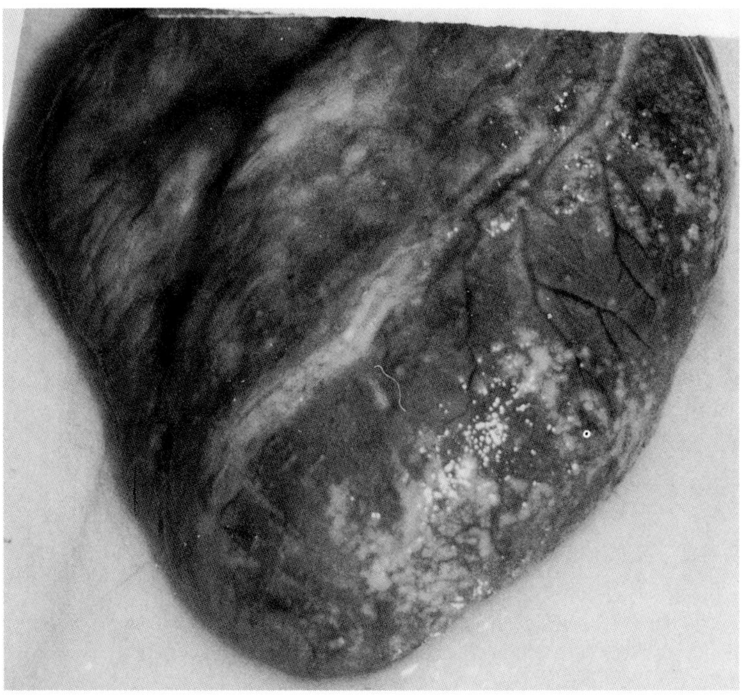

FIGURE 11.8 Heart from a 32-year-old African-American male who had suffered a mild electrical shock at work about 2 months before his death. While undergoing a routine physical examination the day he received the shock, he was told by the examining physician that he had suffered cardiac fibrosis from the electrical injury on the basis of an abnormal electrocardiogram. He was found dead in bed by his young son and there was concern that the death was due to delayed effects of the electrical injury. Autopsy revealed sarcoidosis of the heart and lungs and no evidence of any injury to the body.

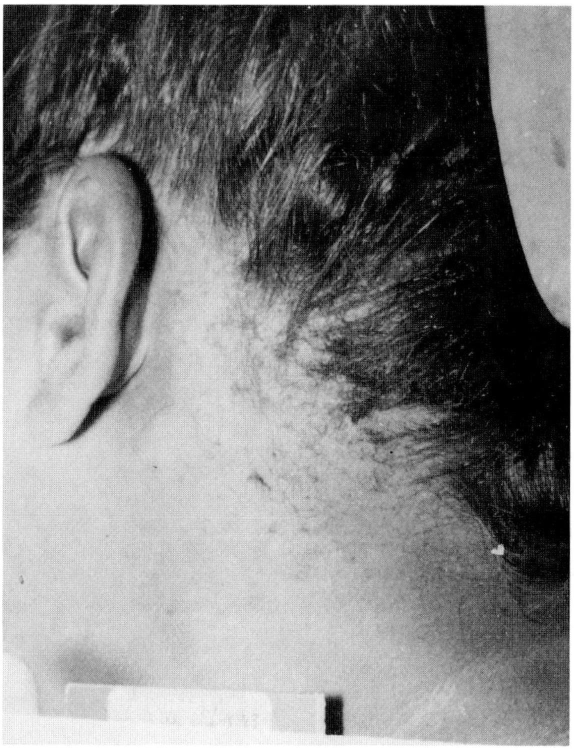

FIGURE 11.9 Singed hair at the entrance site of a lightning bolt which killed this young woman who was attending an outdoor prayer meeting. There was a similar patch of singed hair in the left pubic region and melting of the nylon panties she was wearing. No other marks were found on the body.

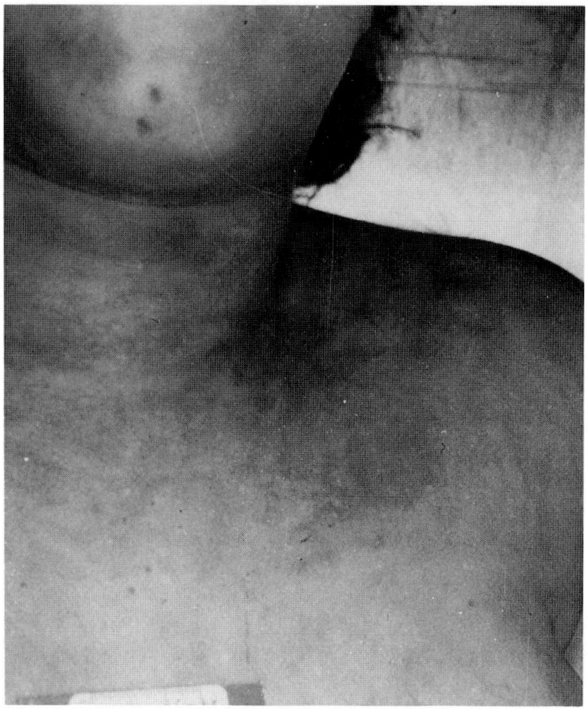

FIGURE 11.10 Dendritic pattern of erythema on the shoulder of a woman struck by lightning.

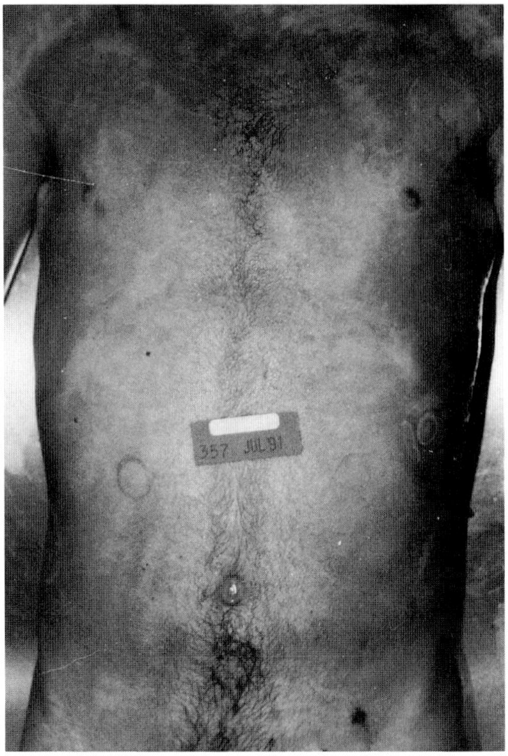

FIGURE 11.11 Singed chest and pubic hair and small electrical burns in the left lower quadrant of the abdomen due to lightning.

12

Postmortem Artifacts

EARLY POSTMORTEM PERIOD

Rigor mortis, the stiffening of muscle following death, is a chemical change that occurs in all muscles of the body over time, resulting from postmortem reduction in adenosine 5′-triphosphate (ATP) levels. Rigor can appear in a very short period of time or may never occur in some individuals. Determination of time of death using rigor as a guide is difficult at best. The formation of rigor in the small muscles in the hair follicles produces "goose bumps" on the skin which can be most clearly seen on the skin of the thighs in the early postmortem period. This is not a sign of cold exposure.

Livor mortis, the pooling of blood within the dependent portions of the body, has a somewhat blotchy appearance in the early stages. Small, irregular, purple-red or red areas of lividity can be seen on the nondependent areas of the body as well as in the dependent areas. These blotches can sometimes be misinterpreted as bruising if one is unfamiliar with this phenomenon. If a body is prone or the head is dangling for a period of time, postmortem scleral hemorrhages may form, which must not be confused with evidence of asphyxia.

Purging, the release of blood-stained fluids from the mouth, nose, or other body orifices, is most commonly seen during the later postmortem period. In some individuals, this can occur very early, especially from the nose and mouth where blood-tinged fluids from the lungs escape through the airways. This is seen most often in infants, and is commonly described in crib death. It is not evidence of asphyxia or abuse. Drying of the skin of the scrotum, which has the appearance of an antemortem abrasion, occurs in the early postmortem period.

Chemical burns from a urine- or feces-filled diaper can occur in infants and toddlers, leaving blisters on the genitals and buttocks which resemble scald burns. The anal sphincter muscle can relax in death in all age groups, resulting in a lax open anus. Cleaning the area by emergency medical personnel during resuscitation can cause the anus to gape more. Care must be taken not to misinterpret this as evidence of sexual abuse.

DECOMPOSITION CHANGE

As decomposition begins to occur, the amount of purge increases, with accumulation of large amounts of blood-tinged fluids about the body. It is not uncommon for forensic pathologists to be called to the scene of what is thought to be a homicide, only to find large pools of tissue fluids around the body due to the onset of putrefaction. Telephone calls from family members convinced their loved one was murdered are also common in such cases. The discoloration of the body due to the release of pigmented products of bacterial metabolism can be misidentified as bruising. Dark discoloration of the face, with gaseous distention of the tongue and the globes of the eyes, can lead to misinterpretation of strangulation. Knowledge of the position of the body at the scene is helpful, as there may be postmortem swelling and discoloration, due to blood accumulation, of the soft tissue around the eyes or in other parts, if the body has been in a prone position or if portions of the body have been dangling, such as over the edge of the bed. Internal organs, the undersurface of the scalp, and the linings of the body cavities can be stained with the products of hemolysis. The dependent portions of the body, where blood pooled (lividity), frequently show such discoloration. It is important to be aware that decomposition changes can occur at different rates in different parts of the body, so that one area may be darkly discolored and bloated and other areas may be intact. Flies will lay eggs near body orifices within minutes of death. The eggs will hatch into the larva, maggots, usually within 24 hours. The maggots create holes as they feed and can skeletalize a body completely. Flies will also lay eggs next to injury sites on the body where blood is found. The developing maggots will feed in these areas, making it difficult to interpret the injury.

INSECT, RODENT, AND LARGE ANIMAL INJURY

Roach bites are small, bland orange or red areas where the keratin layer has been eaten away, usually found around the eyes, mouth, and nose. Roaches will begin to feed on the skin in the immediate postmortem period and these bite marks are often misinterpreted as antemortem abrasions. Other insects, such as ants, can leave similar markings on the body. Similarly, rodents such as mice or rats leave injuries on the body from their feeding activities. Larger animals, such as dogs or cats, leave larger injuries on the body and can completely skeletalize the hands or feet. Examination of the ends of exposed bones will frequently reveal small triangular-shaped defects left by the teeth. Bodies found outdoors have similar defects caused by wild predators. Portions of the body may be dragged off by predators, leaving a partially dismembered body to be examined.

Autopsy examinations of embalmed human remains are sometimes done. There are injuries to the surface of the body caused by embalming, such as trocar holes and abrasions that occur from moving the body after death which must be recognized. Also, the use of the trocar to remove fluids from the chest and abdominal organs causes lacerations of the organs which must not be misinterpreted as antemortem injury nor should any antemortem injury be written off as the result of embalming. Autopsies are always best done on the recently dead, unembalmed body.

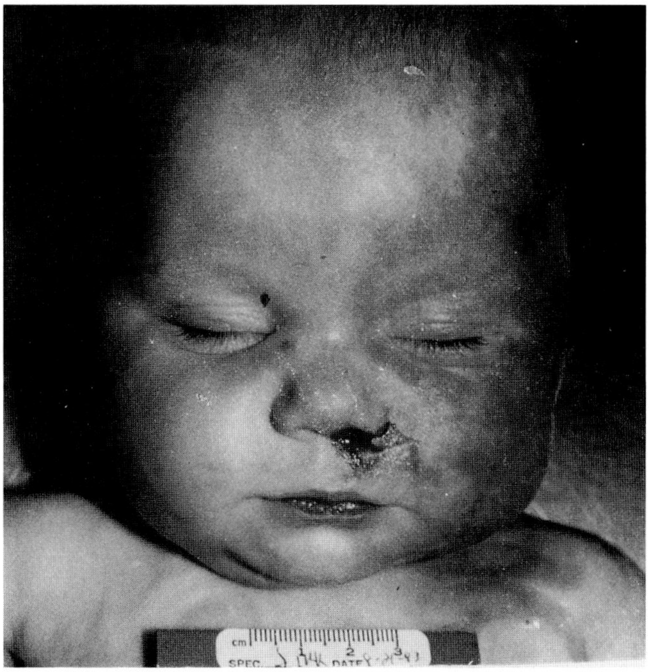

FIGURE 12.1 Young victim of sudden infant death syndrome showing commonly described bloody purge from the left nostril. The discoloration on the left side of the face and chest is livor mortis, also known as lividity or hypostasis.

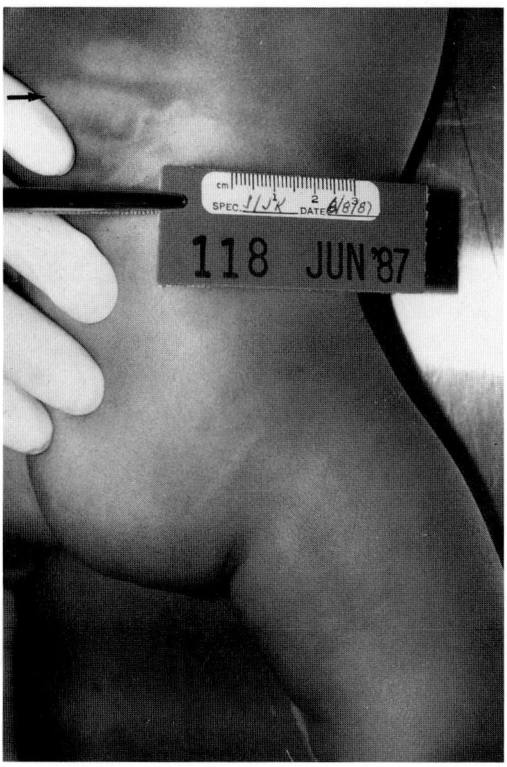

a

FIGURE 12.2a Lividity begins to form immediately upon cessation of heartbeat. It becomes visible over time, depending on factors such as blood volume and skin tones. The lividity on this infant is non-fixed, that is, blanching of the area occurred when pressure was applied with the fingers (*arrow*). This indicates that death probably occurred less than 6 to 8 hours before the examination. (A faint mongolian spot, a blue-black birthmark common in African-American, Hispanic, and Oriental infants, is noted on the right lower buttock area.)

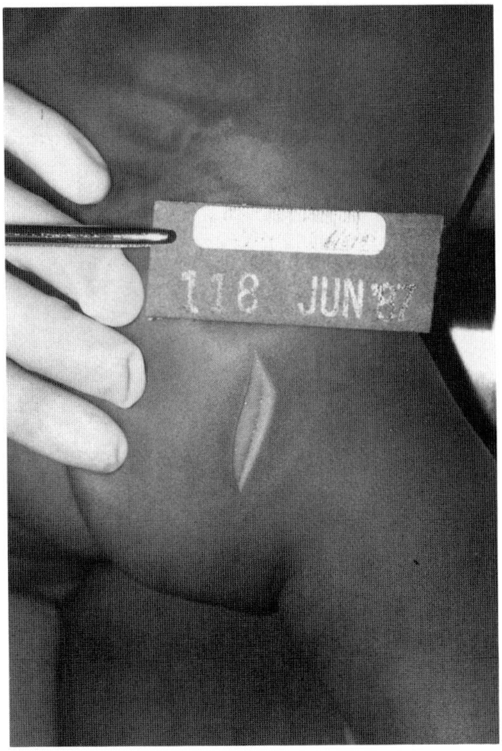

b

FIGURE 12.2b An incision is made through the mongolian spot to show the absence of underlying hemorrhage. Mongolian spots are frequently misidentified as bruises by inexperienced police investigators, emergency room personnel, and pathologists, leading to false allegations of child abuse.

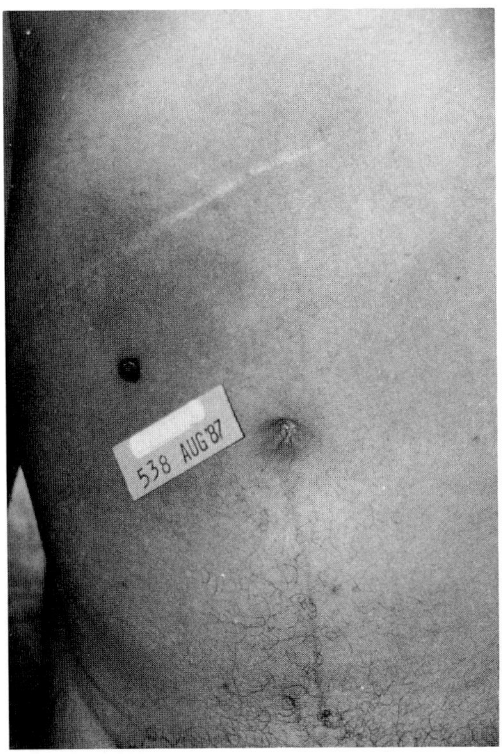

FIGURE 12.3 Trocar wound to the right upper quadrant of the abdomen in an embalmed body with striking resemblance to distant gunshot wound of entry. There is a round central defect with collar of abrasion.

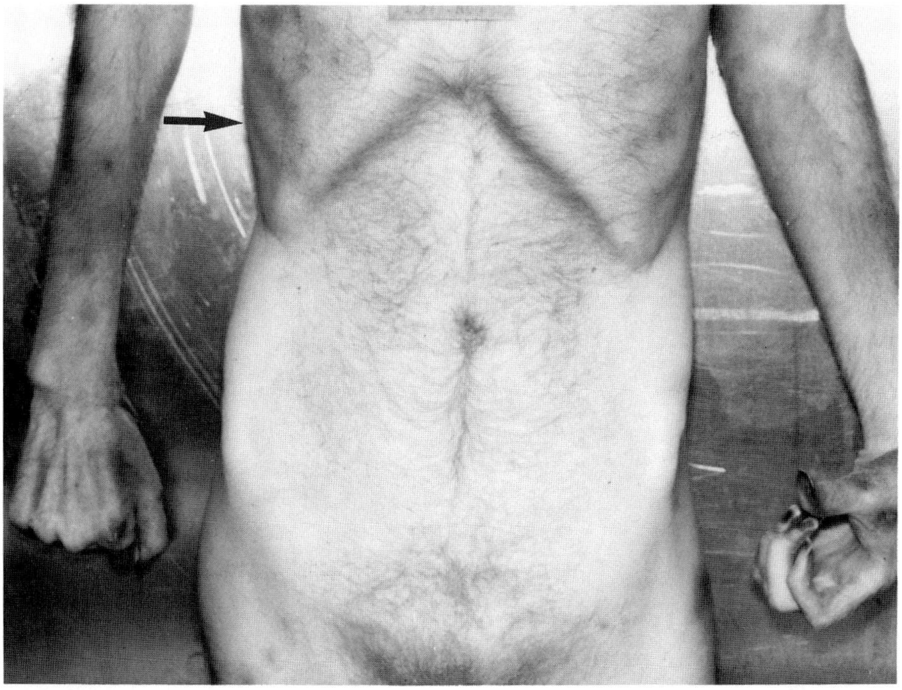

FIGURE 12.4 One of the early signs of decomposition is greenish discoloration of the skin of the abdomen and lower chest which can be mistaken for bruising by individuals unfamiliar with this phenomenon. Small patches of drying artifact, early mummification seen in these same areas resemble abrasions (*arrow*). Note the mummification of the hands.

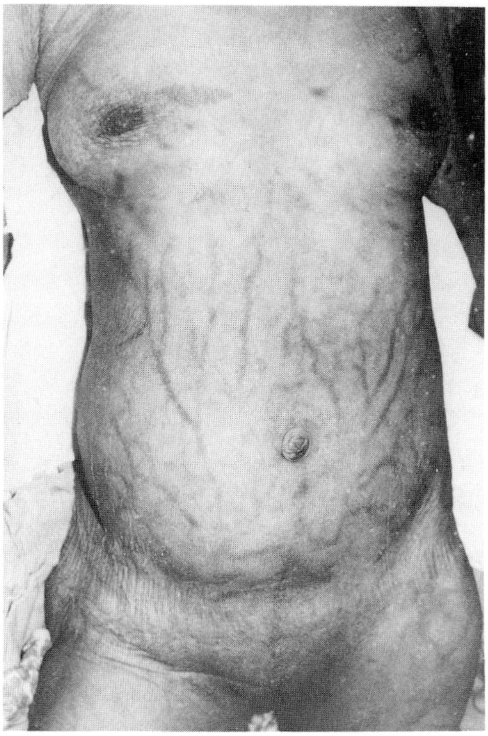

FIGURE 12.5 As decomposition progresses, the abdomen becomes distended by gases forming within the gastrointestinal system due to bacterial action. The red cells within the blood vessels begin to lyse and stain the endothelial surface leaving an arborizing vascular pattern which can be seen through the skin. This is called marbling.

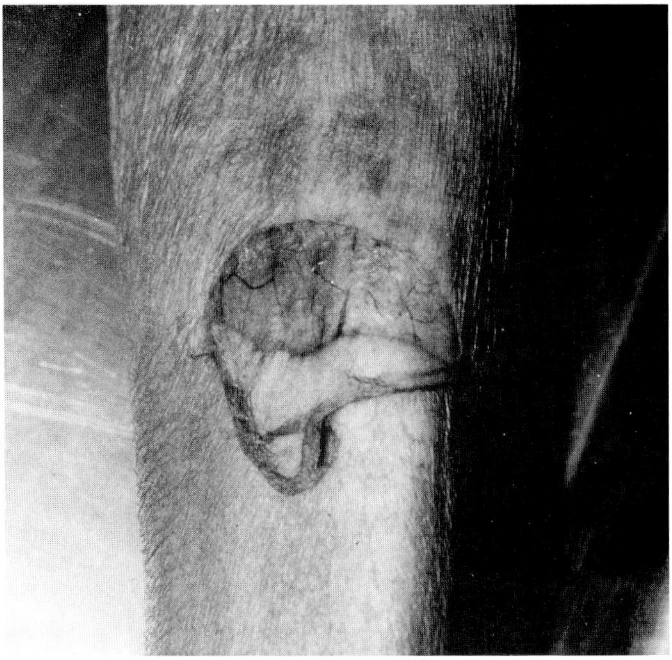

FIGURE 12.6 Skin slippage from a ruptured bulla on the arm of a man found in an early stage of postmortem decomposition. This can occur within a short period of time following death in the obese, in warm environments, in deaths where body temperature is elevated, or where bacteria is present throughout the body, such as sepsis.

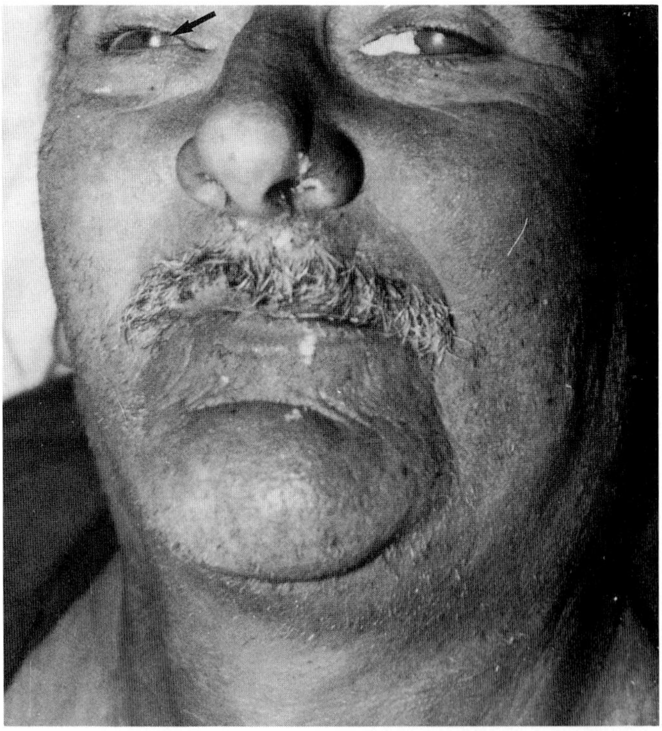

FIGURE 12.7 Time of death can be estimated based on examination and identification of insect life found on or within the body. Fly eggs have been laid in the inner canthus of the left eye, on the left nostril, and near the mouth. Note also the presence of a tache noir artifact (*arrow*) on the right eye. This dark discoloration results from drying of the cornea.

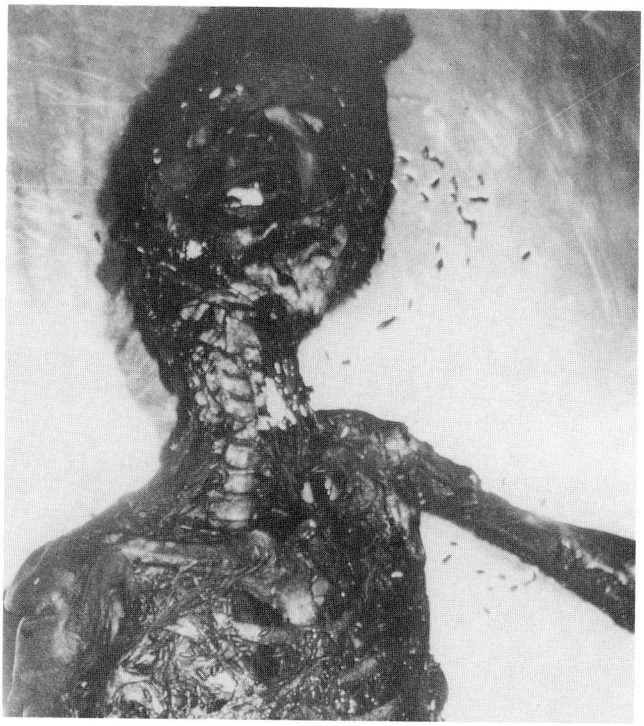

FIGURE 12.8 Near total skeletonization due to maggot infestation and decomposition. The maggots can be examined by an entomologist who may be able to give a better estimation of the time of death than could be done just by examination of the body. The largest maggots should be collected and preserved. Maggots can be killed by boiling and can then be refrigerated until sent for examination. It is also possible to collect maggots and utilize them for toxicologic examination if no soft tissue remains. It is helpful to contact the toxicology laboratory before sending the specimen to ensure that there is methodology available.

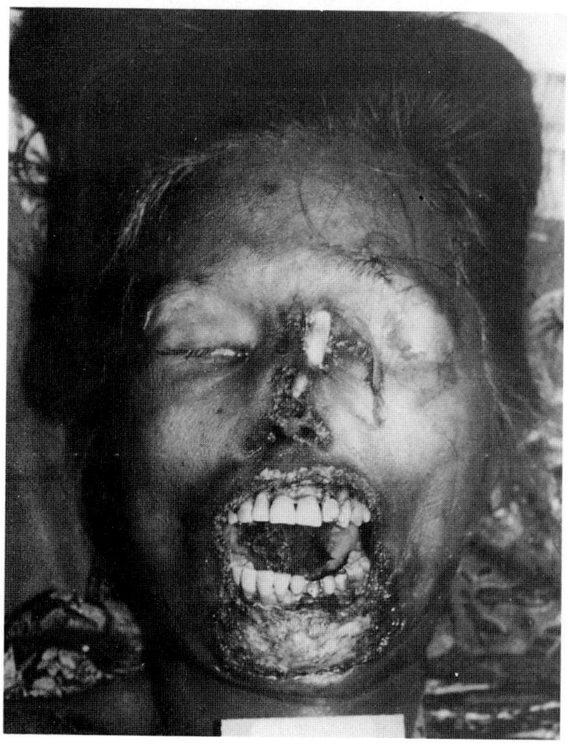

FIGURE 12.9 Bodies found in cool, dry environments can mummify. The skin will become dry, leathery and have a brown color. The skin of the hands and feet will undergo this mummification change first. Note the anthropophagy about the mouth and nose. Insects, domestic and wild animals as well as rodents will feed on human remains. The injuries are clearly postmortem and show no bleeding or redness but have a bland appearance.

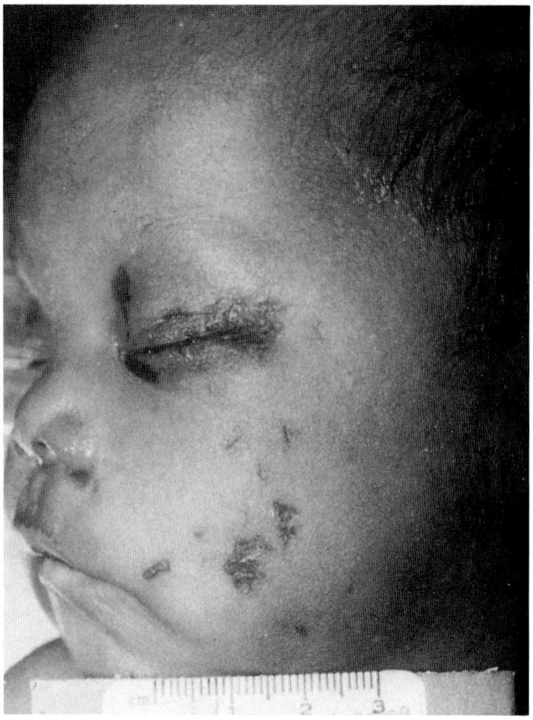

FIGURE 12.10 Roach bites such as these found on the face of a victim of sudden infant death syndrome are sometimes misinterpreted as abrasions and evidence of antemortem trauma. If present on the corners of the mouth or near the nostrils, suffocation or smothering is sometimes wrongly suspected.

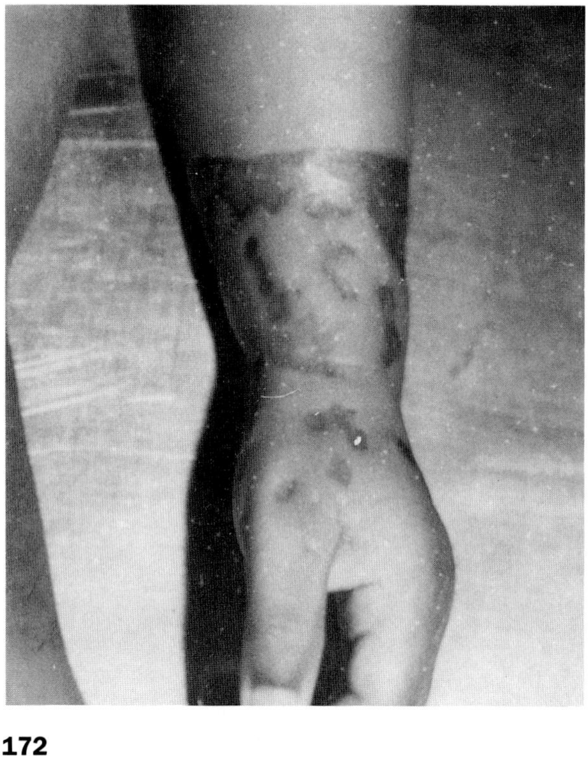

FIGURE 12.11 The pattern of the roach bites on the arm of this 1-year-old caused a pediatrician who had special training in the diagnosis and treatment of child abuse in the living to misidentify this postmortem injury as antemortem ligature marks. The child's sibling, who had no marks on his body, was removed into protective custody. Autopsy showed numerous roach bites on the face, extremities, and diaper area and bronchopneumonia as the cause of death. The pattern on the wrist was due to the elastic cuffs of the jacket the child was wearing. The roaches were able to eat up to the cuff, but not under it. Scene investigation showed that the mattress the two boys slept on was infested with roaches. False allegations of child abuse create problems for the family as well as for the pathologist who must now convince the court and the child protective agencies that another physician misinterpreted marks found on a body.

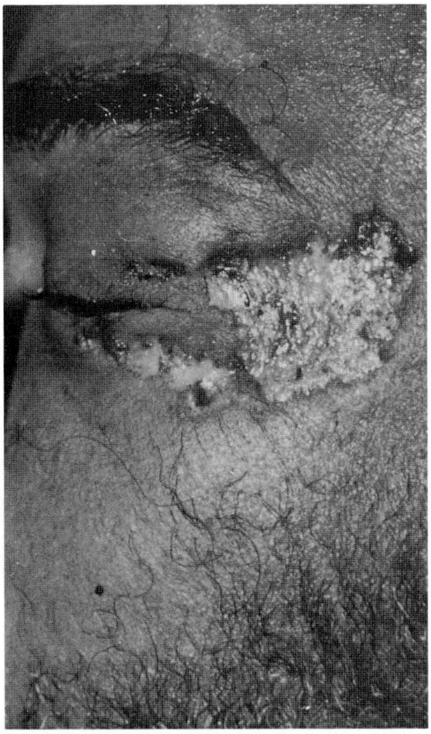

FIGURE 12.12 Postmortem rat bites next to the eye. Note the lack of bleeding or vital reaction around the wound. Also note the fine triangular appearance at the wound margins and the fine striations in the wound from the teeth being dragged across the soft tissues while the rodents gnawed at the tissue.

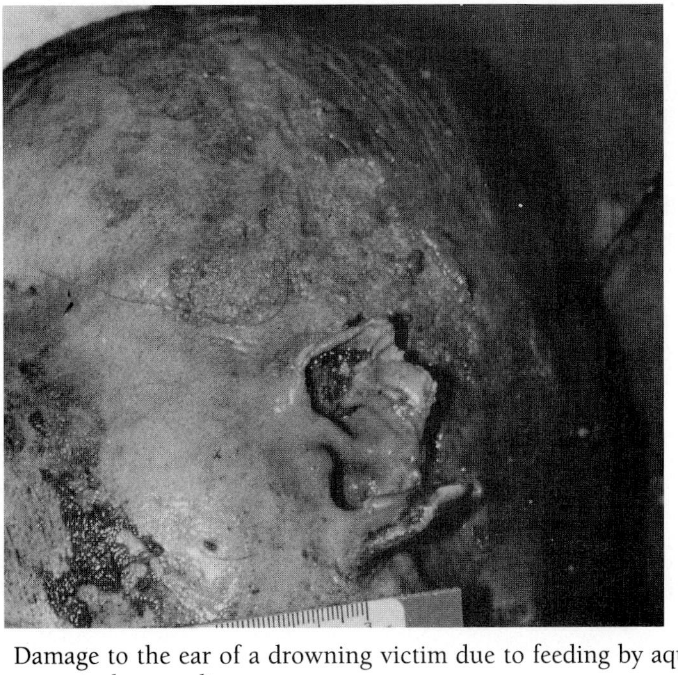

FIGURE 12.13 Damage to the ear of a drowning victim due to feeding by aquatic life. The gray, waxy appearance is due to adipocere.

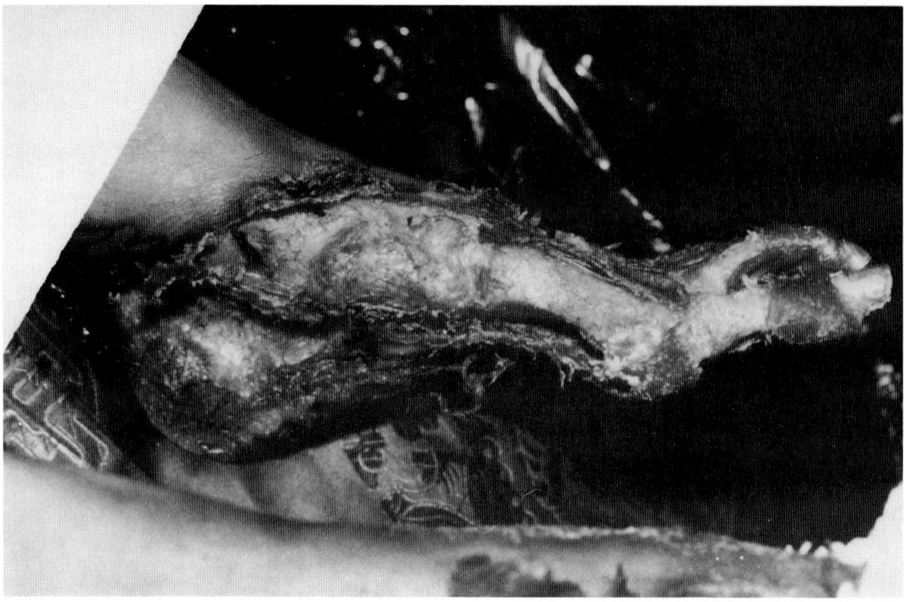

FIGURE 12.14 Postmortem partial skeletonization due to victim's pet dog gnawing on the foot for food. The wound margins are dry and appear dark due to drying.

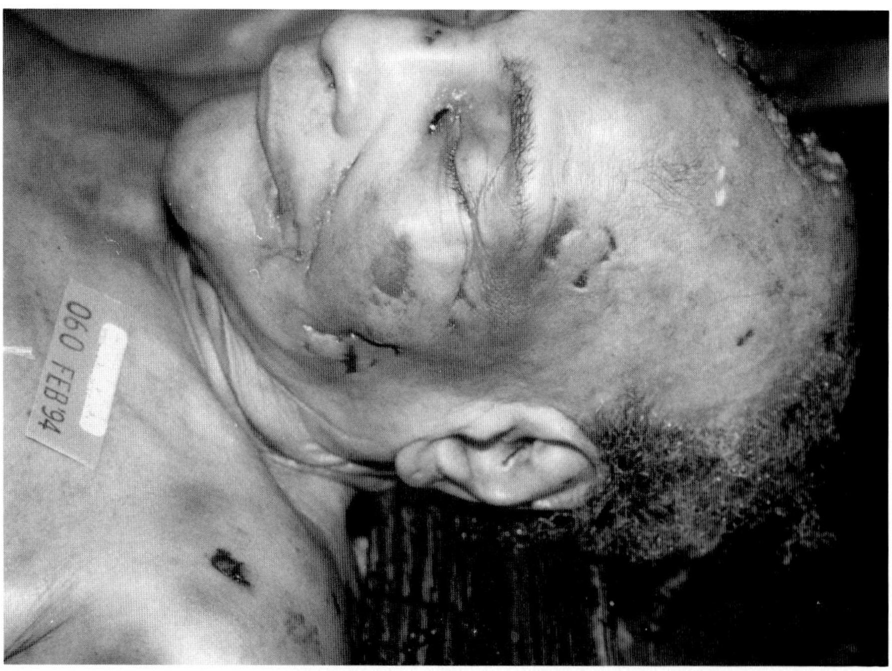

FIGURE 12.15 Antemortem bite marks on the face of an elderly woman who was attacked and killed by two rottweiler guard dogs. Contrast these injuries with the postmortem injuries seen in Figure 12.14.

13

Skeletal Remains

Forensic pathologists are frequently required to examine and identify skeletal remains. This may mean receiving an intact, severely decomposed human body, or just small fragments of bone or partial skeletons. When skeletal remains are discovered, careful sifting of the dirt and debris at the scene can often result in recovery of the teeth which fall out postmortem, as well as recovery of small bones of the hands, feet, the hyoid bone, and occasionally the thyroid and cricoid cartilages. Fingernails can also be recovered.

The first step in examining a bone is to determine whether or not the specimen received is human or nonhuman in origin. Once the specimen is determined to be human, the identification process and the determination of cause and manner of death begins. This examination requires that the bone be cleaned sufficiently of adherent soft tissue, which can be utilized for toxicologic study, and retained for subsequent burial, to allow good visualization of the shape and size of the bone, as well as to allow identification of any injury to the bone. A segment of femur, or other bone containing marrow can be preserved by freezing to allow for later DNA fingerprinting. The bones may be further cleaned by boiling or by soaking them in bleach. Antemortem injuries, such as fractures, holes, or other injury due to gunshot wounds, or fractures or incisions of bone from stab wounds can be identified once the bone has been cleaned. Care must be used while removing the soft tissue to avoid leaving knife or scalpel marks on the bone. Leaving the bones in the bleach too long can also lead to artifactual holes, especially in the thinner bones such as the scapulae, nasal, or orbital bones.

In any skeletal remains, the age, race, and sex are the most important determinations to be made, as this will reduce the number of possible identities. Height of the victim can be estimated from the long bones, but this is not as helpful in making an identification. There are several anthropologic textbooks available which describe the methods for making these determinations and which provide charts and mathematical formulas to be used. Age can be estimated from the degree of cranial suture fusion, the degree of fusion of the epiphyses of the long bones (Table 13.1), the topography of the opposing surfaces of the pubic symphysis, and from the teeth. Race can be determined by examination of the skull (Table 13.2), especially the jaw and the forehead, and the long bones. Sex is most easily determined by examination of the pelvis, with the female pelvis showing a wide inlet and sciatic notch and a flat, wide and short sacrum. Evidence of prior pregnancy, the so-called parturition pits, may also be identified in the female pelvis. Sex determination can also be made from the skull. Consultation with a physical anthropologist, especially an experienced forensic anthropologist, should be done in all cases. It is usually necessary to provide some preliminary data so the police can begin an investigation and local missing persons files can be gone through. An odontologist should examine the teeth, to assist in age and race determination and to chart the teeth so that the dental chart and age, race, and sex information can be placed into the National Crime Information Center (NCIC) system.

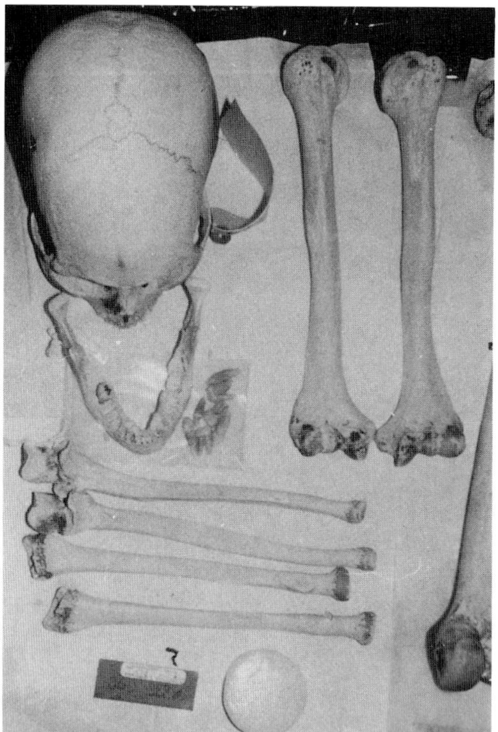

FIGURE 13.1 Skull, mandible, and arm bones of a 22-year-old black male who was found severely decomposed. The bones have been soaked in bleach to remove the soft tissues. The cranial sutures can be clearly seen allowing for an age determination to be made. Many of the teeth have fallen out of the mandible and maxilla and are preserved in a small plastic bag. The teeth can be glued back into the appropriate socket so that a dental examination to determine age can be done. Dental radiographs can be done for comparison with antemortem dental or skull radiographs. The circular object seen in the photograph is a deodorizer.

a

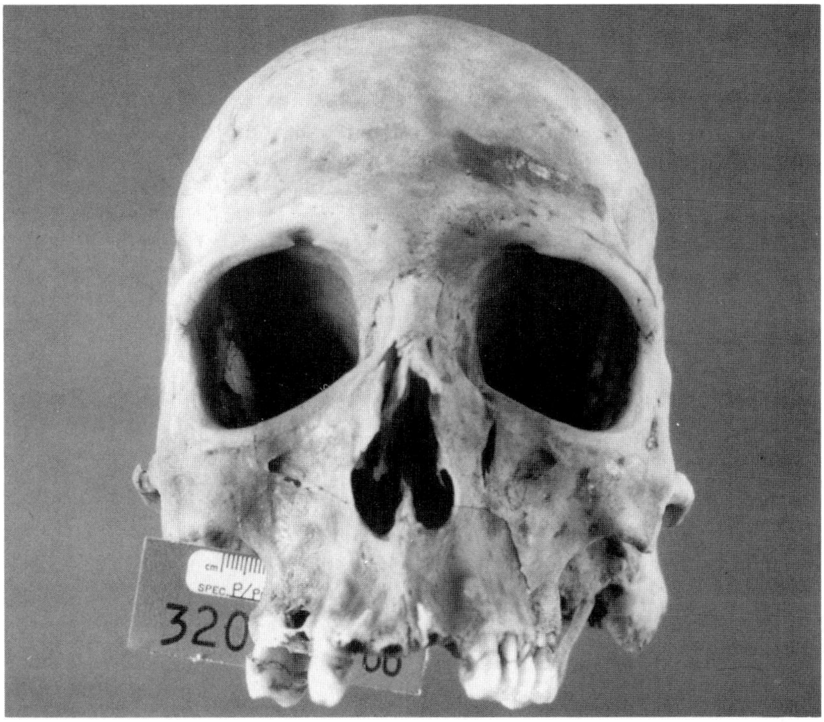

FIGURE 13.2a Facial view of a skull from an intact skeletalized remains found in the basement, under a vaulted sidewalk, of a building undergoing renovation. The skull is from a white male between the ages of 55 and 70. There are multiple old fractures of the face and nose. There is also a recent fracture of the left side of the face which extends to the left temporal bone.

b

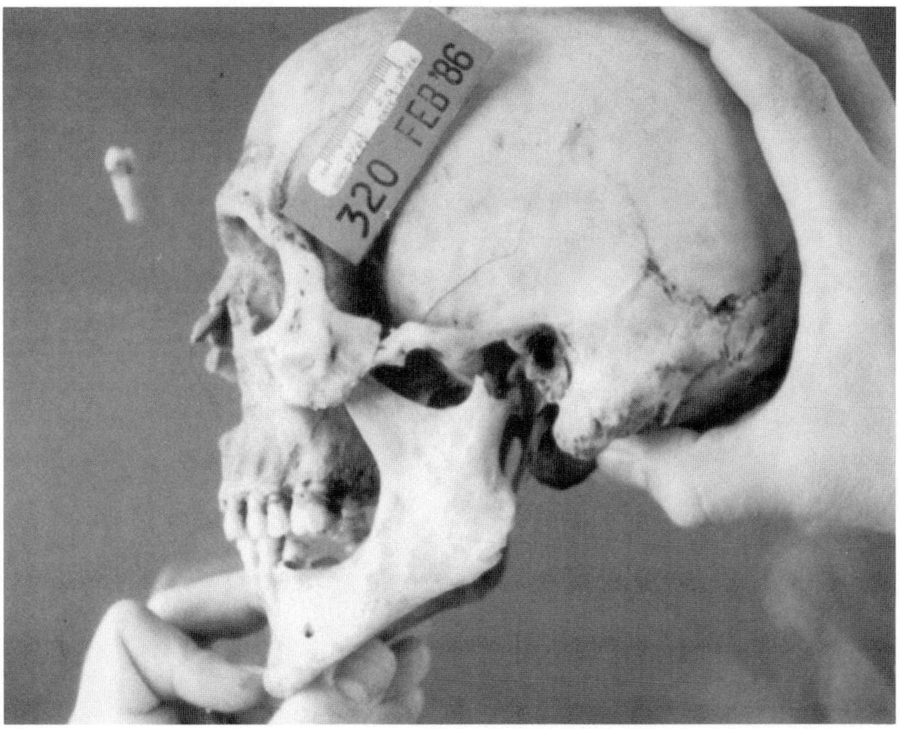

FIGURE 13.2b Lateral view of same skull and mandible. The recent fracture on the left side of the face and head can be seen. The jaw shows evidence of antemortem tooth loss where the bone has healed over the empty tooth socket. The remaining teeth showed caries.

c

FIGURE 13.2c Three ribs from the same individual which show fracture callous from old, healed rib fractures.

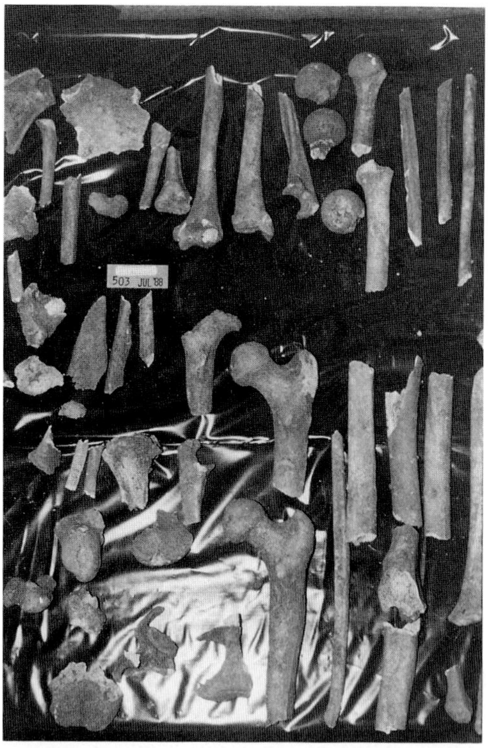

FIGURE 13.3 Skeletal remains from an ossuary, unearthed during construction. The bones were fragmented and contained the remains of multiple individuals of many ages and sexes. The appearance of the specimens was consistent with the bones being over 100 years old and the racial characteristics those of Native Americans.

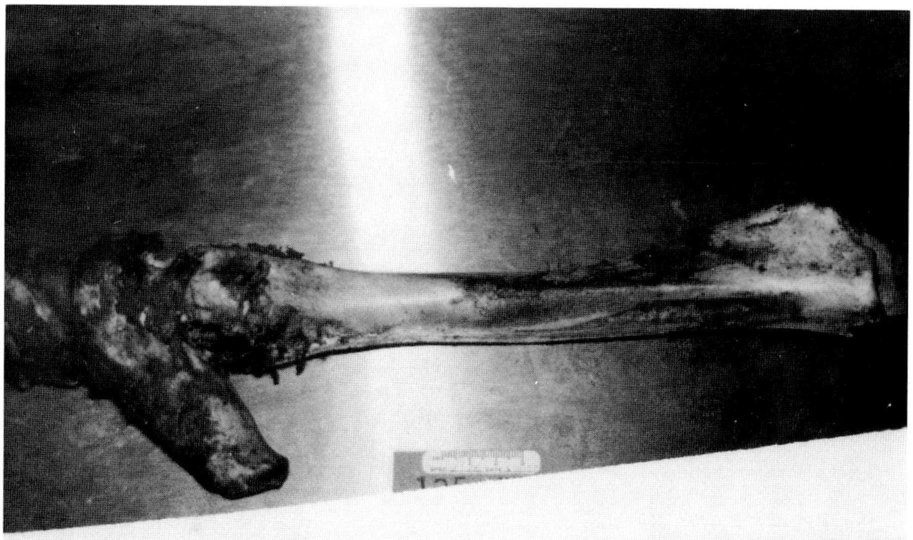

FIGURE 13.4 Not all skeletal remains recovered are human. This bone was unearthed by a citizen preparing ground for a garden. The specimen is a leg bone and partial foot from a large animal. Note the very prominent, thin blade like tibial tuberosity as well as the thick, heavy appearance of the bone.

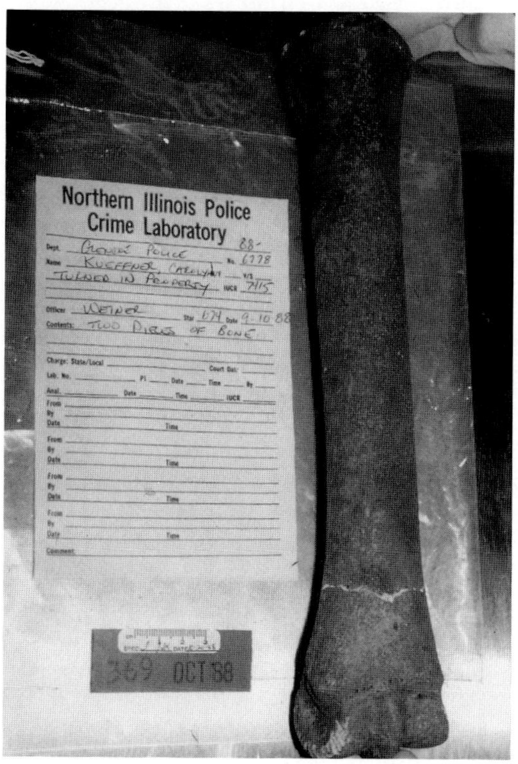

FIGURE 13.5 Another nonhuman leg bone. Note the marked thickness of the bone in relation to its length.

14

Natural Deaths

A full-time practicing forensic pathologist finds that the majority of examinations are performed on individuals who die from natural disease processes. These examinations may be necessary because the death occurred under unusual or obscure circumstances, there is trauma on the body when the body is found which may be due to collapse or falls at the time the subject became unresponsive, or the victim is a child or an otherwise healthy young or middle-aged adult without medical history. These examinations are done to rule out violence or unnatural events as well as to serve the community and protect the living from infectious disease, workplace health hazards, and environmental problems.

Unsuspected heart disease is found in very young individuals who collapse suddenly. This includes the various forms of cardiomyopathy, cardiac hypertrophy, anomalous coronary artery circulation, coronary thromboses, arteriosclerotic and hypertensive cardiovascular disease, and congenital heart disease. Vascular malformations and aneurysms that have ruptured are also common findings.

Infectious disease processes, such as bacterial and viral pneumonia, meningitis, myocarditis, tuberculosis, and sepsis are found in all age groups. Notification of the appropriate health agency should be done in all cases of communicable disease.

Undiagnosed metabolic disorders, such as diabetes, should always be considered when performing an examination as the appropriate fluids, that is vitreous humor, must be collected so that postmortem glucose and electrolyte analysis can be performed. Many alcoholics and drug addicts die, not from acute intoxication or from injury, but from natural disease processes such as cirrhosis or gastrointestinal hemorrhage in alcoholism, or acquired immune deficiency syndrome, endocarditis, hepatitis, or sepsis in chronic narcotism.

Bruising or fatal hemorrhages associated with tumors such as lung cancer or the hematologic malignancies often raise suspicion of a violent death when the medical history of an individual is not known by the persons discovering a body, or if the disease has not been diagnosed.

Though progress has been made in the treatment of asthma, many young asthmatics come to the attention of forensic pathologists due to sudden and unexpected death. The autopsy usually reveals hyperinflated, pale, doughy lungs and mucus plugs. Toxicology studies, especially for cocaine, should always be done as cocaine is known to induce asthmatic attacks.

In all deaths involving seizure activity, the mouth and tongue should be examined for bite marks. A careful examination of the brain, with histology of the hippocampi, should be done in order to identify the seizure focus. Alcoholics suffer seizures during withdrawal as well as from elevated levels of alcohol. Individuals with no seizure history may have terminal seizures due to hypoxia on the basis of a myocardial infarction or other vascular disorders. Toxicology should be done in all cases, especially for alcohol and cocaine.

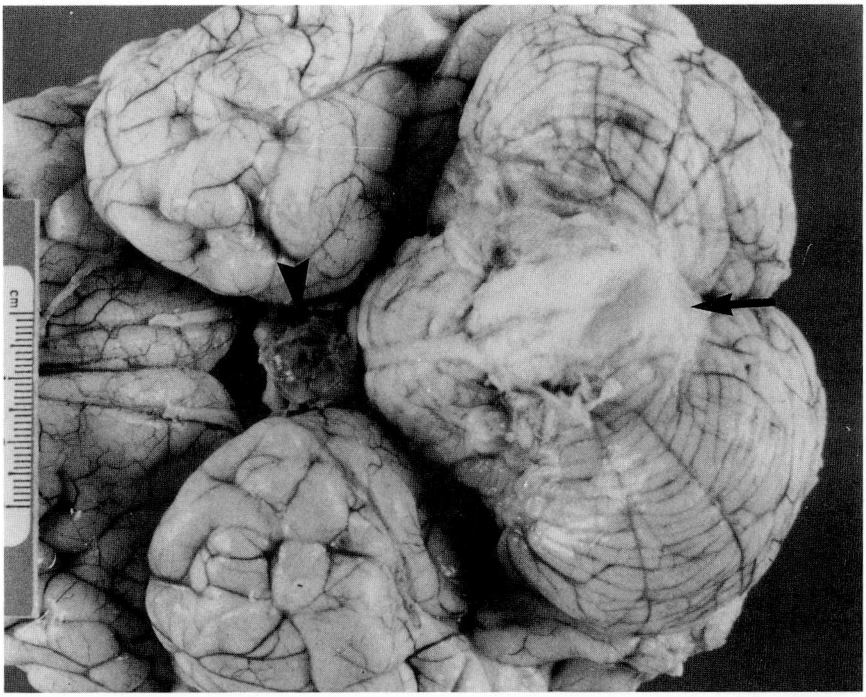

FIGURE 14.1 A cerebellar subarachnoid cyst (*arrow*) and a suprasellar cyst (*arrow head*) found at autopsy examination of a 22-year-old white female who collapsed suddenly at home after complaining of a headache, nausea, and vomiting. There was no other medical history.

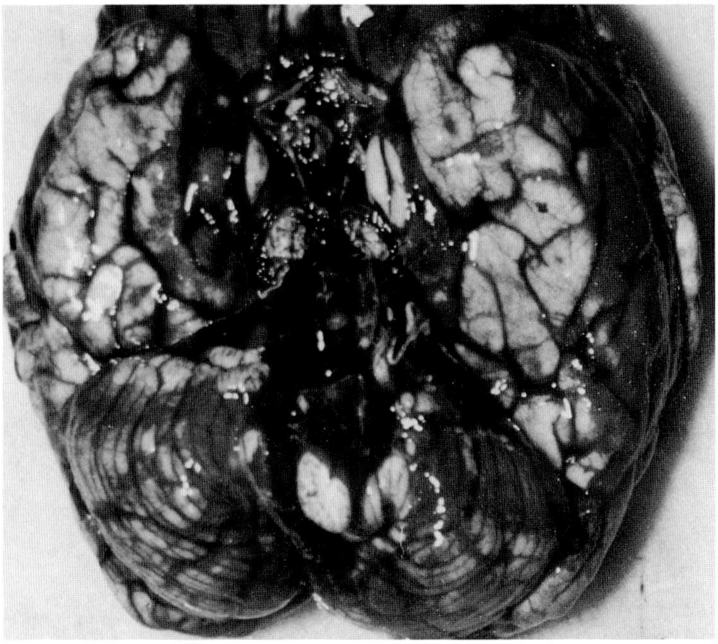

a

FIGURE 14.2a Basal subarachnoid hemorrhage found in a young woman who complained of a sudden and severe headache and then collapsed in front of coworkers.

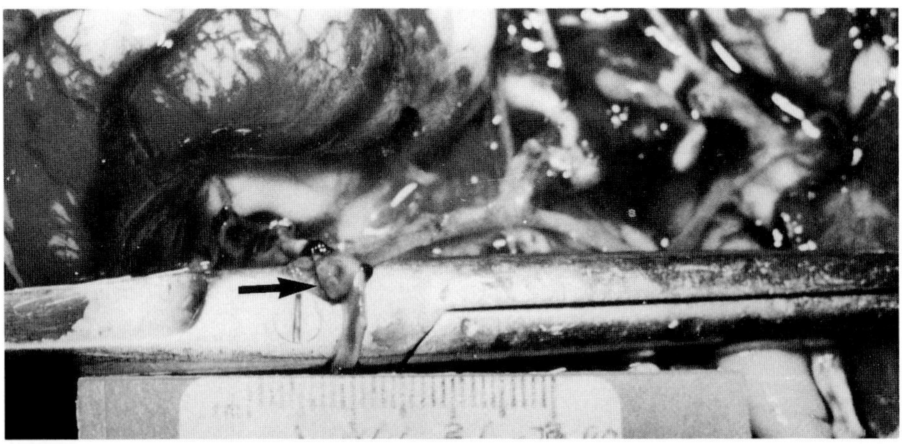

b

FIGURE 14.2b Ruptured berry aneurysm (*arrow*) found during careful examination of the cerebral blood vessels. Compare these findings to those of the traumatic basal subarachnoid hemorrhage in Figures 3.42 and 3.43.

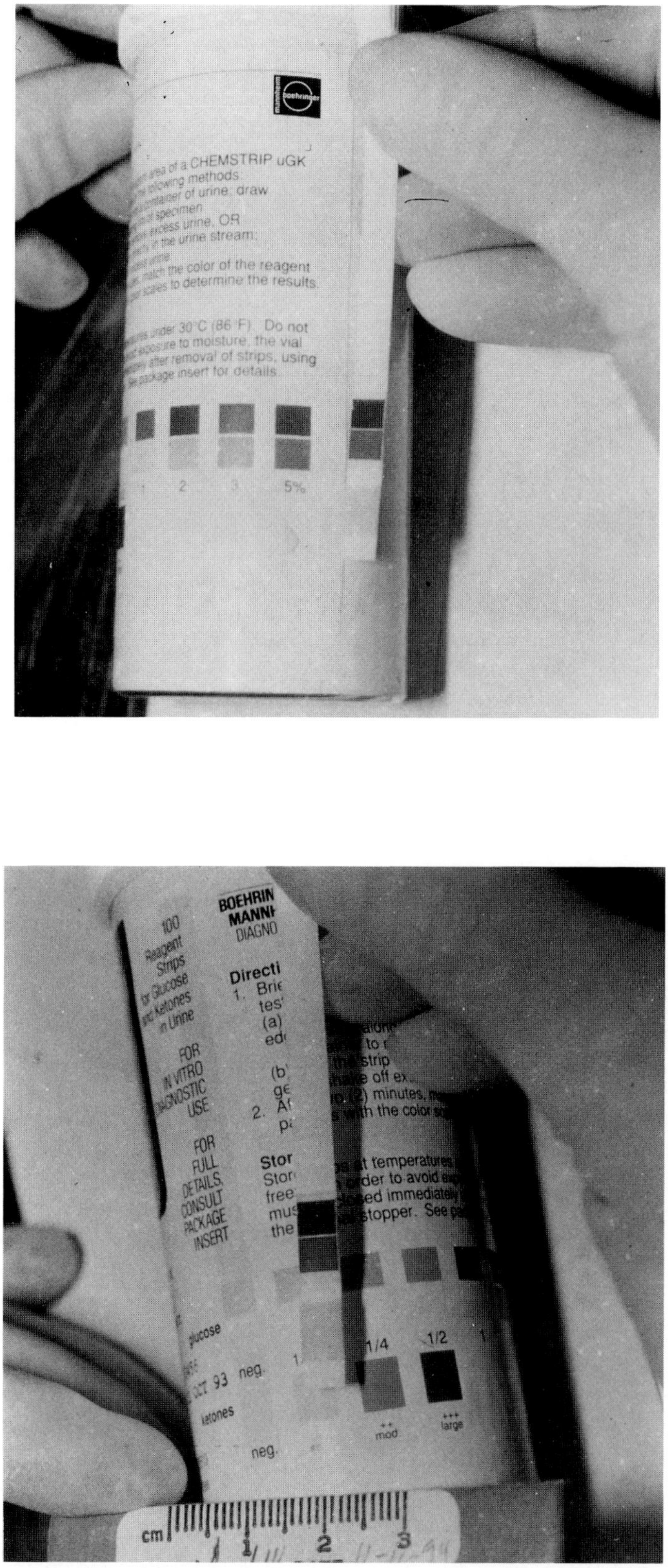

a

b

FIGURE 14.3a, b Urine glucose and ketone dip sticks commonly used by diabetics can be used at autopsy examination to make a rapid diagnosis of diabetic ketoacidosis. The chemical strip may be dipped into urine, or it may be dipped into vitreous humor if no urine is available. The results from vitreous humor are as reliable as the urine results. The glucose results are shown in Figure 14.3 a and the ketone results in Figure 14.3 b.

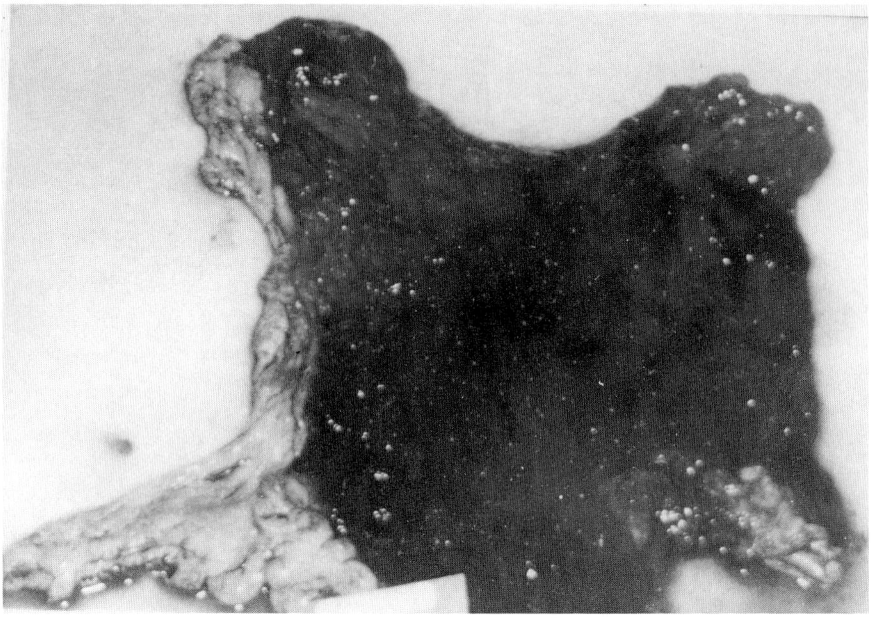

FIGURE 14.4 Hemorrhagic gastritis in a 43-year-old chronic alcoholic who died from a massive gastrointestinal hemorrhage. The victim was found at home in a pool of blood. Blood alcohol was less than 30 mg/dl.

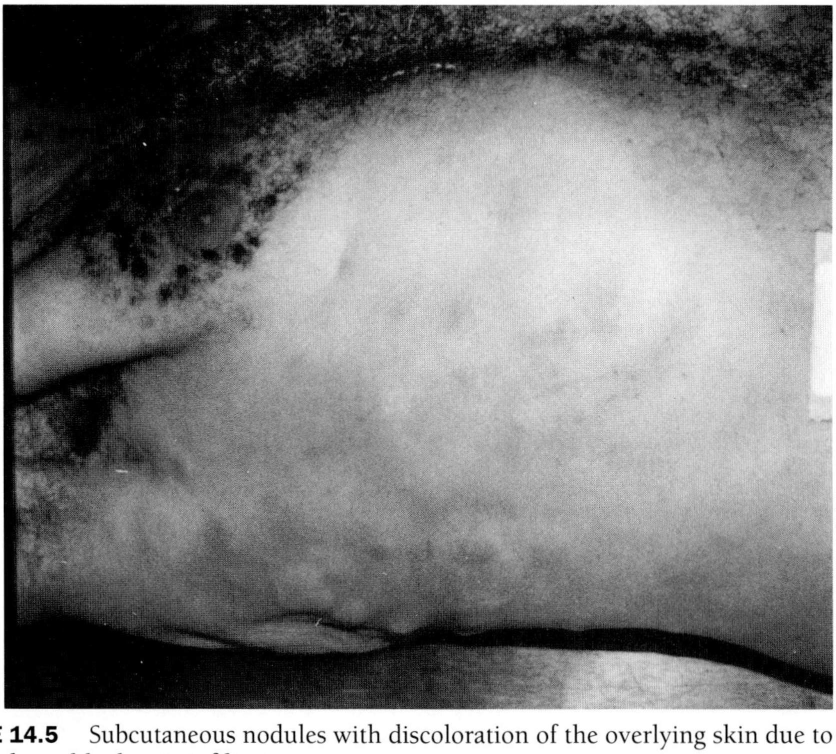

FIGURE 14.5 Subcutaneous nodules with discoloration of the overlying skin due to dermal and epidermal leukemic infiltrates.

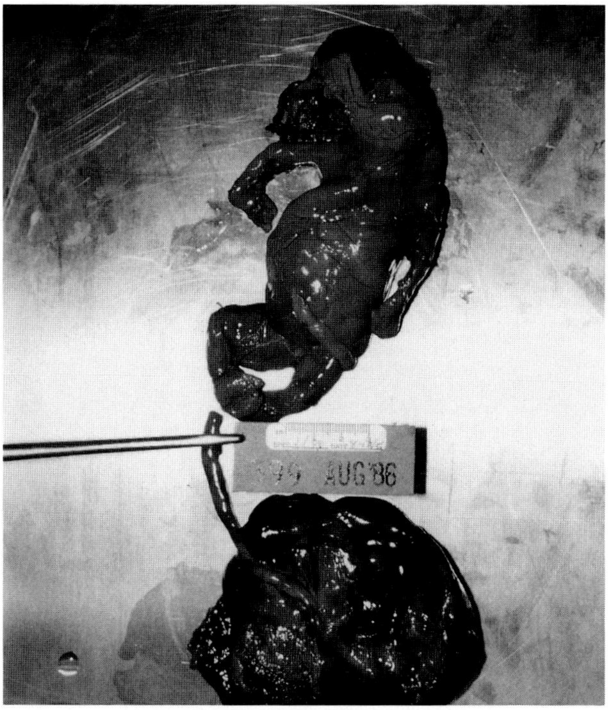

FIGURE 14.6 Macerated stillborn fetus delivered at home. The mother reported that she had not felt the fetus move for some time. The determination of live birth must be made by forensic pathologists whenever a dead newborn or fetus is discovered. In a nondecomposed, nonresuscitated infant, this can be done by looking for air in the trachea, lungs, or the gastrointestinal tract in an x-ray, or by dropping the intact neck organ, lung, and heart block into a container of water to see if the block of organs floats. The only unequivocal proof of a live birth is finding food in the stomach.

References

Baselt RC: *Disposition of Toxic Drugs and Chemicals in Man,* ed 4. Foster City, California, Chemical Toxicology Institute, 1995.

Cooper PR (ed): *Head Injury,* ed 2. Baltimore, Williams & Wilkins, 1987.

Cottone JA, Standish SM (eds): *Outline of Forensic Dentistry.* Chicago, Year Book Medical Publishers, 1982.

Damask AC, Damask JB, Damask JN: *Injury Causation Analysis: Case Studies and Data Sources.* Charlottesville, Virginia, The Mitchie Company, 1990.

Demling RH, LaLonde C: *Burn Trauma.* New York, Theime Medical Publishers, 1989.

DiMaio VJM: *Gunshot Wounds: Practical Aspects of Firearms, Ballistics, and Forensic Techniques.* New York, Elsevier, 1985.

Fischer H, Kirkpatrick CJ: *Color Atlas of Trauma Pathology.* St. Louis, Mosby, 1991.

Guntheroth WG: *Crib Death: The Sudden Infant Death Syndrome.* Mount Kisco, NY, Futura Publishing Company, 1989.

Karch SB: *The Pathology of Drug Abuse.* Boca Raton, CRC Press, 1993.

Kleinman PK: *Diagnostic Imaging of Child Abuse.* Baltimore, Williams & Wilkins, 1987.

Knight B: *Forensic Pathology.* New York, Oxford University Press, 1991.

Knight B (ed): *The Estimation of the Time Since Death in the Early Postmortem Period.* London, Arnold, 1995.

Krogman WC, Iscan MY: *The Human Skeleton in Forensic Medicine,* ed 2. Springfield, Illinois, Charles C. Thomas, Publisher, 1986.

Limpert R: *Motor Vehicle Accident Reconstruction and Cause Analysis.* Charlottesville, Virginia, The Mitchie Company, 1978.

Ludwig S, Kornberg AE (eds): *Child Abuse: A Medical Reference,* ed 2. New York, Churchill Livingstone, 1992.

Marshall EP, Sanow EJ: *Handgun Stopping Power: The Definitive Study.* Boulder, Colorado, Paladin Press, 1992.

Mason JK (ed): *The Pathology of Trauma,* ed 2. London, Arnold, 1993.

Mathog RH: *Atlas of Craniofacial Trauma.* Philadelphia, WB Saunders, 1992.

Moore EE, Mattox KL, Feliciano DV (eds): *Trauma,* ed 2. Norwalk, Connecticut, Appleton & Lange, 1991.

National Research Council: *DNA Technology in Forensic Science.* Washington, DC, National Academy Press, 1992.

Raimondi AJ, Choux M, DiRocco C: *Head Injuries in the Newborn and Infant.* New York, Springer Verlag, 1986.

Schoen FJ (managing ed): *Robbins Pathologic Basis of Disease,* ed 5. Philadelphia, WB Saunders, 1994.

Spitz WU (ed): *Spitz and Fisher's Medicolegal Investigation of Death.* ed 3. Springfield, Illinois, Charles C. Thomas Publisher, 1993.

Sullivan Jr JB, Krieger GR: *Hazardous Materials Toxicology: Clinical Principles of Environmental Health.* Baltimore, Williams & Wilkins, 1992.

Viccellio P: *Handbook of Medical Toxicology.* Boston, Little, Brown, 1993.

White TD: *Human Osteology.* San Diego, Academic Press, 1991.

Glossary

Abrasion: a scrape or a scratch. A blunt trauma injury where the superficial layers of the epidermis are removed by tangential friction forces or a perpendicular blow.

Abrasion collar (ring): an abrasion found around a gunshot wound of entrance caused by the bullet rubbing the edges of the hole created as it indents and then perforates the skin as it enters the body. In fresh wounds, it will have a pink fleshy appearance. As the wound dries, it will appear dry and dark.

Acute: severe; or when used to describe the age of an injury, meaning new-onset or very recent.

Addiction: a mental or physical dependence on drugs or an habitual or compulsive use of a substance.

Adipocere: conversion, in decomposition, of the soft tissues of the body to a gray-white, waxy substance in moist or wet environments.

Adipose tissue: tissue composed of fat cells, blood vessels, and connective tissue.

Air embolism: a bubble of air present in the vascular system disrupting blood flow. May occur in scuba diving, during an abortion, following a stab wound to the neck, or in cunnilingus where air is blown into the vagina, especially during pregnancy.

Alopecia: hair loss. Traumatic alopecia is hair loss due to yanking or pulling.

Ammunition: bullets for a gun, or explosives or materials used for an assault or for defense.

Anaphylaxis: a hypersensitivity, or allergic, reaction to a drug or food item, leading to massive release of histamine and other chemicals from mast cells and basophils which can cause death from laryngeal edema or vascular collapse.

Anoxia: complete absence of oxygen.

Anthropophagy: postmortem destruction of human remains due to feeding by insects and other predators.

Aorta: the main blood vessel which carries blood from the heart to the rest of the body.

A-P: anterior to posterior radiograph; that is, the x-rays will pass through the body from front to back.

Asphyxia: the occlusion, blockage, or exclusion of oxygen.

Aspiration: inhalation of fluid or other foreign material into the airway and lungs.

Atypical gunshot wound: a gunshot wound of entry caused by a deformed or tumbling bullet which has a "P" or "D" shape instead of the typical round or oval shape to the central defect.

Autoerotic asphyxia: a form of masturbation and self-gratification where cerebral hypoxia, brought on by pressure to the neck by the application of a ligature, or the inhalation of a substance, is used to enhance euphoria. Bondage and pornographic materials are frequently part of the act.

Autolysis: the enzymatic digestion of a cell or an organ, especially the pancreas, stomach, or bowel, after death.

Automatic weapon: a weapon in which the mechanism that extracts and ejects the expended casing, loads the fresh cartridge and returns the mechanism into position to fire the next round is powered by the forces generated by firing a cartridge.

Autopsy: an examination of human remains which includes an external examination, an internal examination of all organs, and laboratory studies such as toxicology, performed to document any injury or natural disease processes in order to determine the cause of death. Literally defined as "to see for oneself."

Ballistics: the science of objects in motion. Most commonly used to refer to the study of the motion of bullets. This involves the movement of bullets within the weapon, in the air after the weapon is fired, and the behavior of bullets as they penetrate the target.

Bearing surface: the portion of the bullet that comes in contact with the inside of a gun barrel and that will show the rifling pattern left by the lands and grooves in the gun barrel.

Birdshot: the smallest shotgun pellets which range from a diameter of 0.05 inch up to 0.18 inch in diameter, and range from an average weight of 0.18 grain up to 8.75 grains.

Bite marks: Patterned, opposing semilunar or crescent-shaped abrasions, bruises, or a combination of both, caused by biting or sucking.

Blast wave: a wave of compressed air, caused by an explosion which passes outward from the epicenter or blast point.

Blow back: blood droplets, hair, or tissue fragments which are blown back out of an entrance wound, especially in contact-range or high-velocity wounds.

Blunt trauma: injury sustained due to the impact of an object with the body, or the impact of the body with an object.

Bone marrow embolism: microscopic pieces of bone marrow released into the circulation due to fractures of marrow-containing bones. These are frequently seen in the lungs or kidney where they become trapped in the small vessels of these organs. May also be seen in the brain.

Bore: the interior of a gun barrel.

Bruise: a blunt trauma injury where blood vessels are crushed and blood released into the surrounding tissues appearing as an area of color change on the surface. A black-and-blue mark. The color changes as the injury heals over time.

Bucket handle fracture: a fracture of the metaphysis of the long bone of a child which is pathognomonic of abuse; so called because of the appearance of the fracture, which is curved and resembles a bucket handle on radiographs.

Bulla: a blister, or fluid-filled, raised area of the skin found in thermal or electrical injury as well as in carbon monoxide intoxication and decomposition.

Bullet: a lead or a metal-jacketed lead core or projectile to be fired from a gun.

Bullet wipe: lead or a combination of lead, lubricating oil, metal fragments, and gunpowder which is transferred from a bullet onto clothing, the skin, or bone as it passes through that object.

Bumper injuries: fractures or other blunt trauma injuries, usually found on the legs, caused by the impact of a car bumper with the body of a pedestrian.

Burns: damage to the skin caused by high temperatures; divided into partial thickness and full-thickness depending on depth of injury, with full-thickness burns having damage completely through the epidermis and the dermis. May be caused by flames, contact with hot objects, hot water, or steam. The latter injuries are called scald burns.

Caliber: the diameter of the barrel of a firearm or a bullet.

Calvarium: the top portion of the skull, or the skull cap.

Cartridge: a bullet within a metal case containing gunpowder and primer.

Cartridge case or casing: the metal case, usually brass, into which a bullet, gunpowder, and primer are loaded.

Cause of death: the disease process or injury that initiates a chain of events, regardless of time frame, which results in the death of an individual.

Central defect: the hole in a gunshot or shotgun wound of entry caused by the passage of the bullet or lead shot through the skin.

Cerebral vascular accident: a stroke. An area of hemorrhage or ischemia in the brain leading to destruction of brain tissue.

Cervical vertebrae: refers to the individual bones that make up the neck segment of the backbone. There are normally seven cervical vertebrae. The first is called the atlas. The second, called the axis, has a small upright portion called the dens or the odontoid process which articulates or joins with the atlas.

Chemical burns: injuries caused by the caustic or corrosive actions of various chemicals when they come in contact with the skin or the mucosal surfaces, the linings, of the mouth, esophagus, stomach, or the trachea.

Child abuse: physical or mental mistreatment of a child, including physical, medical, or emotional neglect.

Choke: a narrowing of the muzzle end of a shotgun barrel which modifies the spread of the shot pellets as they exit the barrel.

Choking: asphyxia due to the blockage of the airways by a foreign object.

Chop wounds: wound caused by a heavy sharp weapon, such as an axe or cleaver which has both sharp and blunt characteristics.

Chronic: of long duration.

Chronic narcotism: the use of narcotics over a prolonged period of time which leads to multiple physical complications and addiction.

Compressional asphyxia: a form of asphyxia due to mechanical compression of the chest impeding the normal expansion of the chest which occurs during breathing.

Confined or closed space asphyxia: a form of asphyxia due to the lack of oxygen in a confined area or enclosed space, such as a plastic bag, well, or a sewer resulting from consumption by breathing, fire, oxidation (rust), or decomposition, or due to replacement of oxygen by gases that are heavier than air.

Contusion: a bruise on the skin or an internal organ due to blunt trauma.

Coup contusion: a contusion found directly under a point of impact.

Contre coup contusion: a contusion found in an area opposite the point of impact.

Corner fracture: a fracture of the metaphysis of the long bone of a child which is pathognomonic of abuse; so called because of the appearance of the fracture, which resembles a chip or corner on radiographs.

Coroner: an elected public official whose chief duty is to investigate the cause of death, especially when due to unnatural events.

Cylinder gap: a small space which may be found between the barrel and the cylinder, the rotatable part of a revolver where the bullets are chambered or loaded, from which lead, powder particles, soot, and gases may escape when the gun is fired. In close-range gunshot wounds, this material may strike and leave marks on the body of the victim a short distance from the entrance wound.

Decomposition: the breakdown or decay of the human body following death.

Decompression sickness: the "bends". The formation of bubbles from dissolved nitrogen, carbon dioxide, and oxygen which occurs in the blood of divers who ascend too quickly from depths.

Defense wounds: sharp or blunt trauma injuries to the arms, hands, legs, or feet which are sustained while trying to defend oneself from an attacker.

Drowning: asphyxial death due to inhalation of fluid or due to laryngospasm, caused by the inhalation of the fluid, closing the airway.

Drug abuse: the experimental or recreational use of drugs, or the use of drugs to relieve problems or perceived problems, which leads to a physical or psychological dependence on the drug.

Ecchymosis: a contusion or a bruise.

Ejection rod: mechanism in an automatic or semiautomatic weapon that removes the spent cartridge case of the bullet just fired to allow the next round to be chambered.

Embolism: a foreign object moving within blood vessels from one place in the body to another. Commonly refers to blood clots that form in veins in one part of the body and then travel to and through the heart and occlude arteries in the lung.

Endocarditis: an inflammation or an infection of the lining of the chambers or valves of the heart.

Endocardium: the lining of the chambers of the heart and the surface lining of the heart valves.

Endothelium: the innermost layer of blood vessels.

Epidural hematoma (hemorrhage): bleeding into the space between the inner table of the skull and the dura mater, a tough leathery membrane which protects the brain. Epidural hematomas are commonly associated with skull fractures, accumulate rapidly and are usually due to damage to arteries. Posterior fossa epidural hematomas are usually due to damage to the dural sinus which is a vein.

Epiglottitis: inflammation or infection of the epiglottis, the structure that seals over the larynx when swallowing occurs to prevent foreign matter from entering the lungs.

Erythema: redness due to inflammation where the blood vessels surrounding an injury become dilated and engorged with blood in response to the injury.

Extradural hematoma (hemorrhage): see *epidural hematoma.*

Fat embolism: small bolus or globule of fat from the bone marrow or from the subcutaneous fatty tissue which gets into the bloodstream following trauma.

Forensic medicine: literally means "of the forum," where the law courts of Rome were found, or more commonly, legal medicine. The science and practice of medicine to the purpose of the law.

Forensic pathology: a subspecialty of pathology which deals with the investigation of sudden, unexpected, mysterious, or violent deaths.

Fracture: a break in something; usually refers to a broken bone.

Frangible bullet: a bullet designed to break apart into multiple small pieces upon striking a hard surface. They were originally designed for target practice and stunning cattle. These bullets are capable of entering a human body and causing death.

Gauge: the diameter of the bore of a shotgun or the caliber of shot shell or cartridges a shotgun fires.

Gingiva: the moist, pink, soft tissue of the gums.

Graze wound: a gunshot wound created when a bullet strikes and abrades along the surface of the body but does not penetrate into the body.

Grooves: helical depressions in the bore of a rifle or handgun designed to give rotary motion to a bullet.

Gunshot residue (GSR): residue of the primer deposited on the back of the hand when a gun is fired. It consists of various proportions of barium, antimony, and lead.

Hangman's fracture: a fracture of the odontoid process, the dens, of the second cervical vertebra which occurs in judicial hangings. It is a result of the careful placement of the knot of the noose and the length of the distance the body is dropped in combination with the weight of the body.

Hard contact wound: gunshot or shotgun wound of entry where the muzzle of the weapon is pressed tightly against the body.

Hematoma: a blood clot. A term also used to refer to large bruises where there is a palpable mass in the skin.

Hemoglobin: the red, iron-containing compound in red blood cells which carries oxygen.

Hemopericardium: collection of blood within the sac, the pericardium, which surrounds the heart.

Hemoperitoneum: collection of blood within the abdominal cavity.

Hemorrhage: bleeding.

Hemosiderin: a storage form of iron in the body.

Hemothorax: collection of blood within the chest cavity.

Hepatitis: inflammation or infection of the cells of the liver.

Hesitation wounds: superficial incised wounds found in combination with deeper wounds on the neck or on the wrists of suicides which represent trial or practice strokes done to work up courage or to determine the amount of force necessary to inflict a deeper wound which will sever blood vessels.

Homicide: a manner of death where one individual dies at the hands of another individual who intended to do harm or to kill the victim. This is a medicolegal term as used by the forensic pathologist and must not be confused with the legal term *homicide* or *murder.*

Hyoid bone: horseshoe-shaped bone at the base of the tongue to which strap muscles of the neck and muscles of the tongue are attached. Always examined in forensic autopsies to look for evidence of injury. In strangulation, the hyoid bone may be broken or the muscles and soft tissue attached to the bone may show hemorrhage from the compression of the neck. In young adults, the bone is pliable and does not usually fracture.

Hypertension: high blood pressure.

Immersion burns: burns on the body or a body part such as the hands or feet, due to being held in a hot liquid such as water as a form of abuse or punishment.

Incised wound: an injury caused by a sharp object which is longer on the surface of the body than the wound penetrates into the body.

Infanticide: the killing of an infant or young child.

Inhalation injury: injury to the upper and lower respiratory tract as a result of inhaling super-heated air, fumes, soot, smoke, and noxious gases, leading to direct damage to the lining of the tracheobronchial tree and the alveoli.

Intermediate (intervening) target: an object that is struck or perforated by a bullet before the bullet enters a second target.

Intracerebral hemorrhage: bleeding within the brain tissue.

Intracranial hemorrhage: bleeding within the skull; may be in the brain tissue or in the epidural, subdural or subarachnoid space.

Intraventricular hemorrhage: bleeding within the ventricular system of the brain.

Ischemia: local deficiency of the blood supply.

Jacketed bullet: lead core, or bullet, partially or completely encased in a harder metal, such as copper, to protect the soft lead.

Keyhole wound of bone: an oval defect in the bone created when a bullet strikes the bone tangentially. One edge of the defect will be beveled on the outer table and the other edge beveled on the inner table.

Kinetic energy: force or energy of an object due to the mass of that object multiplied by the square of the velocity of that object.

Laceration: a blunt trauma injury where the skin or an organ is torn due to overstretching of the tissues. The margins of a laceration are irregular and may be abraded or bruised. Tissue bridges, small intact strands of tissue, can be seen stretching from one side of the injury to the other.

Lands: the raised portions between the grooves in a rifled gun barrel.

Larynx: the upper part of the trachea where the vocal cords are located.

Lead snowstorm: multiple small radiopaque lead fragments seen on x-ray along the path of a bullet through the body. Not usually seen in jacketed bullets as the lead core is protected by the jacket. More common in high-velocity wounds.

Ligature: a thing used to bind or to tie someone or something. A rope, cord, etc., which is used in a strangulation or a hanging.

Ligature abrasion: the mark left on the body from friction between the surface of the skin and a ligature.

Livor mortis: lividity or hypostasis. A purple red discoloration of the dependent portions of a dead body resulting from the settling of the blood due to the forces of gravity.

Maceration: the decomposition of a fetus within the uterus following the death of the fetus.

Maggot: a wormlike larval form of a fly.

Manner of death: the circumstances or fashion through which a death came about. May be natural or unnatural, with unnatural deaths further divided into accident, suicide, homicide, or undetermined.

Mechanism of death: the physiologic derangement, chemical or biochemical disturbance brought about by the cause of death which is incompatible with continued life.

Medical examiner: A pathologist trained in forensic medicine appointed to investigate deaths and perform autopsies and postmortem examinations in order to determine cause and manner of death.

Meninges: The linings of the brain and spinal cord which include the pia mater, arachnoid membrane, and dura mater. The pia and arachnoid mater together are called the leptomeninges; they are thin and transparent and are on the surface of the brain. The dura mater is a leathery membrane between the inner table of the skull and the brain, and also between the spinal cord and the bones of the spinal column.

Meningitis: An inflammation or infection of the leptomeninges of the brain or spinal cord.

Methadone: A synthetic narcotic created during World War II by the Germans and called Dolophine. It is used in drug rehabilitation programs, but also used as a drug of abuse itself.

Missile: A projectile fired or thrown from a weapon such as a gun or a bow.

Mongolian spot: a blue-gray birthmark commonly located on the buttock or thigh region of infants and children of African-American, Asian, or Hispanic origin.

Mummification: a type of decomposition in dry environments where the body is converted to a dry, leathery mass of skin and tissue encasing the skeleton.

Münchausen syndrome by proxy: a form of child abuse where a caregiver asphyxiates or causes obscure medical illnesses to occur in a child which require medical treatment, providing gratification to the caregiver and threatening the life of the child.

Muzzle: the opening at the end of the barrel of a gun.

Muzzle abrasion: an abrasion seen in contact- or near-contact-range gunshot entry wounds which is caused by the skin being rubbed against the muzzle of the gun by the expanding gases blown into the tissue at the same time the bullet enters the body.

Muzzle velocity: the speed at which a bullet leaves the muzzle of a gun. An important factor in determining the kinetic energy or wounding capability of a bullet.

Myocardial infarction: a heart attack. An episode of ischemia or reduced oxygen delivery to the muscle of the heart causing injury to the muscle. May be due to atherosclerosis or fatty deposits in the coronary arteries or due to a blood clot blocking a vessel or a spasm of a coronary artery.

Myocardium: the muscle cells of the heart.

Narcotism: abuse of narcotic drugs or opiate derivatives such as heroin or morphine.

Neglect: to fail to provide adequate shelter, food, medical treatment, or emotional support.

Odontology: the study or science of teeth and the surrounding tissue. Forensic odontology also deals with bite mark evidence and identifying individuals by examination of the teeth.

Orbital plate: thin bone in the base of the skull, over the eyes, which forms the roof of the orbits, which is easily fractured from blunt trauma or gunshot wounds to the head or face.

Pancreas: a combined exocrine and endocrine organ found in the upper mid abdomen which produces insulin and digestive enzymes.

Pedestrian injury: an injury caused by a motor vehicle striking a pedestrian. Usually refers to fractures of the lower extremities from the impact of the vehicle with the body. Also refers to the injuries sustained from secondary impacts of the pedestrian's body with the vehicle or tertiary impact with the pavement.

Penetrating injury: an injury to a body part, or a body cavity resulting from a gunshot wound or a stab wound where a foreign object, the bullet or a knife, goes through the skin and into the underlying structures.

Pericardium: a leathery sac of connective tissue which is found around the heart.

Perimortem: referring to the period immediately around the time of death.

Peritonitis: an infection or inflammation of the lining of the abdominal cavity called the peritoneum. This can be due to natural diseases, such as appendicitis, or may follow blunt or penetrating injury to the abdomen.

Petechial hemorrhage: small pinpoint hemorrhages of the skin, sclera, conjunctiva, mucus or serous membranes due to leakage of blood from venules. A nonspecific finding which can be evidence of an asphyxial death, but also commonly found on the thymus, heart, and lungs in sudden infant death syndrome.

Pistol: a firearm in which the chamber, where the bullet is loaded, is part of the barrel of the weapon.

Positional asphyxia: a form of asphyxia that occurs when the body is in a position that blocks or impedes normal breathing or the respiratory movement of the chest.

Postmortem: referring to the period after death.

Primer: the component of a cartridge that ignites when struck by the firing pin of a weapon causing the gunpowder within the cartridge to explode and propel the bullet down and out of the gun barrel.

Pugilistic attitude: position of the arms and legs of a victim of a fire that results from the contraction of muscle and soft tissue due to thermal injury, which leads to flexion of the arms and legs to a position resembling that taken by a boxer or pugilist.

Putrefaction: decomposition or decay of a body.

Radiograph: an x-ray.

Range of fire: the distance that the muzzle of a gun is from the intended target at the time the weapon is fired. Classified as contact-range, where the muzzle is touching the body, close- or intermediate-range, where the muzzle is close enough, usually less than 18 to 24 inches away from the body, to allow the deposition of powder, soot, or stippling on the body or the clothing, and distant-range where the muzzle is far enough away to leave no powder, soot, or stippling around a wound, either on the body or on the clothing.

Reentry wound: an atypical gunshot wound of entry which is found when a bullet first perforates, goes through, one part of the body, such as an arm or hand, and then goes back into (reenters) another part of the body such as the chest or abdomen.

Retinal hemorrhage: bleeding into the lining of the back of the eye associated with severe head injury, such as the subdural hematomas found in "shaken baby syndrome".

Revolver: a handgun that has a cylinder with several chambers for loading bullets, which rotates (revolves) around an axis as the bullets are fired successively.

Ricochet: the deflection of a bullet or other projectile after it strikes an object.

Rifle: a firearm with a long rifled barrel which is fired from the shoulder.

Rifled slug: a large projectile with spiral grooves (rifling) and a hollow base intended for use in shotguns for hunting large game. The rifling is thought to cause the slug to rotate and have improved accuracy.

Rifling: spiral or helical grooves on the inside surface of the barrel of a handgun or rifle designed to give a rotary motion, or spin, to the bullet.

Rigor mortis: a stiffening or contraction of the muscles of the body which occurs after death due to the postmortem reduction in adenosine 5′-triphosphate (ATP), a chemical substance in the body which is needed for muscle relaxation. Rigor begins after death, gradually increases until it becomes full and then gradually declines as the muscle cells begin to undergo decomposition. The time required for this process varies from individual to individual depending on a number of factors both in the individual and in the environment.

Sarcoidosis: a granulomatous disease of unknown cause which is characterized by the presence of epithelioid tubercles or nodules (granulomas) in various organs which lead to dysfunction of the organ.

Scald burns: thermal burns due to hot liquid or steam.

Scuba: equipment worn by divers for breathing underwater; acronym for self-contained underwater breathing apparatus.

Shored entrance wound: a gunshot wound of entry with an irregular appearing abrasion due to rubbing of overlying clothing, such as a belt, against the skin around the bullet hole caused by the bullet pressing the clothing against the body as it enters the body.

Shored exit wound: a gunshot wound of exit which shows an irregular appearing abrasion around the exit hole due to the rubbing of the skin against an overlying object, such as clothing, a wall, or other hard object, as the bullet pushes the skin outward as it exits the body.

Shot cup: a plastic cup that holds the lead shot pellets which are fired from a shotgun.

Shotgun: a gun with a smooth barrel, which has no internal rifling, designed to fire shells or cartridges that contain multiple lead pellets or a single rifled slug.

Shotgun shell: a cartridge made of paper, plastic, or metal, containing projectiles, lead shot, designed to be used in a shotgun.

Skin slippage: the formation of bullae or blisters and the sloughing of the skin found in decomposed bodies and in deaths due to carbon monoxide.

Slash wound: an incised wound which is long and shallow.

Smothering: a form of asphyxia due to the occlusion of oxygen by blocking the mouth and nose with a hand or other object. May also occur if a parent or sibling lies on top of an infant when sleeping in the same bed.

Soot: a gray or black carbon substance created when something burns. In gunshot wounds, it contains vaporized metals from the primer, bullet, and cartridge case.

Stab wound: a wound caused by a sharp object which penetrates deeper into the body than the length of the wound on the surface of the body.

Stillbirth: a fetus or infant that is born dead, having died within the uterus prior to delivery, or dies during the delivery process due to some unforeseen or undiagnosed problem.

Stippling: small abrasions found around close-range gunshot wounds of entry which are due to fragments of unburned gunpowder, and pieces of metal from the bullet or the gun barrel that strike and abrade the skin.

Strangulation: a form of asphyxia resulting from the application of pressure to the neck using the hands or a ligature.

Subarachnoid hemorrhage: bleeding that occurs between the surface of the brain and the arachnoid membrane, a thin transparent covering over the surface of the brain. The term is also used to describe bleeding under the pia mater, the innermost meningeal layer on the brain.

Subdural hematoma (hemorrhage): bleeding that occurs between the outer surface of the brain and the inner surface of the dura mater. It is a result of damage to the bridging veins which extend from the brain to the sinuses, the large venous channels, of the dura mater.

Subgaleal hemorrhage: bleeding that occurs on the undersurface of the scalp due to blunt injury or a blow to the head. May also occur when the hair is pulled and blood vessels in the inner layer on the scalp are torn by the traction forces.

Sudden infant death syndrome (SIDS): The sudden, unexpected death of an infant between the ages of 2 weeks and 1 year, most common between 2 to 6 months, where no cause of death can be found after a complete autopsy examination, including histology and toxicology investigation and an examination of the scene are done.

Suffocation: a form of asphyxia characterized by exclusion of oxygen from the environment by consumption or replacement by other gases, or due to a mechanical disruption of breathing.

Suicide: death at one's own hand.

Tangential wound: a wound caused by a bullet or other missile striking the body at an angle or a glancing blow.

Tardieu spot: a minute area of intense lividity due to the overdistension and rupture of small blood vessels such as is seen in the legs of hanging victims.

Tattoo: a body adornment made by injecting colored inks into the dermis to form a picture or a message. Tattoos can be used to confirm the suspected identity of an individual who is in a state of decomposition or otherwise not viewable due to injury to the face. As tattoo ink is in cells in the dermis, they are still viewable in decomposed bodies where the epidermis has sloughed.

Tattooing: see *stippling*. Small abrasions of the skin found in close-range gunshot wounds.

Test firing: studies done by firing a recovered weapon, using identical ammunition, at a target from several known distances and then comparing the pattern of stippling to that seen on the body of a gunshot victim to determine range of fire. Also done to compare the rifling marks on the bullet fired from a recovered weapon with the markings on a bullet recovered from a gunshot victim to determine if the bullet came from that weapon.

Toxicology: a science which deals with drugs and poisons and their effects on the body. Tests performed on body fluids or organs to detect and measure the amount of drugs or poisons.

Vitreous humor: fluid within the eye which can be withdrawn at autopsy using a small syringe for chemical and toxicology studies such as testing for electrolytes, alcohol, or glucose.

Wadding: a disk of paper, fiber, or plastic which is placed between the shot pellets and the gunpowder in a shotgun shell or cartridge. These can be found within the body in contact- and close-range shotgun wounds.

Wound ballistics: the motion and effects that projectiles, such as bullets, have in tissue.

Yaw: an erratic side-to-side deviation from the path or trajectory by a bullet after it has been fired.

Tables

TABLE 2.1 Comparison of Hospital and Forensic Autopsy

HOSPITAL AUTOPSY	FORENSIC AUTOPSY
Medical history, chart	Police report, terminal event
Patient identified	Identity frequently in question
Deals with natural deaths	Deals with unnatural as well as natural deaths
Academic orientation	Legal purposes Examination of clothing and personal effects Collection and preservation of evidence
Determine mechanism of death	Determine cause and manner of death
Permission of kin required	Legal authorization, permission of kin not required
External examination	External examination more detailed
Internal examination	Internal examination
Histology always done	Histology done for confirmation
Laboratory studies	Toxicology and laboratory tests
May be done by physician assistant	Must be done by pathologist
Clinical pathologic correlation discussed in report	Report is objective
Confidentiality applies	Public record

TABLE 2.2 Format for Forensic Autopsies

External examination:	Include height, weight and general description of body and all scars, tattoos, and marks. Always examine the back.
External evidence of injury:	List all injuries one at a time. May be further divided into recent, healing, and old injuries. (In penetrating or perforating injuries, the external and internal injuries should be described together.)
Internal evidence of injury:	Separate listing of internal injuries found in blunt trauma from motor vehicle accidents, falls, and child abuse.
Evidence of medical treatment:	Injuries from CPR, surgical intervention, both external and internal, venipuncture sites, and other evidence of medical care.
Internal examination:	Description of body cavities and all organ systems done in an organized manner detailing appearance and presence of natural disease. (Injury or therapy to organs has already been addressed and should not be repeated here.)
Diagnoses or findings:	A list of objective findings including injury and natural diseases.
Opinion:	Conclusion based on the autopsy findings as to cause and manner of death.

TABLE 2.3 Specimens Useful for DNA Studies

EDTA-preserved (purple top tube), pretransfusion whole blood
Dried blood on fabric or clothing
Seminal fluid
Brain
Spleen
Bone marrow (in decomposed and skeletal remains)
Muscle
Skin
Dental pulp (in decomposed and skeletal remains)
Saliva

Specimens should be frozen at −20° C if they can not be sent to the laboratory immediately

TABLE 2.4 Quick Estimate of Time Since Death*

BODY TEMPERATURE	DEGREE OF RIGOR	TIME
warm	flaccid	less than 3 hours
warm	stiff	3 to 8 hours
cold	stiff	8 to 36 hours
cold	flaccid	over 36 hours

*Body found indoors at average room temperature.

TABLE 2.5 Procedures in Suspected Sexual Assault

Photographs
- —Identification
- —Position of clothing
- —Trace evidence, hair, fibers, stains on clothing or inner thighs
- —Injury to genitalia, breasts, anus, or inner thighs
- —Any bite mark injuries

Collect and preserve evidence and obtain receipt to maintain chain of custody
- —Clothing
- —Swabs and/or washings from mouth, genitalia, and anus
  Place swabs in separate cardboard boxes with air holes.
  Try to not use plastic containers or plastic bags in order to prevent bacterial growth.
- —Refrigerate swabs if they can not be sent to the laboratory immediately.
- —Swabs from possible semen stains on inner thighs
- —Combed and pulled head hair and pubic hair placed in separate labeled envelopes
- —Blood sample for police for typing victim
- —Fingernail scrapings or nail tips

TABLE 3.1 Procedures in Deaths Due to Blunt Force Injury

Radiographs
- —all areas of injury
- —arms and hands in homicides to document defense fractures, if present

Photographs
- —identification
- —all injuries
  - unwashed
  - washed and with surrounding hair shaved
  - internal and external
- —any trace evidence,
  i.e., hairs, fibers, glass, metal, paint chips to be used as evidence

Complete body chart
- —Localize and measure all wounds.
- —Describe appearance of abrasions, i.e., brush burn or crush or if tissue is piled up on one margin.
- —Describe color of all bruises and note any swelling present.
- —Describe evidence of healing, such as crusting or scab formation.
- —Describe abrasions or bruises on margins of lacerations.
- —Describe tissue bridges or undermining of margins of lacerations.

Obtain blood preserved in sodium fluoride and body fluids for toxicology.

Obtain blood sample and pulled head hair samples (beard hair if facial trauma noted) for police in homicides or hit-and-run cases, and fingernail scrapings or nail tips in assaults and obtain receipt.

Examine all organ systems in the usual fashion.

TABLE 3.2 Special Procedures in Child Abuse Deaths

Radiographs
- —Total body radiographs, both A-P and lateral with cone down views of all joints.
- —Consult radiologist if fractures are found or if there are any unusual findings.

Photographs
- —Identification.
- —Overall views of front and back of body unwashed and washed.
- —Any evidence of neglect such as diaper rash.
- —Close-up of all injuries—new, healing, and old.
- —Close-up of any patterned injury or burn.

Measure and record height, weight, head circumference, chest circumference, and abdominal circumference in infants and children less than 5 years of age.

Examine inside of mouth, eyes, genitalia, and anus for injury.

Look for evidence of bite mark injury or fingerprint bruises on arms, chest, or back. If bite marks are found, call odontologist. Be sure that odontologist examines all individuals who have contact with child, not just the alleged offender.

Assess cleanliness, hydration, and nutritional status.

Look for evidence of traumatic alopecia.

Perform posterior dissection to identify injuries not seen on body surface.

Remove and examine eyes for retinal hemorrhages in all cases of head trauma or suspected "shaken baby syndrome".

Examine all organ systems in the usual fashion.

Obtain blood and body fluids for toxicology, especially test for cocaine, alcohol, and opiates.

Perform histologic examination.

Remove and preserve any fractures, replace long bones with a wooden dowel to preserve body shape.

TABLE 3.3 Types of Skull Fracture

Comminuted:	the bone is fragmented
Depressed:	the bone is driven into the cranial cavity
Diasteal:	widening of a cranial suture
Hinge:	linear fracture through the base of the skull
Linear:	straight or curved line
Ping-pong:	dimpled, shallow depression in the pliable skull of an infant
Ring:	circular fracture around the foramen magnum

TABLE 3.4 Histologic Dating of Subdural Hematoma

Up to 24 hours	Thin fibrin layer on dural surface, dilated blood vessels in dura; few polymorphonuclear leukocytes in hematoma; swelling of endothelial cells of dural blood vessels and dural cells.
2 to 5 days	Rare fibroblasts in outer fibrin layer (adjacent to dura); mononuclear cells in fibrin layer; rare hemosiderin-laden macrophages seen in later time frame. The fibrin layer is thicker and there is laking of the red blood cells.
	May see thin fibrin layer with mononuclear cells on inner surface (facing arachnoid membrane).
5 to 10 days	There is now a 3- to 5-cell layer of fibroblasts; some sinusoidal capillaries are seen in the 7- to 10-day range. More hemosiderin-laden cells.
	Rare fibroblasts extending processes to the inner fibrin layer.
10 to 20 days	Fibroblast layers increase in thickness. There are now well-formed capillaries and the red blood cells stain poorly.
3 to 4 weeks	The fibroblast layer may now be the same thickness as the dura mater in the outer membrane while the inner membrane fibroblast layer is only 2 to 4 cell layers thick.
1 to 3 months	Outer membrane is complete and there are aggregates of hemosiderin-laden macrophages present.

TABLE 4.1 Procedures in Deaths Due to Firearms

Radiographs
- —All areas with gunshot wounds, even if exit wound present
- —Total body fluoroscopy if an available option; this is especially helpful if bullets embolize
- —National Association of Medical Examiners (NAME) recommends that the number of shotgun pellets seen in radiographs be counted.

Photographs
- —Identification
- —All wounds
  unwashed and washed
- —Internal injuries, especially bevelling of bone

Measure and record location of all wounds on body chart.
- —Number all wounds.
- —Use of inches in measurements is preferred over centimeters as most lay people are unfamiliar with metric distances.
- —Measure and describe size and shape of entrance and exit holes.
- —Measure and describe size, shape, and appearance of abrasion collar in entrance wounds.
- —Measure and describe size, shape, and appearance of evidence of close-range or contact-range fire, i.e., charring, gunpowder, soot, or stippling.
- —Take histologic sections of entrance wounds.

Examine clothing for evidence of holes, burning, or gunpowder.
- —Photograph.
- —Submit to police and obtain receipt.

Recover bullets or sampling of shotgun pellets and wadding material preferably with gloved hands, or Teflon-coated instruments
- —Wash.
- —Photograph.
- —Place in sealed labeled evidence envelope.
- —Submit to police and obtain receipt.

Describe internal injuries and path of bullet, listing all tissues and organs affected.

Obtain blood preserved in sodium fluoride and body fluids for toxicology.

Obtain blood sample for police and obtain receipt.

Examine all organ systems in the usual fashion.

TABLE 5.1 Procedures in Deaths Due to Blast Injury

Radiographs
- —Preferably total body to look for foreign objects and to document fractures

Photographs
- —Identification
- —Tattoos or identifying marks on body if face is severely injured or missing
- —All injuries both external and internal
- —Any foreign material recovered

Collection and preservation of physical evidence
- —Any metal or plastic material found on or within the body

Localize, measure, and record all injuries on body chart.

Examine all organ systems in the usual fashion.

Obtain and preserve blood or bone marrow or other materials for DNA identification, if necessary.

TABLE 6.1 Procedures in Death Due to Sharp Force Injury

Radiographs
- —In areas where wounds are present to look for any retained foreign objects

Photographs
- —Identification
- —All wounds
  - unwashed and washed
  - as found, if gaping
  - with reapproximation of wound margins
- —Internal injuries
- —Arms and hands even if no defense wounds are present
- —Any foreign object recovered

Localize and record all injuries on body chart.
- —Number all wounds.
- —Measure, in inches, all wounds, both gaping and with margins reapproximated.
- —Describe margins of wound if sharp or blunt.
- —Describe any irregularities of wounds.
- —Describe and measure abrasions if present on margins of wounds.

Perform internal examination of wound path.
- —Document all tissues and organs affected.
- —Measure depth of penetration (remember this is not a measurement of the length of the knife blade).
- —Recover, photograph, and submit any foreign object to the police and obtain a receipt.

Obtain blood and body fluids for toxicology.

Obtain blood sample for police and obtain receipt.

Exam all organ systems in the usual fashion.

TABLE 7.1 Procedures in Asphyxial Deaths

Radiographs
- —Total body in cases of hanging deaths in custody
- —Lateral neck in suicidal deaths involving a long drop
- —Hyoid bone in hanging and strangulation

Photographs
- —Identification
- —Ligature in situ and removed from the body in hangings and ligature strangulations
- —Ligature abrasions on body
- —Petechial hemorrhages or scleral hemorrhages
- —Abrasions and bruises on the neck in manual strangulation
- —Pressure marks on body in compressional asphyxia
- —Evidence of cyanosis or cherry red lividity
- —Hemorrhages found in neck dissection, fractures of hyoid bone, or neck cartilages
- —Foam cone in drowning deaths
- —Foreign object removed from airways in choking

Preservation of evidence
- —Obtain blood sample for police and obtain receipt.
- —Submit ligature to police and obtain receipt.
- —Place fingernail scrapings or cut nail tips in labeled envelopes, submit to police and obtain receipt.

Complete body chart
- —Measure, localize and record all ligature marks and other injury on the body.
- —Measure length and width or thickness of ligature.
- —Compare ligature with any pattern marks on body.
- —Examine mouth and tongue for abrasions, lacerations, or hemorrhages from biting the tongue or anoxia-induced seizure activity.
- —Look for fingernail abrasions on neck; compare to victim's own nails.

Perform internal examination
- —DO NECK DISSECTION LAST in cases of hanging or strangulation. This is done in a layer-by-layer fashion with the organs still in situ, and then after removal of the tongue and neck structures from the body. Look for congestion of the base of the tongue, petechial hemorrhages of the mucosal surfaces, and hemorrhages in the strap muscles.
- —Retain fractured hyoid bone.
- —Examine gastric contents and material in airways in deaths due to drowning or aspiration of foreign objects; retain.

Obtain blood and body fluids for toxicology.

Examine all organ systems in the usual fashion.

TABLE 8.1 Procedures in Deaths Due to Thermal Injury

Radiographs
- —Total body radiographs or fluoroscopy in badly burned or charred bodies to look for foreign objects
- —Head, chest, and pelvis films in badly burned bodies for identification purposes prior to autopsy

Photographs
- —Identification
- —Area of burns or overall if charred
- —Soot in mouth or nostrils
- —Airways to document presence or absence of soot or inhalation injury
- —Discoloration due to carbon monoxide intoxication

Complete body chart
- —Record location, size, and degree of burns and the percentage of total body surface area involved.
- —Note any pattern to burns, such as: stocking and glove burns to the feet and hands; pour pattern.

Internal examination
- —Note any heat-related epidural hemorrhages.
- —Obtain blood for carbon monoxide and cyanide determination.

Examine all organ systems in the usual fashion.

TABLE 8.2 Percentage of Total Body Surface Area in Burns

	INFANT (%)	CHILD (%)	ADULT (%)
Half of head	9.5	8.5	3.5
Half of neck	1.0	1.0	1.0
Chest and abdomen	13.0	13.0	13.0
Genitalia	1.0	1.0	1.0
Back and buttocks	17.0	17.0	17.0
Half of arm and hand	4.25	4.25	4.75
Half of leg and foot	6.25	6.75	10.0

TABLE 8.3 Common Burn Characteristics

CAUSE	EXPOSURE	DEGREE	APPEARANCE
Scalds	Short	Second	Wet, pink blisters
	Long	Second, third	Wet, dark red
Flames	Short	Second	Wet, pink blisters
	Long	Third	Dry, white, waxy or brown, black leathery
Chemicals Acid, alkali		Second, but may convert to third	Light brown to light gray

TABLE 9.1 Procedures in Suspected Drug or Chemical Deaths

Photographs
- —Identification
- —Evidence of drug abuse, i.e. track marks, skin pop scars
- —Any drugs or drug paraphernalia on body
- —Discoloration of hands, mouth, or mucosa of GI tract
- —Foam cone
- —Scars on wrists or neck from prior suicide attempts

Special examinations
- —Mouth and tongue for evidence of seizures
- —Nostrils and nasal septum for powder or perforations
- —Color and contents of any vomitus

Complete body chart

Internal examination
- —Examine lymph nodes for drug-related lymphadenopathy, especially in the porta hepatis and celiac axis.
- —Note any unusual odors in gastric contents and describe contents.
- —Obtain specimens for toxicology:
  - vitreous fluid
  - blood preserved in sodium fluoride*
  - bile
  - urine
  - liver
  - spleen
  - brain
  - kidney
  - gastric contents, all, and if possible, contents of small bowel in a separate container
- —Perform histologic examination.
- —Examine all organ systems in the usual fashion.

*May obtain blood from heart or aorta, may also obtain a second specimen from the periphery if concerned about postmortem redistribution of drugs, such as digoxin from heart muscle.

TABLE 9.2 Fatal Concentrations of Barbiturates (from Baselt)

	BLOOD (MG/L)	LIVER (MG/KG)
Amobarbital		
average	47	219
range	(22–68)	(106–580)
Phenobarbital		
range	78–116	89–266
Secobarbital		
average	21	115
range	(5–52)	(15–330)

TABLE 9.3 Fatal Concentrations of Drugs of Abuse (from Baselt)

	BLOOD (MG/L)	LIVER (MG/KG)	URINE (MG/L)
Amphetamine			
average	8.6	30	237
range	(0.5–41)	(4.3–74)	(25–700)
Cocaine			
average	5.3	4.2	42
range	(0.9–21)	(0.1–20)	(0.1–215)
Codeine			
average	2.8	6.8	104
range	(1.0–8.8)	(0.6–45)	(29–229)
Methadone*			
average	1.0	3.8	—
range	(0.4–1.8)	(1.8–7.5)	
Morphine			
average	0.7	3.0	52
range	(0.2–2.3)	(0.4–18)	(14–81)
Phencyclidine			
average	4.8	23	35
	(0.3–25)	(0.9–170)	(0.4–120)

*Therapeutic and toxic levels of methadone are very close and it is helpful to know if the victim is in a methadone program or a habitual user.

TABLE 9.4 Fatal Concentration of Antidepressants (from Baselt)

	BLOOD (MG/L)	LIVER (MG/KG)	URINE (MG/L)
Amitriptyline			
average	3.7	130	3.4
range	(2.7–4.7)	(13–317)	(0.4–7.9)
Amoxapine			
average	6.9	97	0.5
range	(0.9–20)	(17–348)	(11–22)
Desipramine			
average	10*	125	0.2
Dothiepin			
average	1.5	8.0	3.2
range	(0.3–2.5)	(2–14)	(0.4–5.1)
Doxepin			
average	9.3	32	7.5
range	(0.7–29)	(22–38)	(2.1–12)
Fluoxetine			
average	3.8	70	12
range	(1.3–6.8)	(29–128)	(5.5–19)
Imipramine			
average	7.3	166	20
range	(6–8.5)	(33–381)	(0.6–54)
Nortriptyline			
average	11	90	79
range	(12–26)	(8–220)	(25–120)
Trazodone	15	57	2.5
Tranylcypromine	3.7	7.3	25

*Plasma level.

TABLE 11.1 Procedures in Deaths Due to Electrical Injury

Photographs
—Identification
—All injury
—Burn marks in clothing or personal effects

Complete body chart
—Localize and measure all injury on body, both electrical and blunt trauma.
—Take histologic sections of all suspected electrical burns.

Obtain blood and body fluids for toxicology.

Examine all organ systems in the usual fashion.

Have suspect electrical appliances, equipment, wiring, or outlets preserved and tested for faulty wiring, current leakage, or tampering with protective devices such as ground-fault circuit interrupters or three-prong plugs.

TABLE 13.1 Age of Epiphyseal Union*

EPIPHYSIS	AGE
Acromion	17–19
Clavicle	
medial	23–28
lateral	18–21
Femur	
head	16–19
distal	17–20
Fibula	
proximal	16–21
distal	16–19
Humerus	
head	16–23
distal	13–16
Iliac crest	18–22
Metacarpals	14–17
Metatarsals	15–17
Pelvis	14–16
Radius	
proximal	14–17
distal	18–21
Tibia	
proximal	17–19
distal	16–19
Ulna	
proximal	14–17
distal	18–21

*Age for males; in females, the age is slightly younger.

TABLE 13.2 Racial Features of the Skull

	CAUCASOID	NEGROID	MONGOLOID
Height	high	low	medium
Length	long	long	long
Width	narrow	narrow	wide
Orbit	angular	rectangular	rounded
Nasal opening	narrow	wide	narrow
Palate shape	narrow	wide	medium

Index